T0354742

CORN
SHELLING
TIME

CORN
SHELLING
TIME

"GOD'S SUPER BOWL ON A SUNDAY"

MICHAEL DUISHKA

CORN SHELLING TIME
"GOD'S SUPER BOWL ON A SUNDAY"

iUniverse books may be ordered through booksellers or by contacting:

iUniverse
1663 Liberty Drive
Bloomington, IN 47403
www.iuniverse.com
1-800-Authors (1-800-288-4677)

ISBN: 978-1-5320-0174-1 (sc)
ISBN: 978-1-5320-0196-3 (e)

Library of Congress Control Number: 2016910808

Print information available on the last page.

iUniverse rev. date: 07/12/2016

Table of Contents

Foreword

NIKITA KRUSHCHEV TOLD AMERICA; "We will bury you". Michael Duishka could not find anyone to endorse or sanction this book. Nevertheless the combination of political lies from the News Media, (television, computers, news papers, radio), but most of all, ungodly lying politicians is making Nikita Krushchev' prophecy come to pass. All of the above evil inventions are being used to not only bury America, but also the whole world, The anti-Christ, anti-moral, Satan possessed pirates have stolen, destroyed, and murdered, (killed) all of the moral foundation of this world. Satan the god of this world has blinded the minds of the mass majority of his subjects with the pleasures of sin until they have reached the point of no return.(PNR). This is the reason Michael Duishka could not allow anyone of the blind guides to endorse this book. This book cannot be understood by any of the apostate *church* goers, so called *"Christians"*, because they have turned God's WORD of TRUTH into their lies. Are they condemned because of their unbelief, which is the unpardonable sin? The only one this book would benefit would be a person that has suffered all of the plagues of sin and has contemplated suicide, or divorce, or maybe has a need to be free from any kind of addiction, or sin. This book will instruct you how to achieve a happy life here on earth, and also life eternal. This book will show you how to heal your broken heart, and how to save your children and family. You cannot see Him, but CHRIST JESUS has endorsed this book with

His anointing. If there is a great storm raging inside of you, Duishka calls it a Euroaquilo. This book has the answer on how to calm that storm that is tearing the heart out of you. If you have tried every man made snake oil solution and none of them worked, before you take the coward's way out, read this book. Just like DUISHKA found deliverance from the great storm inside of him, you can also find deliverance from that great Euroaquilo inside of you, no matter what the symptoms are. Learn what it means to "Shell Down the Corn" to Christ Jesus. God gave us all His only begotten Son to seek and to save the lost. Duishka was lost and could not find my way. Christ Jesus found me and showed me that He is the **ONLY Way**. CHRIST JESUS is looking for you. Krushchev also said; "We spoon fed you socialism until you are a communist and do not even know it". He was right, the president, Vice president, all democrats,and the majority of liberal republican congress, and the Supreme Court Judges are "communists". The answer to any question you can ask is in this book. The answer to all of your questions is CHRIST JESUS!

Preface

WHEN THIS WRITER FOUND out there was not anything he could do for God except do something for one of His people, the most important thing He told me to do was to go into all the world and be a witness for Him. The only way to do that is to write a message to the world. This writer does not have any credentials that are degrees from worldly institutions like BA, MA, PHD or DDV; but he has some threadbare pants where he earned a degree in kneeology and prayer to his Creator. He has studied to show himself approved unto God, a workman that need not be ashamed, rightly dividing the Word of Truth. The only way you can verify that is to ask God. Do you know how to ask God anything? Do you know how to hear His answer? Read this book, **"Corn Shelling Time"**

Preface

Acknowledgments

FIRST, GOD IS ACKNOWLEDGED as the LORD and master of Michael Duishka. God the Holy Spirit inspired the words that Michael Duishka has written in this book. He, (The Holy Spirit), is the anointing Michael Duishka received of Him, and was taught by no man about God. Christ Jesus, The Son of The Living God, prayed that His disciples would receive this teacher from God Almighty, (PANTAKRATOR).

Next, the writer, Michael Duishka wants to acknowledge his darling wife, Mavis, that used her special skills of typing and shorthand, and grammar to compile this manuscript. There are places in this book that are not grammatically, or politically correct, which were intentionally by design to inflect a point of truth, or to emphasize a thought. If you detect one of those flaws, please do not blame or criticize Mavis. OK? OK. Mavis, I thank you so very much for enduring the loneliness while this book was being written. I LUV U!

Acknowledgments and thanks are being given to all of the editors and evaluating personnel and employees of this Publishing Company for evaluating and correcting a lot of mistakes due to my inexperience of being an author. This team of supporters were great!

The outside sources of material used in this book are public domain and from class notes on bible studies at the Ekklesia of the Bride. Recognition and thanks are being given Rick Meyers and his contribution of E Sword, which is public domain. **"Corn Shelling Time"** used parts of the KJV+ Bible, and corrected them with parts of Greek obtained from the Greek New Testament with Dictionary by B. F. Westcott and F. J. A. Hort.

Credit and gratitude also go to my daddy and my mama for the conception of the title of this book, and the SPA Method of Correction my daddy used, which was, **S**eize, **P**ossess, **A**pply. He would **S**eize me with his left hand, **P**ossess the razor strop with his right hand and then **A**pply it to my butt until all of the ADHD, (Attention Deficit Hyperactivity Disorder), also known as the devil, was gone out of me. My mama taught me the sayings, "What goes around comes around," and "Give him enough rope and he will hang himself." They are both asleep in Jesus, and the only treasure that they left me was common sense, which is worth more to me than gold and silver.

Anyone that I missed recognizing is purely unintentional. Please forgive me. Most of all I give thanks to God, The Holy Spirit, for the inspiration to write **"Corn Shelling Time"**.

Introduction

"For then will I turn to the people a pure language that they may call upon the name of the Lord to serve Him with one consent." (Zephaniah 3:9) **"Corn Shelling Time"** wants to introduce you, the reader, to that pure language, so when the time of this age expires, you will know what the pure Word of the LORD is.

The children of Israel were in bondage physically to the Egyptians for 400 years before God sent them a deliverer, Moses. The children of God have been in bondage spiritually to the King James version of the Bible for 400 years, from 1611 A.D. To 2011 A.D., when God sent them a deliverer, Michael Duishka, to instruct only the believers of Christ Jesus, who is the Word of God, a pure spiritual language, not cognate words that are Anti-Christ words that Jesus or His disciples never used. Some of the impure, misleading words are Church, Saint, Cross, Easter, Christmas, Halloween, Good Friday, or Lent. The real pure words respectively are Ekklesia, (Called Out Ones), or congregation, or assembly, but never *Church*, Holy, Holy Ones, but never *Saint*. The definition of *Saint* is someone that is dead; and not any Holy Ones are dead, but <u>all</u> are alive. Jesus was hung on a tree called a torture stake, but never a *Cross* (Crux), signifying Tammuz, a pagan god. The worst word is *Easter*, which is a pagan word substituted for The Holy Passover. This is blasphemy of God, THE CHRIST. The rest of the words are just pagan man made words. Michael Duishka introduced the pure words used in the Holy Scriptures in the Greek New Testament by B. F. Westcott and F. J. A. Hort.

Freedom from being bound by false pagan, heathen, man made words from 1611 A.D. To 2011 A.D. Can be achieved by reading "Please Do Not Call Me A Christian" by Michael Duishka, or reading this book, **"Corn Shelling Time"**. **"And you shall know the truth, and the truth shall make you free."** (John 8:32) All politically correct words are false pagan lies. Anyone that uses these words cannot show themselves approved of God.

Let me introduce you to Christ Jesus, the WORD, which is God, that was hung on a tree, a torture stake, that was Holy, that is calling you out of the *churches*, governments, the world, and the things that are in the world, the Mystery of Iniquity, which is Mystery, Babylon. He is calling you out with a loud voice, and telling you it is **"Corn Shelling Time"**

Chapter 1

THIS LAST GENERATION IS the most intelligent generation in the things of the world since six thousand years ago when God created man. But with all their knowledge, they do not know what **"Corn Shelling Time"** means, unless they have read the book entitled, "Please Do Not Call Me A "Christian". Nor will they ever know what **"Corn Shelling Time"** means unless they read the book, "Please Do Not Call Me A "Christian"; or someone who has read the book tells them. The other option to knowing what **"Corn Shelling Time"** means is to read this book, which tells in it's entirety what is meant by **"Corn Shelling Time"**.

"But, you, O Daniel, shut up the words, and seal the book, even to the time of the end. Many shall run to and fro, and knowledge shall be increased." (Daniel 12:4)

Could it be Daniel was talking about a different kind of knowledge? Are there different kinds of knowledge? There is worldly knowledge, and there is heavenly knowledge. There is knowledge of the natural man; and there is spiritual knowledge, that is given only by God The Holy Spirit. The only way anyone can receive the spiritual knowledge from God is to know God. One can study the scriptures and know all the scriptures have to say about God, and all the knowledge they will have is about God. One can know all about God and still not have any spiritual knowledge. God has to be revealed to someone and be introduced to God before they can know Him. Only a chosen few have known God.

The knowledge Daniel was talking about was knowledge of the Natural Man. This last generation is the most knowledgeable species that ever lived in Natural Man's knowledge. But this last generation is destitute of spiritual knowledge. Since knowledge has increased in the Natural Man, we can conclude that we are in the last generation before the dispensation of the Gentiles comes to an end.

The Holy Bible is the book of knowledge that tells about the only one and the only way that God can be revealed to anyone. We read in the scriptures about the Christ, which in the Hebrew language is called Messiah. Two thousand years ago God's Christ was manifested in human flesh and was called the Son of God. The Christ of God was sent to the earth to be made flesh and to reveal God to whosoever He willed. The only one that can reveal God to anyone is that, Christ, The Son of the Living God. That Son was telling this in the Book of Matthew. To wit: **"All things are delivered unto Me of My Father; and no man knows the Son, but the Father; neither knows any man the Father, save (except) the Son and to whomsoever the Son will reveal Him."** (Matthew 11:27)So the Christ, Jesus, the Son of the Living God, started telling knowledge to whomsoever wanted spiritual knowledge instead of worldly knowledge, that Daniel spoke of in (Daniel 12:4).

So, <u>**"Corn Shelling Time"**</u> is to impart some spiritual knowledge to whomsoever desires knowledge. **"Corn Shelling Time"** is spiritual knowledge that gives life, and that life is everlasting, forever. That knowledge of everlasting life can come only through Christ Jesus. Amen!

There are many many things the Christ said to reveal His Father, God, to whosoever. The first thing He said to do was written in

(Matthew 11:28), where He said, **"Come unto Me all you that labor and are heavy laden, and I will give you rest."**

But wait a minute. He said in another place, **"No man can come to me, except the Father, which has sent Me, draw him; and I will raise him up at the last day."** (John 6:44)

So how can anyone come to Jesus? They cannot come to Jesus when they decide they want to, but have to wait until God draws them to Jesus. How does God draw someone to Jesus? God draws the ones to Jesus by His Holy Spirit. The Father is one entity of God, the Son is the second entity of God, the Holy Spirit is the third entity of God. So, if you can count, that makes God a *triune* God, or as most people say, a trinity. So God uses His Spirit, which is Holy, to draw a person to Jesus, who in turn reveals the Father to the person.

So God uses all of Himself to free a person from the bondage of the wicked one, and adopt him into the family of God. God the Father draws a candidate to God the Son, (Jesus), by God the Spirit. (John 6:44). God draws one to Jesus, then Jesus says, **"No man can come to the Father but by Me."** (John 14:6). So we can conclude that the three entities are never separated in parts. They are always together, and the three together make **One** God.

Does God draw everyone to Christ Jesus? No, but God is no respecter of persons. He gives everyone the opportunity to accept His drawing, or to reject His drawing. God created man to have a free agency either to accept His calling, or to reject His calling.

There was a young man about nineteen that had never been to a church or ever listened to a preacher. This particular day this young man was invited to a church; and as the preacher was talking in riddles that this young man knew nothing of, the Spirit of God kept pulling at the young man as the invitation was given to come to Jesus. The young man confessed later that he felt as though a powerful force was pulling on him; but he nearly pushed a hole through the floor with his foot; and he had to hold on to the pew to keep from going down to the altar. The young man rejected God that day, and was told later that God would only tug or draw a person two times in the person's lifetime. Many years passed after that opportunity to meet God Almighty (PANTAKRATOR) in person; but God did not forget the young man; and seventeen years later the opportunity came again for the Holy Spirit of God to draw this man to Jesus; and this time the man, still young, ran tearfully, with a broken heart down to the altar of repentance, and never rejected God again.. Hallelujah! If the man had rejected the drawing of God's Holy Spirit this time, it is doubtful if He would ever have come again.

Notwithstanding, this is how the trinity of the One God works together for good to them that love God, to them who are called according to His purpose. (Romans 8:28) This action has to happen before any spiritual knowledge can be taught by God the Holy Spirit, (Paraclete). God draws the person to Jesus. Jesus reveals the Father to the person, and pleads as an intercessor, and the third entity teaches knowledge to the recipient.

This is what Daniel was talking about, many shall run to and fro seeking worldly knowledge; and they increase in worldly knowledge; but spiritual knowledge is only given by the Spirit of God; and only to those that are seeking the Kingdom of God and His righteousness. (Matthew 6:33)

Who does God choose to be heirs of salvation? **"Blessed are they which do hunger and thirst after righteousness, for they shall be filled."** (Matthew 5:6) The ones that hunger and thirst after righteousness are going to be seeking the Kingdom of God and His righteousness, seeking the Kingdom and God's righteousness, which is Christ Jesus. The one that seeks and keeps on seeking, and does not tire out from seeking, is the one that God chooses to draw to Jesus, and calls him out to be His Holy One. **"For many are**

called, but few are chosen." (Matthew 20:16) Daniel sealed the book till the time of the end, but this is the time of the end. The book has become unsealed to the chosen ones. What is the book that Daniel sealed? The book that Daniel sealed up, held all the mysteries for the children of Israel, (Jacob), that were to come upon them from then until the end time.

This book, **"Corn Shelling Time",** is the revealing of not only the mysteries sealed up in Daniel's book, but also the mystery of the plan of God's salvation, not only for the children of Israel, but also for you, the reader, of **"Corn Shelling Time."** God is a big God; and whenever He talks, He speaks about events that affect the entire universe. Then God has scribes, like the writer of

"Corn Shelling Time", to reveal the trickle down events that come after the great events that He said would occur.

The book that Daniel sealed up until the end time was visions that would happen to Daniel's people until the Prince, Michael, would intervene for the children of Israel, before they would be annihilated. But keep in mind someone has to bring about the attempted annihilation of the people of Daniel. That someone is the remainder of nations called Gentiles, which we read of in the scriptures, where God calls it the time of the Gentiles.

"Woe unto the world because of offenses, for it must needs be that offenses come, but woe to that man by whom the offense comes." (Matthew 18:7) That man that Jesus was referring to in that particular scripture was the Man of Sin in (II Thessalonians 2:3), alias, Anti Christ, AKA the Beast.

"Corn Shelling Time" will reveal what is meant by the scripture in (Jeremiah 30:7); "Alas for that day is great, so that none is like it: It is even the time of Jacob's trouble, but he shall be saved out of it." Jacob's trouble is bigger than natural man can comprehend. Daniel said, "Trouble such as never was since there was a nation." **"For then shall be great tribulation, such as was not since the beginning of the world to this time, no, nor ever shall be."** (Matthew 24:21)

Daniel said knowledge shall increase, but he was not talking about knowing about the end time, tribulation, or knowing anything about Jesus. Daniel was talking about worldly knowledge, such as radios, computers, televisions, phones, etc. All worldly knowledge is natural. The worldly knowledge has rapidly increased via the air. The knowledgeable vessels of corruption in this age do not have the faintest idea where all these evil inventions originate from. But the spiritual vessels of this age know exactly where all these evil inventions came from. "Wherein in time past, you walked according to the course of this world, according to the Prince of the Power of the Air, the spirit that now works in the children of disobedience." (Ephesians 2:2) The knowledgeable natural ones are the children of disobedience, that do not know they are operating the tools of the King of the Powers in the Air. The powers of the air being Evil Spirits that give power to Evil Rulers of the world.

The believers know how to put on the whole armor of God, and they have spiritual knowledge of how to withstand the spiritual wickedness of the air ways. "Put on the whole armor of God, that you may be able to stand against the wiles of the Devil." (Ephesians 6:11)

While the children of God, that obey Him, are called children of obedience. For we wrestle not against flesh and blood, but against principalities, against powers, against the rulers of the darkness of this world, against spiritual wickedness in high places. We are not wrestling against the children of disobedience that have myriads of worldly knowledge; but we, (The Believers), are wrestling against the spiritual wickedness, the ones that rule the children of disobedience. The children of disobedience are slaves of the Prince (King) of the Powers in the Air, because they are working for the Devil, when they use the evil inventions. "Thus they provoked Him to anger with their inventions, and the plague brake in upon them." (Psalms 106:29)

"But the very elect of Christ Jesus have studied to show themselves approved of God, a workman that needs not to be ashamed, rightly dividing the Word of Truth." (II Timothy 2:15) The very elect were given power to wrestle against the wicked spirits that possess the children of disobedience. "Behold I give unto you power to tread on serpents and scorpions, and over all the power of the enemy, and nothing shall by any means hurt you." (Luke 10:19)

This is the knowledge received that can only be learned from God the Holy Spirit. So we, the very elect, are wrestling with the rulers of the children of disobedience, until they recover themselves from the snare of the Devil; and then they will join the Army of God; and we will have some allies to fight against the spiritual wickedness in high places.

If the children of disobedience do not get the plague before they join forces with Christ and His army, they will be valuable assets to Christ; and they can use the evil inventions, (radios, televisions, computers, phones, transmitters) to fight the principalities and powers of the air. With all of the knowledge the natural man has acquired from the ruler of this world (Satan), think how much more powerful they would be if they had all the worldly knowledge plus spiritual knowledge combined.

They would be a top ranked soldier for God in His army. The problem with the natural man is he does not desire to be a soldier in God's army. The knowledge and wisdom about which we speak, are not received by the natural man, because his knowledge is acquired by a study of worldly things; and the spiritual man receives his knowledge and wisdom freely from God by the Holy Ghost. (I Corinthians 2:13) "But the natural man receives not the things of the Spirit of God, for they are foolishness unto him: Neither can he know them, because they are spiritually discerned." (I Corinthians 2:14)"But he that is spiritual judges all things, yet he himself is judged of no man." (I Corinthians 2:15)

"Corn Shelling Time" is words of wisdom for the ones that hunger and thirst after righteousness. (Matthew 5:6) and for those that are seeking the Kingdom of God and His righteousness. (Matthew 6:33) How bright is the firmament? "And they that be wise shall shine as the brightness of the firmament." (Daniel 12:3) "And they that turn many to righteousness as the stars forever and ever." (Daniel 12:3)

"Corn Shelling Time" is written for those that are wise and can discern (judge) spiritual from natural. **"Corn Shelling Time"** is written by inspiration of the Holy Ghost and cannot be understood by the natural or the unlearned. **"Corn Shelling Time"** is for the wise ones that stand by faith, to be not high minded, but fear; "and let us hear the conclusion of the whole matter. Fear God, and keep His commandments, for this is the whole duty of man." (Ecclesiastes 12:13)

"Corn Shelling Time" is for the ones that not only seek the Kingdom of God and His righteousness, but also those that want to work in the Kingdom and rule and reign with Christ Jesus.

"Corn Shelling Time" is for those that fear the Lord, for this is the beginning of wisdom.

(Psalms 111:10) **"Corn Shelling Time"** is for the "Christians" and every other sinner that wants to be sanctified by the Holy Spirit of God, and become holy, without which, (holiness), no man shall see the Lord. (Hebrews 12:14) Every time this writer has preached a sermon it has always included the commandment of Christ Jesus, when He said; **"But seek you first the kingdom of God and His righteousness and all these things will be added unto**

you". (Matthew 6:33) I asked the LORD, if that is the first thing to do, what is the second thing to do? He told me there is not any second thing. So this ole country boy is still seeking the kingdom of God and His righteousness.

Chapter 2

"CORN SHELLING TIME" WAS a metaphor that my daddy had a private patent on. (First Duishka 1:1) I have permission from Michael Duishka, the author of "Please Do Not Call Me A "Christian", to use the title, **"Corn Shelling Time".**

My daddy was to me as God is to every person that was ever born. My daddy taught me many many things about life; but he never taught me anything about God the Father, or God the Son (Jesus), or God the Holy Spirit, the One God Almighty (PANTAKRATOR), that created the heavens and the earth and the seas, and all the things that are in them. But here is the story of **"Corn Shelling Time",** which is a metaphor for everyone to come to Christ.

My daddy was the best man I ever knew, although I never was taught anything about God and Christ Jesus. I was taught many traits of Jesus, only it never was related to the creator, but it was traits of right from wrong. It came natural to my dad to keep God's Commandments, even though he never related doing the right thing to God. I never knew of dad ever telling a lie or stealing, committing adultery or fornication, or coveting his neighbors' possessions. He did not remember the sabbath to keep it holy. He has on a few occasions as I remember used the name of God in vain.

But here is the heart of the most important thing he taught me called **"Corn Shelling Time".** When I would violate some rule that dad had told us kids not to do as we were growing up, he would call me to him and ask me if I was guilty? Immediately I would automatically deny it and lie about it, and say I did not do whatever it was. Dad would say "Mick", (my nickname), you may as well "Shell Down the Corn", (confess), and tell me the truth. I would keep on lying and denying it, thinking dad would believe me. No such luck. Back in those days, dad shaved with a straight razor, and he had a double razor strop that he sharpened his razor with, among other things. On one end of the strop was a hook to hang it on a nail, and on the other end was a hand hold to hold it tight while he was stropping his razor.

So when I persisted in lying, dad would get up and go over to the nail, the razor strop was hanging on, and unhook it off the nail; and all this time I was like the rich man in hell, I could already feel the flames of fire! Dad would unhook the double razor strop from the nail, and turn and start to slowly walk back in my direction; and I already knew what the bottom line was. I had a thought of running; but then I had another thought about what he had told me before, that if I ran, the punishment would be twice as severe. So, the only thing I could do was this: I would start to do the Saint Vitus Dance that dad taught me, although he did not know he taught me. It just came automatically to jump up and down on one foot and then the other, all the time crying to dad telling him, "Daddy, I'll be good. I won't do it any more. Oh, daddy, give me another chance. I'll be good. I won't do it any more." (I did not worry about using proper English. I used contractions.) But dad just kept on coming, telling me, "I know you will not do it anymore when I get through with you." When he got to me, he took his left hand and grabbed me by the arm; and with the razor strop in his right hand, we started going in a circle; and my bottom would not hold shucks. All the time we were going in a circle and every time the double strop would go whack on my back side, I would holler, "I've had enuff. I've had enuff"; but dad would just keep on until he thought I had enough. After he got through laying the stripes on me, he would walk back over to the nail and hang up the double razor strop until the next necessity.

I could not see it then, because I was too busy licking my own wounds; but I remember now that I am older, there would be a trace of tears in daddy's eyes; and I know it must have hurt dad more than me. He would say, "Come here, boy, and sit down." I would sit down, and he would say to me, "If you had not lied, and "Shelled Down the Corn", (confessed), I would not have whipped you."

The story you have just read is a true story; and it is a metaphor as to how our Father God is to us about our sins; "If we confess our sins, He is faithful and just to forgive us our sins, and to cleanse us from all unrighteousness." (I John 1:9)

One time my younger sister and I had to watch over a lone milch cow we had and let her graze on open range land by the side of the road, because we did not have enough money to buy feed for the old milch cow. We passed by a farm house; and since no one was home, we went in to get a drink of water. While we were in the house, we saw some little trinkets, and took them home with us. The next day I saw the neighbor talking to daddy, and I knew the jig was up. Daddy called me and said, "Mick, that neighbor told me someone came in his house and took some trinkets. If you know anything about it, you may as well "Shell Down the Corn". Do you know anything about it?" I thought about the time he told me if I would have "Shelled Down the Corn", (confessed), he would not have whipped me. Since I knew I was caught anyway, I thought I would test him out, so I "Shelled Down the Corn" and said, "I did it." He asked me where the loot was, and I showed it to him. He said, "I want you to take it and give it back to the neighbor, and tell him you are sorry, and then come back home; and I will deal with you." I did just what he told me to do, which was hard enough to just face the neighbor that I had burglarized his house. Then I had to ponder if dad would use the razor strop or not. When I got back home, dad called me and said;

"Since you "Shelled Down the Corn", I am not going to whip you; but I want you to promise me you will never do that again." I said; "I promise you, daddy, I will never do that again."

But, that is just the way "Christians" do, they promise God if He will save them, they will go and sin no more. But their promise is just lip service, and turns out they lied to God. They think that just because Jesus is merciful, He will forgive them when they go willfully sin: (Read Hebrews 6th Chapter).

If my daddy had lived in this generation, he would be tried and convicted by the heathen laws of the land for child abuse. I am so thankful to God Almighty (PANTAKRATOR) for the stripes my daddy gave me with the double, wide, razor strop. Even though my daddy never taught me a thing about Christ Jesus, when the time came for the Spirit of God to draw me to Jesus (John 6:44), I had enough teaching from daddy to know I had to "Shell Down the Corn" to God. I knew by the conviction of the Holy Spirit of God that flooded my soul, that it was **"Corn Shelling Time".**

My tears washed my black heart, (Spirit). and I knew the Lord was whipping me in a different way than dad; but it had the same effect. What got to me the most is when the evangelist preached that whatever I had done to people to pay them back for what they had done to me was doing evil to Christ Jesus. The evangelist said Jesus paid a debt for me, and I could never repay Jesus for the debt I owed Him. Up until that night as the evangelist preached, and God the Holy Spirit was bringing me under conviction, and He was drawing me to Jesus, I had always paid back whatever someone or anyone had done to me; and the evangelist said the only thing I could do was to confess my sins to God; and He was faithful and just to forgive me of my sins. So, my daddy taught me enough to know the jig was up, that it was **"Corn Shelling Time".**

I "Shelled Down the Corn" and confessed what seemed like a million sins to Jesus; and I know that there was a million more I could not remember. I had a broken heart and a contrite spirit, and I must have shed a million tears. I heard someone say there was something I must do called restitution, and a lot of other things, like I was supposed to forgive my enemies and feed them if they were hungry. I assessed what it would take to make restitution for what I had stolen and destroyed from God's people, and the value was more than my human calculator could sum up. The next thing was forgive and ask for forgiveness. As I was walking in a shopping center, going to the grocery store, I saw one of my enemies that his fists were still sore from beating on my head; so I thought this would be a good place to start; and it was. I yelled his name, and he was reluctant to respond, because he supposed I was a glutton for punishment. I had to tell the whole shopping center I was so sorry for offending him, and would he please forgive me. I think he thought I was setting him up to get revenge, so he just said, "Uh huh", and kept on walking. I had many enemies and also friendly acquaintances I had to ask would they please forgive me; and it will never end, because I treated some so badly, I cannot get close enough to them to apologize.

The Lord Jesus said in (Matthew 11:28); **"Come unto Me all you that labor and are heavy laden, and I will give you rest."** I had accomplished the first commandment when I felt the Holy Spirit of God draw me to Jesus. (John 6:44) I responded to His call to come unto Him, and I did. (Matthew 11:28)

The next thing was: **"Take My yoke upon you and learn of Me, for I am meek and lowly in heart, and you shall find rest unto your souls (lives)."** (Matthew 11:29) Well, when I came to Jesus, I "Shelled Down the Corn", (I confessed I was a sinner), I took His yoke upon me, and I am learning of Him, which is a continual learning, that will never be complete; but I will continue learning of Jesus on into eternity. There are a multitude of people that think that is the sum of the whole matter, to just come to Jesus, "Shell Down the Corn", (confess), and they are saved. Wrong!

No one that is breathing, walking, living in this world is saved. When I asked the Lord, "Will you save me?" His answer was, "Yea and amen **if** you will do what you said you would do Go and sin no more." But, how was a new convert supposed to know what the bible, that he had never read, said about sin, or about sanctification, or about holiness, or about the one doctrine of Christ Jesus.

How is a new convert supposed to know which *church* to attend or to join? I asked God in the Name of Jesus to show me which *church* to go to; and I never got an answer from God until many years later; and I was amazed when the answer came. The teacher, the Holy Spirit, gave me the answer just as plain as day. He said, "Come out of all the *churches* and do not join any *church.*""What? Know you not that he which is joined to an harlot is one body?" (I Corinthians 6:16 and Revelation 17:5) "And upon "Her" forehead was a name written, Mystery Babylon The Great, The Mother Of Harlots And Abominations Of The Earth." (Revelation 17;5)

How is any New Convert to know about the conditions of salvation, when the preachers and theologians do not know themselves; or if they do know, they do not preach or teach sanctification, holiness, the second work of grace, Baptism into the Holy Spirit.

But what they do teach is a false doctrine, like give ten percent (tithe) to the *church* of their doctrine. **"And Jesus knew their thoughts and said to them, every kingdom divided against itself is brought to desolation, and every city or house divided against itself cannot stand. "** (Matthew12; 25)

Every *church* and every one in a *church* is divided against the Word, against Jesus who is the Word. Father God, I pray in the name of Christ Jesus for the ones that desire to be one with You that they would not be marked as the ones that cause divisions and offenses contrary to the doctrine of Christ Jesus and be separated from those that do such things, in the name of Jesus, Amen and Amen.

There is no such word as *church* in my bible, which is the closest thing in existence to the original Word of Truth, which is The Greek New Testament, by B. F. Westcott and F. J. A. Hort. In the Greek New Testament there is no such word as *church*; but there is the true word Ekklesia, which means, (1) Called Out Ones, (2) Congregation, (3) Assembly, but never *church*. *Church* is a word made by man. "But in vain they do worship me, teaching for doctrines the commandments of men." (Matthew 15:9).There are no such thing as the separated doctrines (denominations) made by men, but there is only one doctrine, and that one doctrine is the doctrine of God Almighty, (PANTAKRATOR).

"Now, I beseech you, brethren, mark them which cause divisions and offenses, contrary to the doctrine, which you have learned, and avoid them." (Romans 16:17)

He was speaking of Baptist, Catholic, Methodist, Assembly of God, Episcopal, Apostolic, Christian, Church of Christ, Church of God, Presbyterian, Jehovah's Witnesses, Anglican, Church of Jesus Christ of Latter Day Saints, Nazarene, Eastern Orthodox, Foursquare, Full Gospel, Independent, Church on the Rock, Jewish Christian, Krishna, Lutheran, Pentecostal, Holiness, Seventh Day Adventist, Christian Fellowship, Word of God, and any other *church*. I have marked them for you, and the scripture says you are to avoid them. (Romans 16:17) They are all divided and cause offenses, or cause to sin. No where in the scriptures does God's Word say, "Go to *church*."No where in the New Testament does God's Word say, "Give a tithe, (ten percent)." These are all false doctrines that are to be marked and avoided. (Romans 16:17)

"Beware lest any man spoil you through philosophy and vain deceit, after the rudiments of the world, and not after Christ." (Colossians 2:8)

It took this writer many years to discover he was being taught the traditions of men. And then it took many years to unlearn the false doctrines that were rooted and grounded into me.

"For in Him (Christ Jesus) dwells all the fulness of the Godhead bodily." (Colossians 2:9) "And you are complete in Him, which is the head of all principality and power." (Colossians 2:10)

Which is one of the Mysteries of Godliness, how God can be three entities. God the Father,God the Son, and God the Holy Spirit, and still be One God Almighty (PANTAKRATOR).

"Corn Shelling Time" is to make God's Word simple and plain to understand. If you are a new convert, it will be much easier for you to believe the true Word Of God, than if you had to unlearn a bunch of false doctrines. If you are indoctrinated with a lot of politically correct lies,**"Corn Shelling Time"** will be a challenge, and a golden opportunity for you to learn the truth of Christ Jesus, and "put off the old man, (Ephesians 4:22), which is corrupt and deceitful lusts."

Father God, in the name of your son Jesus, I give you thanks for many many things, but Lord Jesus I am so thankful for your written Word that you inspired your beloved Disciple John to write in (1 John 2; 26,27) your promise of the anointing, which is your Holy Spirit, that would teach me all things, and I had not any need of any man teaching me anything. I give you thanks for the promise **yo**u made me in (John 16:13), that The Spirit Of Truth would come and show me things to come, and He came to me and fulfilled that promise. In the Name of Jesus, Amen and Amen.

Chapter 3

GOD IS NO RESPECTER of persons; and whatever He requires of one person, He requires of all. Then Peter opened *his* mouth, and said, "Of a truth I perceive that God is no respecter of persons." (Acts 10:34)

Now, at this moment in **"Corn Shelling Time".** God used the word, "Confess." "That, if you shall confess with your mouth the Lord Jesus, and shall believe in your heart that God has raisedHim, (Jesus), from the dead, you <u>shall</u> be saved." (Romans 10:9)

So the first requirement of God for all is to "Shell Down The Corn", (confess) that you are guilty of sin, and now is the time to do it. "For He says, "I have heard you in a time accepted, and in the day of salvation have I succoured you. Behold, now is the accepted time. Behold, now is the day of salvation." (II Corinthians 6:2)

That was one of the problems this writer had with God's requirements to be saved. I tried to learn every requirement all at once, and it is impossible. You notice that I said I tried, and tried is not in the true Word of God, because God never tried to do anything. So He expects you to either do it or not. That is the problem with most people. They think all they have to do is to confess the Lord Jesus, and they are saved. Wrong! That is a good start. Just do one thing at a time, and right now confess to the Lord Jesus that you are a sinner and ask Him to save you, just like Peter did. He cried, "Lord save me." (Matthew 14:30) Peter was drowning in the sea of Galilee.

There are over 1,000 commandments in the New Testament; and to be perfect as the Father is perfect, we find it is necessary to keep all those commandments. **"If you love me, keep My Commandments." (John 14:15) "Be you therefore perfect, even as your Father, which is in heaven is perfect."** (Matthew 5:48) This is one of the commandments of Christ Jesus, and He would not have told you to be perfect if it were not possible. It takes a lifetime, but Paul attained, so you can too.

Since God is no respecter of persons, and requires that all "Shell Down the Corn", (Confess), let us observe how some of our brothers reacted when it came **"Corn Shelling Time".** Take brother Isaiah, one of God's greatest prophets; but he was useless until he "Shelled Down the Corn". Isaiah's confession went down like this. "He had a vision of the Lord sitting on His throne in the temple, with the Seraphim crying "Holy, holy", and the whole earth was full of His glory. And the doorposts moved at the voice of him that cried, and the house was filled with smoke." (Isaiah 6:3,4) Right here is where Isaiah "Shelled Down the Corn". "Then said I, "Woe is me! For I am undone, because I am a man of unclean lips, for mine eyes have seen the King, the Lord of Hosts." (Isaiah 6:5)

Then after Isaiah confessed that he was unclean, as we all are, God used him. Then flew one of the Seraphim unto me, having a live coal in his hand, which he had taken with the tongs from off the altar: And he laid it upon my mouth and said, "Lo, this has touched thy lips, and thine iniquity is taken away and thy sin is purged." (Isaiah 6:6,7) "Also, I heard the voice of the Lord saying, "Whom shall I send, and who will go for us?" (Who is us?) "Then said I, "Here am I. Send me."-(Isaiah 6:8) "And He said, "Go, and tell this people. Hear you indeed, but understand not, and you see indeed, but perceive not." (Isaiah 6:9) By the way, the Us is the Trinity, the Father, the Son, the Holy Spirit.

This is one example of Isaiah, one of God's greatest children, "Shelling Down the Corn", confessing that he was unclean. The Seraphim said, "Your iniquity, (which is lawlessness), has been purged with your sin. All of us have to be purged from our lawlessness and our sin, just like Isaiah.   We see that after Isaiah "Shelled Down the Corn" to God, that God used Isaiah to go to warn the Jews of their upcoming persecutions. But they were without understanding, as they had eyes to see, and yet were blind, ears to hear, and yet were deaf, a heart of stone, and could not perceive or understand. (Isaiah 6)

So, now, we will take for an example, my hero, which was Paul, and how Paul "Shelled Down the Corn" to God. The blind yet had eyes to see, and had ears yet were deaf, and had a cold heart of stone that could not understand the law of faith; and mercy, was Paul. His given name was actually Saul, named after the king from the tribe of Benjamin, which was Jacob's youngest son. Paul did not "Shell Down the Corn" to Christ when he saw the light, because he was a strict law keeper; and he knew nothing about the Spirit and another law called Grace.

Christ Jesus is no respecter of persons, and He has to get everyone's attention before they know He is calling them out. Calling them out of what? Calling them out of sin and death and everlasting fire, that was prepared for the Devil and his angels. (Matthew 25:41) When Saul, later called Paul, first saw the light, he did not confess anything to Jesus, until many years later. He was in the stage as "Christians" are in this present time, which is the stage of justification, which is not saved, but only called out, (Ekklesia), Greek for Called Out Ones. **"Many are called, but few are chosen."** (Matthew 20:16)

In order to get Saul's attention, Jesus came to him on the road to Damascus, with His glory so bright that it burned Saul's eyes and blinded him with scales over his eyes, which is just like the "Christians" that have scales over their eyes and cannot see the Truth, which is the Lord Christ Jesus. But, Praise God, the scales fell off Saul's eyes, and he was on the road to becoming a believer and a possessor instead of a professor.

God gave Saul a new name and called him an apostle, changed his name from Saul to Paul. But even after Paul had been regenerated, even after Paul was *(born again)*, even after they called Paul a "Christian", Greek (Xpistiavos) (Kristeeanos) (Acts 26:28), Paul was still filled with inbred sin. Paul, himself is the one that said: "O wretched man that I am! Who shall deliver me from the body of this death?" (Romans 7:24) Paul was looking at the body of a dead one that he was still carrying around inside of him that was offensive, or causing him to sin. The body of sin that was dead inside of him had already been crucified with Christ, but he had not put off the old man that he was still carrying around inside of his members. (Ephesians 4:22) and (Romans 6:6)

"Knowing this, that our old man is crucified with Him, that the body of sin might be destroyed, that henceforth we should not serve sin." (Romans 6:6) "That you put off the former conversation concerning the old man, which is corrupt according to the deceitful lusts." (Ephesians 4:22) Continuing on with the instruction of Paul, in the next verse he puts on: "And be renewed in the Spirit of your mind; And that you put on the new man, which after God is created in righteousness and true holiness." (Ephesians 4:23,24)

After Paul "Shells Down the Corn" and asks who can and who shall deliver him from this body of death? Paul gives thanks to God, through Christ Jesus Our Lord. "So then with the mind I myself serve the law of God, but with the flesh the law of sin." (Romans 7:25)

The only way to put off the old man that was crucified, is to consecrate yourself to God Almighty (PANTAKRATOR); and plead the blood of Jesus, and stay into Christ Jesus, until the second blessing comes from God, in the Name of Jesus. That is what hinders so many "Christians" from receiving the Holy Ghost, because they profess to have the Holy Spirit; and they do have the Holy Spirit with them; whereby if they would humble themselves, and quit acting like they are something, when they are nothing, (Galatians 6:3), it could be, the Holy Spirit would come and dwell into them and sanctify them and crucify the old man in them. "Christians" are all the time professing things that they are, like: "He has made us to be kings and priests"; when the truth of the matter is, they are just professors and not possessors. They profess to be "Christians", when all the time they are nothing. They cannot overcome the old man in them, because they do not consecrate themselves to a purpose, and to God. "Christians" do not even know how to be a "Christian", devoting themselves to following Jesus and keeping His commandments, instead of just professing to recognize Him as Lord, except just when they need something in the things of this world. They stopped short of putting off the old man, which is corrupt according to the deceitful lusts or covetousness.

Newly converted readers, beware of the doctrines of "Christians", and glue yourselves to the One Doctrine of Christ Jesus. **"Take my yoke upon you and learn of Me, for I Am meek and lowly in heart** (Spirit); **and you shall find rest unto your souls,** (lives)." (Matthew 11:29) **"For My yoke is easy, and My burden is light."** (Matthew 11:30)

Paul said; "I beseech you, be followers of me." (I Corinthians 4:16) When Paul "Shelled Down the Corn", (confessed), and Jesus crucified the old man in Paul, it is our imperative duty to follow him. Warning to all: Do not try to exalt yourselves; but on the contrary, you must humble (abase) yourselves. "And whosoever shall exalt himself, shall be abased; and he that shall humble himself, shall be exalted." (Matthew 23:12)

This is the Word of the Lord, and He said: **"And why call you Me, Lord, Lord, and do not the things I say?"** (Luke 6:46) It is very crucial that you keep the Commandments of Christ, which are over 1,000! "All of the promises of God are yea and amen to those that are in Christ Jesus." (II Corinthians 1:20) Notice the scripture did not say the promises are yea to everybody, but yea and amen only to those that are in Christ Jesus.

Everyone that wants to enter the Kingdom of God, or desires to go to heaven, must "Shell Down the Corn", (confess) to Christ Jesus before they can come to God. One of the most touching confessions in the Holy Scriptures to this writer is the account that Luke wrote about in Chapter 5 of his book. "The two boats and their crews had fished all night and never caught any fish. The crowd of people pressed upon Jesus to hear the Word of God as Jesus stood by the Lake Gennesaret. The fishermen were gone out of the boats washing their nets. And Jesus entered into one of the ships, which was Simon's, and prayed him that he would thrust out a little from the land. And He sat down, and taught the people out of the ship." (Luke 5:3) "Now when He had left speaking, He said unto Simon, **"Launch out into the deep and let down your nets for a draught."** (Luke 5:4) "And Simon said unto Him, "Master, we have toiled all the night, and have taken nothing: Nevertheless, at your Word, I will let down the net." (Luke 5:5) "And when they had this done, they enclosed a great multitude of fishes; And their net brake." (Luke 5:6) "And they beckoned to their partners, which were in the other ship, that they should come and help them. And they came, and filled both the ships, so that they began to sink." (Luke 5:7)

Now, the writer wants to interject his imagination as to how Peter must have felt before God's Holy Spirit convicted Simon Peter and drew him to Jesus and "Shelled Down the Corn", (confessed). Peter was a professional fisherman; and if you have ever stayed up all night and toiled, (worked), then you must know how tired and exhausted Peter must have been; and probably was more than a little put out with Jesus telling Peter to launch out into the deep. Nevertheless, here is how the "Corn was Shelled Down" to the Son of God.

"When Simon Peter saw it, he fell down at Jesus' knees, saying, "Depart from me, for I am a sinful man, O Lord." (Luke 5:8) Jesus had already told Peter and others to follow Him, and He would make them fishers of men; and now Jesus had just taught a professional fisherman how to be a fisher of fish. (Matthew 4:19) and (Luke 5:8) Simon Peter "Shelled Down the Corn". Look at the increase in the faith of each one of the ones that "Shelled Down the Corn", (confessed their guilt). Isaiah became one of the greatest prophets in the Old Testament and even prophesied about the Savior being born for us. (Isaiah 9:6) "Then I said, "Woe is me! For I am undone, because I am a man of unclean lips; and I dwell in the midst of a people of unclean lips, for mine eyes have seen the King, The Lord of Hosts." (Isaiah 6:5) Notice when Isaiah "Shelled the Corn Down", he not only confessed for himself, but also for the people that he lived in the midst of that also were undone. Isaiah' example was for you, if you will confess your guilt and quit sinning, God will use you for an example to show all the people you live in the midst of. Instead of the Seraphim carrying a coal of fire to clean your lips, God will baptize your body, soul, and your spirit (heart) with the Holy Spirit and fire. Not only will the *Triune* God clean up your lips and your tongue, but He will clean your heart (spirit), and help you to have a pure heart (spirit), and will prepare you and make you fit for the Master"s use.

Instead of you saying negative words that pronounce death, the Holy Spirit will teach you to say the Words that Jesus spoke, which were all Words of life. The Holy Spirit is the only teacher you need. You have no need of man teaching you. 1 John 2;26,27.

Paul was my hero, because he was not taught by any man of what to eat, or what to say, or how to live. The Lord, Christ Jesus, taught Paul by the Holy Spirit, and by angels, and by revelations, and by visions, and by the risen Christ Himself. In (Galatians 1:16) Paul said he conferred not with flesh and blood, (mankind). God said to Paul: **"My grace is sufficient for you: For My strength is made perfect in weakness."** (II Corinthians 12:9)

Most people think that when Paul sought the Lord three times to take the thorn out of his flesh it was some kind of infirmity, but it was sent by Satan to keep him from exalting himself, because of the many revelations God had given him. (II Corinthians 12:7,8) All the revelation, visions, works, came to Paul after he had "Shelled Down the Corn".

After Simon Peter "Shelled Down the Corn" to Jesus and fell down to his knees and confessed his guilt to Jesus, Peter fed the Sheep of Jesus with many morsels of God's food that was nourishing to Jesus' Sheep. One of the meals that was nourishing that Peter prepared was the one in (I Peter 3:19), "where he told about Jesus preaching to the spirits in prison, which sometime were disobedient, when once the long suffering of God waited in the days of Noah, while the Ark was a preparing, wherein few, that is, eight souls (lives) were saved by water. The like figure where unto even baptism does also now save us, (not the putting away of the filth of the flesh, but the answer of a good conscience toward God) by the resurrection of Christ Jesus." (I Peter 3:20,21) The rest of the mystery is following in **"Corn Shelling Time."**

Father God, in the name of Christ Jesus please draw the readers of **"Corn Shelling Time"** to Christ Jesus by Your Holy Spirit; and, dear Jesus, please reveal the Father to them and send Your Holy Spirit, which is The Comforter, Counselor, Advocate, and the only teacher they will ever need. Send The Spirit Of Truth into them to bring to their memory all the things You said and show them things to come. Above all things Father I ask You to save them in the last day, and Lord Jesus I ask You to raise them up, in the name of Jesus. Amen!

Chapter 4

"IN THE BEGINNING WAS the Word, and the Word was with God, and the Word was God." (John 1:1)

This was not the beginning of the earth with man inhabiting the earth. There are millions of years in between Genesis 1:1 and Genesis 1:2.

The Word that God spoke was God. God spoke the creation into existence before He created man. God created angels and the universe before He created man.

The arch angel Lucifer was cast down to the ground by the Word. (Isaiah 14:12) After Lucifer was cast down to the ground, then we pick up the Word Of God in (Genesis 1:2)

After these things began the 6 days of creation of the world and all the things in it. God spoke the Word. The Spirit moved upon the face of the waters and brought whatever the Word said to come to pass.. "God said, "Let there be light." (Genesis 1:3)

After God spoke all the things in the seas and the earth into existence, and God said: "Let **us** make man." (Genesis 1:26) "And God blessed them, and God said to them: "Be fruitful, and multiply, and <u>replenish</u> the earth, and subdue it, and have dominion over the fish of the sea, and over the fowl of the air, and over every living thing that moves upon the earth." (Genesis 1:27,28) Direct your attention to the words underlined, because they never pass away; and they are active and pertain to life forever. Who was God talking to when He said: "Let us make man?" Since God is the only One that can create life, He had to be talking to God the Father, God the Son, and God the Holy Spirit. God spoke the Word, the Holy Spirit brought to pass whatever the Word formed that God said. So the **Us** was the *Triune* God, or the Trinity, or the Father, the Son, the Holy Spirit, which is **One** God. The next underlined word is replenish, meaning that the earth was plentiful before, so God said to replenish it. What was on the earth before it became void, without form and total darkness? Was there humanity on the earth before? Since God's Word is Truth, we can rule out human kind ever being anywhere on any planet anywhere in the whole universe.

Adam was the first man that God ever created, Created He them in His own image. "Let **Us** make man in **Our** image after **Our** likeness." (Genesis 1:26)

So **Us** and **Our** was the Trinity, Father, Son, Holy Spirit. Amen. So God did not say to replenish the earth with humans; but He told the humans to multiply.

The things that were on the earth before were animals, fish, birds, and angels to raise the herbs and tend the trees and to cause the earth to be a garden, which the Arch Angel, Lucifer, was the chief overseer, until he wanted to rise up and be equal to God. (Isaiah 14:12)

Please understand this insert in this book is not the Word of God, but is fiction from the mind of the writer. (First Duishka 1:1) To Wit: When Lucifer rose up to declare that he would ascend (go up) into heaven, and would exalt his throne above the stars of God; he said, "I will sit upon the mount of the congregation in; the sides of the north: I will ascend above the heights of the clouds, I will be like the

Most High." (Isaiah 14:14) Lucifer has been doing the talking until now, when the Word of God said: "How art you fallen from heaven, O Lucifer, son of the morning. Are you cut down to the ground, which did weaken the nations?" (Isaiah 14:12) (Genesis 1:2) says the earth was without form, and void and darkness was upon the face of the deep, meaning the earth was flooded and totally dark, void of any light. Lucifer was the Arch Angel, and angels are flames of fire, and Lucifer was cut down to the ground. How did the earth become darkness and flooded with water? (First Duishka 1:1) says it happened on this wise. Lucifer tried to be equal with the Most High, and there ensued a great war in heaven with God and His Hosts of two thirds of the angels and Lucifer and one third of the angels. God cast Lucifer and one third of the angels down to the ground, and flooded the entire earth with water, putting out the flames of fire on Lucifer and his one third of angels, leaving Lucifer and his angels black and dark. So the earth was flooded and dark. Lucifer was black. (Duishka 1:1)

The above that you have just read is only a figment of Duishka's imagination. That was just thrown in, and you can just throw it out. (a theory)

Back to the Word of God and thus saith the Lord. All this quoting of scripture is to follow the Word, which is God, from the beginning to the end.

Because of the ignorance of some that do not know that the Word was in the beginning, and the Word was God. (John 1:1) Since the Word of God created every living thing, and the sun and the moon, and the stars, for signs in the heavens, did you read where He gave man dominion over everything that was alive, over every living thing. The other underlined word was living. The Word gave life.God created every living thing, so that made God the owner of everything that has life in it.Included in all the things God owned was mankind. He gave man dominion over all the other living things. Actually God gave man dominion over himself, which is called a free moral agent to choose for himself who he (man) wills to have dominion over him. When Adam and Eve disobeyed God, they gave themselves to Satan to have dominion over them. Satan is the executioner of the death sentence Adam and Eve brought upon all mankind, when they disobeyed the Law of God, which was do not eat the fruit of the tree of knowledge. The sentence for that crime is death. They chose to disobey the Law of God and received the sentence of death.

They not only turned their free moral agency over to Satan, the executioner of the death sentence; but they also turned you and I and all mankind over to the executioner, Satan, to carry out the death sentence, which is upon all mankind. That is the legacy Adam left you and I and all mankind, which is called our Adamic nature, the law of sin, the body of sin, the body of death, the carnal mind, or our old man. That is our inbred sin that we inherited from father Adam.

There is only one way mankind can get redeemed from that death sentence; and that is by the blood sacrifice; the ransom that was paid by the Word, Jesus, Lamb Of God, our Redeemer. It takes thousands of years for God's plan of redemption to be manifested; because God wills to not only clean the hearts of the redeemed people, but also clean the heavens and the earth from all filthiness and impure things. That is why the earth and all the works of it will be purified by fire. That is how your heart (spirit) is purified by the Holy Ghost (Spirit) and fire.

All the people on earth do not belong to God, because most of the people on earth are walking dead people that Satan has claim on. God only owns the sanctified, Holy Ghost filled, that have the old man purged out of them by the fire of purification and are living. The walking dead people are on probation; and God and all of the living are praying for the dead that are on probation that they will repent and apply the blood of Jesus to their hearts (spirits) and be pure in heart, and be Holy as God is Holy, without which no one can see God. (Hebrews 14:12)

Michael Duishka

It is **<u>"Corn Shelling Time"</u>** for you if you are one of the walking around dead, that thinks he is alive, just because he is walking; when all the time you are on probation until you run out of time. If you think the writer of this, is pointing a finger at you, remember his thumb is pointing back at himself. This writer is not ashamed of My Lord Jesus, and remembers very well when he "Shelled Down the Corn" to Jesus with a broken spirit and a contrite heart with tears, and snot pouring out flooding the place, crying out to Jesus to have mercy on me, a sinner, and save me in the Name of Jesus. I believe that I shall be saved, if I endure to the end. (Matthew 24:13)

I "Shelled Down the Corn" to God and confessed I was guilty of being a sinner; just like I "Shelled Down the Corn" to my daddy; and God was faithful and just and forgave me of my sins, and cleansed me from all my unrighteousness. (I John 1;9)

But, I point out there was still the sin I inherited from Adam in my heart. There is a difference in sins and sin. Sins are the trespasses I committed myself, and God is faithful and just to forgive these sins, if I "Shell Down the Corn", (confess). But, sin, is not something you committed; but it is sin you inherited from Adam; and God cannot forgive you for something you did not do. This sin has to be crucified by Christ Jesus; and then purged, or put off, by you. (Ephesians 4:22)

In order for Jesus to crucify and destroy the old man of inbred sin, you must surrender your all, your body, soul, and spirit, and all your members, and senses to Christ Jesus. "For I am persuaded that He is able to keep that which I have committed unto Him against that day." (II Timothy 1:12) That Day, being the Lord's Day of Judgment.

Pay attention, dear reader, I am not writing this for monetary reasons, or to be haughty or rude, or to build me up in pride, because my pride fell a long time ago, never to be proud again. I am writing this to you by commandment to warn you of the deceitfulness of Satan, your enemy, and your master, and to show you how to change masters,

| 30 |

and submit yourselves to The Master, Lord Christ Jesus, who washed our sins away in His Own Blood.

Satan deceived Eve. So he can and already has you deceived. Satan tried to deceive the Word, (Jesus), with the Word. Jesus was the Word, and knew every Word He had said, clear back to the beginning. So when Satan quoted Psalms 91 to Jesus, Jesus just told Satan some more Word that He had said in another place in time past.

But you are not the Word; and if the KJV gets close to the scripture, but misinterprets or misconstrues, or substitutes, or just plain changes the Word of Life, you do not know the difference. Satan has succeeded in deceiving you by what you believe to be the Word of God. Satan caused the scholars of the King James Bible, because they were under duress from the king, to write what had already been written in the Catholic Bible, which was the Lie from Satan himself, that caused the Catholic people to worship Pagan gods, and have festivals of Devil gods.

The Catholic Church of Rome killed millions of Holy Ones; and the Kings of England did the same thing, and intimidated the scholars, writers of the KJV to appease the king; or they would get their head lifted off. Tyndale wrote the first Truthful Bible and translated the most original Greek New Testament scriptures into English; and he was seduced into coming back to England, where he was killed by the king.

There is very little difference between Catholics and Protestants. Both cults are deceived by Satan, by using a few words that Jesus' disciples used, mixed with doctrines of Devils, and causing "Christians" and church goers to believe they are saved on their way to heaven; when all the time, Satan is shouting victory.

The only hope for the deceived people of the churches is to keep God's Commandment in (Revelation 18:4), which is: **"Come out of**

"Her", My People, that you be not partakers of "Her" sins; and that you receive not of "Her" plagues." (Revelation 18:4)

The last previous word that was underlined was living, but that was before Adam fell from the protection of God. When Adam fell, he caused the entire sum of mankind to fall and come under condemnation, which is death. So every child that is born of a woman, from Eve until the end of the age is walking around dead men. All humans are born with an allotted time of probation, which is; the time that is allotted to each one, he is walking around dead; but there is a way to overcome death; and that is to apply the blood of Jesus to your heart, and let the blood of Jesus that was paid as a ransom for us to be redeemed from the penalty of death that Adam gave us for an inheritance.

How can you apply the blood of Jesus to your heart? It is simple in one way, and difficult in another. The simple way is to believe Him. The difficult way is to believe in Him. You may think this is just a play on words, Not So. It is very important to live by every Word that proceeds out of the mouth of God. (Luke 4:4)

The Devil used the KJV of the Bible to seduce you and mislead you, so he will not loose you. He owns you until you apply the blood of Jesus over you to cleanse you from your sins and all unrighteousness. (I John 1:9). But you have to "Shell Down the Corn", (confess); and that is the first step in applying the blood of Christ Jesus to your heart.

The way you will know if the blood has been applied to your heart is, after you have "Shelled Down the Corn" to God with a broken spirit and a contrite heart, if you love your brethren. Then you will know you have passed from death to life, because he that loves not his brother abides in death. (I John 3:14)

That is not all that is required of you. After you have passed from death to life, comes the difficult part; and you do not know that you have beat the executioner out of an execution of a soul (Life) that was condemned to die; but you passed from death to life; but you waged war with Satan; and the fight is on.

When you passed from death to life, you do not know how to fight a spiritual warfare; but that is exactly what you are involved in. "For we wrestle not against flesh and blood, but against principalities, against powers, against the rulers of the darkness of this world, against spiritual wickedness in high places." (Ephesians 6:12)

You do not know how to overcome all the spirits of darkness, and you cannot learn by going or joining any church, because that is what Satan wants you to do, because churches are his fortress. He is in every church every Sunday morning deceiving the fearful and the abominable. They think they are hid from Satan, because they never cast him out, but fellowship with the filth of the world. Dear reader, it is imperative that you overcome all these unclean spirits of Satan that are in the Harlot churches if you desire to rule and reign in the kingdom of God with Christ Jesus.

"To him that overcomes and keeps my works to the end to him will I give power over the nations And he shall rule them with a rod of iron: as the vessels of a potter shall they be broken to shivers: even as I received of My Father." (Revelation 2:26,27)

How can you overcome all the unclean spirits of darkness when you fellowship and assemble yourself together with them every Sunday? He said to come out from among them and be you separate from them. (II Corinthians 6:17) Thus saith the Lord and touch not the unclean thing. (II Corinthians 6:17) Here is His answer and commandment; "Come out of "Her", My people, that you be not partakers of "Her" sins, and you receive not of "Her" plagues." (Revelation 18;4)

Chapter 5

JESUS SAID: "COME UNTO Him, and learn of Him." You cannot learn how to overcome the enemy in *church*, because they do not know how to fight a spiritual battle in a *church*. It does not make any difference which denomination you go to. All they know how to do is to pray for Jesus to give them something, or pray for Jesus to rebuke Satan for them. Jesus is not going to rebuke Satan for you, because He has already overcome Satan Himself, and He has given you all the weapons to fight a spiritual warfare, and overcome the wiles of Satan. (Ephesians 6:11)

But you do not know how to learn of Jesus. You know how to learn about Jesus by going to *church*. But that is all you will ever know by going to *church*, is learn about Jesus. You will never know Jesus Himself, because you will not find Jesus in *church*. Listen and pay attention to what the Bible says, instead of what the blind guides in *churches* tell you, because they have just read about the Holy Spirit and fire. They have not been sanctified and become holy, or they would not break the commandments of God. They would come out of "Her." (Revelation 18:4)

All, say: **"All"**, *churches* break the laws of God! Jesus never said in His Word to go to *church*. Jesus did say, **"Come unto Me." "Learn of Me."** (Matthew 11:28,29)

How do you come to Jesus? How do you learn of Him? Answer: Believe Him! You say, "I do believe Him"; but what did He say? **"Every Word that proceeds out of the mouth of God."** (Matthew 4:4)

You cannot find Jesus by clicking on to Jesus.com Search with your mouse. You cannot be filled with the Holy Spirit by clicking on to Holy Spirit.com Search. You cannot SKYPE Jesus. You cannot send Jesus a text message or send Him any E-mail, because Jesus does not have an E-mail address. You can call unto Him. His number is JER.33:3 "Call unto Me, and I will answer you, and show you great and mighty things, which you know not." (Jeremiah 33:3)

"If you love Me, keep My Commandments; and I will pray the Father; and He shall give you another Comforter, that He may abide with you forever." (John 14:16,17)

"Howbeit when He, the Spirit of Truth, is come, He will guide you into all Truth; for He shall not speak of Himself; but whatsoever He shall hear, that shall He speak; and He will show you things to come." (John 16:13)

This Spirit of Truth is called in the Original Greek in the New Testament, (Parakletos), which means an intercessor, or counselor, or an advocate. (John 14:16)

This Parakletos is the only teacher this writer ever had that taught me the Truth. Preachers in *churches* did their best to teach and preach the Truth; but they were ignorant and unlearned in the tongue Jesus and His Apostles spoke in, so all the teaching I received from preachers was false. After many years of being filled with false teaching, the Lord Christ Jesus sent His Spirit of Truth to me to teach me in the **TRUTH.** He told me to unlearn all the false doctrines I had been taught, and learn of Him: Here is the Word He showed to me, and I will pass it on to you:

"These things have I written to you concerning them that seduce you. But the anointing, which you have received of Him, abides in you; and you need not that any man teach you; but as the same anointing teaches you of all things, and is Truth, and is no lie; and even as He has taught you, you shall abide in Him." (I John 2:26,27) "The anointing is the Holy Spirit that in layman's terms is called a gut feeling." (First Duishka) The anointing told me to unlearn all the false teaching I had rooted and grounded in me; and learn of Him, which I did; and now I pass it on to whosoever has ears to hear, let him hear; and whosoever has a heart to perceive, let him understand what the Lord told me; and **"Come out of "Her."** (Revelation 18:4)

"And I heard another voice from heaven saying, **"Come out of "Her", My people, that you be not partakers of "Her" sins, and that you receive not of "Her" plagues."** (Revelation 18:4)

The reason the former teachings were false and had to be unlearned is because they came from English KJV of the Bible, which is a sequel of the Catholic Unholy Bible. Both the KJV and the Latin Catholic Bible contain false scriptures pertaining to worship of Pagan gods and doctrines of Devils, which is false "Christ-*ians*." It took this writer many years of trial and error, mostly error, to find out the KJV of the Bible is very misleading and misinterpreted and intimidated scriptures.

"Now the Spirit speaks expressly, that in the latter times some shall depart from the faith, giving heed to seducing spirits and doctrines of Devils." (I Timothy 4:1) This is the latter (last) times, and many false "Christ-*ians*"have already departed from the faith in Jesus.

"This is the latter Times, speaking lies in hypocrisy, having their conscience seared with a hot iron." (I Timothy 4:2)

This is the time of the end, when Daniel's book will be opened, that he shut up. I will open it in a later chapter of this book; but let him that reads this please understand, it is **"Corn Shelling Time"**.

For the ones that believe Christ Jesus, and know what the anointing has taught them, and what the Holy Spirit has given them in a gut feeling, this latter time is a very exciting time. Shakespear said, "The world is a stage"; and I say, "The last scene is about to be presented in living color; and the curtain is close to rising on the last scene; and you are about to be witnessing God's Grand Finale'."

Jesus said: **"And you shall hear of wars and rumors of wars. See that you be not troubled for all these things must come to pass, but the end is not yet."** (Matthew 24:6)

"For nation shall rise against nation and kingdom against kingdom; and there shall be famines and pestilences and earthquakes in different places." (Matthew 24:7)

"All these are the beginning of sorrows." (Matthew 24:8)

The beginning of sorrows escalated to a significant start in the year 2011, when all these things Jesus prophesied started increasing like never before.

This is the time for you, dear reader, to "Shell Down the Corn", (confess) that you are a sinner, and be baptized with the Holy Ghost and fire, so you can fight against those wicked spirits in the air that are causing anger and hate in the hearts of the children of darkness. The enemy (Satan) has filled the hearts of the deceived ones, most especially the so called "Christians" that make the church house their god. We need to pray fervently for God's people to come out of "Her", just like Lot came out of Sodom and Gomorrah.

Because I was taught by no man, and because I was taught by the same anointing I received at first, which was God's Holy Spirit, I can see so many prophecies fulfilling right before my eyes. Oh, how I pray that you, dear reader, would read it for yourselves, so you could see and understand the Truth that He told us would come to pass in the latter days, which we are now in this untoward (*perverse*) generation. (Acts 2:40)

You cannot hear how to repent of your sins in *church* anymore. You cannot hear how to apply the blood of Jesus to your heart (spirit) to cleanse your black heart from all unrighteousness. The *churches* just want your attendance and what you can do for them. Such as give them all the money you can, or do some theatrical act, such as sing, dance, or play, anything to add to the mystery of iniquity. The *churches* are theaters that portray the filth and abominations of the world in all ungodliness in one way or another, carrying on their corruption in the name of God (Jesus). That is why Jesus said to **"come out of "Her", My people, that you be not partakers of "Her" sins, and that you receive not of "Her" plagues.** (Revelation 18:4)

Every kind of plague that is known of and many that are not known of are coming upon *church* goers, simply because they did not go to Jesus; instead they went to *church*. It is **"Corn Shelling Time."**

The leaders in *churches* do not have any discipline. That is why they do not discipline the church goers; and that is why the churches are just like a circus, with wild animals that are trained how to act and what to say, that sounds like the Devil when he was tempting Jesus. (Luke 4:4)

Jesus called the Gentiles in Sodom and Gomorrah dogs. They were men lying with men (*queers*) committing all kinds of acts of fornication, just like the children of darkness that fill up the *churches* of Satan in this present time. They say Jesus is Lord, but obey the conversation of Satan. You know what they say is, always a lie. **"And why call**

you Me, Lord, Lord; and do not the things which I say?"
(Luke 6:46)

The *churches* use the name of Jesus, and the *church* is a cloak *(covering)* for their many sins:

"The scribes *(theologians)* and the pharisees *(preachers)* sit in Moses' seat." (Matthew 23:2)

"All therefore whatsoever they bid you observe, that observe and do; but do you not after their works; for they say and do Not." (Matthew 23:3)

That is why you need to read the book entitled "Please Do Not Call Me A "Christian", by Michael Duishka.

"And call no man your father upon the earth. For one is your Father, which is in heaven."

(Matthew 23:9)

"Neither be you called masters *(teachers)*, **for one is your master** *even* **Christ."** (Matthew 23:10)

After you "Shell Down the Corn" to Christ Jesus, (confess your sins), He will be your master *(teacher)*, and will teach you all things. (I John 2:26,27)

"The thief comes not but for to steal, and to kill, and to destroy. I am come that they might have life, and that they might have it more abundantly." (John 10:10) Jesus (The Word) doing the talking. Without Jesus you cannot have life in you. You may think that because your body is functioning you are alive. You say I am reading this, so I am alive; or because you are walking and breathing you are alive. The Word, (Jesus) said you are dead, because you do not have the giver of life. (John 1:4) Says; "In Him, (The Word), was life."

So, if you do not have the Word, you do not have any life; but you are dead, just waiting until you fall down and some other dead person buries you. "But Jesus said unto him. **"Follow Me. Let the dead bury the dead."** (Matthew 8:22)

So the Word says He is life, and the Word says follow Him. That is what we need to do to live and have life now and forever. Let us begin following the Word, which was with God and was God. (John 1:1) **"In the beginning was the Word, and the Word was with God, and the Word was God."** (John 1:1)

So, we are following the Word, which said in Him was life. (John 1:4) So follow the Word on down to (John 1:14): "And the Word was made flesh and dwelt among us." So the Word was made flesh and received another name, called Jesus. So, Jesus, the Word, God are the same, Life.

The beginning means the first thing that God spoke was the Word, and the Word was God that we must follow. Following the Word, He spoke the heavens into existence. Of course, in the heavens was the host of the planets and the angels and other creations; and we follow the Word on into the creation of the things to be planted on the planet earth. Of course we know the earth did not have any living thing upon it, because it was void and covered with darkness. Then we see the Word for the first time on the earth, as God spoke the Word and said: "Let there be light." And it was so. He created the ruler of the daylight, and named Him Sun, and the ruler of the night light, He named Him Moon.

We will not go through the whole creation, but we will show that the Word of God created life; and life did not evolve; and God created the whales and every living creature that moves, which the waters brought forth abundantly. (Genesis 1:21)

God then spoke the Word, saying: **"Bless you, be fruitful and multiply, and fill the waters in the seas; and let fowl multiply in the earth, everything after it's kind."** (Genesis 1:22)

Now the Word of God has blessed all the life He created up to this point, and still has not made man yet. After God commanded the beasts of the earth to be made after their kind and cattle after their kind, God said: (What did He say?) He said: **"Let us make man in our image, after our likeness, and let them** (*mankind*) **have dominion over all the earth and every living thing that moves upon the earth."**

The sixth day He finished all His work; and on the seventh day God rested. God, the Word, sanctified the seventh day and rested. The word sanctified means holy and pure, undefiled.

Then God planted a garden and called it Eden, and God took the man and put him in the garden to dress and keep it. God gave the man one commandment, and the man could not keep the one commandment; and he caused death to come upon you and me and all mankind from that time until the heavens and the earth are made new.

God spoke the Word and said: **"You may eat of every tree of the garden freely; but of the tree of the knowledge of good and evil, you shall not eat of it; for in the day you eat thereof, you shall surely die."** Then God caused a deep sleep to come upon Adam and took one of Adam's ribs and made a woman, and God brought the woman unto the man. Then up jumps the Devil! Remember Lucifer was a ministering spirit that was cast out of heaven down to the ground. So God called Lucifer a different name after He threw Lucifer out of heaven, and called him Devil, and Serpent.

Understand what a spirit is: A spirit is an unseen force that is more powerful than the air and does not have a substance that can be seen with natural eyes. A spirit does not have any form, but can enter anything that does have a form and force the thing that does have form to do his will.

That is exactly what Lucifer, the wicked spirit, did. He entered into the most subtle of all the creatures that God created, the serpent. God created the serpent to walk on two legs, upright like a human, until the Devil used the serpent's body to enter into. After the serpent allowed the Devil to use his body, God cursed the serpent and caused him to crawl on the ground and eat the dust all the days of his life.

But the Devil knew that Adam could not be deceived into disobeying God, so he used the serpent to hide in, and went to the weaker vessel to deceive, which was the woman. While Adam was out tilling the ground, the Devil entered into the serpent, and caused the serpent to go to the woman, who was in the orchard where the forbidden fruit tree was; and the devil caused the serpent to talk to the woman. This is the first deception. The Devil caused the serpent to say to the woman subtle words that deceived her, causing her to disobey God and eat from the tree of death.

This is the same force of evil spirits that man has to overcome in these last days. These evil spirits come into a person and put thoughts into his brain, and make him think that God caused him to think those evil thoughts. God could foresee that all men had evil hearts (spirits) and would eventually destroy all creation, but God provided a way of escape for the ones that obey His commandments and believe Him, and love Him. But for those that just believe that Christ Jesus was just a good man and a prophet, they will be destroyed with the evil men that destroy; but the next chapter shows you how to overcome.

Father God, in the name of Jesus, the one that paid the ransom with His blood to save the whosoever that believes Him, I ask You to do for them the same thing You did for me, which was to make me a whole person again by healing all my infirmities, and healing my spirit, and giving me a bath by the washing of the water of the Word, and cleansing my black heart by applying the blood of Jesus to my heart, and making my heart pure and holy, and giving me all the promises of God; and I am not forgetting all Your benefits and most especially the power You gave to me to tread on serpents and scorpions and over all the power of the enemy; and nothing shall by any means hurt me; and Father baptize them in the Holy Ghost and fire just like You did me; and since I know You are no respecter of persons, I believe You will do for these that believe You the same thing You did for me. Father teach them by the Comforter, Your Holy Spirit. Father I give You thanks in the name of Christ Jesus; and I believe You will do what I ask You in the name of Christ Jesus, Amen and Amen.

Chapter 6

THE FIRST DECEPTION THAT seduced the woman, Eve, did not go away, but escalated into a force that brings eternal death to everyone that does not overcome the evil wicked one. "And Adam was not deceived; but the woman being deceived, was in the transgression." (I Timothy 2:14)

Repeat: You must, it is imperative. You cannot overcome sin, Satan, sickness, lusts, doubt, envy, pride, wrath, anger, impatience, or any other offense or stumbling block, unless, except, you "Shell Down the Corn" to Christ Jesus. Except you confess Your sins to Jesus and beg His forgiveness for your black heart, you will die in your sins. Listen! Pay attention! "Shell Down the Corn" to Christ Jesus. "Submit yourselves to God. Resist the Devil, and he will flee from you." (James 4:7)

If you are offended by any part of this book, you are dying, because this book is come to give life; and, "Except you drink the blood of the Son of Man, (Jesus), you have no life in you." (John 6:53)

"From that time many of His disciples went back and walked no more with Him." (**John 6:66**) They were offended at this saying, and they backslid. "Then Jesus said unto the twelve: "Will you also go away?" (John 6:67) Jesus is saying the same thing to you, dear reader, so repent of your unbelief and "Shell Down the Corn". (confess Christ Jesus)

If you are not offended by any part of this book, then you are being perfected for the Kingdom of God. It takes a lot of time to submit yourselves to God, and a lot longer to resist the Devil.

The mistake that most people make, most especially "Christians", is they think God is going to do something for them. God is not going to do anything for you, because He has already done everything for you; and has given everything He had for you, even the ultimate sacrifice, His life. Jesus will help you do any Godly thing if you "Shell Down the Corn", and confess, and repent of your sins, and be baptized in the Holy Spirit, which is your Helper.

There are too many things the Devil has given you, for you to overcome all at once. So, you need to recognize and identify what are the things of the world you need to shuck off. There are too many evil inventions that are your idols that cause you to sin. I personally know Couch Potatoes that just keep on getting fatter by sitting and lying on the couch, eating and watching television (*Idolatry*). I personally know men and women that have restored antique automobiles that hardly ever leave the automobile for fear that someone will steal it, or destroy it. (*idolatry*)

I personally know so called "Christians" that give tithes and offerings to their denominational *church*, and give thousands of dollars to so called "Christian" funds; and they let their unfortunate neighbors lie in pain, because their neighbors do not have money or insurance to go to a doctor; and the doctors hide, and any one that needs help cannot find them. (*idolatry*) The oaths they take that they will not turn anyone away are vanity; and they turn everyone away that cannot pay enormous prices, or that does not have insurance that they can overcharge thousands upon thousands to make them richer. I have permission from the author of "Please Do Not Call Me A "Christian"" to use his quote, "Please Do Not Call Me A "Christian.""

These are some of the pitfalls to keep you from overcoming sins and Satan and being holy. "Without holiness you cannot ever see God". (Hebrews 12:14) That is why so called "Christians" do not have any power to overcome sin, because they talk a good show, but underneath, it is all hype. Kapeesh?

You, dear reader, cannot overcome anything in your allotted time here on planet earth, unless you "Shell Down the Corn"*(confess sins)*, and seek the Kingdom of God earnestly with a broken heart and a contrite spirit; and quit playing with false doctrines, and your worldly, pagan days of idolatry, such as *Sunday, Easter, Christmas, Halloween, Martin Luther King Day, Lent, Good Friday,* and many, many more forms of *idolatry*, that are doctrines of Devils, and traditions of men. (Colossians 2:8)

First, before you can have any power, you have to read the gospel for yourselves. "For I am not ashamed of the gospel of Christ: For it is the power of God unto salvation to everyone that believes, to the Jew first, and also to the Greek." (Romans 1:16) All these scriptures you need to read them for yourselves; and do not say, "I do not understand." The reason you say you do not understand is simply because you are too lazy to understand. "Study to show yourself approved unto God, a workman that needs not to be ashamed, rightly dividing the Word of Truth." (II Timothy 2:15)

Remember you do not need a man to teach you anything, according to the Word of Truth. (I John 2:27) Read this scripture until you believe Jesus, that His anointing, which is the Holy Ghost, will teach you all the things Jesus said; and also He will show you things to come. (John 16:13) If you would read the Word of God for yourselves, the Words that are written are Jesus, and He is Life. It is the spirit that quickens, *(makes alive)*, the flesh profits nothing. "**The Words that**

I speak unto you, they are Spirit and they are Life." (John 6:63) So listen and pay close attention: The more Words of God you retain in you, the more spirit you have in you; and the more Spirit you have in you, the more Life you have in you.

The Words in (I John 2:27) learn them and know them in a flash. Say: "I do not need any man to teach me anything." Say: "Father, I thank you for the Holy Spirit teaching me the Truth, instead of a lie, in the Name of Christ Jesus, Amen."

This is all instruction on how to overcome the world, the false doctrinal *churches*, the unclean associations. Learn to say, instead of pray. **"Have the faith of God."** (Mark 11:22) **"For verily I say unto you, that whosoever shall say unto this mountain, be thou removed, and be thou cast into the sea, and shall not doubt in his heart, but believe that these things which he says, shall come to pass, he shall have whatsoever he says."** (Mark 11:23) Remember Jesus was talking to His disciples, which were blood bought believers, that not only believed into Jesus, but also believed Him! There is a big difference in believing in Jesus, as the Devils also do, and believing Him. But if you believe Him, you can say: "In the Name of Jesus, you unclean spirits get behind me, and go; and they should obey." Please remember, you have to be into Christ Jesus, and have His blood applied to your heart (spirit), and be washed in His blood; and remember there is nothing that can wash away your sins, except the blood of Christ Jesus. **"And when you stand praying, forgive if you have ought against any, that your Father also, which is in heaven, may forgive you your trespasses."** (Mark 11:25) **"But if you do not forgive, neither will your Father which is in heaven forgive your trespasses."** (Mark 11:26)

There are two contingencies before what you say will come to pass: One is forgiveness. Do not remember anything someone may have said to you, or about you, or do not hold a grudge, or any malice against any; but, rather, forgive. The next hindrance that will keep you from having what you say is doubt. But if you have "Shelled Down the Corn" to Jesus (confessed your sins) and applied His blood to your heart, and do not doubt, you should have whatsoever you say. (James 1:6) calls it wavering. Do not waver, but believe what Jesus said. He cannot lie. Trust Him instead of the *church,* or any man! Including Preachers!

My sayings are no different from my Lord Christ Jesus. His words offended the Pharisees (*churchgoers*) and the rulers: and when I use His same words, they offend the rulers, "Christians" "hypocrites", and any established religions.

But His Words mean the same thing today, as they did yesterday; and you will be judged by His Words on that great and terrible judgment day of the Lord. The *church* cannot save you. All they can do is take up your tithes and offerings, and sell you what they call salvation. Jesus, nor any of His disciples ever took any tithe.

"Woe unto you, Scribes and Pharisees, hypocrites, for you compass sea and land to make one proselyte; and when he is made, you make him two fold more the child of Hell than yourselves." (Matthew 23:15) There are not any Scribes and Pharisees around in this day and time, where I am writing this book; but there are millions of hypocrites; and they do just what the Savior said, compass sea and land to proselyte *church* members; and when they have made him, they make him "Christians" two fold more a child of Hell than they are. If this offends any, you have need to repent and Come Out of "Her". (Revelation 18:4)

Churches and Preachers say no one can be saved outside of the *church.* I say no one can be saved if they do not come out of "Her", because they are partakers of "Her" sins and will receive "Her" plagues. (Revelation 18:4) *The churches* are worldly *churches;* and the "Christians" are still in the world. The lust of the flesh, and the lust of the eyes, and the pride of life, are not of the Father, but are of the world. (I John 2:16)

You cannot show me any "Christian" in any denominational *church* that is not lusting to satisfy his flesh, or his eyes, or is puffed up with pride. All "Christians" do not keep the Commandments of God.

"Here is the patience of the Holy Ones, here are they that keep the Commandments of God, and the faith of Christ Jesus." (Revelation 14:12)

Jesus said it, and I am just repeating His Words. If His Words offend you, do not keep on sinning; but repent and come out of "Her", and come to Jesus, instead of *Church*. (Matthew 11:28) This is one more thing that is necessary for you to overcome, the commandments of men. **"But in vain they do worship Me, teaching for doctrines the commandments of men".** (Matthew 15:9) This is the Mystery of Iniquity at work.

This is a continuation of the deception that the Devil deceived Eve with; that is now manifest in the *churches* of Satan by examples of every kind of filth and abomination filling up the *churches* that disobey the law of God. Satan has deceived the leaders of the *churches* to let every kind of fornication and uncleanness darken the doorways to the so called sanctuaries, and welcome men lying with men, (*queers*), and lesbians (*lizzies*), idolaters, and any kind of sinner that makes the coffer ring.

Oh, dear reader, do not be taken in by the snare of the Devil, to be fellow shipping with the unbelievers. "Be not unequally yoked with unbelievers, for what fellowship has righteousness with unrighteousness, and what communion has light with darkness?" (II Corinthians 6:14)

"And what concord has Christ with Beliar? Or what part has he that believes with an infidel?" (II Corinthians 6:15)

"And what agreement has the temple of God with idols? For <u>you</u> are the temple of the living God. As God has said, "I will dwell in them, and walk in them, and I will be their God, and they shall be My people." (II Corinthians 6:16)

"Wherefore come out from among them, and be you separate, saith the Lord, and touch not the unclean thing and I will receive you and will be a Father unto you; and you shall be My sons and daughters, saith the Lord Almighty, (PANTAKRATOR)" (II Corinthians 6:17,18)

All the above is a Commandment of God; and if you stay yoked together with lawbreakers, you are just as guilty of sin as Adam and Eve, when they disobeyed God's Commandment. The only way to overcome fellow shipping with unrighteousness is to come out of "Her"; and do what God said, "Be you separate."

"He that overcomes, the same shall be clothed in white raiment; and I will not blot out his name out of the Book of Life; but I will confess his name before My Father, and before His angels."
(Revelation 3:5)

There is not any difference in a "Christian" and a heathen. They dress with their nakedness showing the same way. They celebrate pagan unholy days the same way. They fellowship with murderers, robbers, and destroyers of God's creation alike. "(And should destroy them that destroy the earth)" (Revelation 11:12) They vote for murdering, robbing, destroying, lying politicians.

Just like Eve enticed Adam to eat the fruit that was forbidden, do not let the unbelievers, "Christians", entice you. Read it (scriptures) for yourselves. "Study to show thyself approved unto God, a workman that needs not to be ashamed, rightly dividing the Word of Truth." (II Timothy 2:15)

Since it is a fact that the gospel of the New Testament was written in the Koine' Greek language, it would be better for you and everyone to learn the Koine' Greek language, because that is the only way you will ever rightly divide the Word of Truth. For the ones that do not know Koine' Greek, this writer has used mostly the KJV Bible. There are some words that are man made perverted words that would be blasphemy if the writer used them in relation to the gospel. Some of these words are *church, saint, cross, Jesus Christ, Sunday, lent, good Friday*. These are words of blasphemy. To explain more fully why these words should not be used is because they are words of deception the Devil caused the Catholics to use to deceive "Christian" church goers. People use the word Jesus Christ, thinking Christ is Jesus' last name; when they should say what the Greek says, which is Christ Jesus, or Jesus THE Christ, which He was God's Christ, God. There is no such thing as God's *Church* or *Church* of God, no such thing as *Church* of Christ, or any *church* connected to God or His Christ. God used the word, Ekklesia, which means individually called out ones. If a group of called out ones ever had a meeting together, the Ekklesia was called a congregation, or an assembly, but never *church*.

The word *saint* is a Roman Catholic word used to cover up all their murders, stealing, idolatry, fornication and whoredoms. Every time some pope, bishop, cardinal, or any catholic died, the leftover ones canonized him as a *saint* to cover up all the sins he had committed.

The apostles would be offended if they knew the Roman Catholic heathen dubbed them into *sainthood*. For example *St.* Peter, *St.* John, St. Paul and so on. To be a *saint*, the definition says: A dead one; and I'll guarantee you that the apostles are alive. So the Roman Catholic *Church*, the Mother of Harlots, canonized the Holy Ones (Hagios) as *saints*. There is a big difference in the Greek word Hagios and the cult word *saint*. The difference being the *saint* is a murderer, or an idolater, or a robber, or all the above; whereas a Holy One is pure, sanctified, without sin.

The word *cross* has misled many, because every Roman Catholic and protestant also think Jesus was nailed to a *cross*. The Greek alphabet does not have any C's. So the Truth was nailed to a tree (Xulon) made into a stake (stauros), then Pilate had a sign board nailed across the tree above Jesus' head, that made the ignorant and unlearned Catholics think the tree was made that way. When Jesus was nailed to the tree, it was a perpendicular to the earth, not a horizontal *cross*. It was called a stake of suffering.

Among the other false words of blasphemy is the pagan, "Christian" heathen word *Sunday*, which means the day of the sun god. The Roman Catholic Ruler declared the first day of the week as *Sunday*, which came from heathen worship of Ishtar and Baal. The heathen Catholics adopted the *Sun day* as the Holy Sabbath Day, and the heathen "Christians" followed suit; and the scholars that put together the KJV Bible changed very little from the Catholic Text to the KJ Text. Now the heathen day to worship the *sun god* for "Christians" is chiseled in stone; and they blaspheme the Holy Father God and His Christ Jesus every *Sunday*, because they fail to remember the Sabbath day to keep it Holy.(Exodus 20:8) "For whosoever shall keep the whole law, and yet offend in one point, he is guilty of all." (James 2:10)

Heathen "Christians" are quick to say, "We are not under the law anymore." Then they are not in His love anymore. "If you love Me, keep My Commandments." (John 14:15)

So come out of "Her", so you can receive power from on high. You cannot receive power from on high until you shuck off the worldly stumbling stones. To name a few: Sports, pagan gods, *Christmas, Easter, Halloween, Martin Luther King Day, television, pornography, voting,* any job that contributes to killing, robbing, or destroying God's people, God's earth, or any of God's creation, trees, herbs, birds, animals, water and more.

(I John 2:27) speaks of the anointing, which is the Holy Ghost, which a natural man cannot receive. Which things also we speak, not in the words which man's wisdom teaches, but which the Holy Ghost teaches, comparing spiritual things with spiritual. (I Corinthians 2:13)

"But the natural man receives not the things of the Spirit of God: For they are foolishness unto him, neither can he know *them*." (I Corinthians 2:14) "But he that is spiritual judges all things." (I Corinthians 2:15)

So unless you have the same anointing that the believers received at first, which is the Holy Ghost, it is impossible to overcome Satan, until you be endued with power from on high. But on the other hand, if you have had a personal Pentecost, then brother you are ready for the front lines in this spiritual war we are engaged in.

"Because you have kept the Word of My patience, I also will keep you from the hour of temptation, which shall come upon all the world to test them that dwell upon the earth." (Revelation 3:10)

If you do not have a pure heart yet, it is because of self. Self lusts, which are self desires and what the Devil's crowd has enticed you to do. Come out from among them and be separate from the worldly *church*, and let Him teach you.

Dear Heavenly Father, in the name of your Living Son, Christ Jesus, I am praying for the weak ones that cannot latch on to your **Word** and disassociate themselves from the unclean filth and abominable ones that profess to be "Christians", yet You and I know they are not.

Father, I ask you to give these weak ones a greater measure of your Holy Spirit, and, Father, give them the gift of discernment so they can recognize the wiles of the enemy; and, Father, would you help them to overcome the things that are in this world, that are not of

God, like the lust of the flesh, and the lust of the eyes, and the pride of life. Father, for the ones you have sanctified, I pray you would put your seal on them; and I ask this in the Name of Christ Jesus, The Son of the Living God. Amen and Amen.

THIS is an insert in the book, **"CORN SHELLING TIME"** and **MICHAEL DUISHKA** with some of his belief, and the iteration of the **WORD** of **GOD ALMIGHTY, (PANTAKRATOR).** All Churches are a tool of Satan, because they do not proclaim the ONE doctrine of GOD. There is only ONE true doctrine (teaching) of GOD. Not thousands of doctrines (teachings) of men, the traditions of men, and the doctrines of devils. (1 Timothy:4:1) Now the SPIRIT speaks expressly, that in the latter times some shall depart from the faith, giving heed to seducing spirits, and doctrines of devils. Another teaching of CHRIST JESUS is to eat His flesh and drink His blood,(JOHN: 6;53) which is speaking Spiritually, which no natural man can understand, only a man that is Spiritual and judges all things. (1 Corinthians 2:13,15). The false teachings (doctrines of devils),that the UNHOLY Catholic *Church*, (*THE MOTHER OF HARLOTS)* teaches that when they go through the ritual of the sacrament the wafer and the wine literally turns into real flesh and blood of Jesus. WRONG! But the LORD sent me to iterate His **WORD**, and now **"CORN SHELLING TIME"** will show you the **WORD** with the bark on it, straight from the *horses'* mouth, here is what HE said about His body, (*flesh)* and HIS blood. And as they were eating, Jesus took bread, and blessed *it*, and brake *it*, and gave *it* to the disciples and said,

"Take,eat,: this is my body". And He took the cup, and gave thanks, and gave *it* to them, saying, **Drink you all of it: For this is my blood of the new testament, which is shed for many for the remission of sins, But I say unto you, I will not drink hereafter of this fruit of the vine, until that day when I drink it new with you in my Father's kingdom.** (Matthew 26:26,27,28,29,30).

DO not think that this correction was only to the MOTHER HARLOT, it was also to the protestant Harlot daughters of the MOTHER. This writer has been to many *churches* observing their doctrines, seeking to find just one that did not give heed to seducing Spirits, and doctrines of devils, not one could this writer find. On the ritual of the sacrament, every church that observes this ritual is as phony as a three dollar bill. The biggest problem with many of the harlots is Repentance, and the blood that Jesus gave me and you for a precious gift to cover our sins. Also to wash our sins away. Many souls will spend eternity in which ever compartment of Hell they are judged to abide in, because some preacher of darkness is ashamed to tell the ignorant congregation about the blood, that without being covered by that blood of HIS that He shed on that torture stake you can never, never, never, be forgiven for your sins, or the SIN your Father Adam And Eve left you for an inheritance. Many of the Harlot Churches are abandoning Repentance, which is another commandment of Jesus, that without Repentance there can be no forgiveness of sins. **"But you go learn what that means, I will have mercy and not sacrifice, For I am not come to call the righteous, but sinners to Repentance"**. (Matthew 9:13). That means All, For all have sinned and come short of the glory of GOD. (Romans 3:23). As it is written, there is none righteous no not one. (Romans 3:10). **"CORN SHELLING TIME"** is iterating the three imperative things that is necessary for anyone to be saved. The first step is to shell down the corn, which means in plain language to confess your sins. If we confess our sins He is faithful and just to forgive us *our* sins, and cleanse us from all unrighteousness. The second thing is to Repent, and turn from your wicked ways, and ask GOD to forgive you. The third thing to do is Believe Him, when He just said He would forgive you. That if you shall confess with your mouth the LORD JESUS, and believe in your heart that God has raised him from the dead you shall be saved. (Romans 10: 9). AMEN

Chapter 7

THE BOOK THAT WAS sealed up in Daniel's ministry was hidden from the beloved prophet, because Daniel would not be able to view all the marvelous things that were to happen to Daniel's people, so that is the reason why the angel told Daniel to go his way, because these things were closed up and sealed until the time of the end, which is this present time that we are living in. The very end is still yet to come. The very end is in the future, but these days are the days of the end time.

In 2011 opened up the beginning of sorrows that Jesus said would come to pass in (Matthew 24:8). Jesus said a lot of things would trigger the beginning of sorrows, which would lead on into the end times. (Matthew 24:8) These things started being more prevalent in 2011 than ever before, since records started being kept. There are so many disasters that this book would not hold the details of all that began to occur in 2011 A.D.

"For many shall come in My Name, saying I am Christ, and shall deceive many." (Matthew 24:5) This is one of the beginning of sorrows that Jesus said would manifest in the end time, but He said, **"The end is not yet."** (Matthew 24:6)

Satan has deceived many in his *churches;* and they all say they are "Christians"; but they say is always a lie. Paul told the Corinthians they were carnal. (I Corinthians 5:1) Why did Paul tell them they were carnal? Because they were just like *churches,* divided up into different doctrines: Catholic, Baptist, Pentecostal, *(but all "Christians").* I do not think so. How can they be divided and be one with Christ Jesus. They can quote Matthew 18:19, where it says; **"If any two of you shall agree on earth as touching anything they shall ask, it shall be done for them of My Father, which is in heaven."**

Maybe they think they can agree after they get into heaven, because nothing has been done for them. They do not have any power, no healing, no Holy Spirit, no holiness; but only filth, corruption, and sin. They do not want to read the scriptures for themselves, but just want to argue and say they have all these things; but all they have is a form of Godliness, but are denying the power thereof. "From such turn away." (II Timothy 3:5) Pay attention: This is one of the many places in the scriptures that tell you to turn away from them. "Come out of "Her", My People." (Revelation 18:4)

They argue that they are filled with the Holy Spirit; but they show signs of being dead, walking around with all kinds of infirmities, from being a lazy fat sluggard with diabetes, high blood pressure, gall stones, high cholesterol, osteoporosis, cancer, and all kinds of heart problems, still saying they are saved "Christians"; but going to Satan's *Church* giving their tithes and offerings, with the preacher telling them (I Peter 2:24); "By whose stripes you were healed." Satan has them deceived, telling them they are healed and a "Christian", when the truth says they are dead.

Father, God, in the name of Jesus, I pray for your people to come out of "Her", so they can be saved and made ever to wit whole from the top of their head to the soles of their feet. In the Name of Jesus. Amen.

"But the Spirit speaks expressly that in the latter times some shall depart from the faith, giving heed to seducing spirits and doctrines of devils." (I Timothy 4:1) Another thing that was sealed up in the book of Daniel, was what Jesus said about wars and rumors of wars. "See that you be not troubled." He was talking to His blood bought believers, that believed what He said in (Exodus 20:13): "Thou shall not kill." Now, the "Christians" are sacrificing their young men to the Devil in wars, and wars, and wars, all in the name of "Christianity"; and because the heathen "Christian" leaders of the "Christian" people say: "Kill, kill, kill. Or the "Christian" harlots have their babies aborted, because they committed fornication, or adultery, or whoredom. So kill your baby during the week and go to *Satan's church* on *Sunday.*

The "Christian" police are killing, stealing, and destroying God's people in the name of the law, and going to *Satan's churches* on the *Sun god day*; and the preacher praises the killers for doing such a wonderful job of protecting and serving themselves by killing, stealing, and destroying in the name of God. Oh me!

Another thing that Jesus said was there would be kingdom against kingdom, which is obviously happening all over; also nation (Gentile) against nation (Gentile), which is occurring all over; also famines, pestilences, and earthquakes in divers places. (Matthew 24:7)

All of these things escalated to being at the apex of fulfillment in 2011. "But He said: "The end is not yet." But it is plain to see we are in the days of the end time. Before I get this written, there will be great disasters. Jesus said all these things were the beginning of sorrows. (Matthew 24:8) How long will these sorrows last? They will last until the end of the dispensation of the nations (Gentiles). They just keep on escalating and getting worse until Christ Jesus comes back to stop them.

The angel talking to Daniel knew all the horrible things that were pronounced to come upon Daniel's people; and he wanted to spare Daniel from all the morbid events of slaughter and destruction that were coming upon not only Daniel's people, the Jews, but also on the nations (Gentiles).

Daniel had read the book of Jeremiah and Isaiah, and the books of Moses and psalms, that told of all the major events that were to come upon the whole entire earth; but he had not read the New Covenant. Daniel "Shelled Down the Corn" to God Almighty, (PANTAKRATOR), in the ninth chapter of Daniel; not only confessing his sins, but also confessing the sins of Israel, (Jacob), and was making supplications for them, and was asking forgiveness. Then the angel, Gabriel, flew swiftly and touched Daniel.

"The angel, Gabriel, told Daniel, for the overspreading of abominations, the city and the sanctuary shall be destroyed by the people of the Prince that is to come." The city and the sanctuary indeed were destroyed in the year 70 A.D.; but Gabriel is a ministering spirit; and his words have a twofold meaning; so the Prince he is speaking of is the Prince of the powers of the air, (Ephesians 2:2), which is the Prince of principalities, rulers of darkness of this world, and spiritual wickedness in high places, which is spiritual powers that believers of Jesus wrestle against, (Ephesians 6:12), that the unbelievers know nothing about. The Prince that Gabriel is telling Daniel about is Lucifer himself, that will incarnate himself into the man, Anti-Christ, and will confirm the covenant with many for one week (*7 years*); but this is talking about the overspreading of abominations that are happening today in this present time.

Gabriel, the angel messenger, is telling Daniel what is going to happen to the Israelites; but **"Corn Shelling Time"** will tell what will happen to the nations, (Gentiles), all at the same time the people of God are tested. "I will call them, My People, which were not My People, and her beloved which was not beloved." (Hosea 1:10) Some Gentiles will be spiritual Jews.

Michael Duishka

The Prince, Gabriel told Daniel, would come and confirm the covenant with many for one week, which is the Anti-Christ that will obtain the kingdom by flattery. (Daniel 11:21) But the Prince will obtain the kingdom by peace and be peaceable until the middle of the week. "He will exalt himself above all that is called God or that is worshiped, so that he, as God, sits in the temple of God, showing himself that he is God." (II Thessalonians 2:4)

In the middle of the week he will cause all hell to break loose, and he, (the Anti-Christ), will break the agreement, or covenant, he has made with Israel. For the readers that do not have understanding of the mysteries of the bible, a spiritual week is seven literal years; and the angel, or the man, Gabriel, told Daniel that seventy weeks had been determined for Daniel's people and upon the holy city to finish the transgression and to make an end of sins. In plain natural man's language: For the second coming of the Most Holy, which is Christ Jesus. (Daniel 9:24) Please understand, all of this vision did not come to Daniel until after he had "Shelled Down the Corn" and confessed his sins and also the sins of his people.

If you, the reader of **"Corn Shelling Time"**, will use some *kneeology,* that is bend your knee; or if you are not able to get down upon your knees, just humble your heart and confess just like Daniel did to the Lord Christ Jesus your sins, and have a broken heart for your sins, and let the blood of Jesus cover your sins, you will receive an enlightening of the Lord Christ Jesus; and the Word of God will cause life to come to what you read; and you will be taught by revelations, just like the Apostle Paul and the Apostle John were taught by the anointing. (I John 2:27)

The seventy weeks that have been determined do not occur consecutively, but happen at different intervals in time. Without going into the different events that determine the seventy weeks, the writer will cut right through to the chase. Sixty-Nine weeks have already come to pass, and this present time is between the sixty-ninth week and the seventieth week, which is the last week, or the last 7 years of sins, or transgressions.

We are coming to the mysteries that Daniel sealed up unto the end, because it was too gross and bloody to show Daniel what was going to happen to, not only the Israelites, but also the entire culmination of every Gentile race, color, or creed on the face of the earth.

"When you therefore shall see the abomination of desolation, spoken of by Daniel the prophet, stand in the Holy Place, (whoso reads let him understand)." (Matthew 24:15)

Daniel had read the book of Jeremiah, where; "In that day a man shall go around with his hands on his loins in so much pain, like a woman in travail." (Jeremiah 30:6) "Alas for that day is great, so that none is like it. It is even the time of Jacob's trouble; but he shall be saved out of it." (Jeremiah 30:7) Daniel knew of this, even Jacob's trouble, which begins in the midst of Daniel's seventieth week, or the last three and a half years of Jacob's trouble.

"Daniel lifted up his eyes and saw a male person *(man,)(angel)*; and he went into a deep sleep, and put his face to the ground; when a hand touched him and set him upon his knees, and upon the palms of his hands."

"The man, *(angel)*, said to Daniel; "Stand upright, because you are greatly loved. Understand these words that I speak to you." "Fear not, Daniel, for from the first day you did set your heart to understand and to chasten yourself, "S*hell Down the Corn*", before God, your words were heard; and I am come for your words." "But the Prince of the kingdom of Persia, *(modern day Iran)*, withstood me one and twenty days; but Lo Michael, one of the Chief Princes, came to help me; and I remained there with the Kings of Persia." (Daniel 10:9,10,11,12,13)

The writer of this book is going to intervene at this point to make you, the reader, understand the spiritual warfare that has been going on since Lucifer was cast out of the Highest Place is still going on until this present time, and will continue until Satan, (Lucifer), is bound for one thousand years.

The angel was talking and telling Daniel about the spirits and principalities, and rulers of the airways that hindered him from coming to answer Daniel's prayer. But Michael, the fighting angel that has been commissioned by God to fight the spiritual warfare in the heavens, came and caused the spiritual kings of Persia, *(modern day Iran)*, to release Gabriel, the messenger angel, so he could come through the airways to Daniel to give Daniel instructions from God.

If the so called "Christians" would join with Christ's sanctified holy believers and learn how to fight a spiritual warfare, we could overcome the powers and principalities and spiritual wickedness in high places and the rulers of darkness. O that they were wise, that they understood this, that they were wise and not steal, kill, and destroy.

Gabriel told Daniel: "And now will I return to fight with the Prince of Persia, *(modern day Iran)*; And when I am gone forth, lo the Prince of Grecia shall come." (Daniel 10:20) So Gabriel knew which spirits of the air ways would win; and he told Daniel the outcome of his people on up to the end of the age, even to the abomination that makes desolate. (Daniel 11:31)

Daniel prayed three times a day, morning, noon, and evening. But his prayers were enough to keep the enemy from destroying him. If the so called "Christians" would do the same as Daniel, we could overcome the Prince of Persia, *(modern day* Iran); and also the wicked spirit that rules the President of the United States of America. But, instead, the Prince of the USA has given America to every foreign terrorist country on the earth; and the so called "Christians" plaudit him for destroying their own country. America, the ObomaNation of Desolation. (1ˢᵗ DUISHKA)

But every nation has an evil spirit ruling over them called a prince or a king. These are the powers of the airways that Jesus' chosen ones wrestle against. That is, "He who will let will let until He be taken out of the way." (II Thessalonians 2:7)

The beginning of sorrows began to escalate in 2011 A.D. and will keep right on escalating until Jacob's trouble starts. (Jeremiah 30:7) Jacob's trouble starts in the middle of Daniel's seventieth week, or in the midst of the seven year treaty the Anti-Christ makes with Daniel's people, which are the Israelis or Jews.

Just to mention a few of the sorrows: The worst natural disaster up to date happened on March 11. 2011, in Japan, the earthquake and tsunami, where 15,000 died. Then on April 27, 2011, a tornado in Alabama killed 240 people. Then an E-5 tornado killed many in Joplin Missouri on May 20, 2011.

In the Philippine Islands a tropical storm, Was hi, left 1500 dead. 30,000 children died due to a famine in Ethiopia, Somalia, Kenya, and Eastern Africa, not to mention 3 million that needed medical assistance. We could go on and on telling of the wild fires in Texas and Oklahoma, that destroyed many animals and thousands of acres of hay. All this is just a minor part of the sorrows of the world that happened in 2011 and is still going on, and will go on, until the prophecy is fulfilled in Revelation 11:18, when "the Lord will destroy them that destroy the earth." (Revelation 11:18)

What is shut up in Daniel's book is a twofold meaning of Daniel's vision of the great image that King Nebuchadnezzar saw in his dream. "That the second beast of (Revelation 13:14) causes to be made the image of the first beast (Anti-Christ); and he had power to cause the image to speak and cause as many as would not worship him to be killed." (Revelation 13:15)

Also shut up in Daniel's book is the mysteries and prophecies of the New Testament, including Jesus and His apostles, including Paul and John. **"When you therefore shall see the abomination of desolation spoken of by Daniel the prophet stand in the Holy Place, (whoso reads let him understand)."** (Matthew 24:15)

Just in case you do not understand, in the entirety of this book, you will be showed plainly the truth. "But, Jesus said: **"I told you, and you believed not."** (John 10:25)

But there are two that are choosing up sides. One is Satan, the executioner of death. The other one is Christ Jesus, the giver of Life. Which one you obey is the one that gets you. Christ Jesus chooses those that obey His Commandments, or His Word.

We have followed the Word from the beginning up to the New Covenant of grace: That the Lamb of God appeared on the earth to be a sacrifice for the sins of the world.

The Word was the **I AM** in (Exodus 3:14). The Word was what opened up the Red Sea in (Exodus 14:21) It was the Word that caused the death angel to pass over the children and not kill the children of Israel, like he did every first born thing in Egypt. (Exodus 12:29) The Word was That Prophet that Moses prophesied would be raised up by God in (Deuteronomy 18:15). The Word was God (John 1:1). The Word was made flesh (human). (John 1:14) The Word was Jesus. (Luke 1:31) The Word was Christ. (John 1:17) The Word is Truth. (John 14:6)

So, as we open the book that was sealed until the time of the end, we ask you, Father God, in the Name of Jesus, the Christ, the Son of the

Living God, to reveal to the reader the urgency of "Shelling Down the Corn", (confessing his sins) before he is destroyed. Amen, Amen.

Father God, in the name of The Christ Jesus, I plead the blood of Jesus over the unskilled ones in the Word; and I ask You, Father, to draw them to the scriptures, to read them for themselves and I say the same anointing I received of Him that abides in me will abide in them; and they will receive the Holy Spirit of God to help them understand the living Word of God Almighty, (PANTAKRATOR); and He will teach them and bring to their remembrance all the Words of Christ Jesus; and they will not have a need to be taught by any man. (I John 2:27) Also, Lord Jesus, I pray for those that have hardened their heart and their minds have been blinded by the god of this world that they would fall upon the stone Christ Jesus; and their hearts would be broken; and their spirits would be contrite; and they would apply the blood of the sacrificial Lamb to their heart; and just like blind Bartimaeus and myself cried out to Jesus and said you son of David, Lord, have mercy on me; and you would raise them up in the last day. I ask this in the name of Jesus The Christ, The Son Of The Living God. Amen and Amen!

Chapter 8

"BEHOLD YOUR HOUSE IS left unto you desolate." (Matthew 23:38)

That was a prophecy to the Israelite s and also to the "Christians" that are now unbelievers that are still Gentiles. *THE CHURCHHOUSE is left unto you desolate!*

Jesus left the temple never to return until you shall say, **"Blessed is He that comes in the Name of The Lord."** (Matthew 23:39) Jesus at that time was talking about the temple of the Jews at Jerusalem; but He was also talking to the man made *churches* that "Christians" worship. Their church building (*church house*) is left unto them desolate. The only temple that survives (continues to live) is your body, if you are a landlord for the Holy Spirit of God. "What, know you not that your body is the temple of the Holy Ghost (God) in you, which you have of God; and you are not your own? For you are bought with a price." (I Corinthians 6:19,20) The price that was paid for you was the blood of Jesus.

This is a warning to all you "Christians" that think the church house is going to save you from the abomination of desolation. Do you not know that your *house* is left unto you desolate; and you, the *churches*, are the abomination of desolation? "And upon "Her" forehead a name written, Mystery, Babylon The Great, The Mother Of Harlots And Abominations Of The Earth." (Revelation 17:5) The Mother being the *Unholy Roman Catholic Church* and all the other *churches* being "Her" *daughters,* which are the abominations of the earth.

Only the believers that come out from among them and are not unequally yoked to the unbelievers will be saved from the hour of temptation that is coming upon the whole world. (II Corinthians 6:14) (Revelation 3:10)

Oh, you foolish deceived ones, do you not know that your house that is left unto you desolate is your body, which is supposed to be the temple that God the Holy Spirit lives in? Know you not that your bodies are the members of Christ? Shall I then take the members of Christ and make them the members of an Harlot *(church)*? God forbid. What? Know you not that he which is joined to an harlot, (church), is one body? (I Corinthians 6:15,16)

If you are a member of a *church*, you are joined to an Harlot, because the Catholic *Church* is the Mother Of Harlots. (Revelation 17:5)

The book that Daniel sealed up until the end times is talking about this specific thing, when he is speaking about the abomination that is going to leave you desolate, because the Mother of Harlots, *(churches),* is the abominations of the earth. (Revelation 17:5) The abomination of desolation that Daniel and Jesus talked about is the people of the Prince, *(Anti-Christ),* which are the Gentile (Nations) that persecutes Daniels people, which is you, the ones that have joined their membership to a church, (Harlot). You are already marked by the true believers, the sanctified Holy Ones, that have separated themselves from the unbelievers. (II Corinthians 6:17)

The Gentile (Nations) are the people of the Prince, that Satan has raised the Prince, *(Anti-Christ),* up out of. There is not any difference in the heathen and the so called "Christians". They all voted for the immoral leaders of the USA that have destroyed the country and given the country to every kind of filth and abominable thing on this earth. "And it shall come to pass, if you shall hearken diligently unto the voice of the Lord, thy God, to observe *and* to do all His Commandments, which I command you this day, that the Lord, thy God, will set you on high above all nations of the earth." (Deuteronomy 28:1)

Please listen, I am showing you, dear reader, what you are guilty of, because this *NewNited States of America* used to be exactly like the promise said: He set this nation on high above every nation on earth. That was then, and this is now. America, the ObomaNation of Desolation!

"But it shall come to pass, if you will not hearken to the voice of the Lord, thy God, to observe to do all His Commandments and His Statutes, which I command you this day, that all these curses shall come upon you and overtake you." (Deuteronomy 28:15)

Since you, "Christians", and heathen alike voted for the unholy abominable filth, that means you chose to destroy this *NewNited States of America*. The country that was above every nation on God's earth has become cursed above all other nations on God's earth. "The Lord shall make the pestilence cleave unto you until He have consumed you from off the land, where ever you go to possess it." (Deuteronomy 28:21)

Since the so called "Christians" and heathens voted for the lawless ones that steal, kill, and destroy, they will be consumed off this land. You are cursed above everything on this earth; and all these curses have already come upon this heathen nation; and if you do not have the pestilence cleaving to you, that is what will be revealed in the opening up of Daniel's book that he sealed up. "The Lord shall smite you with a consumption, and with a fever, and with an inflammation, and with an extreme burning, and with the sword, and with blasting, and with mildew; and they shall pursue you until you perish." (Deuteronomy 28:22)

There are some of you readers that the curse has already manifested on you, and you are still too stiff necked and stubborn to "*Shell Down the Corn*" (*confess your sins*)to God Almighty and repent, and be saved. The only way for you to have entrance into the Kingdom of God is to "*Shell Down the Corn*"(*confess*) to God in the Name of Jesus and confess that you are a sinful person; and perhaps the Lord Jesus will forgive you and raise you up on the last day. "But if you do not repent, the heaven that is over your head shall be brass; and the earth that is under you shall be iron." (Deuteronomy 28:23)

"The Lord shall make the rain of your land powder and dust: From heaven it shall come down upon you, until you be destroyed." (Deuteronomy 28:24) This will not affect the majority of you directly, because you are too lazy to try to grow anything on the land anyway. But it is already affecting you Indirectly, because your President is giving aid to all the lazy terrorist countries, that will not break the ground if it was not like iron. But it is getting closer to a world-wide famine every day, because sorrows have already begun to accelerate to their apex.

In 2011 the beginning of sorrows escalated to great heights, which Jesus said there would be famines. (Matthew 24:7)

Daniel's book will open up all the great plagues that are double dog dead sure to come upon the whole earth, and there is a way you can escape. "The Lord shall cause you to be smitten before your enemies. You shall go out one way against them, and flee seven ways before them, and shall be removed into all the Kingdoms of the earth." (Deuteronomy 28:25) This next verse is a way of escape. "And your carcase shall be meat unto all fowls of the air and unto the beasts of the earth; and no man shall fray them away." (Deuteronomy 28:26) ""You shall betroth a wife, and another man shall lie with her."

Because you let your wife go to work on a heathen job with vile men, that will flatter her, and tell her how beautiful she is, until he lies with her, then comes the divorce; and the law of the land takes authority over every law of God; and you are guilty of lawlessness.

"There has no temptation taken you, but such as is common to man. But God is faithful, who will not suffer (*let*) you to be tempted above that you are able; but will with the temptation also make a way to escape, that you may be able to bear it." (I Corinthians 10:13)

There is a way to escape the greater temptations that are double dog dead sure to come upon you, before you are taken up in them; and God sent His only begotten Son down here to earth to tell you how to escape the hour of temptation which shall come upon the world to test them that dwell upon the earth. (Revelation 3:10)

This writer of this book has been tested and tempted with some of the most heartbreaking troubles, that at the time they were happening, it seemed impossible to bear. I did not have anyone to tell me how to bear the pain in my heart and escape. I thought: That is from the Devil himself, I thought: That is the way the Devil deceives you and me, just like he deceived Eve in the Garden, he puts thoughts into your mind; and you think they are your thoughts, or God has caused you to think the thoughts. Thoughts are from the wicked one himself, and have destroyed many of God's children by deceiving them with thoughts. But, thank God for (I John 2:26,27) that I had no need of a man to tell me how to escape the tribulations I was being subjected to; but the Holy Spirit of God came to me and strengthened me, before my evil thoughts caused me to kill myself. That was one of the promises that God's only begotten Son, Christ Jesus, made to His loved ones, the ones that do His Commandments, that He would pray the Father; and He would give you another comforter, that He may abide with you forever. (John 14:16) Since I knew I was doing His Commandments, I knew He loved me; and He would provide a way of escape for me. That is the reason Christ Jesus was sent from

God to reveal the Father to the ones keeping His Commandments. If you are being tested with any kind of temptation, trial, persecution, tribulation, trouble, or anything, there is a sure way of deliverance that will work a way of escape for everyone that believes Jesus. Do the same thing all the prophets did, and myself also, and that is to humble yourself before God Almighty, and in the Name of Jesus, *"Shell Down the Corn"*. Confess to Him that you are a sinner, and you repent from your wrong doings, and you will quit doing sinful things, which are breaking the laws of God; and you renounce Satan and all his unclean spirits; and you promise to trust Christ Jesus instead of trusting in man for your deliverance and your way of escape.

If you do what you promise, the Lord Jesus is faithful to do what He said He would do, and will provide a way for you to escape the trial you are going through at this present time; but also He will keep you from the future hour of temptation that is coming upon the whole world, that this book, **"Corn Shelling Time"**, will reveal in detail about all the major events that Daniel did not have time to go into each detail of each event that was to come upon his people, and also the Gentiles, and the whole world.

When you receive your deliverance, and the Holy Spirit shows you a way of escape, the worst thing you can do is give glory to a *Harlot church*, or to a doctor, or a preacher, or any men; but give honor where it belongs, give thanks to God, the Father, God the Son, God the Holy Spirit. If you do not give thanks to God, and confess that He is the one that provided a way for you to escape, a worse calamity will come upon you. If you still do not listen to God to do His Commandments, you will have the stranger that is in your land to get up above you, very high, and you shall come down very low. (Deuteronomy 28:43) *(that has already happened to America)*.

This has already come to pass and is being fulfilled at this very moment. You have a stranger, a foreigner, as your ruler, and that is as high up as he can get. That is as low down as you can get.

The stranger took control of all your goods; and he is lending to you; and you are not lending to him. He shall be [correction], he is *already* your head; and you are *already* the tail. This is because you did not obey God and keep His Commandments. America is now an ObomaNation of desolation. The stranger has made America an ObomaNation of denominations.

"The Lord shall send upon you cursing and vexation and rebuke in all that you set your hand to do, until you be destroyed, and until you perish quickly, because of the wickedness of your doings, whereby you have forsaken Me." (Deuteronomy 28:20)

This nation, and every nation on the earth are falling; and the only hope is for you and every individual to read the Word of God for themselves and to "come out of "Her", My people," thus saith the Lord. (Revelation 18:4) God is pleading with His people through this book, **"Corn Shelling Time"**. God sent me to plead with His people in this time of the end; and please understand, it is every man for himself. If you think your apostate church is your salvation, the god of this world has blinded your mind. If you are living just for the fishes and loaves, and what the stranger gives you on welfare, unemployment benefits, loans that you do not have to pay back, then you are lost; and the only hope for you to miss the flames of Hell is to *"Shell Down the Corn"*, and confess to God Almighty that your master was Satan, and confess that your idol was the heathen ruler of this country, or the apostate *church*, (*Harlot*), or the principal of the flock, or whatever your idol is, and renounce Satan, and beg Christ Jesus to forgive you; and come out of "Her" and consecrate yourself to Christ Jesus. Amen.

The reason the 28th Chapter of Deuteronomy is quoted, is because that is the Word of the great I AM_that gave to Moses the Word of Life that none of God's scribes deviate from; and it is the same rules from Deuteronomy to Revelation; and the Word of God does not ever change.

"Corn Shelling Time" is revealing to you what was sealed up in the book that Gabriel told Daniel to seal up until the end times; and we are definitely in the latter days; and the time of the end is coming up. Daniel knew what Moses and the prophets had written, and the book of Psalms, plus Daniel was shown visions from his time until the end, which **"Corn Shelling Time"** will reveal to the world, as a warning to "Come out of "Her", My People. You be not partakers of "Her" sins, and that you receive not of "Her" plagues." (Revelation 18:4)

"O, the depth of the riches, both of wisdom and knowledge of God! How unsearchable are His judgments; and His ways past finding out!" (Romans 11:33)

When Gabriel, *(the angel from God)*, told Daniel: "O Daniel, I am come forth to give you skill and understanding. At the beginning of your supplications (prayers) the Commandment came forth; and I am come to show you, for you are greatly beloved. Therefore, understand the matter, and consider the vision." (Daniel 9:23)

That was before the Holy Ghost fell on the ones at Jerusalem on the Day of Pentecost after the resurrection. So God deployed a special Angel, Gabriel, the Messenger Angel, to carry instructions to Daniel. (Daniel 9:22)

In another vision Gabriel told Daniel to stand upon his feet, after Daniel had fasted for 21 days, and was so weak he could not stand until Gabriel touched him and gave him strength to stand. Then Gabriel told Daniel, "The Prince of the Kingdom of Persia, *(modern day Iran)*, withstood me, *(Gabriel)*, one and twenty days." The evil spirits of the air ways did not want God's message to get through to Daniel; but Michael, one of God's Chief Angels, came to help Gabriel; but Gabriel still remained there with the Kings of Persia. (21 days) That does not mean earthly kings, but it means the spirits in the air that are the spiritual rulers over the earthly kings of Persia. "Now,

I am come to make you understand what will befall your people in the latter days, for yet the vision is for *many* days." (Daniel 10:13,14) Daniel did not repeat what Gabriel told him would befall his people in latter days; but Christ Jesus, the Holy Spirit, will reveal the things that will befall Daniel's people in latter days in the following Chapters of **"Corn Shelling Time".**

"Gabriel told Daniel, "Now you know why I have come to you; and now I will return to fight with the Prince of Persia; and when I am gone forth, Lo, the Prince of Grecia shall come." (Daniel 10:20)

Reader, please understand, the way Gabriel told Daniel to understand about the spirits that rule the air and the waves that go through the air. A couple of examples of God's power over the evil spirits that work in the air waves. There were a couple of God's children, that had come out of "Her", *(Mystery Babylon),* that had an answering machine with this message answering the phone. "Hello, we are out working for Jesus, at the tone leave your message, and we will return your call shortly, thank you." When they would return and play back the messages, there would be messages from the children of darkness with some message from Satan blaspheming the God of heaven and His children. The two believers immediately agreed with Matthew 18:19: **"Again I say unto you, that if two of you shall agree on earth as touching anything, that they shall ask, it shall be done for them of My Father, which is in heaven. For where two or three are gathered together in My Name, there AM I in the midst of them."** (Matthew 18:19,20) So the couple of believers agreed together and did not doubt and said: "you Prince of the powers of the air, I rebuke you and command you, in the Name of Christ Jesus to stay off this phone, and get out of the lines to this phone, and stay out. I bind you in the Name of Christ Jesus. The Prince of the air powers obeyed the Name of Jesus; and to this present time, has entered no more on the phone. Praise God! The radio, telephone, television, and computer are all tools of Satan, unless one of God's people is using them for the glory of God to communicate God's Word to warn more people to "Shell Down the Corn", and "Come out of "Her", My People." (Revelation 18:4) So Gabriel and Michael are Chief Angels of God. "And of the angels He says, who makes His angels spirits, and His minister a flame of fire." (Hebrews 1:7) So, Gabriel and Michael are spirits; and they are fighting with spiritual wickedness in high places. Where are the high places that spirits battle in? There are only 3 heavens that the scriptures speak of. We know that Lucifer and 1/3, one third, of the angels have been cast out of the 3rd heaven, where Paradise is, so that only leaves two heavens for the Prince of the power of the air to rule; and there is nothing in the 2nd heaven for the wicked to steal, kill, or destroy; so he rules over the wicked spirits, *(one third of the angels, demons, and disembodied spirits)*, that can come into humans from the first 1st heaven, which is above our heads, that we call space. The demons and all the unclean spirits are in competition with each other to see who is the strongest, and which ones are the most deceptive. **"When the unclean spirit is gone out of a man, he walks through dry places, seeking rest; and finding none, he saith, "I will return unto my house where I came out." ** (Luke 11:24) **"And when he comes, he finds it swept and garnished."** (Luke 11:25) **"Then he goes and takes unto him seven other spirits more wicked than himself; and they enter in, and dwell there; and the last state of that man is worse that the first."** (Luke 11:26)

So you can see, if Daniel and Jesus told about fighting unclean spirits, it is a fact that the unclean spirits are fighting to see which one is the strongest, so he can rule over your body, soul, and spirit; and if the unclean spirit can deceive you, you will be the landlord of the Unholy Spirit, instead of the temple of the Holy Ghost.

If you have any doubt, pride, envy, hate, fear, anger or lust, you have unclean spirits in you; and you need to be delivered from the demons fighting in you to see which one rules your body. The only way you can be delivered is to "Shell Down the Corn", and confess, and repent, and be baptized into Christ Jesus, and cast those demons out in the Name of Christ Jesus. Then the most important is <u>BELIEVE.</u>

Father God, I pray for the reader of this book, **"Corn Shelling Time"**, in the Name of Christ Jesus, I submit the reader of this book to you; and I resist the devil in him, and rebuke the unclean spirits; and I say to all you unclean spirits, Come out of this person in the Name of Jesus. My mate and I say to you unclean spirits, Loose this person in the Name of Christ Jesus; and we bind you Devil from coming back into this person in the Name of Jesus. Amen and Amen.

In the Old Contract (*Testament*) the Holy Spirit was given only to men of God that were Holy. In the New Contract (*Testament*) the Holy Spirit is given to whoever is baptized into Jesus. (Acts 2:38) In the Old Testament they fought against flesh and blood, (humans). In the New Testament, believers fight against spirits and not against flesh and blood (humans). Gabriel, the angel and Michael, the angel, fought spiritual rulers of kingdoms; and ever since Christ Jesus gave the believers power over the enemy, which is the devil, and all unclean spirits, we were expected to use that power to join the ranks of Jesus to fight against spiritual wickedness in high places; but the weak could not muster up enough power to cast the demons out of themselves, much less out of kingdoms. Now the principalities and powers of the air, the rulers of the darkness of this world, the spiritual wickedness in high places, rule every kingdom, every city mayor, every president, every government, every governor, every *church*, even every school that is subsidized by the government. The ministers of Satan disguised (*transformed*) themselves into ministers of righteousness; and those invisible spirits rule every ruler of the world; and they rule every human being that is not sanctified, holy, and baptized in the Holy Spirit of God Almighty, (PANTAKRATOR). Every professor of Christ Jesus is being deceived by Satan and the gods of this world, if he is not a possessor of Christ Jesus.

Professors, "Christians", *church goers*, are enemies of Christ Jesus by the fact that they are killing, stealing and destroying God's people, when they vote. It does not matter if they vote for a democrat, republican, or a prime minister, or any ruler. They all kill in wars, steal by the laws of the land, and destroy by pollution. The spirit that has rule over you puts thoughts into your mind that causes you to believe you are doing the right thing, when all along you are allied with one of Satan's ministers, that has transformed himself into a minister of righteousness to seduce you, because he is going to pass a law of the land to promote wars, abortions, all kinds of murders, whether by police, soldiers, doctors, capitol punishment, (*lethal injection*), *queers* (homosexuals) men marrying men, women that have left their natural affection, teachers of children that are perverting their tender minds, having sex with them and teaching them how to commit safe fornication. Laws of the land that tax everything God gave to His people, and not leaving the working class enough to live on, but giving all the working man's wages to the lazy shiftless dopers, whores, thieves on welfare, that do not have to work; but just let the president and congress, that are on big time welfare, give them money, food, and clothing to sell for dope, fornication, and not even have to pay for murdering their babies and their young men in wars. All kinds of filth and corruption and abominations; and you, mister and misses "Christian" are the guilty ones that will have to stand before the Great Judge on the White Throne, while the Books are opened, and the Book of Life will be searched to try to find your name, because you not only did all the above mentioned abominations; but you had pleasure in those that did do them. (Romans 1:32) Judgment: Death (*Second*) Please, if you say I am silent, then you have assented to the evil deed.

But, God the Father, God the Son, God the Holy Spirit is giving you a gift, and is providing you a way of escape. **<u>"Corn Shelling Time"</u>** is your way of escape. But the prescription has to be followed to a tee. First humble yourself to God Almighty, like get on your knees, called *kneeology*. **Say,** "Father God, be merciful to me, a sinner.

In the name of Jesus, I "Shell Down the Corn"; and I confess all my sins before you and ask you to save me; and please forgive me for all my sins; and I promise I will not knowingly sin anymore. Father God, I renounce Satan and all the world and all the things that are in the world. I repent and I turn from my wicked ways; and I surrender everything I have over to you, in the Name of Christ Jesus. I believe the blood of Jesus covers my sins; and I thank you, Lord Jesus, for paying the price of my redemption with your blood. Thank You. Amen. I BELIEVE CHRIST JESUS.

Chapter 9

"**WHEN YOU THEREFORE SHALL** see the abomination of desolation, spoken of by Daniel the prophet, stand in the Holy Place, (whoso reads let him understand.**")** (Matthew 24:1)

Like the Angel, Gabriel, came to Daniel to give Daniel skill and understanding, the Lord God Almighty, (PANTAKRATOR), has anointed this writer of **"Corn Shelling Time"** to give His people skill and understanding to whoso reads and believes and turns from darkness to the light, Christ Jesus.

"These things have I written unto you concerning them that seduce you; but the anointing which you have received of Him, abides in you; and you need not that any man teach you; but as the same anointing teaches you of all things, and is Truth and is no lie, and even as He has taught you, you shall abide in Him." (I John 2:26,27) This is what will give you understanding.

"But you, O Daniel, shut up your words and seal the book even to the time of the end. Many shall run to and fro, and knowledge shall be increased." (Daniel 12:4) This is the time. The end is nearing. Every door will be shut and every human will be judged shortly.

Let us start with Jesus opening up Daniel's book. (Matthew 24:15). The abomination that makes desolate that Daniel sealed is speaking of the image the false prophet made in Revelation 13:15.

"And he had power to give life unto the image of the beast, that the image of the beast should both speak and cause that as many as would not worship the image of the beast should be killed." (Revelation 13:15) This is the abomination (*image*) that is set up in the Holy Place for the Jews; but you have got to remember that there are now believers out of the Gentiles; and the image, or the statue of the beast must be worshiped over the entire earth. So the image will be in all *churches*, mosques, and synagogues, shrines, and any other place that worships a cow, Buddha, or anything else.

We are opening up Daniel's book, because we are coming to Daniel's seventieth week, which is the last seven years of the times of the Gentiles. The first half of the seven years is peaceful, as the Prince, or Anti Christ is flattering the Jews. After three and one-half years, or in the middle of the seven years, the Anti Christ will set himself up in the Jew's Holy Place and declare he is God; and he will cause the daily sacrifice to cease, or be taken out of the way; and the beast's image will be placed there instead. This is the abomination of desolation. This is when, "The Prince who opposes and exalts himself above all that is called God, or that is worshiped, so that he as God, sits In the temple of God, showing himself that he is God." (II Thessalonians 2:4)

"When ye therefore shall see the abomination of desolation, spoken of by Daniel the prophet, stand in the Holy Place, (whoso reads, let him understand) Then let them which be in Judea flee into the mountains." (Matthew 24:15,16)

The Prince, (*Anti Christ*), will break his covenant that he had with the Jews in the middle of the week, or at the end of three and one-half years. Then in the middle of the week the trouble is so bad that "At that time Michael the chief fighting angel for the Jews shall stand up for Daniel's people, the Jews; and there shall be a time of trouble such as never was since there was a nation, even to that same time; and at that time thy people shall be delivered, which are found written in the Book (*of Life*)." (Daniel 12:1)

"And there was war in heaven, (*first and second heavens*). Michael and his angels fought against the dragon (*Satan*), and the dragon fought and his angels, and prevailed not, neither was their place found anymore in heaven." (Revelation 12:7,8)

Keep in mind, all this war in the heavens is spiritual warfare; and you cannot see the dragon and his angels. When the dragon, (Satan), and his angels are cast out of the first and second heavens to the earth, it will be just like it is right now, only worse, you cannot see the spirits come into you, so whatever you cannot see, you do not believe.

You cannot see the Christ, so you do not believe Him. He is spirit and will not dwell in you, if you have any unclean spirits in you, such as envy, hate, self, fear, pride, idolatry, or any kind of sins that have the world, or anything of the world in you. God owns the earth and all life. If you have the Word, (Jesus), in you, you have life in you. If you have any of the sins of the world in you, such as unforgiveness, idolatry, worship of other gods, such as *church*, politics, sports, *Christmas, Easter, MLK, Sunday, television, computers, phones*, you are dead and belong to Satan. All of the god's of this world are made of material that is dead and are idols, such as silver, gold, wood, stone, plastic, anything synthetic, are all dead and have no feelings of any kind, and is an evil invention of the wicked one, and are dead.

Anything that has life, including you, belongs to God; and whoever you obey is your master. If you obey Christ and come out of "Her", then you are free to choose whom you wish to serve. But as long as you are in "Her", you are a partaker of "Her" sins; and you will receive "Her" plagues, which you already have; and you belong to

Satan, even if you say you belong to Christ. They say is always a lie. (Revelation 18:4)

Ask yourself what is the reason you have the calamities that you have? What is the reason you have the wounds that have befallen you? What is the reason you are receiving stripes, which the bible calls plagues? Is it not because you are not keeping the commandments of God? God promised that you would be destroyed from this earth. (Deuteronomy 28:21)

"The Lord of that servant will come in a day when he is not aware, and will cut him in sunder, and will appoint him his portion with the unbelievers." (Luke 12:46)

"And that servant which knew his Lord's will, and prepared not himself, neither did according to His will, shall be beaten with many stripes." (Luke 12:47)

I want to interject that for those that do not know what the original Greek word for stripes; *It is plague, or wound, or calamity.* (Luke 12:48) **"But he that knew not, and did commit things worthy of stripes, (wounds, calamities, stripes), shall be beaten with few stripes,** *(wounds, calamities).* **"For unto whomsoever much is given, of him shall be much required; and to whom men have committed much, of him they will ask the more."** (Luke 12:48)

So if you have any kind of plague, or if you have had any kind of calamity, ask yourself why? It just said because you are not doing God's will.

"But remember there has no temptation taken you but such as is common to man; but God is faithful, who will not suffer (*let*) you to be tempted above that you are able; but will with the temptation also make a way to escape, that you may be able to bear it." (I Corinthians 10:13)

"But if we say that we have no sin, we deceive ourselves, and the Truth is not in us." (I John 1:8) But the next verse tells the way of escape, to-wit: "If we confess our sins, *"Shell Down the Corn"*, He is faithful and just to forgive us our sins and to cleanse us from all unrighteousness." (I John 1:9)

All the plagues, sicknesses, infirmities, diseases, wars, famines, earthquakes, tornadoes, hail, floods, fires, and stripes are because of your sins and rebellion against God. Not only you, dear reader, are guilty, but the entire human race is guilty of despising God's laws and hatred of God's Commandments; and let it be known, that I told you in the first of this book, and I am telling you again, and I will continue to tell you until the end of **"Corn Shelling Time"**, and warn you to: "Come out of "Her", My people, and not be partakers of "Her" sins, and that you receive not of "Her" plagues," which are all the above plagues just mentioned, and many more not mentioned yet. (Revelation 18:4)

The only way of escape, that Jesus has provided for you is to: "Come unto Me, and I will give you rest." Jesus doing the talking. (Matthew 11:28) You cannot be healed of the stripes, (plagues), because it is a promise from Jesus, that whoever does not do His will is double dog dead sure to receive stripes or plagues. (Luke 12:46-48)

I am not to be called a prophet; but I can prophesy to you; and it will not be a false prophesy, because God cannot lie; and you, dear reader, have either received one of these plagues, or you will receive one or more of the plagues, until you be destroyed from off the land. (Deuteronomy 28:20)

The only way for you to escape destruction is to repent and *"Shell Down the Corn"*, *(confess)*, and quit forsaking God. Keep His Commandments and quit hatred of His Covenant, which is Love. **BELIEVE!**

America is falling from being the greatest nation on earth to the least of all nations and will soon perish, because you brought a plague on it whenever you elected a president that is destroying America by spreading our borrowed wealth around mostly to the lazy Obamaites on welfare, and to the terrorist nations that burn the American flag, and call America what it is, "The Great Satan,"ObomaNation of desolation. The book that Jesus opened and read what Daniel prophesied would come to pass is coming to pass at this present time. The ObomaNation of desolation is happening as I write.

Jesus is pleading with you in this book, **"Corn Shelling Time"**, and showing you His mercy, so He will not have to plead with you in the valley of Jehoshaphat, where God will plead with all nations for His people so (Joel 3:2) says. "And God will plead with all nations with the great winepress of the wrath of God, and will be trodden down until blood flows up to the horse's bridles." And I pray your blood will not be part of that blood. (Revelation 14:19,20)

"And I saw when the Lamb opened one of the seals, and I heard, as it were the noise of thunder one of the four beasts saying, "Come and see". (Revelation 6:1) This is one of the things that was sealed up in Daniel's book that makes desolate. Let us see what John saw in Revelation 6:2.

"And I saw a white horse, and he that sat on him had a bow, and a crown was given unto him, and he went forth conquering and to conquer." (Revelation 6:2) This is the Prince of the people which gained control of the people with flattery and gift giving, in the same manner Obama is giving America's wealth to every lazy and shiftless bum in the world. Because of his flattery and generosity with OPM (other peoples' money).

But right at this point God is pleading with the lazy shiftless ones to get a decent job, and "let him that stole, steal no more; but rather let him labor (work) working with his hands the thing which is good, that he may have to give to him that needs." (Ephesians 4:28)

This white horse rider is the Anti-Christ that steals, kills, and destroys, just like all the leaders of the war mongering countries of the world do. God is pleading with you, dear reader, to repent and be not partakers of "Her" sins. You that put your trust in any leader are cursed. "Thus saith the Lord: Cursed be the man that trusts in man and makes flesh his arm, and whose heart departs from the Lord. (Jeremiah 17:5)

All the lazy shiftless welfare recipients are so ignorant they do not know they sold their soul to the Devil when they put their trust in Obama, and made America an ObomaNation of desolation. Not only DHS recipients, but also fluent white people that sold their birthright to Satan for a promised bowl of soup. All these fools are Anti-American and Anti-Christs. Just like God said to Pharaoh, "I have raised you up to show my power;" and God has raised Obama up to be a plague to God's people to chasten His people for disobedience and profaning the sabbath of God, which is the seventh day of the week, and not the first day of the week. "Remember the Sabbath Day to keep it holy."

(Exodus 20:8) ""For whosoever shall keep the whole law, and yet offend in one point, he is guilty of all." (James 2:10)

God gave His people a new land of America flowing with riches, and milk and honey. God's people turned into heathen idolaters, and God said He would let the plagues overtake you until you be destroyed from off the land. The President, and the Congress, and the Supreme Judges are just one of the many, many plagues that have overtaken you; and you had pleasure and approved in the ObomaNation of desolation they brought on the whole world. These black hearted children of darkness have robbed, killed, and destroyed God's children, and held them captive in bondage of sin; and God sent the author of **"Corn Shelling Time"** to expose the children of darkness, and to warn God's people to come out of "Her", which is Mystery, Babylon, and renounce Satan and all of Satan's ministers.

Listen and pay attention, all you people of Spain and Italy, and all European Countries that are under the yoke of Catholicism. You need to come out of "Her" and take the yoke of Jesus upon you. (Matthew 11:29), because His burden is light. I know that the plagues have overtaken the whole world, because the whole world has disobeyed God's Commandments and have not kept His statutes, and are not holy, which it is imperative to be holy, "For those that are not holy cannot see God."
(Hebrews 12:14)

This is not the days of Inquisition, where "Her" slaughtered millions of blood bought believers in every manner of torture Satan could cause man to think of. "Her" is still promoting deception by causing the *Harlot Government sanctioned churches* to hide their filth and sins in the name of "Christianity". In the name of suppression of heresy, the heretics themselves slaughtered multiplied millions of God's people, until the remainder of the people joined the heretics to keep from being killed; and the unholy office of the Whore at Rome is once more raising "Her" wounded head to cause "Her" Harlot Daughters *(churches)* to be deceived by ecclesiastical lies.

That is why God is calling His people, if He has any people in "Her", to come out of "Her". "Her" is not confined to the Mother Harlot, (*The Church of Rome)* or the Harlot Daughters, *(Churches),* Protestants, or any other Church, but also to the governments of the world, and also to the world itself, and be separated from these heretics, so God Almighty (PANTAKRATOR) will accept you and call you His Sons and Daughters. (II Corinthians 6:17,18)

God Almighty, (PANTARATOR), the Father, Son, Holy Spirit is not the ruler of this world, yet. Satan is the ruler of this world and all the things of the world, until the judgment.

"Hereafter, I will not talk much with you! For the Prince of the World comes and has nothing in Me." (John 14:30) **"Of judgment, because the Prince** (Ruler) **of this world is judged."** (John 16:11)

"But if our gospel be hid, it is hid to them that are lost." (II Corinthians 4:3) "In whom the god of this world has blinded the minds of them which believe not, lest the light of the glorious gospel of Christ, who is the image of God, should shine unto them." (II Corinthians 4:4)

The above scriptures have established for a fact that Satan is the ruler, god, prince, king of this world and the things of this world.

The problem with want-to-be believers is they cannot judge the difference between the world and the earth. They cannot judge between the things of this world and the things of this earth. They cannot judge themselves. If they could judge themselves, they would know they are walking dead, because they do not know how to come out of the world, because all the world and the things of the world are dead, including the want-to-be believers. The organized religions are of this world, the governments are of this world. All *churches* are of this world. All the people that are joined to any of the things above are worldly people and belong to the god of this world, Satan. If any person is joined to any of the above mentioned things, he or she is the property of Satan.

"No man can serve two masters; for either he will hate the one, and love the other; or else he will hold to the one and despise the other. You cannot serve God and mammon, *(money, things, world)*" (Matthew 6:24) Jesus nor any of His disciples never belonged to any *church*, or government, or had any fellowship with any worldly person.

That is the reason the command said to Come out of "Her", My people. The writer of all this knows that there are some good honest people in the *churches;* but they have been deceived by the glamor and enticing words of man's wisdom and cannot judge with their heart and heed the Word of God, because their minds have been blinded by the god of this world. Satan is the power that <u>all</u> *pagan churches* succumb to by yielding to the traditions of men that Constantine escalated when he unionized the pagan gods with the *"Christian" god*, and started the *Catholic church*, which started the persecution of anyone that did not agree with the heretics, calling the dissenters heresy; "and in "Her" was found the blood of prophets, and of Holy Ones, and of all that were slain upon the earth." (Revelation 18:24)

Then the Mother Church, Mother of Harlots, taught "Her" Daughters how to be Harlots, which are the *"Churches" (Harlots)* all over the world system. The protestants only revised some of the pagan beliefs in the Catholic Bible and pretended to keep God's laws and statutes, when all the time they made their proselytes a two fold child of Hell more than them. God's command is to: "Come out of "Her." (Revelation 18:4)

To understand rank and file, is to understand who rules you. Satan is the ruler of all unclean things. He is the head over the one third of the angels that got cast out of the third heaven with Lucifer. Some of the angels of the Devil have higher ranks than other angels. The angels have authority over the demons and all unclean spirits. The unclean spirits go into anyone that is not filled up with the Holy Spirit of God. The unbelievers do not have the spirit of God in them.

Christ Jesus has been raised up to be the authority and head over all things, including you. But the Holy Spirit of Jesus is a gentleman and will not force Himself on anyone. You have to have a pure clean heart *(spirit)* in order for the Holy Spirit to abide *(live)* in you. So until you are sanctified, *(pure, clean, holy)*, the old man still abides in you, which is anger, wrath, envy, pride, covetousness, which is promoted by Satan and his spirits of darkness, making you a child of darkness, and causing you not to believe Christ Jesus.

All these unclean spirits have already been bound out of the third heaven, and now inhabit the air of the first heaven, and can inhabit you, if you give place to one of these unclean spirits, and allow him to come into your body, soul, or spirit. The way you give place to Satan or any of his demons of Hell is to disobey what Jesus (God) said, which is called sin.

After you allow the unclean spirit to come into you, the unclean spirit starts destroying your members with all kinds of maladies and steals your joy, until ultimately he destroys you completely in the first Death!

God's way of escape from all these calamities, Satan, sin, sickness, death, is to simply "Shell Down the Corn" to Christ Jesus and believe what He said and do what He said, which is to confess your sins to Him and tell Him you are sorry for your trespasses; and you forgive everyone that has trespassed against you; and that you will go and sin no more; and that you repent: and you have just been transformed from death to life.

But now that you have been transformed from death to life, you can receive the promises that Christ Jesus gave His blood bought believers, and one of those promises is: **"Behold I give unto you power to tread on serpents, and scorpions, and over all the power of the enemy, and nothing shall by any means hurt you."** (Luke 10:19)

But until you *"Shell Down the Corn", (confess),* to Christ Jesus, the Prince of the Powers of the Air pulls his rank and authority over you and his angels, and causes you to be "deceived by false apostles, deceitful workers, transforming themselves into the apostles of Christ." (II Corinthians 11:13)

"And no marvel for Satan himself is transformed into an angel of light." (II Corinthians 11:14)

"Therefore it is no great thing if his ministers also be transformed as the ministers of righteousness. Whose end shall be according to their works." (II Corinthians 11:15)

All of the plagues, wounds, stripes, infirmities, disasters, calamities, diseases, heartaches, sickness, deceptions, disappointments will continue to come upon you until you "Shell Down the Corn" to Christ Jesus, *(confess)*, and repent, and BELIEVE HIM.

But the moment you come out of "Her" and come unto Christ Jesus with your hat in your hand, you will be changed in a moment in the twinkling of an eye and transformed from death to eternal life.

Christ Jesus has the power to overcome Satan for you; but He will not do it for you, because He has already done it for you, when He shed His blood for you, and bought you with the price of His own blood, and He gave you the power to have the authority over Satan, *(the god of this world)*, and all unclean spirits, and principalities, and powers, and rulers of darkness of this world, and spiritual wickedness in high places (*your thoughts)*; and that is all that Christ can do for you. The rest is up to you, whatever you do with that power.

Remember, children of darkness, until you "Shell Down the Corn" to Christ Jesus, *(confess your sins)*. "You are having a form of Godliness, but denying the power thereof. From such turn away." That is what all *churches (Harlots)* do; and that is why people that have "Shelled Down the Corn" and confessed to Christ Jesus, they want to be sanctified, which means to be holy, and pure of heart, and baptized into the Holy Spirit. They have to turn away from the *churches* and all other unclean things. (II Timothy 3:5)

Sanctified does not only mean set apart for God's use; but it means holy and pure and baptized into Jesus and the Holy Spirit of Christ Jesus; and then you are eligible to be set apart for God's use. Until you meet all the contingencies of God, you have not any power over the enemy, Satan!

Now you know who rules the world and the airways, and all the evil inventions, (Psalms 99:8, Psalms 106:29), and all the idols of the world. But you can confess Godliness until you be destroyed from off the land; but you will not inherit the Kingdom of God as long as you yield your members to a Harlot. "Know you not that your bodies are the members of Christ? Shall I then take the members of Christ and make *them* the members of an Harlot? God forbid." (I Corinthians 6:15)

"What? Know you not he which is joined to an Harlot *(church)* is one body?" So if you are a member of a *church,* you are joined to an Harlot; and you are one. (I Corinthians 6:16)

But, if you are "God's people, Come out of "Her", and be separate from the unclean filth that fellowships with fornicators, *queers,* idolaters, and all ObomaNations of the earth. (Revelation 18:4:17:5) "Having a golden cup in "Her" hand full of abominations and filthiness of "Her" fornication." (Revelation 17:4)

"Wherefore, come out from among them and be you separate, saith the Lord, and touch not the unclean thing; and I will receive you." (II Corinthians 6:17)

"And will be a Father unto you, and you shall be My Sons and Daughters, saith the Lord Almighty, (PANTAKRATOR)" (II Corinthians 6:18)

"Satan, the Devil, took Jesus up into an high mountain, and showed unto Him all the kingdoms of the world in a moment of time. And the Devil said unto Him, "All this power will I give you and the glory of them for that is delivered unto me, and to whomsoever I will I give it. If you therefore will worship me, all shall be yours." And

Jesus answered and said unto him: **"Get you behind me, Satan: For it is written, you shall worship the Lord thy God, and Him only shall you serve."** (Luke 4:5,6,7,8)

So Jesus rejected the temptation to have this world and all the kingdoms of the world. He rebuked the Devil and kept the written Word in remembrance, so He could be lifted up on the stake of suffering, and be obedient unto death, so that you and the writer of **"Corn Shelling Time"** could be like Him, and resist the temptations of this world."

"Love not the world, neither the things that are in the world. If any man love the world, the love of the Father is not in him. For all that is in the world, the lust of the flesh, and the lust of the eyes, and the pride of life, is not of the Father, but is of the world." (I John 2:15,16) So you, dear reader, come out of the world.

You have read the written word of what Satan owns, including you, because your father, Adam, forfeited his life that God gave him to be a slave of Satan to death. When Adam disobeyed God and broke the Commandment of God, he forfeited all mankind to the executioner to carry out the death sentence. The only way you can be redeemed from the penalty of death, is to believe Jesus.

"He said: Likewise also the cup after supper, saying, **"this cup is the New Testament in My blood, which is shed for you."** (Luke 22:20)

It is imperative that you *"Shell Down the Corn"* and "Confess with your mouth the Lord Jesus, and shall believe in your heart that God has raised Him from the dead, you shall be saved."(Romans 10:9) This is a good start, but there are a lot more contingencies required to be saved. Satan owns the kingdoms of the world at this present time. God said: "The earth is the Lord's and the fulness thereof, the world and they that dwell therein." (Psalms 24:1) This appears to be a contradiction, but it is speaking futuristic.

Satan is ruler of this world until the 2nd coming of Christ Jesus; then Christ will take the world and all the evil inventions and turn them into plowshares. (Isaiah 3:4)

God gave Adam and Eve dominion over every living thing on earth. They were the rulers of the world at that time. But when they disobeyed God and broke God's Commandment, they gave up their ruler ship to the Devil. The Devil kills, steals, and destroys; and everyone that has not the seal of God is the property of the ruler of this world, which is Lucifer, the old serpent, the Devil, Satan.

God owns the earth and the light, the seas, the firmament, which He called heaven, all vegetation, the sun, moon, stars, the moving creatures in the water that have life, fowl that may fly above the earth, cattle, creeping things, and beasts of the earth, man that has been regenerated to new life to live forever. The man that has not the approval of God is a dead man that is in the Land of Nod, walking around until he is buried; and then he dies the second death. "God the Father, God the Son, God the Holy Spirit created the heavens and the earth." (Genesis 1:1) And nothing was made without Him. God owns only the people that believes His shed blood was the price He bought the believer with. All the unbelievers belong to Satan. Only the ones that come out of "Her" are God's people.

So, as we look into the very near future, as we have an insight into Daniel's book that we are having a revelation of the Lamb of God that is worthy to unseal Daniel's book that has seven seals inside of it. We have already discerned that the abomination of desolation occurs in the middle of Daniel's seventieth week. "When the Lamb opened the first seal, we saw a king of the earth riding on a white horse, going out to conquer and be conquering; and God gave him a fanfare with a loud noise as it were thunder." (Revelation 6:1)

Michael Duishka

Father God, I ask you in the Name of Christ Jesus, to let your light of the good news written in the Holy Scriptures shine in the hearts of the unbelievers, and open the minds of the ones that believe not, whom the god of this world has blinded. Father cause them to read (I John 2:26,27), so they will know. In the Name of Jesus. Amen.

This is an insert in the book, **"CORN SHELLING TIME"** and **MICHAEL DUISHKA** with some of his belief. The king James bible has enough truth in it that a sinner can be justified and receive the first work of grace, which is justification. But it does not seem probable that the justified one can meet the requirements to advance into the second work of grace, which is holiness and sanctification if the justified one continues to assemble himself together with unrighteous ones which all *churches* are filled with fornicators,Idolaters,adulterers,effeminate,abusers of themselves with mankind, thieves, covetous, drunkards, revilers, extortioners, men lying with men, and women with women, and the supposedly justified one having pleasure in those that do these sins. That you may with one mind *and* one mouth glorify GOD,even the Father of our LORD CHRIST JESUS. (Romans 15:6). How could one be holy and sanctified in a filthy place as this? Now I beseech you brethren, MARK them which cause divisions and offenses contrary to the doctrine which you have learned and AVOID them.

(Romans 16:18). How can you mark them and avoid them without coming out from among them and be separate from them. (2Corinthians 6:17) thus saith the LORD. The *Churches* are all cults, that reject the every word that proceeds out of the mouth of God. Some are bloodless cults, that do not believe the blood of Jesus was a sacrifice He made to buy back the lost souls that belong to Satan and these bloodless cults are still the possessions of Satan, because they do not believe CHRIST JESUS. It is my belief that all the *churches* that do not keep the commandments of God are cults of infidels, masquerading as "Christians". God is pleading with you to come out of her and Repent!

Chapter 10

NOWHERE IN THE SCRIPTURES does Daniel's sealed book get opened. Jesus, (The Lamb), and I are going to open the book, so we can see what will befall Daniel's people in the times of the end.

The Lamb opened the first seal to reveal the rider on the white horse, which went forth conquering and to conquer. The rider on the white horse signifies peace; "But when they shall say peace and safety, then sudden destruction comes upon them, as travail upon a woman with child; and they shall not escape." (I Thessalonians 5:3)

So the rider on the white horse is the Anti-Christ, which gets his power from the dragon, which is Satan. "Even him whose coming is after the working of Satan with all power and signs and lying wonders, and with all deceiving of unrighteousness in them that perish, because they received not the love of the Truth, that they might be saved." (I Thessalonians 2:9,10)

So this rider on the white horse not only deceives Daniel's people; but he deceives the whole world, and goes out to conquer and to be conquering all the nations, tribes, kindreds, tongues, races of gentiles and fools of the whole world with his flattery and lying promises of giving the world what they want, until he becomes the ruler of the whole world; just like Obama did with America, and promised every evil faction of America what they wanted with America's wealth, until it became an ObomaNation of Desolation. This Anti-Christ on the white horse will get his pattern from Obama; and Satan will deceive the fools all over the world, just like Obama deceived the fools in the *NewNited States of America*. **"There will be wailing and gnashing of teeth."** (Luke 13:28)

After the rider on the white horse in Revelation 6:2 spends three and one-half years deceiving Daniel's people, He sets himself up in the temple, or Holy Place, and declares he is God. Even he, himself, believes he is God. (II Thessalonians 2:4)

Then he spends the next three and one-half years conquering the rest of the world. Which brings us back to the Lamb of God opening the second seal in the sealed up book of Daniel and the revelation being shown to John, the beloved disciple of Jesus.

"And there went out another horse *that was* red; and power was given to him that sat thereon to take peace from the earth, and that they should kill one another; and there was given to him a great sword." (Revelation 6:3,4)

Please understand, dear reader, that this killer is not only killing Jews; but he is given power to steal, kill, and destroy the entire earth. Daniel said, "This will be a time of trouble, such as never was since there was a nation, *even* to that same time; and at that time, your people shall be delivered."

(Daniel 12:1) But the angel, Gabriel, is talking about the end of the age, or the end of the seventy weeks that Daniel prophesied. Until the seventieth week has ended, we are talking trouble that is past your imagination, because in the same scripture, the angel said that at that time Michael shall stand up, which Daniel sealed up. (Daniel 12:1)

So when we open Daniel's seal, we read: "There was war in heaven, (first and second heaven). Michael and his angels fought against the dragon, and the dragon fought and his angels, and prevailed not. Neither was their place found any more in heaven." (Revelation 12:7,8)

So, not only are there wars on earth, but also there will be war in the high places, (heavens). "And the great dragon was cast out, that old serpent, called the Devil, and Satan, which deceives the whole world. He was cast out into the earth, and his angels were cast out with him." (Revelation 12:9)

So this war in heaven is the same time that Daniel 12:1 said Michael would stand up. So we see where Michael and his angels won the war in heaven. "But woe to the inhabitants of the earth and of the sea, for the devil is come down unto you, having great wrath, because he knows he has but a short time." (Revelation 12:12)

"And they that be wise shall shine as the brightness of the firmament, and they that turn many to righteousness as the stars forever and forever." (Daniel 12:3)

At the time of the tribulation, there are going to be believers that lead many wicked out of unbelief to truly believing. "Many shall be purified and made white, and tried; but the wicked shall do wickedly; and none of the wicked shall understand; but the wise shall understand." (Daniel 12:10)

"And such as do wickedly against the covenant shall he corrupt by flattery, but the people that do know their God shall be strong and do, exploits. And they that understand among the people shall instruct many; yet they shall fall by the sword, and by the flame, by captivity, and by spoil many days." (Daniel 11:32,33)

"Now when they shall fall, they shall be holpen (helped) with a little help; but many shall cleave to them with flattery" (Daniel 11:34)

"And some of them of understanding shall fall, to try *(test)* them and to purge, and to make them white, *even* to the time of the end; because *it is* yet for a time appointed." (Daniel 11:35)

Daniel's sealed up book is being opened by the Lamb of God, only to show Daniel's people and God's people what must befall them, so they can be worthy to inherit the Kingdom of God. Daniel said; "And they that understand shall instruct many, yet they shall fall by the sword first." "Which means by the one that sat upon the red horse; because power was given him to take peace from the whole earth; and a great sword was given him to cause the understanding ones to fall by his great sword." (Revelation 6:3,4) This falling by the great sword means God's people that have come out of "Her", and understand the mysteries of the bible. If you do not understand the mysteries of the bible, then you have not studied enough to be approved unto God; and you are a workman ashamed, and cannot rightly divide the Word Of Truth. (II Timothy 2:15)

There will not be any *churches* or "Christians" that can instruct the ones that do not understand, because the "Christians" do not understand themselves; or they would not be joined to a Harlot *(Church)*. You cannot be approved of God if you cannot rightly divide the Word Of Truth. No "Christian" that has joined his members to a Harlot is keeping the Commandments of Christ; and therefore they belong to the *Harlot Church,* and do not belong to Jesus. So they will not be killed by the Anti-Christ, but will die with the plagues of the Whore, which is the sinful Mother of the Harlots.

So, whenever the "Christians" study enough to be approved of God, they will come out of "Her", which is the whole worldly system, churches, governments, self, idolatry, greediness, hate, false gods, Ishtar *(Easter)*, *Christ-Mass, Halloween, MLK, Obama Care, Welfare,*

DHS, Sports, television, PC's, fascination gambling, pharmaceutical assistance, druggery (legal or illegal), drunkenness, or any kind of dependency other than Christ Jesus. When they come out of "Her" and come to Jesus (Matthew 11:28), they will "Shell Down the Corn", (Confess) to Jesus that they are sinners, and ask God to save them in the Name of Jesus. (1 John 1:9) says if we do that, *(Shell Down the Corn)* confess, He is faithful and just to forgive our sins and cleanse us from all unrighteousness.

Listen, dear reader, do not judge this writer as a holier-than-thou person, one that has a beam in his eye, because he washed his eyes in the water of the Word, and found the eye salve (balm) in Gilead. But this writer is as compassionate as any of God's children, just warning everyone of the awesome and terrible plagues that have already come upon you, because you are not keeping the Commandments of Christ Jesus. You say, "How do you know that?" I know that, because you go to *church.* Jesus never did say, *"Go to church." Church* is a Harlot that is unified with every abominable, filthy, deceived sinner that uses the church and Jesus for a cloak *(covering)* to try to seduce the very elect if possible.(John 15:22)

"If I had not come and spoken to them, they had not had sin; but now they have no cloak for their sin. Then shall arise false Christs and false prophets, and shall show great signs and wonders, insomuch that, if it were possible, they should deceive the very elect." (Matthew 24:22)

This writer has seen the ones that worldly knowledge was increased to on their deathbed, crying: "Oh God save me". But God did not hear their cry, because they were ashamed to call on God's only begotten Son, Christ Jesus, when they were able.

There was one wealthy man that gave ten thousand dollars to his church every year, and he really believed he was feeding the poor, because his preacher told him that is what his money went for, to feed the poor. Yeah, right! It is an awful scene to see the "Christians" die that have been deceived by the traditions of men, that lived their allotted time believing their *church* could save them.

That is the reason this writer is warning you to "Shell Down the Corn" to Christ Jesus and renounce your idols, whatever they may be, and come out of "Her", and come to Christ Jesus, and fall upon; the stone, and be broken, and join your members to eternal life, instead of eternal damnation. **"Corn Shelling Time"** is bringing a broader meaning to the plagues that the Lamb of God is opening up that were sealed up in Daniel's book. All because they did not keep the Commandments of God."Take head to yourselves and bear no burden on the Sabbath Day." (Jeremiah 17:21)

Now, the "Christians" do not even know what day the Sabbath Day is, much less keep it holy. Jeremiah also said: "Thus saith the Lord: "Cursed is the man that trusts in man, and makes flesh his arm, and whose heart departs from the Lord." (Jeremiah 17:5)

Just look at the plagues, too numerous to mention, yet everyone I talk to says: "Oh, I have good insurance, or I have a good doctor", yet the trust they put in man could not save them from the plague, or from eternal death. This writer has Christ Jesus for a doctor and insurance.

The laws of the land are making the choice more binding for God's believers to keep the Commandments of God, because the laws of the land are an abomination to Christ Jesus, who never did vote, or never had mandatory insurance, or pay tithes. But if you want to make the Kingdom of God, you have to shuck off the laws of the land, and start obeying the laws of God Almighty, (PANTAKRATOR).

Take this Opportunity to confess the Lord Christ Jesus. Repeat after me. Say: My Lord Jesus, I confess I am a sinner, and I ask you to save me; and you said you would save whosoever calls on your Name. I believe you, and I thank you for saving me. In the Name of Jesus, I believe you will save me. Amen." This writer agrees with you in the Name of Jesus. Amen."

Warning! If you have already received one of "Her" plagues, you can go to your doctor, and the doctor may give you a prescription to relieve the symptoms of the one plague, but the prescription will cause another infirmity in another part of your body; and you will only prolong your destruction from off the land; and the doctor will give you medicine for your pain, until you are addicted to the drugs, and have to depend on people to take you to the restroom, and depend on someone to dress and undress you, and depend on man to take you to the doctor; and that goes on until you are destroyed from off the land, because you will not put your trust in Christ Jesus to save you from the plague, and forgive you your sins. "Thus saith the Lord: Cursed is the man that trusts in man." (Jeremiah 17:5)

This writer is not telling you to do something that he himself has not already tested to see if the Word Of God be true. I could not name as many perils that I have overcome that would be as many as the Apostle Paul; but I can name you six, yea even seven times Satan has tried to kill this anointed one of God; but God's grace was sufficient to help me overcome each death sentence of the Devil. Thank you, Lord Jesus for giving me the measure of faith to trust you and believe you. God is no respecter of persons, what He did for me, He will do for you, if you have faith enough to trust Him. If you belong to Satan, he will destroy you, because he came to rob, kill, and destroy. (John 10:10)

Even as I write this, a disaster just occurred in a heathen country, that has been killing "Christians"; and now thousands are crying for help, and do not know where to get help, because they killed the missionaries that were sent to tell them how to call on Jesus. Thus will be the same with every soul on earth, or in this world that rejects the Savior, Christ Jesus.

A few chapters back in this book the writer said a disaster would happen before the book was finished, and it happened. But this is not the time of trouble that Daniel and Jeremiah were talking about. This is the beginning of sorrows that Jesus talked about in (Matthew 24); and the sorrows intensified in the year 2011, and will accelerate until the tribulation period that Jesus said would be worse than ever before, and never would be again. (Matthew 24:21)

Father God, in the Name of your Son, Jesus *The* Christ, I pray for your people that are like just Lot, when he came out of Sodom and Gomorrah. Cause your people to come out of "Her", in the Name of Jesus. (Revelation 18:4)

The heathen all over the world, including "Christians", are victims of the plagues that destroy them from off the land. Some are destroyed suddenly, and some are allowed to suffer a slow death, to give them more time to "Shell Down the Corn" and confess their sins; and some do, and some don't. Some would, but do not know how to have faith in Christ Jesus, and believe Him. Some have sinned away their days of grace and are taken suddenly by fire, water, earthquake, or wind, (tornado, cyclone, hurricane, tsunami, typhoon or flood). They are gone, too late to pray for them.

Someone a long time ago called them educated fools, and was right. "And the King lamented over Abner and said: "Abner died as a fool dies." (II Samuel 3:33) For Abner came out of the City of Refuge to die as a fool, just like God's people come out of Christ Jesus to die as fools. God's people are accursed, because they believe every other gospel beside the one Paul preached. "But though we or an angel from heaven preach any other gospel unto you than that which we have preached unto you, let him be accursed." (Galatians 1:8)

Yet God's people are misled by every kind of denomination and false doctrine that comes along.

"That we henceforth be no more children, tossed to and fro, and carried about with every wind of doctrine, by the sleight of men, and cunning craftiness, whereby they lie in wait to deceive." (Ephesians 4:14)

"And why call you Me, Lord, Lord, and do not the things which I say?" (Luke 6:46) Church people say "Jesus is Lord, and do not do what He said to do. He did not say *go to church*. He did say to feed the hungry, and give drink to the thirsty, visit the sick, visit the prisoners, and to entertain strangers.

"Be not forgetful to entertain strangers, for thereby some have entertained angels unawares."
(Hebrews 13:2)

In this *NewNited States of America*, there is a conspiracy to talk trash against the Mexican strangers in this country. The Mexicans are the majority of hard workers that: "In the sweat of your face shall you eat bread til you return unto the ground." (Genesis 3:19) They make their living by working fast and hard, and the stupid whites are afraid to call the shots the way they are, where the fat lazy blacks and whites just lay back and receive welfare checks and food stamps, and months and months of unemployment that their black president buys their votes with, by giving the hardworking people's money away to the lazy bums. "For even when we were with you, this we commanded you, that if any would not work, neither should he eat." (II Thessalonians 3:10)

The way the government got around this Commandment of God, was to pass a mandatory law, that so many blacks had to be hired at every job site in the USA, whether he was qualified or not, and they never were qualified to do the job they were given by the law of the land. Even the leaders of our God given Country are unqualified blacks that kill, steal, and destroy the wealth of the USA to the tune of trillions of dollars in debt to other countries.

The black president and his majority congress just keep printing those worthless 100 dollar bills. I agree with the late great President of these United States of America, Richard Nixon, when he said quote, "Black people are incapable of running Jamaica, or anywhere else. Blacks can't run it nowhere, and they won't be able to for a hundred years; and maybe not for a thousand." He says: "Do you know, maybe one black country that's well run?" *(From the Nixon Tapes)* No, is the answer to Nixon's question. There are not any countries that are led by a black that did not go down instead of up, including these *NewNited States of America*. Since Obama went into the office of presidency, this country has speedily went down hill just like a snowball headed for Hell!

So get ready you lazy, shiftless, fat parasites, your gravy train is about to derail. Obama is spreading the wealth of the hard working people around to the lazy shiftless thieves, killers, and destroyers of America for the *ObomaNation of desolation of America*. "And the nations were angry, and your wrath is come, and the time of the dead that they should be judged, and that you should give reward, unto your servants the prophets, and to the Holy Ones, and them that fear Your Name, small and great, and should destroy them which destroy the earth." (Revelation 11:18)

The last warning Christ Jesus gave to His People, not to the heathen, or the pagans, or the "Christians", but to the people that believe Him is: "And I heard another voice from heaven saying, "Come out of "Her", My people, that you be not partakers of "Her" sins, and that you receive not of "Her" plagues." (Revelation 18:4)

This is talking about, "Mystery, Babylon, which is the Mother of Harlots and abominations of the earth." (Revelation 17:5)

The angel is talking about the *Mother Church of Rome, The Catholic Church* and Her Harlot Daughters, all the other *churches* of the world, including the *Protestant Harlot Churches:* Also, the governments of the world and also the world itself. "Love not the world neither the things that are in the world. If any man love the world, the love of the Father is not in him. For all that is in the world, the lust of the flesh, and the lust of the eyes, and the pride of life, is not of the Father, but is of the world." (I John 2:15,16)

Father God, in the Name of Christ Jesus, I pray for the ones that do not understand the Mysteries of the Bible, because I love them and you love them; and it is written, "it is not your will that any should perish, but that all should repent and *"Shell Down the Corn"*, (confess) to you in the Name of Jesus." Amen and Amen.

THIS is an insert in the book, **"CORN SHELLING TIME"** and **MICHAEL DUISHKA** with some of his belief. There was some kind poll conducted, which is always a big made up lie to promote the poll taker's agenda. The poll taker asks his partner, and his family, and his friends, who are biased and the poll always comes up the way the liar wants it to come up. The poll said that sixty per cent of the people favored same sex marriage. Actually it really said equality marriage, but I cannot write that lie, because the words that Satan and his subjects use, is right the opposite of every word that proceeds out of the mouth of God, which is GOD'S WORD, which is CHRIST, which is JESUS, which is GOD. There is no such thing as men marrying men in the kingdom of GOD, or women marrying women in the kingdom of GOD. GOD sent MICHAEL DUISHKA into this world to reiterate the true WORD of GOD, not the word of Satan or his followers. If 60% of the world are queers,that would mean the escalation of the great apostasy, (falling away from God) is rapidly reaching the apex of the great and terrible day of God, which is the day God starts to pour out His wrath on the wicked people that will not understand what is causing their destruction. They will continue, as they are, as **"CORN SHELLING TIME"** is being written. But the wise ones will understand and come out of the Harlot *Churches*, governments of the world, wars, Idolatry,police, voting, marching, protesting, disobedient to parents, hollering for equality and justice, pornography, all evil inventions except to use them working for Jesus, eradicate hate from your spirit, do not do anything that consents to robbing, killing, or destroying anything, or anybody, always prefer your neighbor before yourself, take your children or grandchildren out of any government funded public school, teach them only every WORD that proceeds out of the mouth of GOD, do not learn, or let your children learn any heathen,pagan, religion, such as Islam, Muslim, Quran, Catholicism, or any other false proclamation, such as evolution,secular humanism,modernist teachings, or be a part of anything that blasphemes God, be a loner if you cannot find another believer of CHRIST JESUS, not one that professes to believe in Jesus, but one that believes CHRIST JESUS and POSSESSES HIM, there are many false professors, but only a very few POSSESSORS of HIM, shun the very appearance of evil. Submit yourself to GOD, Resist the devil and he will flee from you in the name of JESUS.(James 4:7) **"Behold I give unto you power to tread on serpents and scorpions, and over all the power of the enemy: and nothing by any means shall hurt you"**. (Luke 10:19) Remember we are not fighting against humans, (flesh and blood) but do not be fooled we are double dog dead sure fighting against those unclean spirits that are in humans, (flesh and blood) and you just read the promise of the power you can use over these unclean spirits that Jesus gave to you in Luke 10: 19, so you as a believer of Jesus have the authority to bind and cast out all the spirits of the devil. **" Again I say unto you whatsoever you shall bind on earth shall be bound in heaven: and whatsoever you shall loose on earth shall be loosed in heaven."** (Matthew 18:18) SO what is your problem that you do not obey the commandment of Jesus when He commanded you to come out of all the things mentioned above, which is MYSTERY, BABYLON,and JESUS said: **"COME OUT OF HER, MY PEOPLE, THAT YOU BE NOT PARTAKERS OF HER SINS, THAT YOU RECEIVE NOT OF HER PLAGUES"**. (Revelation 18:4) JESUS only gave those promises to holy ghost filled, blood covered, sanctified, commandment keeping, BELIEVERS! AMEN.

Chapter 11

"And though I have the gift of prophecy and understand all mysteries, and all knowledge, and though I have all faith, so that I could remove mountains, and have not charity, I am nothing." (1Corinthians 13:2)

The reason this writer is spending hour after hour of his time writing this warning to ignorant worldly people, how to understand, how to have life and life more abundantly, is because he has love and charity for the children of darkness that are perishing by being disobedient to their Creator, Christ Jesus.

This disobedience to Christ Jesus is just one of many mysteries of life. Satan has many glamorous deceptions that appeal to the soul, or fleshly desires, or lusts of natural man; but Christ Jesus pleads with the spirit of man to desire things eternal. Satan's children are seeking the temporal worldly desires.

God's children are seeking the Kingdom of God, which is eternal, forever. The mystery is why would millions upon millions trade eternal life in paradise for the kingdoms of this world, which brings eternal death?

Believers understand the mysteries of God and the secrets that God's Holy Spirit only shares with the spiritual man, because the spiritual man is seeking the revelation that only the Holy Spirit can reveal. The natural man thinks these spiritual things are foolishness, which brings us to the mysteries of God, which Jesus told His disciples that it was given to them to understand the secrets and mysteries of God. (Matthew 13:11) But to the natural people He spoke in parables. All of the mysteries of the Kingdom of God are summed up in two mysteries. One is the mystery of Godliness. (I Timothy 3:16)

"And without controversy, great is the mystery of Godliness. **God was manifest in the flesh**; justified in the spirit; seen of angels; preached unto the Gentiles; believed on in the world; received into glory." (I Timothy 3:16)

"In the beginning was the Word, and the Word was with God, and the Word was God." (John1:1)**"And the Word was made flesh and dwelt among us. (And we beheld His (*The*) Glory, the Glory as of the only begotten of the Father), full of grace and Truth."** (John 1:14)

Just in case some historian, or any other idiot, believes John was illiterate and could not read or write, Isaiah said: "Therefore the Lord himself shall give you a sign. Behold a virgin shall conceive, and bear a Son, and shall call His Name Emmanuel." (Isaiah 7:14) There are many more scriptures that bear out that Jesus was God in the flesh; but the above scriptures are sufficient for believers.

Next is **He was justified in the spirit:** "Concerning His Son Jesus The Christ, our Lord, which was made of the seed of David, according to the flesh." (Romans 1:3) "And declared to be the Son of God with power, according to the Spirit of Holiness, by the resurrection from the dead." (Romans 1:4)

"Seen of angels: And to make all men see what *is* the fellowship of the mystery, which from the beginning of the world, has been hid in God, who created all things by Christ Jesus." (Ephesians 3:9)

To the intent that now unto the principalities and powers in the heavenly places might be known by the Called Out Ones (Ekklesia) the manifold Wisdom of God." (Ephesians 3:10)

"Preached unto the Gentiles: For by one Spirit we are all baptized into one Body, whether we be Jews or Gentiles, whether we be bond or free; and all have been made to drink into one Spirit." (I Corinthians 12:13)

"Where there is neither Greek nor Jew, circumcision nor uncircumcision, barbarian nor Scythian, bond *nor* free; but Christ *is* all and in all." (Colossians 3:11)

Believed on in the world: And there was delivered unto Him the book of the Prophet Isaiah; and when He had opened the book, He found the place where it is written: **"The Spirit of the Lord is upon Me, because He has anointed Me to preach the gospel to the poor. He has sent Me to heal the broken hearted, to preach deliverance to the captives, and recovering of sight to the blind, to set at liberty them that are bruised, to preach the acceptable year of the LORD/"** (Luke 4:17,18,19)

Received up into Glory: "And their eyes were opened, and they knew Him, and He vanished out of their sight." (Luke 24:31) "He was manifest in a fleshly body. He was received up into Glory in a Spiritual Body." The mysteries of Godliness are summed up in (I Timothy 3:16)

But there are other Mysteries that come out of the Mystery of Godliness, that need to be understood. God trusted certain men to become stewards of the Mysteries of Godliness. That is why Jesus said to His disciples: "It is given to you to understand the Mysteries of the Kingdom of God and heaven."

Paul said: "Let a man so account of us, as of the ministers of Christ, and stewards of the Mysteries of God." (I Corinthians 4:1)

"Moreover it is required in stewards of the Mysteries of God, that a man be found faithful."(1 Corinthians 4:2) Being a faithful steward, means not giving heed to seducing spirits, or not giving heed to doctrines of devils, which every *Harlot church* has a different doctrine than the one doctrine of God.

Having the faith of God. (Mark 11:22)

This writer cannot translate the mysteries of Christ from his spiritual knowledge to worldly knowledge, because even though Christ explained in writing the meaning of some of the parables, the deep things still remain a mystery to the natural man; and they are past finding out, except the Holy Spirit of God reveals them. (I Corinthians 2:14) They are secret. They are hidden to all sensual intellect. They are only revealed to whom Christ chooses to know them.

Father God, in the name of Jesus, I ask you to fill the person reading this with your Holy Spirit, so all the Mysteries of God will be revealed to him or her. In Christ Jesus. Amen. Amen.

This is the mystery of iniquity, or lawlessness. "For the mystery of iniquity does already work." (II Thessalonians 2:7) So, Paul said the mystery of iniquity was working in the time Paul was writing the letter, or the epistle to the Thessalonians. Now, we know that iniquity means lawlessness, or disobedience to the law of God. Since the disobedience was already working in Paul's time, what made it a mystery? What made it a mystery is the people of God, "Christians", that had the Truth preached to them; and at first they believed and were glad to have the opportunity to receive the seed, (*The Word*), sown into their hearts. Their faith was strong at first; but as time went on, they let the agents of Satan, or his ministers, lead them astray from the faith they had in the Seed, (*Word)*, that they had first received. That is the mystery of lawlessness, or iniquity. The mystery is not talking about the rank sinner that never has "Shelled Down the Corn" to Christ Jesus; but on the contrary, it is talking about the so called "Christians" that have tasted the heavenly gift of God, Christ Jesus, and have partaken in the Holy Spirit; and then let the false apostles, deceitful workers, transforming themselves into ministers of righteousness, seduce *(lead them astray)* them into believing the Lie and be condemned. They turned back into iniquity by many things of this world, which is idolatry. Here is the way the wicked one (Satan) works to deceive the so called churches that are filled with so called "Christians". He puts thoughts into the ministers that cause them to think the Word of God means for "Christians" to prosper and be in good health, and yet continue in sin, which is iniquity, or lawlessness.

So, the spirit of Satan causes the ministers of righteousness to transform themselves into ministers of unrighteousness. So they are preaching (Anti-Christ) instead of preaching what Christ Jesus commanded, which was humbleness, and to be rich in the Word of God, and to shuck off prosperity of this world, and all the things that are in the world. The false apostles, deceitful workers that are Anti-Christs deceive the ignorant so called "Christians" to keep them joined to the Whore and "Her" Harlot Daughters, *the churches of Satan.* These are the works of the mystery of iniquity. "And no marvel, for Satan, himself is transformed into an angel of light." (II Corinthians 11:14) This is the mystery of iniquity, lawlessness. The two mysteries are, of Godliness, and of Iniquity.

Paul, the apostle of Christ, said: "The mystery of iniquity was already at work in his time." (II Thessalonians 2:7) His time was almost two thousand years ago. The lawlessness has escalated in two thousand years, which provoked a great falling away. The question is, falling away from what, or who? Answer: Falling away from the faith they had in Christ Jesus. This great apostasy is escalating at great speed; and to real believers it can be seen plainly in the *Mother Church and all "Her" Daughters, the protestant churches.* It would have to be the *churches* and the "Christians", because the sinners and the common people never had any faith in Christ Jesus to fall away from. The "Christians" in the *churches* are no different from the heathen, or sinners, because they are all idolaters. All this great apostasy is caused by seducing spirits of the transformed ministers of righteousness, who are ministers of Satan. (II Corinthians 11:15) All the *churches* and the so called "Christians" are departing from the faith they once had in Christ Jesus, and turning to faith in doctrines of devils, *(demons)*. This mystery of iniquity is ushering the "Christians" into another mystery of iniquity, which is called Mystery, Babylon. Mystery, Babylon is the *churches* of the world joining the governments of the world to form the beast, with the leader the Anti-Christ. (Revelation 17:5) "And upon "Her" forehead *was* a name written, Mystery, Babylon The Great, The Mother Of Harlots And Abominations Of The Earth." The verses of scripture preceding verse 5 makes it clear who the Mother is who is sitting on many waters. That is what makes the mystery. In spiritual visions, nothing is literal; but everything is symbolic. The angel is one of the 7 vial angels that are showing John the symbol for many waters, which is what the Great Whore is sitting on, which are peoples, and multitudes, and nations, and tongues. (Verse 15)

The woman signifies a religious system that claims to know God, but has committed spiritual fornication, and caused peoples, multitudes, nations, tongues, kings, and inhabitants of the earth to commit fornication, which is being unfaithful to God, by murder of God's Holy Ones and breaking every Commandment of God by profanity of the Sabbath Day, changing the Sabbath Day of God into *Sunday,* the man made day to worship the god of the Sun, and all the other Commandments of God, by causing the Harlots to commit murder and fornication with God's Holy Ones. The Great Whore is the same example the *Catholic Church of Rome* is setting, so she must be the *Roman Catholic Church.*

She is called the Mother; and since the Mother of anything always has children, and this Mother is the Mother of Harlots, the Harlots are the children of the Great Whore. So if the Mother is the Mother of Harlots, the Harlots have to be the Daughters of the Whore, which makes the Daughters,Whores, also, which means all the other *churches* are the Harlots.

The kings of the earth have committed fornication with "Her", and the inhabitants of the earth have been made drunk with the wine *(spirits)* of her fornication. "And John saw the woman drunken with the blood of the Holy Ones, and with the blood of the martyrs of Jesus." (Revelation 17:6) Brother John said, "when I saw "Her", I wondered with great admiration."

The mysteries have been explained, except for the culmination of all of them, which will come later in **"Corn Shelling Time."**

The mystery of the sower of the seed and the mystery of the wheat and the tares were explained by Christ Jesus; and I am sure this writer could not explain the secrets of God any better than the Master. If you want to learn:

The Parable of the sower of the seed, go to (Matthew 13).
The wheat and the tares, go to (Matthew 13:24).
The grain of mustard seed (Matthew 13:31).
The parable of the leaven (Matthew 13:33).
The hidden treasure (Matthew 13:44)
The parable of the pearl. (Matthew 13:45)
The parable of the net and fish. (Matthew 13:47)

These are all mysteries about Godliness and the Kingdom of Heaven. We will get back to the Mystery, Babylon later in **"Corn Shelling Time"**; and also the manifestation of the Mystery of God, which will be the end of all Mysteries.

The angel that warned God's people to come out of "Her" in (Revelation 18:4) was talking to the "Christians" of all *churches,* including the Great Whore, which is the Mother of all Harlots and the *Mother Church* that is in Rome that has deceived the weak minded people for seventeen hundred years, and the strong minded people that were blood bought believers She killed and made them martyrs of Jesus. The Protestants followed in "Her" wickedness in a more subtle way, causing the inhabitants of the earth to commit fornication against God.

FATHER God, I humble myself as I come before your throne of Grace and ask you to save all the people that come out of "HER", and they will be your people. In the Name of Christ Jesus. Amen.

THIS is an insert in the book, **"CORN SHELLING TIME"** and **MICHAEL DUISHKA** with some of his belief. Nearly every time I get the opportunity to speak with a so called "Christian" I know the conversation is going to be short lived. Every time a scripture is quoted the "CHRISTIAN" always gets the soulish, natural interpretation, which is always wrong. When he is asked could it have a spiritual meaning, his reply is always, " I am not going to argue about it" or " that is your interpretation". The most misunderstood text is the one about Peter with the vision of the creeping things. The voice said kill and eat. Then the voice said,do not call anything common or unclean that I have cleaned. The bible plainly shows the voice was talking about taking salvation to the Gentiles. The unlearned wants to argue it is talking about eating unclean animals, which is the natural thought, But the natural man receives not the things of the SPIRIT of God, because they are foolishness to him: neither can he know *them,* because they are spiritually discerned. (1Corinthians 2:14). **If you love me keep my commandments, and I will pray the Father, and He shall give you another comforter, that He may abide with you forever,** *Even* **the Spirit of TRUTH: whom the world cannot receive, because it sees Him not, neither knows Him: For He dwells with**

you, and shall be in you. (JOHN 14:15,16,17). That promise is contingent on, IF you keep His commandments, which no *Church* keeps His commandments. All the commandments the *Churches* keep are man made commandments and traditions of men and doctrine of devils. HE commands you to come out of her. (Revelation 18:4)

Chapter 12

BACK TO THE LAMB of God that is opening the book of Daniel that has been sealed up until the time of the end, which is soon to happen according to the signs of the times that Jesus told His disciples, they would know when the presence *(second coming)* of Jesus was drawing near by the signs of the times.

If this book is offensive to anyone, it would only be offensive to a sinner that is not obeying God's law. "And a stone of stumbling, and a rock of offense, even to them which stumble at the Word, being disobedient. Where unto also they were appointed." (I Peter 2:8)

If **"Corn Shelling Time"** offends or causes anyone to stumble, then he is not my brother. My brothers are the Holy Ones that have come out of the worldly system *(churches, governments, things of this world)* and agree with every Word that proceeds out of the mouth of God.

"It is good neither to eat flesh, or to drink wine, nor anything whereby your brother stumbles, or is offended, or is made weak." (Romans 14:21)

The Apostle Paul is speaking to natural, sensual men that do not discern natural from spiritual, just as some of you, dear readers, are guilty of. Because I eat flesh and drink blood, which was not only offensive; but it drove away the natural, weak followers of Jesus. I am talking spiritually; and the sinners and "Christians" hear with the natural, or sensual ear. (John **6:66**) "From that time many of His disciples went back, and walked no more with Him." They took the Mark of the Anti-Christ. (John **6:66**)

The reason they were offended and stumbled, is because they were not brothers. My Lord Jesus had just told them: "**Verily, Verily, I say unto you. Except you eat the flesh of the Son of Man and drink His blood, you have no Life in you.**" (John 6:53) This is the flesh I said I eat, and this is the blood I said I drink. Only the Holy Brothers understand that we do it spiritually. The natural man cannot understand, because he is yet carnal, and only lusts after sensual pleasures and appetites. There are not any visible words that can be written by any man that can make you understand the Word of the Bible. The only way is to do like I did, and did not receive any teaching by any man; but I came out of "Her", (*churches, governments, things of this world*), and went to (I John 2:26,27)

"These things have I written unto you concerning them that seduce you, (*lead you astray*). But the anointing you have received of Him abides in you; and you need not that any man teach you; but as the same anointing teaches you of all things, and is Truth, and is no lie; and even as He has taught you, you shall abide in Him." (I John 2:26,27) AMEN. So Be It.

Thank you, Lord Jesus for the anointing which I received, which is Your Holy Spirit, that taught me all things. You can read every word of the Bible, even memorize portions of it; and unless you have received the anointing of the Master Himself, you will still be a natural man, and cannot understand that the Master said: "**It is the Spirit that quickens** (brings to life). **The flesh** (natural) **profits nothing. The Words that I speak unto you, they are Spirit, and They are life.**"(John 6;63) God inspired man to write the Words, but the Holy Ghost teaches you the meaning.

The Angel, Gabriel, was sent to teach Daniel skill and understanding. "And God, Who at Sundry times and in divers manners spoke in times past unto the fathers by the prophets, has in these last days spoken unto us by His Son, Whom He has appointed heir of all things, by Whom also He made the worlds. Who being the brightness of His Glory, and the express Image of His Person, and upholding all things by the Word of His power, when He had by Himself purged our sins, sat down on the right of The Majesty on High." (Hebrews 1:1,2,3) God is still speaking to us by the Holy Spirit of The Son, teaching us all things; **"And He will show you things to come."** (John 16:13)

Now let us go back to the sealed book of Daniel, and let the Comforter show us some more things when the Lamb of God is opening the seals of the book. We read in previous chapters where some of the people that do know their God and have understanding shall instruct many in this tribulation time; but they shall fall by the sword, which the first and second seal in (Revelation 6:1,2,3,4) showed us two horses, one was white, and one was red; and the riders were to take peace from the earth by weapons of destruction and by the sword, which Daniel's book said in (Daniel 11:33). Also in the same verse it said additional ones would fall by the flame and captivity, and spoil. So, as the Lamb of God is the only one worthy to open Daniel's sealed up book, let us see what the next seal reveals to us as the Lamb of God opens the third seal. John heard the third beast say, "Come and see". And John saw a black horse, and he that sat on him had a yoke in his hand.

The K.J.V. Interpreters reads like this: "And he that sat on him had a pair of balances in his hand." But the Greek word is *Zugon* (Zuyos), being interpreted yoke everywhere else in the Bible. So, I believe the rider on the black horse had a symbol that had a two fold meaning. Daniel's book said some of his people would fall by captivity, which the yoke signifies bondage and captivity. But the rest of the context signifies a famine; and as we continue (Revelation 6:5) "John beheld a black horse, and he that sat on him had a pair of balances (*KJV*) in his hand. And John heard a voice in the midst of the four beasts say, "A measure of wheat for a denarion, *(Penny)* and 3 measures of barley for a denarion *(Penny)*, and see you hurt not the oil and the wine." (Revelation 6:6)

Now, the black horse is a symbol for death. So the first horse, which was white and the second horse, which was red, brought war, and the captivity of the third horse, which is black, and alludes to death by some going into captivity and some dying from starvation, brought on by world wide famine. This is all in Daniel's book that the Lamb of God is unsealing. This not only shows what will be falling on Daniel's people, but also falling upon the Gentiles that do not obey the Anti-Christ. Those that do obey the Anti-Christ and his laws are doomed for Hell. "They must take his mark, or his name, or the number of his name." (Revelation 13:17) These have denied Christ, and do not have the Seal Of God.

"Corn Shelling Time" is not only; to reveal the apostasy, which is the falling away from Christ Jesus, or anything that is connected to God Almighty (PANTAKRATOR); but **"Corn Shelling Time"** is to instruct the entire world how to escape the hour of temptation that is coming upon the entire earth. You cannot afford to wait until it arrives and think to change your ways when it gets here, because it will be too late to observe and do all the instructions in the bible, or the ones in this book.

"Corn Shelling Time" is to warn the readers about the urgency of the signs of the end time, which are rapidly and quietly closing In on us in this present time. As you read this, humble your heart to God Almighty, (PANTAKRATOR), and confess to Him that you are a sinner; and **say**: "Lord Jesus, Please save me." You would be wise to *"Shell Down the Corn"*, which is confess in the presence of a witness, or some witnesses, so you will have a witness when the record books are opened; and the Lamb's Book of Life is opened, to see If your name is written there. **"Whosoever, therefore, shall confess Me before men, him will I also confess before My Father, which is in heaven."** (Matthew 10:32)

So, just as the Lamb of God (Lord Jesus) is the only one worthy to open the sealed book of Daniel and the seals of Revelation, in the same manner He will have the authority to open the Lamb's Book of Life. So, right now do not put it off any longer. "Shell Down the Corn", and ask the Lord Jesus to save you and your whole family. Right now is the accepted time of salvation, before any more plagues come upon you.

"And when the Lamb had opened the fourth seal, John heard a voice of the fourth beast say, "Come and see." John looked, and behold he saw a pale *(Khloros) (Green)* horse, and his name that sat on him was Death, and Hell followed with him. And power was given unto them over the fourth part of the earth, to kill with sword and hunger, and with Death, and with the beasts of the earth."

(Revelation 6:7,8)

These revelations were sealed in Daniel's book, and were included in "the revelation that God gave to Christ Jesus to show His servants, *(doulos)*, slaves, things which shortly must come to pass."

(Revelation 1:1) "And He sent His angel to signify unto His Slave, John." (Revelation 1:1)

So, whenever The Lamb opened the sealed book and the seven seals in the book, He opened a Menu to the hour of temptation that was prophesied to come upon the entire earth. "And the trouble is great, so that none is like it." (Jeremiah 30:7)

"For then shall be great tribulation such as was not since the beginning of the world, to this time, no nor ever shall be; and except those days be shortened, there should no

flesh be saved; but for the elect's (Ekklektos) **sake, those days shall be shortened.**" (Matthew 24:21,22)

So, if you put off " *Shelling Down the Corn", (confessing Christ Jesus),* the wrath of God will be so severe that you can see which selection of the Menu your destruction will be.

"And power was given to the rider of the red horse that they kill one another." (Revelation 6:4)

Daniel's book said some would fall by the flame. The Menu said hail and fire, mingled with blood.

"The first angel sounded, and there followed hail and fire mingled with blood." Since blood cannot inherit the Kingdom of God, the blood could be mingled with the flames that some fall by. (Daniel 11:33) (Revelation 8; 7)

Before we open up the Menu to the trumpets and the vials *(bowls)* and the woes, let me clarify some misconception of *church goers* that have been deceived into thinking the rapture is going to happen to all *church goers*; and they will elude the great tribulation. In the first place, there never was a *church* in the original Word of God. The reason being, all the disciples and Jesus Himself never spoke any English or Latin; and the word, *Church,* is an invented word by man. Jesus called His people (Ekklesia) out. This is a compound Greek word that means a calling out, and never *Church.* The church was started by Satan causing the Great Whore, the *Catholic Church,* organizer of all the Harlots *(churches)* that were drunken with the blood of the Holy Ones, (not *saints*), and with the blood of the martyrs of Jesus. (Revelation 17:6)

Jesus did not say, "And upon this rock I will build my church. The Strong's Hebrew and Greek dictionaries interpret the word, a called out meeting, a religious congregation. But that is why the King

James translators got things falsified, is because they just copied the Catholic Bible, which is mixed with Pagan Worship; and they started in (Matthew 16:18) falsifying the truth (Ekklesia), and also a lot of false words. There was never any word Saint, but Jesus used the Greek word Hagios, which means Holy, and not a dead thing (*Saint*).

So, in 2011 Michael Duishka wrote a book called "Please Co Not Call Me A "Christian", where the English speaking people had been in bondage for 400 years, ever since 1611, year of the King James Bible printing, and the deceived ones, thinking a copy of the Catholic Bible was the true Word of God, did not know they have been in bondage for 400 years, from 1611 A.D. to 2011 A.D., just like the children of Israel were in bondage to the Egyptians for 400 years. And God is calling His people out of "Her", so they would not partake of "Her" sins and receive not of "Her" plagues. But Satan's ministers that transformed themselves into ministers of righteousness have deceived God's people for 1700 years, whenever Constantine mixed Paganism with Catholicism.

All people go to *church* for, now-a-days is to be entertained, or to entertain. That is why Jesus said; **"Verily I say to you, that the Publicans, and the Harlots go into the Kingdom of God before you."**

(Matthew 21:31) The Publicans being the tax collectors, which were thought of the same way they are thought of today. The harlots in that quote of Jesus were literal whores. Whereas the *churches (harlots)* are spiritual whores that are supposed to be in union with Christ Jesus; but are cheating on Him by being in league with the unbelieving crowd of Satan Worshipers. Any *church* that is entered into, is destitute of the Word Of Truth. Because they can come close to quoting ("John 3:16"), they claim to be sanctified, which has a definition of Holy and Pure and Set Apart. When *church* members are asked if they are sanctified? They immediately answer "Oh yes". If you ask them what it means to be sanctified? They leave off the true definition, which is Pure and Holy, and say it means set apart for God's use, which is true if you are Pure and Holy. The historic mistake of the so-called "Christians" is they think they are the body of Christ. If that were so, the body of Christ would be a filthy mess of abominable idolaters that idolize everything from sex symbols, to murderers, to adulteresses, to fornicators. They, *(churches)*, allow any kind of sinner to become a member, not to get the sinner salvation, but rather to get the sinner's money in tithes and offerings. "Not forsaking the assembling of ourselves together." *With sinners?* (Hebrews 10:25)

"And when He had opened the seventh seal, there was silence in heaven about the space of half an hour." (Revelation 8:1)

This page of the Menu means the lull before the storm. So, we go back to the beginning of the events that happen in the last half of the seventieth week of Daniel, when Jacob's trouble begins. Not only does Jacob's trouble begin, but the entire world of nations *(Gentiles)* go into the hour of temptation. Listen! Here is a way to escape the hour of temptation that is coming on the entire earth. "Shell Down the Corn" to God, (confess that you are a sinner and pray); and here is the answer Jesus will give to you. "Because you have kept the Word of My patience, I also will keep you from the hour of temptation, which shall come upon all the world, to prove them that dwell upon the earth." (Revelation 3:10)

God's wise ones that have been called to instruct many to righteousness will fall by the government of the Anti-Christ. They will be imprisoned for 10 days before they are killed; but here is their reward. "You be faithful unto death, and I will give you a crown of Life." (Revelation 2:10)

"He that has an ear, let him hear what the spirit says unto the *Ekklesia, (called out ones)*. He that overcomes shall not be hurt of the second death." (Revelation 2:11)

At this present time we are in the beginning of sorrows, which became more fervent and intense in the year 2011. The sorrows are occurring more rapidly than I can write them down. America is an ObomaNation of Desolation, which is a plague itself, that has come upon the Great Satan Nation. But the sorrows are erupting over this entire earth.

It seems like they are happening to warn the people to "Come out of "Her", (Mystery Babylon) and "Come to Jesus." (Matthew 11:28)

The sorrows are the stripes or the wounds that are being administered to the disobedient ones of the Word of God. To the "Christians" and *church goers* the plagues come in the form of sickness or diseases that cannot be cured; and they have to become drug addicts just to be able to stand the pain.

Queers (homosexuals) are not gay, because they are plagued with a life threatening disease that is carrying out the sentence of death that is pronounced on men lying with men. (Romans 1:32)

Other grievous diseases for being disobedient to God, are cancer, diabetes, obesity, heart trouble of all kinds, ulcers, gall bladder, kidneys, alcoholics, lung diseases, and on and on until you perish.

Other plagues that are weapons of mass destruction are whirlwinds that erupt in different ways, such as tornadoes, cyclones, typhoons, hurricanes, or earthquakes, tsunamis, or floods that cause mud slides, drownings, and property destruction; or maybe fires, that destroy millions of acres of trees or vegetation for animals to eat, which all the above triggers famines, that are happening at this present time; and men repented not.

Father, God, in the Name of Christ Jesus, I do not pray for myself; but Father I pray for the ones that are being victims of the above plagues (*stripes*); And Father draw them by your Holy Spirit to Christ Jesus and cause them to "Shell Down the Corn" and confess their sins, and repent, and receive your salvation and be healed. That they would go and sin no more. In the Name of Jesus. Amen.

So, to burst your bubble, you, nor anyone you know are not going to be raptured alive. There is going to be a great general rapture of all the ones that are asleep that are in Christ Jesus (I Thessalonians 4:13)

Paul tells you not to be ignorant; but some of you deceived KJV readers, persist in being ignorant anyway, and want to make a way of escape, and not come out of "Her". The preachers of Satan have interpreted that every *church goer* is going to be raptured out of this world and escape the tribulation. It will never happen! "As it is appointed unto men once to die; but after this the judgment." (Hebrews 9:27) So, you see all are going to die. So, it is very important that you be into Christ Jesus when you die. If you are one with Christ Jesus, you will only sleep for a while. Listen! The Word of God says: "For if we believe Jesus died and rose again, even so them also which sleep in Christ Jesus, God will bring with Him." (I Thessalonians 4:14) If you have been raptured already, why would God bring you with Him?

Before I answer that question, I need to explain the 3 parts that form you. You have a body, that goes back to the dust, or ground. You have a soul, which is your intellect, or your mind. You have a spirit that God gave you when you were born. This spirit that God gave to you leaves your body at death; and Jesus' angels gather all things that offend out of His Kingdom, also them that do iniquity, *(those spirits that are lawless)*. So, if you do not obey God's laws, but obey the laws of the land, you will be gathered by the angels; and they shall cast you into a furnace of fire. (Matthew 13:41,42)

But, on the other hand, if you had a righteous spirit, and were not in the Mystery of Iniquity, but was one *(in union)* with Christ Jesus, "God will bring your spirit and soul back with Him; and your spirit will be with the Lord Himself up in the air; and your body will rise to meet your spirit; and your spirit and body will come together; and your soul that has been asleep will wake up; and you will be caught up in the clouds to meet the Lord in the air; and so shall we be with the Lord forever." (1Thessalonians 4: 14,15,16,17,18) **"The righteous shall shine forth as the sun in His Kingdom."** (Matthew 13:43) **"Verily, verily, I say unto you, except a grain of wheat fall into the ground and die, it abides alone; but if it die, it brings forth much fruit."** (John 12:24)

"But he that has a spiritual ear, let him understand. When God brings them that are asleep in Jesus with Him, He does not ever touch the earth; but He calls out loud His Own at the last trump of God, and then comes the judgment of your awards, and rewards, and crowns, and jewels in your crown, which will be presented at the marriage of the Lamb." (Revelation 19:7) So if you expect to be at the marriage supper of the Lamb, you will need to *"Shell Down the Corn"*, *(confess)* to God, in the Name of Jesus, and repent (turn from your wicked ways), and pray for the Holy Spirit to make you have a pure heart that will make you Holy. If you do all these contingencies and believe Christ Jesus *(not believe in Him)*; but believe Him, you will be a candidate running for an office in Christ's Government, which will be a Theocracy *(ruled by God)*.

Father God in the name of Jesus I ask you, Lord Jesus, to save every one that reads **"Corn Shelling Time"** and raise them up in the last day. Lord Jesus when you shout with the voice of an archangel I pray that you will bring their spirits back with you and join them with their bodies to be with you forever. Amen and Amen.

This is an insert in the book, **"CORN SHELLING TIME"** and **MICHAEL DUISHKA** with some of his belief. It is my observation, and belief that the Police, and the Churches are synonymous with the scripture robbers of God's people. The Police have a false slogan, TO PROTECT AND SERVE, which is a big masquerade to cover up their stealing, killing, and destroying. The only ones they protect, and serve are themselves. Many times I have called the Police to report me being assaulted, robbed, or attempted to be robbed, and each time I was arrested and put in jail myself. One time I was attacked by a man trying to rob me, but failed,when the Police showed up the robber told them that I was the perpetrator. The Policeman, which was a (*Democrat*) protected me and served me with handcuffs and hauled me to jail. Many times I have been burglarized, Police called and instead of searching for clues, they immediately start investigating me, by wanting to know my SS#, how old am I, where was I when the burglary happened, and many more personal questions that they can sell to thieves, and solicitors. *The Churches* are Cults with different MOs, (*methods of operations*) but the same motives, which are supposedly helping God's people when they are helping themselves, to growing richer and advertising how they help the poor, heal the sick,and many other phony programs that are disguised to entice the misled members to give more money to help the professional scam operators that pose as the poor. The professional Bums go from one *church* to another, then to every other Charity, then to the street corner with their sign, homeless. The *Churches* sell their salvation under the guise of tithe, and freewill offerings. The giver of tithe and offerings think they are justified by not feeding the hungry, giving drink to the thirsty, visiting the sick, visiting the prisoners, taking in strangers, whenever they give to the *church*, but that is just a cloak to try to cover up their slackness. **For the poor always you have with you, but me you have not with you always.** (JOHN 12: 8) And He said unto them; **Go you into all the world, and preach the gospel to every creature. He that believes and is baptized shall be saved, but he that believes nut shall be damned. And these signs shall follow them that believe; IN my name shall they cast out devils; they shall speak with new tongues; They shall take up serpents; and if they drink any deadly thing it shall not hurt them; they shall lay hands on the sick and they shall recover, (Mark 16: 15,16,17,18).** Notice, the first sign that Jesus said would follow the believers, (*not "Christians"*) was in my name, (now Jesus Christ is not his name, HIS name is CHRIST JESUS, because Christ is not his last name,) shall they cast out devils; That is why there are not any sick recovering, because Jesus knew that the devils in a sick one was the reason the one was sick. The reason the devils were in the sick one is because the sick one had sinned. That is why after Jesus cast the devil out of the sick one, He said: **"Go and sin no more".**

Chapter 13

IN THE PREVIOUS CHAPTERS of **"Corn Shelling Time"** we followed the Word from the beginning of God down to the Word creating the earth and the living things on the earth; and now we are going to follow the Word to Hell and back, just to let you know you are required to obey the written Word of God!

God spoke to Adam and Eve by His Word. They were disobedient and caused all mankind to fall. God spoke to Cain and marked Cain with a curse, that is still with the children of darkness to this day. After Cain murdered his brother Abel, God said: (His Word): **"And now you are cursed from the earth, which has opened her mouth to receive your brother's blood from your hand."** (Genesis 4:11) "And the Lord set a mark upon Cain." (Genesis 4:15) DUISHKA, believes the mark was he turned black.

"But Noah found grace in the eyes of the Lord." (Genesis 6:8) And God Said: The Word of God: "Make you an Ark of gopher wood." (Genesis 6:14) "And God told Noah to go out of the Ark, and take your wife and your sons and their wives and multiply." (Genesis 8:17) "And the Word of God said: "Whoso sheds man's blood, by man shall his blood be shed, for in the image of God made He man." (Genesis 9:6)

"And Ham, the father of Canaan, saw the nakedness of his father, and told his two brethren without; and Noah awoke and knew what his younger son had done unto him, and he said: "Cursed be Canaan, a servant of servants shall he be unto his brethren." (Genesis 9:22,23,24,25) Same curse as CAIN.

Now a descendent of the servant of servants, Obama, a descendent of Canaan, is ruler of Shem and Japheth; and they are his servants, the ObamaNation of Desolation.

"And the whole earth was of one language and of one speech." (Genesis 11:1)

"And unto Eber were born two sons. The name of one *was* Peleg, for in his days was the earth divided; and his brother's name *was* Joktan." (Genesis 10:25)

"And it came to pass as they journeyed from the East, that they found a plain in the land of Shinar; and they dwelt there." (Genesis 11:2) This is where the Tower of Babel was started by Nimrod, which was a Hamite, which means he was rebellious toward God's Word. "So they started building the Tower of Babel, until the Lord confounded their language; and they were scattered upon all the face of the earth." (Genesis 11:9) "And the Lord said: "Behold the people is one, and they have all one language, and this they began to do; and now nothing will be restrained from them, which they have imagined to do." (Genesis 11:6)

What goes around, comes around. In this present age, it is a sequel to the Tower of Babel, and Nimrod. This world, with all the evil inventions, has evolved into one language again via the computer. The one language, which allows communication worldwide at your fingertips. The ObomaNation of Desolation has caused The Great Satan, *(America),* to become a third class country, just like the most of the black infested countries that have to beg, borrow, or steal to survive. God allowed Satan to destroy America, just like the fools that voted for the destroyer, to come back into the clean house and bring seven devils with him. (Luke 11:26) The only way there will be any flesh saved, is for the days of ObomaNation to be shortened; **"And for the very Elect's sake, they shall be shortened."** (Matthew 24:22)

But, we are following the Word, so let us go back to the Great City, and the Tower of Babel, and find the Word: "And the Lord said: "Go to, *(means come on),*let Us go down, and there confound their language, that they may not understand one another' speech." (Genesis 11:7) Notice the Word said: "Let Us," which is still plural, and still meaning the Father, the Son, (Word), The Holy Spirit, which we at this present time are going to be confounded or confused, (CONFUSION) which is the meaning of Babel, or Babylon, the great mystery which **"Corn Shelling Time"** is revealing to you, the reader.

So the Word, who is God, who is My Lord and Master, divided the earth, and scattered the people, and put boundaries or borders for every nation to have their own possession of the earth; but greed caused the children of disobedience to cross over their boundaries, and rob, kill, and destroy other nations, which is the working of Satan. **"The thief comes not, but for to steal, and to kill, and to destroy."** (John 10:10)

So, Nimrod, the ruler of Babel, the Mighty Hunter of men, the one that had the Mark of Cain (black), started the Mystery, Babylon, which is the working of the Mystery of Iniquity, which is culminating at this present time; and Oboma is a protege' of Nimrod.

This Mystery will manifest in the last half of Daniel's week. Daniel's seventieth week is the last 7 years of this age. The last three and one half years is the period of tribulation. A time that is so wicked that has never happened before, and will never happen again. That is why the Word is warning His people to "Come out of "Her". Some people have already come out of "Her" and have already gotten the mote out of their eye and can plainly see the beam in their brother's eye; and we are not the ones that are scornful of the ones that are still in "Her"; but the Word sent us to repeat His reproof, and correction, and instruction in righteousness. (II Timothy 3:16)

The only problem with God's people is that they that are in "Her", deny that they are in "Her", because Satan has blinded their minds; and they do not even know what "Her" includes. So the Word told Ezekiel to warn the people, when he sees the sword coming upon the people; and if the people hear the warning, and do not come out of "Her", their blood will be upon their own heads. But, if the people hear the warning and come out of "Her", they will deliver their own soul. But, if the watchman, (writer of **"Corn Shelling Time"**), does not warn God's people to come out of "Her", then the blood of the people will be upon the watchman's head.

But, the writer of **"Corn Shelling Time"** is not condemning the people. The Word is telling them " they are_already condemned, because they did not believe Him." (John 3:18) "because they did not believe in the Name of the only begotten Son of God.." **"And this is the condemnation, that light is come into the world, and men loved darkness rather** (more) **than light, because their deeds were evil."** (John 3:19)

Just in case God has some ignorant people that do not know what "Her" consists of, **"Corn Shelling Time"** is going to draw you a picture, so you will not have an excuse of ignorance, when you stand in Judgment, before the One that can send you to Hellfire, for being a child of darkness, when light came to you; and you loved darkness more than light, and stayed married to the Harlot, instead of coming out of "Her".

The Mystery, Babylon is the "Her" of Revelation 17 and 18. The world system is the Mystery, Babylon, which is the Mystery of

Iniquity, (lawlessness). Anything that is disobedience to God, the Word, is iniquity. To Wit: This world is a kingdom, and this kingdom and all the things that are in the kingdom belong to the ruler of this world. The ruler of this world is the Devil, AKA Satan. "And the Devil, taking Him (Jesus) into an high mountain, showed unto Him all the kingdoms of the world in a moment of time; and the Devil said unto him, (Jesus), "All this power I will give you, and the glory *(things)* of them. For that is delivered unto me, and to whomsoever I will give it." (Luke 4:5,6) **"Hereafter I will not talk much with you, for the prince** (king) **of this world, comes, and has nothing in Me."** (Jesus doing the talking) (John 14:30) This written Word proves ownership of this world belongs to the Devil. All the things, things that are in this world, belongs to the Devil, including you, if you have not come out of "Her". The world, and the glory of all the kingdoms of the world belong to the Devil. (Luke 4:5,6)

All the glory of the kingdoms of this world, to name a few are man made things, such as governments, which are all man made and ruled by the prince of the powers of the air. (Ephesians 2:2) Christ Jesus will rule in the future at His Presence, (Parousia), or His Second Coming; but, that is then, and this is now. Now, all the governments and the members of the governments of the world are children of disobedience; and if you are a member of the government or work for the government in any capacity, you are the property of Satan. If you vote for any politician, you are a partaker of "Her" sins. All the rulers of the kingdoms of this world, *(kings, presidents, prime ministers, heads of any kind)* are ministers of Satan, and are doing a job for the ruler of this world. All the governments of this world come to steal, kill, and destroy anything that belongs to God. If anyone has come out of "Her", the governments of the world are looking for that person to rob him of his possessions, and then kill him and destroy him.

All the politicians took lessons from the Father of Lies, their master, the Devil. The Devil has his ministers deceived, and his ministers are deceiving all the children of disobedience to God's laws. The governments of the world are a part of "Her", Mystery, Babylon, the Mystery of Iniquity. The religious kingdoms of this world are that power Satan offered to give to Jesus in (Luke 4:5,6). When Jesus refused to bow down and worship the Devil, the Devil immediately offered that power to God's people; and they were full of the lust of the flesh, the lust of the eyes, and the pride of life, (I John 2:15,16), and greedy, so they were tempted and could not refuse. So they became the slaves of the Devil, and try to cover it up by saying they are "Christians", and they are members of the Harlot Church. All of these facts are documented by different news media. Moreover, they use the Name of Christ Jesus as a cloak.

The *churches* are the Harlots of the Mother in Mystery, Babylon the Great in (Revelation 17:5) The Mother is the *Catholic Church*. The Mother Church in Rome is another part of Mystery, Babylon the Great in (Revelation 17:5), which is part of the Mystery of Iniquity, or lawlessness, and part of the Anti-Christ's Beast. The *churches,* including the *Mother Catholic Church,* are all man made and not sanctioned by God. God never called anyone to come to *church,* but rather He called His people out of the Mystery, Babylon.

Ekklesia, properly interpreted (calling out loud). **"Corn Shelling Time"** is an echo of Christ Jesus calling out loud to "come out of "Her", My people, that you be not partakers of "Her" sins; and that you receive not of "Her" plagues." (Revelation 18:4)

To the kingdoms of Asia, and Africa, and Europe, and Australia, Antarctica, South America, and North America: You people are all victims of Adam and Eve's death sentence; but there is light come into the world, which is Christ Jesus. So do not love darkness more than this light and be condemned by doing evil; but come to the light, Christ Jesus, and "Shell Down the Corn", "(confess), that you are a sinner, and Christ Jesus will save you from this untoward generation." (Acts 2:40)

It is too late for the North Americans to stay the plague, because they, *(the people)*, have already partook of "Her" sins and already received "Her" plagues. The ObomaNation of Desolation Plague is already upon them, and their only hope is to "Shell Down the Corn" to Christ Jesus. *The Harlot Churches* are responsible for that plague, and Christ Jesus is calling out Loud for His people to "Come out of "Her". (Revelation 18:4)

Many, many deceived souls are joined to organized religion, which is the same thing as a cult. There are not any differences between heathenism and "Christians", as both cults worship pagan gods, and dress the same as harlots, go through the same rituals as the Babylonians, and worship idols, such as *Christmas, Easter, Halloween, Witchcraft,* and turn their man made *churches* into heathen temples, and make heathen gods their objects of worship, such as *Saints, Tammuz, (called the Cross), Saint Nick, (Santa Claus),* and allow any kind of fornication and adultery to be joined to their fellowship. That is the reason God calls the Harlot branches of the Mother Harlot, Mystery, Babylon. Oh, dear reader, listen to Christ, and "Come out of "Her", and no more partake of "Her" sins." The world system is Mystery, Babylon: The world governments, the world organized religion, AKA *churches,* all the idolatry in sports, evil inventions, and any kind of fornication, which is idolatry, and the Great Harlot and "Her" Branches, *Churches,* that hold all the filth and abominations of the entire world.

The sorrows Jesus said would begin have accelerated to the point of no return to normality. Many are coming in His Name, even the harlots in the churches have added Christ to their pseudonym, calling themselves "Christians". The priests themselves are the biggest bunch of sex abusers, being caught as pedophiles and homosexuals, *(Queers)* still saying they are "Christians". But, God is not mocked. The record is broken; and it plays over and over, how the filth and abominable come in Christ's Name. The sorrows just keep on getting worse, with Nation against Nation and the ground opening it's mouth in earthquakes and Tsunamis, and volcanoes,. Pestilences are so rapidly increasing the doctors and scientists cannot find cures. Famine of food is world wide; but the worst famine is for the Word of God. **"Behold I have told you before"** (Matthew 24:25).

"Behold, the days come, saith the Lord God, that I will send a famine in the land, not a famine of bread, nor a thirst for water, but of hearing the Words of the Lord." (Amos 8:11) "And they shall wander from sea to sea, and from the north even to the east. They shall run to and fro to seek the Word of the Lord, and shall not find it." (Amos 8:12) This is the days God is talking about. The famine of the Word is already here. Satan has counterfeited the Word until He (The Word) is obsolete. **"Corn Shelling Time"** is the most pure language that this writer knows of to exist in the world at this present time. "For then will I turn to the people a pure language, that they may all call upon the Name of the Lord, to serve Him with one consent." (Zephaniah 3:9). This is not the millennium, which is the time God is talking about, but this writer is practicing using pure correct words in order to please my Lord.

The language that is spoken in this present time is politically correct lies **"Corn Shelling Time"** does not use the words *church, cross, saints, Easter, gay, pope, father, penance, Christmas, Icons, images, Lent, "Christian", Halloween, no private confessions,* or any other pagan man made words that are counterfeit words for the Pure Word of God.

All the above words are taken from the Catholic Bible, which was written under duress from the Roman Emperors and the Popes to cause pagan gods to be worshiped, instead of the Almighty God, (PANTAKRATOR).

Then the KJV Bible is a sequel, or a continuing story of the added to, and taken away from. The Catholic Bible which have taken away the Pure Word of God. The scholars of the KJV Bible were under duress from the king to put nothing that would offend the king, at the risk of losing their heads.

That is the reason **"Corn Shelling Time"** is offensive only to people that are guilty of transgressions against the Word, (Christ Jesus). The writer of **"Corn Shelling Time"** is not under duress from any man or any organized religion. But this writer is indebted to the Love Christ Jesus showed when He shed His blood to cover me, and wash me, and cleanse me from all unrighteousness.

I apologize to any believers that are sanctified and have put on holiness if I have written anything to offend you. Please forgive me. I do not apologize to any "Christians", using a pseudonym with the Word Christ. I do not apologize to any *church*, which is a harlot, or to any heathen or pagan god worshiper. This writer does not apologize for being politically incorrect and telling the Truth.

Mystery, Babylon is a sequel to the Tower of Babel, a continuing story of sin and rebelliousness to God's Word. The *churches* are the enemy that sowed tares (*weeds)* in the Word of God, which is the wheat. The harvest time is already happening; and God's angels are busy gathering all things that offend, and them which do iniquity out of the world. (Matthew 13:41)

God, the Son of Man, is sending His workers into the harvest to warn His people to come out of Mystery, Babylon, so they do not get snared in the trap of the Devil, that is the destroyer, and can not escape. The destroyer is causing the plagues and the sorrows to come upon God's earth and upon God's people to destroy them.

If you, dear reader, have fallen into Satan's trap and have received the plague of weeds sowed into your wheat, which is the true Word of God, just confess to Christ Jesus; and He will send His angels to gather the weeds out of you, because you are the Kingdom of God, and you are His wheat. So do not try to lie to the Master, just "Shell Down the Corn." (Confess Jesus)

The Word comes to people in different ways. After the flood, God appeared to one of Shem's descendents, a man called Abram, and gave Abram the Word first hand. He, (God), gave Abram's seed the land of Canaan. The only deed to the land of Canaan was the Word of God. But there is still a controversy to this day as to the ownership of that land, which is present day Israel; and the Muslims call it Palestine. But, when God appeared to Abram, He changed his name to Abraham; and told Abraham that the whole families of the earth would be blessed in him. (Genesis 12:3) Later the Word of the Lord came and met Abraham by a man named Melchizedek, King of Salem, and brought forth bread and wine; and He was the priest of the Most High God. (Genesis 14:18) The Priest Melchizedek blessed Abraham and took a tithe from him.

The Word of the Lord came to Abraham again, this time in a vision, (Genesis 15:1), and promised Abraham as many seed as the stars in the sky; and because Abraham believed God, God counted it unto Abraham as righteousness.

So, it still is, to this day, you, dear reader, must believe Jesus, not believe in Him, but believe every Word of Christ. The Lord God appeared to Abraham and changed his name from Abram to Abraham, and made a covenant with Abraham to be the father of many nations. (Genesis 17:4) God gave Abraham all the land of Canaan to be a possession for his seed forever. Abraham was to cut off the foreskin and be circumcised forever as his part of the token. (Genesis 17:10)

"Now when Abraham was 99 years old, the Lord appeared to Abraham, and said, "I am the Almighty (PANTAKRATOR) God. Walk before Me, and you be perfect." (Genesis 17:1)

"And the Lord appeared to him in the plains of Mamre; and he sat in the tent door in the heat of the day; and the Lord told Abraham that Sarah would bear a child; and God went on to destroy Sodom and Gomorrah, the City Lot lived in; and God told Abraham He would not destroy Sodom if ten righteous people be found; but ten were not found. So two angels went to Lot and told him to come out of her, the town of *queers*. The men told Lot to bring the angels out to them so they could know them, *(have sex with them)*. Lot offered the men his two virgin daughters, but they tried to kill Lot, but the angels smote the men with blindness, so they could not find the door. The angels told Lot to get all his people out, because God sent them, (the angels), to destroy the City. Lot warned his sons in law; but they mocked him, so when the morning came, the angels hastened Lot to take his wife and the two daughters that were there, "lest you be consumed in the iniquity of the City." The angels took Lot and his wife and two daughters by the hands and led them out, and said, "Escape for your life.". Then the Lord rained upon Sodom and upon Gomorrah brimstone and fire from the Lord out of Heaven. But Lot's wife looked back from behind him, and she became a pillar of salt." (Genesis the 19th Chapter). The Word appeared in person to Abraham, because Abraham found favor with God.

The pastors, evangelists, preachers, are all hirelings in this present time. They are all in competition with each other to see who can pull the most mammon (personal gain), money, *(filthy lucre)*, out of the sheep. There is no such thing as a shepherd. **"But, he that is a hireling, and not the shepherd, whose own the sheep are not, sees the wolf coming and leaves the sheep, and flees, and the wolf catches them, and scatters the sheep."** (John 10:12) "The hireling flees, because he is an hireling, and cares not for the sheep." (John 10:13) Now a days the hireling is the wolf in sheep's clothing. Instead of warning the flock, they fleece the flock. They never tell the flock to come out of Mystery, Babylon, because they are Mystery, Babylon. They preach against sin, but are guilty of sin themselves. Instead of warning the ignorant ones to be not partakers of "Her" sins, they encourage the *church goers* to vote for the robbers, killers, and destroyers of God's earth, and God's people. Instead of teaching forgiveness, they still believe in revenge. "An eye for an eye, and a tooth for a tooth." All they preach is justice; and that is exactly what they will be judged by at the Great White Throne Judgment. The Judge will say: **"Get away from Me, I never knew you."**

The preachers encourage our young unlearned men to volunteer to go join the Armed Services, boasting how patriotic it is to go killing other ignorant unlearned men in other countries. When they should teach and preach to our young men to follow Jesus and be conscientious objectors, and be no part of killing, robbing, and destroying God's people. Young men have been brain washed into going to war, thinking they are doing so to protect their country. When they realize they were duped, it is too late; and they either get killed, or commit suicide, or come home maimed, lame, blind, naked, and miserable, or do not ever come home. Most of them are dependent on drugs for however long they live. Some are mentally deranged, called shell shocked. All because the people voted a warmonger in as their leader; and they are being led to their destruction. He is just another plague that you are receiving, because you did not come out of Mystery, Babylon. The people are led to slaughter just like dumb sheep. It is not going to get any better; but it will only get worse, until you are destroyed by one of "Her plagues. All you can do at this point of no return is to "Shell Down the Corn" to Christ Jesus. Confess that you bet on the wrong horse, and "Come out of "Her", if you are God's people." (Revelation 18:4)

"Corn Shelling Time" is a way for you to escape the plagues that you have already, and to save face when you stand before Christ Jesus. Come out of governments, come out of *churches,* come out of worldly things, which are the glory of the Kingdom of Satan. Take your children out of the government schools, and teach them about Christ Jesus; and do what Jesus said in (Matthew 11:28) **"Come unto Me."** Father, God, in the Name of Jesus, the ones that believe you, and come out of "Her", please save them; and when they read (I John 2:26,27), you are no respecter of persons, teach them all things by your Word. In the Name of Jesus. Amen.

This is an insert in the book, **"CORN SHELLING TIME"** and **MICHAEL DUISHKA** with some of his belief. The reason there are so many sick people in the world today is because the preachers and the *churches* do not believe Jesus when He promised power from on high. Then when He gave the commandment to go into all the world and preach the gospel, His disciples did just that exhibiting His power with all the signs following until they were killed, and the heathen "Christian" heretics in the Roman Catholic Church slaughtered the believers until there are only a few of us that know how to believe JESUS. He set us an example and a pattern,which big time false preachers are just professors and not possessors of the power (HOLY GHOST) to have the signs following. I remember one world famous preacher that slurred those "devil caster outers" and when he made light of the believers that cast out devils, Satan entered into that preacher, and instead of being a professor of the Holy Spirit, he became a possessor of Satan's demon of lust. Satan set a trap, called a snare for the world famous preacher, because the preacher was winning souls for the kingdom of God, world wide. Through ignorance, or pride, or both the man of God gave place to the devil, and the devil took him, and the preacher fell. Like the majority of preachers today, many excuses are made for not casting out the unclean spirits. The most of the preachers just say they cast out demons, but do not. **"Many will say to me in that day, LORD, LORD, have we not prophesied in your name? And in your name have cast out devils? and done many wonderful works?** (Matthew 7:22). You guess what Jesus said.

Chapter 14

STILL FOLLOWING THE WORD to Hell and back. Yesterday I was reminded of one of the things the Word said in (Matthew 24:7). **"There shall be earthquakes in divers places."**

As this writer was sitting at his table, the table and floor started moving; and I knew it was an earthquake. Two hours later the news reported it was of the magnitude of 4.5, which is not very strong. But it was only twenty miles away from me, and I was reminded of the beginning of sorrows the Word, (Jesus), spoke about in Matthew 24.

The sorrows escalated more vividly in 2011, and the sorrows are rising, and will reach their apex shortly, and then will begin the revealing of the Anti-Christ, because the great apostasy has already happened. The "Christians", who were once loyal to Christ, have abandoned Him. Everything Christ Jesus is, or has, the Anti-Christ has a counterfeit for. One thing is Christ has a body of believers. The counterfeit body of Christ is the *churches*. Christ is coming back to receive His Bride. The Anti-Christ has the "Christians" for his bride; and they are deceived into thinking they are the bride of Christ. But Christ Jesus will have a Bride that is pure and holy, without spot or blemish or any such thing. He would never be married to a whore, which all the *churches* are (*Harlots*). The apostate churches are the counterfeit bride of the Anti-Christ, who sets himself up, and declares he is God (II Thessalonians 2:7)

This writer has personally seen these things happen with "Christians" in *churches;* "Being filled with all unrighteousness, fornication, wickedness, covetousness, maliciousness, full of envy, murder, debate, deceit, malignity, whisperers, backbiters, haters of God, despiteful, proud, boasters, inventors of evil things, disobedient to parents, without understanding, covenant breakers, without natural affection, implacable, unmerciful, who knowing the judgment of God, that they which commit such things are worthy of death, not only do the same, but have pleasure in them that do them." (Romans 1:29,30,31,32) "Also, who changed the Truth of God into a lie." (Romans 1:25)

This is the way the *Mother Church of Rome* and all the Harlot Daughters of "Her" are doing at this present time. There are all kinds of schisms, *(splits)*, in the *churches* at this present time. There are so many divisions just on account of the above mentioned sins, that the whole lump is leavened. The whole body of the counterfeit body of Christ is infected, and the writer of Romans said: "Now I beseech you brethren, mark them which cause divisions and offenses contrary to the doctrine, which you have learned, and avoid them." (Romans 16:17)

"For they that are such serve not our Lord Christ Jesus, but their own belly, and by good words and fair speeches deceive the hearts of the simple." (Romans 16:18) "Your glorying is not good. Know you not that a little leaven leaven the whole lump." (I Corinthians 5:6)

Now in the days of Paul, they purged out the sinner, (leaven), and were supposed to become a new lump; but the leaven (sin) just kept spreading until now-a-days the whole of organized religion is just like a boil, festered up with puss and corruption ready to burst. Paul said to mark them. Which you cannot mark them unless you have the gift of discernment, which this writer has. (I Corinthians 12:10) And as one is sinning in adultery, another is sinning in homosexuality, and another in greed and covetousness, another in murder, another disobedient to parents, which is worse than an infidel, another proud, and another boastful, and another unmerciful, and all of them are guilty of idolatry and fornication.

"If there are any that are pure and holy, they must do like just Lot, and come out from among them, and be you separate, saith the Lord, and touch not the unclean thing, and I will receive you." (II Corinthians 6:17)

So, this writer has marked all of the so called "Christians" in all of the *churches* (*harlots*), which are all divided from the one doctrine of Christ Jesus.

The *queers* are getting married to each other, and sin is running rampant. Instead of the government and the *churches* checking it, they are encouraging it, (sin). "For many walk, of whom I have told you often; and now tell you even weeping, that they are the enemies of the stake of Christ, whose end is destruction, whose God is their belly, and whose glory is in their shame, who mind earthly things." (Philippians 3:18,19)

"Even as Sodom and Gomorrah and the cities about them in like manner, giving themselves over to fornication, and going after strange flesh, are set forth for an example, suffering the vengeance of eternal fire." (Jude 1:7)

Since I do not speak evil of dignities, I will speak about the evil people that voted the "Christian" president of America into office, that approved of *queers* marrying, and among many other sins, turned America into an ObomaNation of Desolation. This writer is not telling you to rebel against the government; but when the law of the land rebels against the laws of God, to steal, kill, and destroy, which are you going to obey, man made laws or God's laws?

The *church,* once was a place that taught the law and commandments of God. This writer "Shelled Down the Corn", (confessed my sins), to Christ Jesus; and I met Christ at the altar of a *church.* That was the most wonderful miracle that ever happened to me. But that was then, and this is now. For there are certain men crept in unawares, who were before ordained to this condemnation, ungodly men, turning the grace of our God into lasciviousness, and denying the only Lord God, and our Lord Christ Jesus. These ungodly men multiplied and the holy men of God let down their guard and allowed false apostles, false prophets, false pastors, false teachers to change the one doctrine of God into many false doctrines and schisms, splits, divisions, discords, dissensions, and denominations, all claiming to be the body of Christ; but doing the unclean sins of Satan. Jesus told His disciples to observe and do what they say, but do not do like they do.

"Wherefore, I take you to record this day, that I am pure from the blood of all men. For I have not shunned to declare unto you, all the counsel of God. Take heed to yourselves, and to all the flock, over the which the Holy Ghost has made you overseers, to feed the Called Out Ones of God, which He has purchased with His own blood." (Acts 20:26,27,28)

Paul said: "For I know this, that after my departing shall grievous wolves enter in among you, not sparing the flock." (Acts 20:29) That is exactly what happened to all the *churches.* The hireling wolves infiltrated the *churches* and turned them into an unholy den of thieves. There are some sincere preachers, but their audiences are small and getting smaller, because they want to have their ears tickled with politically correct lies. "Because you have said, we have made a covenant with death, and with Hell are we at agreement. When the overflowing scourge shall pass through, it shall not come unto us; for we have made lies our refuge, and under falsehood have we hid ourselves." (Isaiah 28:15)

"That is what this wicked and untoward generation has said." (Acts 2:40)

Listen, you ones that are in love with Christ Jesus, to what the Word of God is telling you, before you are destroyed. "And the ten horns which you saw upon the beast, these shall hate the Whore, (*The Catholic Church and 'Her" Daughters)*, and shall make "Her" desolate and naked, and shall eat "Her" flesh, and burn "Her" with fire." (Revelation 17:16) So, God tells you, if you belong to God: "And I heard another voice from heaven saying, Come Out of "Her", My people, That you be not partakers of "Her" sins, and that you receive not of "Her" plagues." (Revelation 18:4)

God told Abraham his seed would be in bondage in another land for 400 years. The Hebrews, which Abraham's seed was called, were slaves to the Egyptians for 400 years. The Angel of the Lord appeared to a Hebrew by the name of Moses. Moses was an exile from the land of Egypt and was herding sheep for his father-in-law, Jethro, who was the priest of Median. Moses took the sheep to the backside of the desert to the foot of a mountain, which is called the mountain of God, "Horeb". Moses watched a bush burning with flames of fire, and the bush was never consumed. When Moses went up on the mountain to see why, we encounter the Word of God that told Moses to take off his shoes, because he was walking on holy ground. (Exodus 3:5) The Word of God commissioned Moses to lead the Hebrews out of Egypt, which he did; but Moses asked God who could he tell the Hebrew children sent him to deliver them; and God said: **"I Am That I Am.** Thus shall you say unto the children of Israel. **"I Am has sent me unto you."** (Exodus 3:14)

These Words are so very important to you, dear reader, because they are the key to everlasting life; because after the Lord used these two Words on the mountain of God, He claimed to be the **I Am** two thousand years later, when Jesus was talking to the scribes and the pharisees; and also He was talking to you. (John 8:24) **"I said**

therefore unto you, that you shall die in your sins, for if you believe not that I Am, you shall die in your sins."

So Moses delivered the Children of Israel out of bondage and came back to the mountain of God; and the **I Am** gave Moses the Law of God; and told the children of Israel: "If you do not hearken to the voice of the Lord, thy God, to observe to do all His Commandments and His Statutes, which I command you this day, then all these curses shall come upon you and overtake you." (Deuteronomy 28:15)

You say, that was just said to the children of Israel. If that be so, how come you are cursed with the plagues that you suffer? You, say it is just a streak of bad luck. Wrong! No such thing as luck, good or bad. Nothing happens by happenstance, but everything happens fulfilling the Word of God. "Jesus said unto them: **Verily I say unto you that the publicans (tax collectors) and the harlots (literal) go into the Kingdom of God before you.**" (Matthew 21:31) Jesus was talking to the rulers of the organized religion of that time; but the Word is also talking to you, if you are any part of Mystery, Babylon. The Word was talking to you, and whosoever believes the Word.

So if you are a sinner that does not go to a *church,* you are in a better position to repent than the multiplied millions of *church goers,* because you are near the Kingdom of God. Wherever you are, no matter, just bend your heart, humble yourself before the Mighty God, and "Shell Down the Corn", (confess), to God Almighty (PANTAKRATOR) that you are a sinner, and you ask Him to save you, in the Name of Christ Jesus; and you believe that Christ came in the flesh, and He died on the stake (tree), and the blood that He shed covers you from, your sins and all unrighteousness, and that He was buried and was resurrected (rose again), and has forgiven you of all your sins. And if you believe what you just said, and go and sin no more, you shall be saved. You are the very one that Jesus (the Christ) came down here to earth to seek and save the lost. **"For the Son of Man** (Jesus) **is come to seek and to save that which was lost.** (Luke 19:10)

You just said with your mouth, the Word (Jesus). Now all you have to do is believe what you said, and it will come to pass.

"But what saith it? The Word is nigh you, even in your mouth and in your heart (*spirit*), that is, the Word of Faith (believe), which we preach: That if you shall (confess), *"Shell Down the Corn"*, with your mouth the Lord Jesus and shall believe in your heart (spirit) that God has raised Him from the dead, you shall be saved." (Romans 10:8,9)

We are still following the Word, and the Word just came into you, your heart, and your mouth, if you believe the Lord Jesus, The Christ (Messiah), you shall be saved. Not only you, but your house. The Word is not talking about the structure or building you stay in; but the Word is talking about your spouse, your children, your dad, your mom, your brothers, sisters, crops, animals, and all things that you believe for.

"And they said: (Paul and Silas) Believe the Lord, Christ Jesus, and you shall be saved and your house" (Acts 16:31)

Pay attention! Listen! My Lord Christ Jesus cannot lie. "His name is Truth." (John 14:6) "He said: Whatever you say with your mouth, you will have it." (Mark 11:23) And you just believed to righteousness, and you just "Shelled Down the Corn", (confessed to salvation). "For with the heart (spirit) man believes unto righteousness, and with the mouth confession is made unto salvation." (Romans 10:10)

For the scripture, (the Word), says: "Whosoever believes Him shall not be ashamed." (Romans 10:11) So, you are now a candidate for the Kingdom of God; and not only the Kingdom, but also to be a ruler in God's Government. And from here on you can write your own check for as much as you believe. So now you do not have to keep on asking Christ Jesus to save you, but you are obligated to Him, to study the Word, and to be a witness to others what Christ Jesus has done for you. **"The Words that I speak are spirit and they are life."** (John 6:63) So the more Words of Jesus that you retain in your mind, or memory, the more of His Holy Spirit you will have in you; and the more Spirit of Christ you have in you, the more Life you will have in you, and Life more abundantly. (John 10:10)

Lord God, I agree with this one that just "Shelled Down the Corn" (Confessed) and believed in the Name of Christ Jesus. (Amen)

So, God sent a deliverer to free the Children of Israel from the Egyptians that was the first nation on earth to oppress Israel. The Word of the Lord was written in the Law of God for the Children of Israel to obey, which they told God they would do all He said; but they turned to other gods, just the way God's people are doing as I write this book. "The Children of Israel had sinned against the Lord, their God, which had brought them up out of the land of Egypt, from under the hand of Pharaoh, King of Egypt, and had feared other gods, and walked in the statutes of the heathen, whom the Lord cast out from before the Children of Israel, and of the Kings of Israel, which they had made." (II Kings 17:7,8) "And the children set them up images and groves in every high hill and under every green tree." (II Kings 17:10)

These are the same sinful acts of the "Christians" at this present time: Setting a green tree on the altar of the *churches* to worship the mass of the Whore and "Her" gods, and using the pseudonym "Christmas". "For they served idols, whereof the Lord had said unto them, you shall not do this thing." (II Kings 17:12) "Yet, the Lord testified against Israel and against Judah, by all the prophets and by all the seers saying: Turn you from your evil ways, and keep My Commandments and My Statutes, according to all the Law, which I commanded your fathers, and which I sent to you by My servants the prophets." (II Kings 17:13) "Notwithstanding, they would not hear, but hardened their necks, like to the neck of their fathers, that did not believe in the Lord their God." (II Kings 17:14)

God is no respecter of persons; and the children of darkness say that this law has been done away with; but they do err; and the Laws of God are just as meaningful now as they were then. And now the Word will show you what will happen to you if you do not keep His Commandments and His Statutes.

"The Children of Israel provoked the Lord to anger, (*just the way the heathen "Christians" are doing*), until the Lord removed Israel out of His sight, as He had said by all His prophets, so was Israel carried away out of their own land to Assyria unto this day." (II Kings 17:23)

So Judah was left in the land, but not for long, because they were evil and worshiped other gods and went into idolatry, and provoked the Lord God; and He sent His Word to Jeremiah the prophet; and the Word said: "Therefore thus saith the Lord of Hosts, because you have not heard my Words, behold I will send and take all the families of the North, saith the Lord, and Nebuchadrezzar, the King of Babylon, My servant, and will bring them against this land and against the inhabitants thereof, and against all those nations round about, and will utterly destroy them, and make them an astonishment, and an hissing and perpetual desolation." (Jeremiah 25:8,9)

God is saying the same thing to you in this warning, called **"Corn Shelling Time"**. He was talking literally to the land of Judah, but He is talking spiritually to the present generation of the whole world, and also to the children of this generation.

The Tribe of Judah was warned about literal Babylon; and you are being warned about Mystery, Babylon. "Come out of "Her", My people." (Revelation 18:4) God used the word perpetual for the desolation of Israel, but America has become a perpetual ObomaNation of Desolation, which means your house is left unto you desolate, and will never be returned to the glory and the splendor that was once enjoyed by the past generations. America has made a pact with the Devil and traded the beauty of a nation of light and riches and opportunity for a slick tongued opportunist that has destroyed the freedom this nation once possessed; and it is going down hill like a snowball headed for Hell, to be a perpetual desolation.

"And no marvel, for Satan himself is transformed into an angel of light. Therefore, it is no great thing if his ministers also be transformed as the ministers of righteousness, whose end shall be according to their works." (II Corinthians 11:14,15)

"And you shall leave your name for a curse unto My Chosen: For the Lord God shall slay you and call His servants by another name." (Isaiah 65:15) God does not say what name will be cursed, or what name He will call His Servants. I believe He is talking about the "Christians" being cursed, because He says: "But, you are they that forsake the Lord that forget My Holy Mountain, that prepare a table for that troop, and that furnish the drink offering unto that number. Therefore, I will number you to the sword; and you shall all bow down to the slaughter, because when I called, you did not answer; when I spake, you did not hear, but did evil before mine eyes, and did choose that wherein I delighted not." (Isaiah 65:12,13)

Thus saith the Lord: **"Corn Shelling Time"** is God calling you and speaking to you; and if you will answer Him, and just say: "Here am I, Lord, Lord." With trembling say: "What will you have me to do?" (Acts 9:6) He, the Holy spirit will change your thinking, and will lift the curse from you; and He will bless you above measure, and make you fit for the Kingdom of God.

Then the Word was sealed up in Daniel's book until we read where: "The Word was made flesh and dwelt among us." (John 1:14) "In the beginning was the Word, and the Word was with God, and the Word was God." (John 1:1)

We have followed the Word of God from the creation of the heavens and the earth, to earth again. (Geneses 1:1)

"And without controversy, great is the Mystery of Godliness. God was manifest in the flesh, justified in the Spirit, seen of angels, preached unto the Gentiles, believed on in the world, received up to glory." (I Timothy 3:16)

"The same was in the beginning with God. Still talking about the Word, which was God." (John 1:2) "All things were made by Him (The Word), and without Him was not anything made that was made." (John 1:3)

We just read where the Word was God and was manifest in the flesh, and was baptized by John the Baptizer; and John called Him the Lamb of God, and we beheld His glory, as the only begotten of the Father, the Son, whom is the only begotten to have seen the Father; "and John saw and bare record that this was the only begotten Son of God." (John 1:34) His name on earth was Jesus; but He was the Christ in the Greek tongue; but He was the Messiah in the Hebrew tongue.

Father God, as we follow your Word, please show us the road your Son, Christ Jesus, took after He was made flesh. In the Name of Jesus. Amen and Amen!

This is an insert in the book "Corn Shelling Time" and Michael Duishka and some of his belief. Thus says The LORD; Cursed *be* the man that trusts in man, that makes flesh his arm, whose heart departs from the LORD.(Jeremiah 17:5) I believe you are cursed, because you trust a lying politician that promises to do a job for you if you will vote for him or HER, and you trust him and make flesh your arm, and he says; Ha Ha Ha I fooled you, I fooled you, and you say; he is so smart and wonderful,all of his or HER mistakes are because of the last president, and we will elect him for another 4 years to steal all the money from us to correct his mistakes. Then it is hard to find someone to say they voted for the lying, murdering, thief. That is why you are cursed. Then you turn right around and elect someone that has already been proven to be a liar and you say, OH She is for the women having equal rights to murder their babies,*(abortion)* then rob you in taxes to give your money to Planed Parenthood to pay for the Murder. OH, ME, that is one reason, God said; You are cursed! **Notwithstanding I have a few things against you, because you let that woman Jezebel, which calls herself a prophetess,to teach and to seduce my servants to commit fornication, these things says the son of God, who has his eyes like unto a flame of fire and his feet like fine brass:** (Revelation 2:19,20) But I let Not a woman to teach nor usurp authority over the man, but to be in silence. (1 Timothy 2:12) But that is why God called her Jezebel, because she does not believe Christ Jesus.

Chapter 15

"**CORN SHELLING TIME**" HAS followed the Word, which is God, all the way from the beginning down through the creation of not only our little earth, but followed Him through the universe to the division of the Archangel, Lucifer, from the abode of God; and the division of the angels themselves, where one third of the angels went with the Wicked One; and two thirds of the angels were retained by God, because these two thirds of the angels that stayed in the heavens of God were obedient and Holy.

To be obedient and Holy is the only way a human can enter into the Kingdom of God, because God and all the host of heaven are Holy. "Follow peace with all men and Holiness, without which no man shall see the Lord." (Hebrews 12:14)

"Corn Shelling Time" followed the Word to prophesy of the seed of the woman, Eve, to bruise the head of the serpent, which is talking to Satan himself. (Genesis 3:15) This is the start of all the **Word** to be a mystery and can be understood only by the coaching of the Holy Ghost. The reason the Holy Spirit is called the Holy Ghost is because you cannot see Him.

The Word is called seed, which is in the parable of the sower in Matthew 13. The Word was the **I Am** on the mountain of God. The

Word was the Melchizedek, King of Salem, the Priest of the Most High God. (Genesis 14:18) The Word, which was God, appeared to Abraham in bodily form; but He came to others by the Holy Spirit, and to some by Holy Angels. But the Holy Spirit caused men to prophesy in parables, or mysteries. Even the prophets, sometime did not know what they were inspired to speak, the Word. But every Word, even down to the jot and tittle was fulfilled by Jesus, who was the Word, who was God.

The reason the Word is spoken in mystery form (parables) is so the enemy, which is Satan, cannot know the plan of God to sabotage His plan to save the ones salvation is given to. The children of darkness do not have the understanding of the Mysteries of God, because if they did, they would tell the enemy every secret of God, not on purpose, but ignorantly, because they cannot bridle their tongue. (James 1:26) They do not discern natural from spiritual. That is why God's Word is spiritual and is written in mystery form, and cannot be discerned by the natural man, because the natural man would betray God's man. "For what man knows the things of a man save the spirit of man, which is in him? Even so the things of God knows no man but the Spirit of God. Now we have received not the spirit of the world, but the Spirit, which is of God, that we might know the things that are freely given to us of God. Which things also we speak, not in the words which man's wisdom teaches, but which the Holy Ghost teaches, comparing spiritual things with spiritual. But the natural man receives not the things of the Spirit of God, for they are foolishness unto him. Neither can he know them, because they are spiritually discerned." (I Corinthians 2:11,12,13,14)

"But he that is spiritual judges all things. Yet he himself is judged of no man." (1 Corinthians 2:15) "For who has known the mind of the Lord that he may instruct Him? But we have the mind of Christ." (I Corinthians 2:16) "And the tongue *is* a fire, a world of iniquity (lawlessness), so is the tongue among our members, that **it** (*the tongue*) defiles the whole body, and sets on fire the course of nature, and it *(the tongue)* is set on fire of Hell." (James 3:6)

"Keep thy foot when you go to the house of God, and be more ready to hear, than to give the sacrifice of fools, for they consider not that they do evil. Be not rash with your mouth *(tongue)* and let not your heart be hasty to utter anything before God. For God is in heaven, and you upon earth. Therefore let your words be few. For a dream comes through the multitude of business, and a fool's voice is known by multitude of words." (Ecclesiastes 5:1,2,3) That is the whole sum of why God cannot trust you with His secrets (mysteries, parables) because you would betray Him, and His servants with the multitude of words with your mouth. (tongue).

So Jesus (**The WORD**) fulfilled every prophesy that was written by the prophets in the scriptures about Him.The Scribes, (lawyers) Pharisees, Sadducees, came tempting Jesus, desired that He would show them a sign from heaven, and Jesus called them a wicked and adulterous generation, and said; the only sign given to it would be the prophet Jonah. (Matthew 16:1-4). Which is a mystery in itself. But since we are following the **WORD,** here is the interpretation of the mystery. **"For as Jonas was three days and three nights in the whale's belly, so shall the Son of Man be three days and three nights in the heart of the earth."** (Matthew 12:40) The discernment of this prophesy is only understood by a country boy, that has "Shelled Down the Corn" (confessed) to Jesus and admitted that he did not have enough sense to come in or go out without the guidance of Christ Jesus; and by the direction of the Holy Spirit of God Almighty, (PANTAKRATOR), this writer has not read all the bibles and all commentaries of the world; but the Catholics, protestants, and other bibles that I have read, and their commentaries cannot count three days and three nights correctly, because there is no such thing as *lent* or *good Friday*. Here is the way the writer of **"Corn Shelling Time"** discerns the three days and three nights in the heart of the earth. In the first of the Creation God did not start with the day, but He started with the night first, and He ended with the end of the day, which was at sunset or around 6:00 o'clock in the evening started a new day at night. And the interpreters of the Catholic bibles did not understand the writing of the Greek scribes. So they interpreted the Greek scriptures falsely. For example, the Greek scriptures did not ever say Jesus Christ, because Christ was not Jesus' last name, on the other hand the holy scriptures, which are only written in Greek did not ever say Jesus Christ; and Jesus did not say three days and three nights in the heart of the earth as the KJV Bible quotes Him as saying. But Jesus said the first shall be last and the last shall be first. So correctly interpreted quotation is three nights and three days in the heart of the earth, because Greek texts are read backward.

So Jesus ate the Passover meal with His disciples on the 14th night of Nissan, and they hung Jesus on the stake (tree) *(not a cross)* on the day of *Wednesday* the 14th of Nissan, until 3:00 o'clock in the evening. At 3:00 o'clock the Joseph of Arimathaia along with Nikodemos, brought about 100 pounds of myrrh and aloes mixed and prepared Jesus' body to be put in a sepulchre, wherein no man had ever lain. So the Jews could not have Jesus still hanging on the tree past 6:00 o'clock in the evening, because that started the night and day of the High Sabbath, which would be *Thursday* night. So by 6:00 o'clock *Wednesday* evening Jesus was buried in the Memorial Tomb, and a stone sealed the mouth of the tomb. So we start the night of *Thursday* with Jesus' spirit in the heart of the earth, which is Hell. *Thursday* night is one night, (keep count), at 6:00 o'clock the next morning starts the daytime of the High Sabbath of Unleavened Bread. So Jesus' spirit spends the day Thursday in Hell. That makes one day at 6:00 o'clock that evening ends *Thursday* and starts the night of *Friday,* which makes (2) nights Jesus is in Hell. At 6:00 o'clock A.M. Starts *Friday* day. At 6:00 o'clock P.M. That evening ended *Friday* day, and started *Saturday* Night, which made 2 Nights and 2 days Jesus' Spirit was in Hell in the Section of Hell that was called Paradises or Paradise in English, because He told one of the malefactors, this day you shall be with Me in Paradises. (Luke 23:43). So at 6:00 o'clock P.M. Ended *Friday* day and started *Saturday* Night, which if you are keeping count makes three nights He has been in Hell. Then at 6:00 o'clock A.M. Starts *Saturday* day until 6:00 o'clock P.M. Makes 3 nights and 3 days Jesus was in the heart of the earth or the belly of the earth, or for short, Hell. So at 6:00 o'clock P.M. On *Saturday* ended the day of the Sabbath (*Saturday*) and started the night of the first day of the week, which in heathen language was *Sunday*.

So to fulfill the prophesy in scriptures it said: "For you will not leave My Soul in Hell, neither will you suffer (*let*) your Holy One to see corruption." (Psalms 16:10) So here is fulfilled two prophesies, because after four days a body starts to stink and be corrupted. So Jesus' body stayed in the tomb until the night of the first day of the week; and Jesus' Spirit was raised up out of Hell; and He picked up His body and waited for Mary Magdalene and the other women to come to put spices on Jesus' body; but His body was not there. But "He is risen." (Luke 24:6) "He is not here, for He is risen." (Matthew 28:6)

"But if the Spirit of Him that raised up CHRIST Jesus from the dead dwell in you, He that raised up Christ from the dead shall also quicken (*make alive, give life*) *to your mortal bodies* by His Spirit that dwells in you." (Romans 8:11)

So we have established that Christ is risen from the dead. What was the reason that Christ Jesus went to the belly of the earth, or Hell, or paradise? There were, and there are different places that spirits and souls and bodies go to in order to wait for the time to be judged. Some are judged before others. Some are judged at the first resurrection of the righteous, and others will be judged 1,000 years after the first resurrection, which is the second resurrection, or the Great White Throne Judgment. The reason that Christ Jesus went to Hell was to preach to the spirits in prison. (I Peter 3:19) Now at that time paradise was a compartment of Hell, being separated from the other compartments of Hell by the Great Gulf, or an expanse Jesus called paradise in the parable of the rich man and Lazarus. (Luke 16:19); Abraham's bosom (Luke 16:22). The abode of all the spirits of men, whether righteous or wicked at that time was in the heart of the earth. The righteous spirits were in paradise, where Jesus told the malefactor; "This day you will be with me in paradise." (Luke 23:43). And the wicked spirits were in another compartment on the other side of the Great Gulf, or expanse, called Hell, or the prison of evil spirits until the Great White Throne Judgment. This is the place where the other malefactor, *(thief)* that was hanged with Jesus went. (I believe). All bodies of righteous or unrighteous were in the ground called a grave. All these in the heart of the earth, whether in paradise or the abode of the wicked were disembodied spirits. Their bodies were in the grave. Their spirit and soul were separated from their bodies. The question is asked: How could the rich man in Hell lift up his eyes if he did not have a body? Jesus was talking about the rich man's spiritual eyes. "The natural man receives not the things of the Spirit of God, for they are foolishness unto him, neither can he know them, because they are spiritually discerned." (I Corinthians 2:14) The rich man was a spirit with spiritual eyes also spiritual ears, which that is what the scripture means when it says "He that has an ear *(spiritual ear)* let him hear what the spirit is saying."

Not only was Jesus the first one to ever be raised from the dead; but after He preached to the spirits in prison, which were in paradise, all the ones that believed Jesus were raised from the dead also. Paradise then was emptied of all the spirits, and some of the spirits picked up their bodies on the way to heaven, and some will God bring with Him to get their bodies at the first resurrection. (1 Thessalonians 4:14,16)

The first fruit was Jesus, and He was raised on the night of the first day of the week, right after the regular Sabbath, and picked up His body, and appeared to Mary Magdalene in bodily form, and then went on up to glory. But before He went up to glory, He said to

Mary **"Woman why weepest thou?** (John 20:15) Then He said: **"Mary".** (John 20:16) "Then Jesus said to her: **Touch Me not, for I Am not yet ascended to My Father, but go to my brethren and say unto them; I ascend unto My Father and your Father, and My God and your God."** (John 20:17)

Now Jesus was the first to be resurrected; "But the graves were opened, and many bodies of the Holy Ones (*not Saints*) which slept arose, and came out of the graves, after His resurrection and went into the Holy City, and appeared unto many." (Matthew 27:52,53) These are called the first fruits. "But now is Christ risen from the dead, and become the first fruits of them that slept." (I Corinthians 15:20)

"Therefore, My people are gone into captivity, because they have no knowledge, and their honorable men are famished, and their multitude dried up with thirst. <u>Therefore Hell has enlarged herself, and opened her mouth without measure; and their glory, and their multitude, and their pomp, and he that rejoices, shall descend into it.</u>" (Isaiah 5:13,14) So when Jesus led captivity captive, out of paradise, Hell enlarged herself. "Wherefore He says when He ascended up on high, He led captivity captive, and gave gifts unto men." (Ephesians 4:8)

"Then Peter said unto them, Repent and be baptized every one of you, in the Name of Christ Jesus, for the remission of sins, and you shall receive the gift of the Holy Ghost." (Acts 2:38) So the gifts that Jesus gave to men was the Holy Spirit and the gifts of the Holy Spirit. (I Corinthians 12:4) The best Gift was Christ Himself. **"For God so loved the world, that He <u>gave</u> His Only Begotten Son, that whosoever believes Him should not perish, but have everlasting life."** (John 3:16)

"He that believes on Him is not condemned, but he that believes not is condemned already, because he has not

believed in the Name of the Only Begotten Son of God." (John 3:18) So believe Him.

"Corn Shelling Time" has followed the Word to Hell and back and found out the Word was God manifest in the flesh. (John 1:1) (I Timothy 3:16) (John 1:14) The Word was God, so we have followed the Word from the beginning, which was before anything was created. We beheld the Word creating all things, and without Him, was not anything made. "He (The Word) was sent and healed them, and delivered them from their destruction." (Psalms 107:20) He was sent to all the prophets to foretell of Him being made flesh by the conception of a virgin, and Him offering Himself as a blood sacrifice upon the altar of a tree. Preaching salvation to a wicked generation that rejected His Testimony, just the same way this perverse and untoward generation is rejecting Him today.

How He (The Word) fulfilled every jot and tittle that was pronounced that He would do by the prophets. How, after He was hung on a tree, and died, His body was buried in a tomb; and He went to a compartment of Hell called paradise, and preached to the prisoners, and led captivity captive back to heaven and moved paradise from Hell to the third heaven. How the spirit raised Him out of the dead ones in Hell and on His ascension, He stopped on earth long enough to pick up His body. Then He went on up to His Father and His God to glorification. How after He was glorified He came to His assembled disciples and gave them instructions about the Mystery of the Plan of Salvation, which was necessary to be preached to every creature in the entire world. How He (The Word) appeared numerous times to His disciples; and after that He appeared to above five hundred brethren at once, and last of all He was seen of Paul, the Apostle, as of one born out of due time. (I Corinthians 15:7,8). "And now, since God raised Christ Jesus from the dead, God set Him at His own right hand in the heavenly places." (Ephesians 1:20) "Far above all principality and power, and might, and dominion, and every name that is named, not only in this world, but also in that which is to come. And has put all things under His feet, and gave Him to be the head over all things to the Ekklesia, (congregation of called out ones)." (Ephesians 1:21,22)

Now the Word, (Christ Jesus) has become our High Priest in heaven. "Seeing then that we have a great High Priest that is passed into the heavens, Jesus the Son of God, let us hold fast our profession." (Hebrews 4:14)

You just read where all power of principalities and powers were given to Him, Our Lord Jesus, and He went back to earth to His disciples and commissioned them to **"Go you therefore and teach all nations, baptizing them in the Name of the Father, and of the Son, and of the Holy Ghost (Spirit)" "Teaching them to observe (*do*) all things whatsoever I have commanded you and Lo, (*look*), I Am with you always, even unto the end of the world."** (Matthew 28:19,20) To continue what He said: **"Go you into all the world, and preach the gospel to every creature. He that believes and is baptized shall be saved; but he that believes not shall be damned."** (Mark 16:15,16) **"And these signs shall follow them that believe, in My Name they shall cast out Devils, they shall speak with new tongues, they shall take up serpents. And if they drink any deadly thing, it shall not hurt them. And they shall lay hands on the sick, and they shall recover."** (Mark 16:17,18)

This is where the *churches* and "Christians" missed the Power that was bestowed upon them. "They having a form of Godliness, but denying the Power thereof. From such turn away." (II Timothy 3:5) The so called "Christians" profess to have the Power, but they do not possess the Power. They do not understand that the Power was given to Christ Jesus and not them. The Power has to work by the Word, because He said: **"In My Name they shall cast out Devils."** not in the Name of the *Church or in the Name of "Christian"*, but only in the Name of Christ Jesus, and He gets the glory. When He said "you shall take up serpents," He did not mean to start playing with snakes, as natural men interprets the Word erroneously; but "All the Words that He speaks, they are Spirit and Life." (John 6:63) So He is talking spiritually about the serpent that deceived Eve, which was the Devil. So Christ Jesus is talking about taking up Devils and casting out sin that causes sickness, and casting out the Devil that deceives people and causes all kinds of sin and sickness. He gave His disciples this Power. **"Behold I give unto you Power to tread on serpents, and scorpions, and over All the Power of the enemy: And nothing shall by any means hurt you."** (Luke 10:19)

"Corn Shelling Time" is reminding you and warning you to obey the Word and "Come Out of "Her". (Revelation 18:4) Satan thought that he was the victor over Jesus. He thought that he killed Jesus. But Jesus made it very clear that no one could take His life, because He voluntarily laid His life down for His sheep. **"As the Father knows Me, even so I know the Father; and I lay down My life for the sheep."** (John 10:15) **"Therefore does My Father love Me, because I lay down My life, that I might take it up again. No man takes it from Me, but I lay it down of Myself. I have Power to lay it down, and I have Power to take it again. This commandment I have received of My Father."** (John 10:17,18)

So the goats are allied with Satan in Mystery, Babylon, stealing, killing, and destroying God's property; but God's sheep have the Kingdom of God within them, and go about doing good. The Good Shepherd is leading His Sheep to green pastures and still water, where they do not steal, kill, or destroy. His sheep know His voice and will not follow any other Shepherd. If anyone is following a false Shepherd, then he, or she, is a goat and will be on the left side of Jesus. If you are greedy, going through this world seeking the glory of the Kingdoms of this world, Satan is willing to give you his worldly things, but you have just given him your soul *(life)* in exchange for the world. If you are joined to any *Harlot Church,* and vote for any politician, you need to "Come out of "Her" and be you separate from the stealing, killing, and destroying of God's people, and God's earth, and the life on and in His earth. Be not unequally yoked *(joined)* together with unbelievers of the Word. (II Corinthians 6:14)

Father God, In the name of Christ Jesus I give you thanks for revealing your secrets and your mysteries to babes that are in Christ Jesus and that are one with you. Thank you for the gifts of the Holy Spirit, but moreover I thank you for the Holy Spirit Himself, which is the anointing I received at first; and I have no need of any man teaching me anything because Jesus said He was the only teacher and I believe Him. I give you thanks for giving your only begotten Son in order that whosoever believes Him might be saved, In the name of Christ Jesus Amen and Amen.

In everything give thanks: for this is the will of God in CHRIST JESUS concerning you.

(1 Thessalonians 5:18)

This is an insert in the book, **"Corn Shelling Time"** and **Michael Duishka** with some of his belief. In my opinion natural fleshly humans do not have a Spiritual ear to hear the voice of the Holy Spirit, which is the way God The Holy Spirit speaks. He that has a spiritual ear can hear God plainly.

Chapter 16

BEFORE DANIEL'S BOOK WAS closed and sealed, he told about how knowledge would be increased. This present generation is the fulfillment of that prophesy. This present generation is so intelligent on all the evil inventions of the world, but so ignorant and destitute about the Word of their Creator. This wicked and perverse generation has been taught to twist words to right the opposite of their truthful meaning, so they can be politically correct liars.

"Woe unto them that call evil good and good evil, that put darkness for light, and light for darkness, that put bitter for sweet, and sweet for bitter. Woe unto them that are wise in their own eyes, and prudent in their own sight." (Isaiah 5:21,22)

This generation even invented cognate words that were similar and related by descent from the same ancestral language of the *Latin Churches, of the lineage of Roman Catholic Church* and the English King James Bibles. These two twisted examples of cognate words joined right into the plan of Satan to deceive the children of God into becoming the children of darkness, calling darkness light, and light darkness.

You send your children to a government owned and curriculum dictated institution under the fear and duress of; *"It is the law of the land."* You are not only sinning against the God that created you, but you are sinning against your children; and not only are you condemned, but you have caused your children to be condemned to the second death, because "he that believes not is condemned already." (John 3:18) You, you "Christian" parent, are commanded to be a watchman for your children. Instead of you being a watchman for your children, you are a watchman of your children, watching them commit fornication, which is idolatry and joining to the *Harlots of Mystery, Babylon,* which is mandatory destruction, The ObomaNation of Desolation.

"And these Words which I Command you this day, shall be in your heart, and you shall teach them diligently unto your children and shall talk of them when you sit in your house, and when you walk by the way, and when you lie down, and when you rise up; and you shall bind them for a sign upon your hand; and they shall be as front-lets between your eyes; and you shall write them upon the posts of your house, and on your gates." (Deuteronomy 6:6,7,8,9) Woe be unto you and to your children if you do not do this.

The writer of **"Corn Shelling Time"** suffered persecution from the government, and the laws of the land, and the schools, and the DHS; (Department of human services),and worst of all from his own household for obeying this commandment of God. But there is one consolation. Their blood will not be upon my hands, because they were warned; and if you have read this, you have been warned.

The laws of the land say it is mandatory for you to send your children to a public government funded school, that only teaches evil, wicked, sin. The *churches* condone the same thing. The commandment of God is right the opposite, so you are obeying the pagan laws of the land, teaching safe sex, which is fornication, and giving little kids dope for something called ADHD, which is Devil Possession. Teaching children to go backward, instead of teaching God's Wisdom. Teaching the young virgins to dress like harlots and dance half naked with their wares showing in order to temp some heathen boy to rape them; and either aborting their illegitimate baby, or having a halfbreed like the president. Woe to ones that do such things. That is why God is pleading with you to "Shell Down the Corn" and Come out of "Her", the government, the *church*, the schools, and most of all the world and things that are in the world. Pay attention: Listen: If **"Corn Shelling Time"** offends you, you had better take heed to yourself and know beyond a shadow of doubt that you are an unbeliever and already condemned. But if you "Shell Down the Corn", (confess), (I John 1;9) "He is faithful and just to forgive us our sins, and cleanse us from all unrighteousness." If you have an ear, (*spiritual*). Please hear.

Let the Lord Jesus warn you of another sacrifice. If you ever make a genuine commitment to serve the Lord Christ Jesus, listen to what He says: **"Think not, that I Am come to send peace on earth. I came not to send peace, but a sword. For I Am come to set a man at variance against his father, and the daughter against her mother, and the daughter in law against her mother in law. And a man's foes shall *be* they of his own household."** (Matthew 10:34,35,36)

So, if you really surrender all to Christ Jesus, be ready to give up your spouse, and your children, if you are true to your commitment to the Lord Christ Jesus. Because you have to sacrifice the worldly things, such as television, sports, dancing, drinking, dope, adultery, fornication, idolatry, and work not only to justification, but most of all to sanctification and holiness.

The only teacher that this writer has, gave these instructions to whosoever will receive them. "He said: **Come unto Me all you that labor and are heavy laden, and I will give you rest. Take My yoke upon you, and learn of Me, for I Am meek and lowly in heart, and you shall find rest unto your souls."** (Matthew 11:28,29)

Instead of schools teaching these Words of life, they teach sports and sex. The boys are taught to be gladiators in some kind of arena, and only a small percentage reach the professional status, where they are paid large sums of money, but it only lasts for a short period, until they become maimed, lame, halt, brain damaged, or some die young. The boys that do not make it to the professionals have to find some other profession; and most usually the one they find turns out to be dishonorable, such as attorneys, politicians, or police, or some other job that steals, kills, and destroys God's people and His earth. Very few turn out to be honorable farmers, ranchers, carpenters, plumbers, electricians, husbandmen, or any other trade that gives life.

Some go to seminaries to learn how to be a hireling preacher that sells salvation. Denominations talk about the door to door witnesses that talk about their bible, looking for donations when they themselves are doing worse when they are more sneaky and subtle selling choice seats in the Harlot Church to the one that pays more tithes and donations. That is like the pot calling the kettle, blackie, right? Right. All the *harlot Churches* scam money in different ways. I have heard that some charge monthly membership dues to be joined to the *Harlot Church*. **"Jesus said to remain in the same house eating and drinking such things as they give."** (Luke 10:7)

But he that is an hireling, and not the Shepherd, whose own the sheep are not, sees the wolf coming and leaves the sheep, and flees, and the wolf catches them and scatters the sheep." (John 10:12)

The scriptures bear out that a minister is due wages, but seminaries have taught them how to pull excessive amounts of money, using the Name of God. The wolf is coming soon; and the hireling preacher will take the mark, number, or his name; and so will the "Christians" or they will be killed. (Revelation 13:15) But some in the *churches* have wisdom. He that has an ear, let him hear.

Many boys that do not make the professional ranks go into trafficking dope or guns or stealing, killing, and destroying.

The girls usually go to work for the DHS as a Social Worker, or the cities, counties, or state government. Very few have honorable jobs, such as housewives, midwives, or nurses. Many get pregnant out of wedlock and wind up murdering their babies in abortions. All the above is what the institutions that are supposed to be teaching Christ Jesus do, not permitting that Name to be voiced.

These students of darkness have a broad and wide way to destruction. If you live in America, you live in an ObomaNation of Desolation, and your house is left unto you desolate. (Matthew 28:38) Jesus called you out loud, (Ekklesia) called out.

There is a beautiful song that says "Softly and tenderly Jesus is calling, calling for you and for me." But the English words are softly spoken, compared to the Greek language that Jesus spoke. English cannot come close to the strong meaning that Greek words emphasize. Just like the Greek word Ekklesia, which means called out in a loud voice; not a Catholic man made word, *church,* that the English bibles copied from the Catholic bible, the same way they did on a lot of very important scriptures that Satan has deceived the pastors, evangelists, and teachers. Jesus said, "and that which you have spoken in the ear, in closets, shall be proclaimed upon the house tops." (Luke 12:3) And that is exactly what Ekklesia is meaning, shout it out loud from the housetops. Come out of "Her", My people." (Revelation18:4)

And He gave some, apostles, which are the ones that saw Jesus in bodily form, that have all passed away; and there are not any true apostles anymore. "For such *are* false apostles, deceitful workers, transforming themselves into the apostles of Christ." (II Corinthians 11:13)

"Unto the angel of the called out ones of Ephesus, write; These things says He that holds the seven stars in His right hand, who walks in the midst of the seven golden candlesticks. I know your works and your labor and your patience, and how you cannot bear them which are evil, and you have tested them which say they are apostles, and are not, and have found them liars." (Revelation 2:1,2) So the apostle Paul was the last one Christ Jesus gave apostleship to. He was the last one to see Christ Jesus. Although a lot of people say they have seen Christ Jesus; but you know what they say is. The same way He gave some to be prophets. There are prophets that are seers into the future to tell about the coming events that are double dog dead sure to come to pass, like Daniel, Ezekiel, Isaiah, Jeremiah, and all the minor prophets, and all the New Testament apostles; but John was the last prophet until the two witnesses that are called prophets in the eleventh chapter of Revelation. Joel said in the last days the sons and daughters will prophesy, and Phillip had some daughters that prophesied, and Agabus had a word of knowledge for Paul, but none of these were prophets. There are a lot of prophesiers that tell of meeting a boyfriend, or a girlfriend, but no true prophets.

"Corn Shelling Time" is telling you before time things that will happen in the future, but they have already been prophesied by the true prophets, and the writer is only reiterating what has already been prophesied. As it has been previously written. I am not a prophet. Paul said seek to prophesy, but he was not talking about being a prophet like himself. "He, (Christ Jesus) gave some to be pastors, teachers, and evangelists", but the ones that are real, God sent them, and the false ones are hirelings that are deceitful workers that just do it for mammon and personal gain. "And no marvel for Satan himself is transformed into an angel of light. Therefore it is no great thing if his ministers also be transformed as the ministers of righteousness, whose end shall be according to their works." (II Corinthians 11:14,15)

"Corn Shelling Time" is God pleading with you to search the scriptures and read the Truth for yourself. All the writer is doing is showing you where to find the Word of life. "Search the scriptures, for in them you think you have eternal life, and they are they which testify of Me." (John 5:39)

This is why you need to read for yourself. Then you would understand the same anointing that I have received of Him would abide in you, and you need not that any man teach you. "But as the same anointing teaches you of all things, He is Truth, and is no lie, and even as <u>He</u> has taught you, you shall abide in Him." (I John 2:27)

The above underlined He is bringing to your attention how the King James Bible slanders the Word of God, calling the anointing, which is the Holy Spirit, <u>it</u>. He is God. Unless you read the Truth for yourself, and unless you have received the anointing of God, which is the Holy Ghost, and He is not an it, you will never know the Truth, which is Christ Jesus, which is **The Christ,** not Jesus Christ. How can anyone with a finite brain, that cannot know how to tell the Truth preach about the Truth, when they do not even know who the Truth is. "Christ Jesus said unto him; I Am the Way, the Truth, and the life. No man comes unto the Father but by Me." (John 14:6) They read the English Bibles, which is cognate words of the Catholic (Vulgate) Revision of Douay, revision of revision of revision, and so on and on. These revisions admittedly made many errors, which have deceived and still are deceiving ignorant clergymen. Because they profess to have the Holy Spirit, but do not possess Him. Just like John the Baptizer came in the same spirit of Elijah, you have to learn to read Greek, if you ever expect to be of Jesus, and all the apostles and prophets and writers of the Holy Scriptures of the Greek New Testament. There is no way any English interpretation can come close to the spirit the Greek writer was relaying in his tongue. The writer of **"Corn Shelling Time"** has been called a backslider and a hypocrite and many other adjectives that he cannot write down here in this book. But I looked at the source that all the name callers were getting their information from; and Lo and Behold they were children of darkness and were not judging righteously like Jesus said to judge, righteously.

So many times this writer has asked the God up in Heaven, the One that created me and you and all things, if I was doing His Will, because I said: Lord Jesus, I am the only one in the whole entire earth that is echoing your Word to come out of "Her", And He said: "Was Moses the only one I sent to deliver the children of Israel? Was Elijah the only one I sent to challenge the prophets of Baal, And the evil king, Ahab and the evil queen, Jezebel? Was Jeremiah the only one I sent to show the children of Israel how they were going to be slaughtered and taken captive by the Babylonians? Was Daniel the only one I showed the statue of the abomination that makes desolate? Was Jesus, My Only Begotten Son, that I sent to be sacrificed for the entire world? Was Paul the only Apostle I sent to the Gentiles? Was John the only Apostle I sent to reveal what you are writing about, to come out of "Her", Mystery Babylon? Was Polycarp faithful to Me until death? Are you the anointed writer of **<u>"Corn Shelling Time"</u>** the only one in the world I sent to tell My people to "Come out of "Her", Mystery Babylon? Did the evil people kill all my prophets that you mentioned and many more of My people? Are you the only one in the world saying "Come out of the *Harlot Churches*? Are you the only one in the world saying Come out of politics? Are you the only one saying come out of the world and all the things of the world? If the answer to all My questions are yea and amen, then Michael Duishka, you have the answer by faith." God asked me all those questions. He said, look at all the politicians all over the entire world. Show Me one that is not a liar. My Word says; **"And all liars shall have their part in the lake which burns with fire and brimstone, which is the second death."** (Revelation 21:8)

God is doing the talking: "He said: Look at all the *churches,* they all profess Jesus Christ. But none of them possess Christ Jesus. He said, I have a few individual people that are zealous to serve Me, but they cannot serve Me, and sit in a *church* all their life. They are the ones that I said, Come out of "Her" to." God said to me, "Just like you were a bench warmer when you played football in high school. You played right end, sitting on the right end of the bench. You rode the pine. You were the number one bench warmer. That is what I liken all *church goers* to. They keep the pews warm and sit on the deacon's benches, and have the number one seats in the *Mother Whore and ""Her" Harlot Daughters.* Many of My people have amassed fortunes and said to themselves, I will leave all this to my children, and they do. The children say the same thing, and they think they are doing Me a service when they give the excess to the *Harlot Churches.* But I never did say, give to a *church;* but I did say to Come out of "Her" and come unto Me; and just like I showed Abraham where to go, I will show you where to go, to feed Me when I hungered, and give Me drink when I was thirsty, when I was a stranger you took Me in, when I was naked and you clothed Me, when I was sick and you visited Me, when I was in prison you came unto Me. But you try to justify your conscience by saying I give to the *church,* to all the funds, and so called ministries, and pacify all the devils, but that is not what I called you to do." God doing the talking. "Here is what I will for you to do. First I called you out with a loud voice, (Ekklesia (called out loud), then humble yourself and come unto Me, and I will give you rest. Then take My yoke upon you and resign and divorce the *Harlot Church you are married to*, and take all the money you have laid back in store, and go where I will show you, feeding Me, and I will give you rest from going to *the church*, working for the devil every *Sunday*, the man made sabbath of the devil worshipers' *Sun God."*

This writer used to be a faithful *church goer* and tithe giver, *Sunday* school teacher, preacher, song leader, and all nine yards, until God showed me I was just riding the pine, and not in the real game of ministering to the hungry, thirsty, naked, sick, stranger, or prisoner, but I was doing what the deceived preacher told me to do, and not what God said to do. I argued with God and told Him He called me to *go to church* to teach *Sunday School,* to give to missionaries, to the prison ministers, etc. God told me flat out: I did not call you or anyone else to do all those things. I said: "All those people cannot be wrong." He said: **"Wide is the gate, and broad is the way**

that leads to destruction, and many there be which go in thereof." (Matthew 7:13)

God said: "I have millions of people all over the earth that will never go to *a church;* but they will read your book, **"Corn Shelling Time,"** and they will Come unto Me," thus saith the Lord God Almighty, (PANTAKRATOR) A lot of "Christians" are deceived and think the *Church* is God, and they think if they come out of "Her" that would be back sliding; but on the other hand they would be doing what the Word of God said to do, and they would go do the work the Holy Spirit of God has called them to do. They went to *Church* and learned what God wants them to do, but they are just sitting on the pew wasting everything they have learned, thinking if they do something for the *church,* they are doing something for God. **Wrong!** How many have you helped in *church?* All you professed sinners, be of good courage, because you are closer to the Kingdom of God, than all the "Christians" that profess Jesus Christ, but do not possess Christ Jesus. But you, professed sinner, are near the Kingdom of God, and the Word is nigh you, even on your tongue. Just say it. Say, Lord Jesus I confess I am a sinner and I ask you to forgive me, and save me, and He is faithful and just to forgive you and cleanse you from all unrighteousness. All you Harlots, if you will say the same thing, Christ will save you and give you another profession, such as a wealthy housewife, and a good many of you harlots, *(whores),* are already housewives; but if you will "Shell Down the Corn" to Christ Jesus, He will take away the lust of the flesh, just like He did for Mary Magdalene. You are physical whores, but you are closer to the Kingdom of God, than the spiritual whores that profess "Christianity", and are unfaithful to Christ Jesus, by committing spiritual fornication, which is Idolatry, being joined to a *Harlot Church* that **"hears the sayings of Christ Jesus and does them not shall be likened to a foolish man, which built his house upon the sand, and when the rain descended, and the floods came, and the winds blew, and beat upon that**

house, and it fell, and great was the fall of it." (Matthew 7:26,27)

But Mary Magdalene was a physical whore, and suddenly Christ Jesus cast out *(threw out)* seven devils and she followed Him; and He is not a respecter of persons, He will do the same for you or anyone that will "Shell Down the Corn" (confess), just like this writer did! Amen.

This writer was the lowest of all sinners; and I mean no one had ever been lower than me. I was the *badest* of all of the bad seed; but when I "Shelled Down The Corn" to God, just like I did to my daddy, Christ Jesus had mercy on me; and caused me to start a new life with all things becoming new; and He said He would not remember the old things anymore. Jesus said the publicans and the harlots would come into the Kingdom before the hypocrites and the pharisees and the self righteous. You, Mister, and Misses sinner, just say the word that is nigh you, and even on your tongue, say like Peter did when he was sinking, Lord save me. He will save anyone that asks Him to save them, but you have to ask Him to save you, a sinner.

The Pope, which is the head of the *Great Whore,* which is the biggest tool Satan has in his arsenal, has voiced his opinion that the population of the *Church* needs to change to the filth and abominations of the world, and gives his power to go along with same sex marriages, which this writer's belief is, *queers marrying queers,* which to my belief is bestiality in its lowest form. "Men lying with men, women changing their natural use into that which is against nature, who, knowing the judgment of God, that they which commit such things are worthy of death, not only do the same, but have pleasure in them that do them." (Romans 1:20-32)

So the daughters of the Great Harlot *(Protestants)* follow suit and have pleasure in them that do them. Because they, the protestants, allow the *queers* membership in their *churches,* when all the time they know full well what the scriptures say to do to such a one, "which is to take anyone committing fornication out from among you and to deliver such an one unto Satan for the destruction of the flesh, that the spirit may be saved in the day of the Lord Jesus." (I Corinthians 5:2,5)

Not only the *Pope* and all the *Harlots* sanction such filth, but the president and the vice-president of these *NewNited States*, which are "Christians" say they believe that homosexuals should be allowed to marry. And the majority of the population voted for such twisted doctrines of Satan. "But no marvel, for Satan himself is transformed into an angel of light. Therefore it *is* no great thing if his ministers also be transformed as the ministers of righteousness, whose end shall be according to their works." (II Corinthians 11:14,15)

"Be not deceived, God is not mocked; for whatsoever a man sows, that shall he also reap."(Galatians 6:7) Not only is God not mocked, but His sanctified believers are not mocked either. His sanctified believers are sealed with the Holy Spirit, which is the comforter, which Jesus promised to send back to His believers that teaches all things. (John 14:26) We, (the blood covered believers) are not deceived, but our motive is the same one all the writers of the Holy Scriptures had, which is to take you by the hand and lead you out of "Her". Just like the angels led Lot, his wife, and two daughters out of Sodom and Gomorrah. "Her" being Mystery, Babylon, which is revealed as the Whore, (*churches*), governments, schools, and the world, and all the worldly things that cause mankind to commit spiritual fornication, which is Idolatry. It is too late for the ones that have known the depths of Satan, that is the ones that have bent their knee to worship the world and all the glory of the kingdoms of Satan. They have already sold their soul to Satan for all the glamor of the gain of this world. **"For what is a man profited, if he shall gain the whole world, and lose his own soul?"** (Matthew 16:26). If you are in Politics, you are making your death bed. Quit, and come out of "Her." If you are joined to a *Harlot (Church)*, you are making you, and your children' death bed. Quit, and come out of "Her". If you love the world and all the worldly things, (*mammon*), Quit and come out of "Her". "Come out of "Her", My people." (Revelation 18:4)

Father, in the name of Christ Jesus, I ask you to draw the one to Jesus by your Holy Spirit that does according to your Word in (I John 1:9) and will simply confess his sins, and Lord Jesus I ask you to cause the one that does this to come to the Father, and Lord Jesus you raise him up in the last day, and all the glory belongs to You. In Christ's Name. Amen. Father God in the name of Christ Jesus I pray for the little children in public schools that have ignorant parents that have subjected their innocent children to devil filled councilors that put evil thoughts into their tender minds to see if they need to change sex genders, also teach them about the Satan filled Islam, Muslim religion, and Sharia Law which turns these children into anti-Christs just like their ignorant parents. Claim all you can for you LORD JESUS I Believe AMEN!

Chapter 17

THIS WRITER IS SORRY that he ever learned the letter and the pronoun I. But to proclaim the miraculous events that Christ Jesus has done in this writer's life, the pronoun I has to be used. But let it be understood that this writer is nothing but an instrument being used by the Maker. And to relate how the Maker is using, and has used His instrument in the past the pronoun I, has to be used to show what Christ Jesus has done, and this vessel is only telling you what Christ did and the clay had nothing to do with the Potter's works.

This writer is documenting the trials and errors that caused him to live past God's guarantee of three score and ten and past by reason of strength, fourscore. Figure it out. I had nothing to do with it. If you have read how daddy taught me to dance with his double razor strop and taught me how to "Shell Down the Corn", (Confess my wrong doings), how I honored my daddy and my mama, and received the promise of long life. (Ephesians 6:2) Says: "Honor your daddy and mama, which is the first commandment with promise." "For God commanded saying, Honor your father and mother, and he that curses father or mother, let him die the death." (Matthew 15:4) Daddy used the double razor strop on all my siblings, and they are all passed. But I gave honor to my daddy for teaching me to "Shell Down the Corn", (Confess my errors), which was instruction how to "Shell Down the Corn", (confess to God Almighty, PANTAKRATOR).

That is the only way that anyone will ever be in the Kingdom of God is to "Shell Down the Corn".

It is easier to believe that Jesus will do more for someone else, than to have faith enough to believe He will do for yourself. The reason being, I knew all the evil deeds I had done in my life, and it was hard to believe Him when He said I forgive you all your sins. I could not believe He would forgive me of all of the evil sins I had committed in my young life. But I tested God and myself out early, after I had asked Him to save me. On account of my indulgence in strong drink, lots of it, and my participation in drugs, I developed cancer of the pancreas, and I was destitute of money. So, I went to the elders of the *church,* and they went through the motions of (James 5:14,15) "Is any sick among you? Let him call for the elders of the *church,* and let them pray over him anointing him with oil, and in the Name of the Lord; and the prayer of faith shall save the sick, and the Lord shall raise him up; and if he have committed sins, they shall be forgiven him." (James 5:14,15) This went on for 3 or 4 *Sundays,* and I would still bend double with pain. Keep in mind, this was before I had read (I John 2:26,27), and before I learned the Holy Scriptures had been written in the Greek, and there is no such Word as *church.* So I started to bisecting the scriptures of (James 5:14). I had called for the elders, they had anointed me with oil, and used the Name of Jesus (Lord). Then in 15, "And the prayer of faith shall save the sick." I was and had been saved already, "And the Lord shall raise him up." I said He will resurrect me after I have died. "And if he have committed sins, they shall be forgiven him." And I said, "I have committed a multitude of sins, and He will forgive them after I am dead, and raise me up in the resurrection of the dead." So that was the extent of my faith; but then I was seeking the Kingdom of God above all things, so I read the verse before (James 5:14), which was (James 5:13) "Is any among you afflicted?" And immediately I answered and "Shelled Down the Corn" to God. I said; "Lord Jesus, I confess I am afflicted, or I never would have went to someone else to do something for me that only you can do. Since I confess I am afflicted in the brain, the

Word says: "Let him pray." "Please forgive me Lord Jesus; and if you heal me, I will be healed; and if you save me, I will be saved. Devil you are a liar, so get out of me in the Name of Christ Jesus. Amen." I was looking for an instant healing; but by faith I just kept using the Name of Jesus to command the Devil to get out of me; and after about 6 months the Devil was gone; and I was healed in the Name of Jesus. That was the beginning of my faith building, and I believed the Lord Jesus would do anything I asked Him to do; but I came up against something that He would not do. The reason is because I was asking amiss. My wife of 27 years decided she wanted a divorce; and I will not go through the two and one half years of praying and binding the Devil; but she was granted the divorce; and I could not believe that Jesus would allow it to happen; but He did. I was mad at God and blasphemed. But Christ never left me, even though I blasphemed. After a short time, I sought forgiveness; and He was there with open arms to forgive me. I asked Him why He allowed the Devil to win; and He told me, he did not win. That she was a free moral agent; and she was not worthy of me. But most importantly for me is the Lord forgave me. The sins I committed gave place to let the devil afflict me with infirmities.

Then the Lord cast some devils out of a few people, and they were healed. Word went across the state that there was a preacher that could cast out the demons out of people. An Assembly of God preacher and a brother of a devil possessed woman came to me and asked me if I would cast the demons out of her? I told them I would let them know. So they drove back to their hometown and waited. The Lord called me to fast. I fasted 8 nights and 8 days before the Lord showed me in a night vision what the woman looked like and the vision went like this. The woman was lying down and all manner of devil spirits were moving in her body, in her arms and her breast was frogs, snakes, and other reptiles; but the biggest one was a big dog, like a German Shepherd dog, that ran across her throat and neck and her face. So in the vision I turned to my wife, that I am married to now; and I said: "Did you see that? Let's cast it out, and I woke up. When morning came, I went to my Bible, and began research on a dog spirit, and I discovered that a Gentile was called a dog, and the Sodomites were called dogs. So I discerned that the strongest demon in the woman was a spirit of fornication, including homosexuality and possibly bestiality. So I called the Assembly of God preacher and the woman's brother and told them the time and date I had set the meeting, and to bring the woman. I had the meeting set up at one of the sister's houses that attended the *church*. All this was before I had learned to "Come Out of "Her", and before I had read (I John 2:26,27), and before I knew that the anointing was the only teacher I would ever need in my life time. So the preacher and the woman's brother deceived the woman and lied to her as to why they were bringing her to me. Nevertheless, I preached a sermon to the woman and asked her if she had ever heard of Christ Jesus? Then I asked her how many demons she had in her? She answered in a guttural voice; and I knew it was the demon talking. The demon said there was 242 demons in the woman. I asked the demon what his name was? He replied, Jesse. And at that time I realized I had made a big mistake, and that mistake was, I had allowed the preacher, the woman's brother, and some more to be present at this meeting. So after the demon said his name was Jesse, I asked him if he was the strong one of all the demons? Before he could answer, the preacher jumped up and said; "Hold your peace, devil, shut up and be quiet, in the Name of Jesus." So, at that moment, the Holy Spirit showed me, and brought to my remembrance what Jesus said: "And when Jesus came into the ruler's house and saw the minstrels and the people making a noise, He said unto them; "Give place, *(leave out)* For the maid is not dead but sleeps. And they laughed him to scorn. But when the people were put forth, He went in." (Matthew 9:24,25) So I remembered I should have put forth the preacher and the woman's brother, and anyone else that were unbelievers. So, when the preacher told the devil to hold his peace in the Name of Jesus, he gave place to the demons to stay in the woman; and they never spoke anymore. The woman jumped up and went outside the house and started railing on her brother and the preacher, saying; "You lied to me, I knew that I had failed the

Michael Duishka

woman by not putting forth the audience and the unlearned. Later I wound up anointing the door post and the furniture in the sister's house, and binding the devil out of her house and her. So the lesson is never have an audience when you are casting out demons. Jesus always went out to a lonely place away from the crowds. So I "Shelled Down the Corn" and asked Christ Jesus to forgive me, and He did.

That was one of the many times that I erred, but there were times that the Word was confirmed by signs following. The motive I have for writing these trials and errors is so anyone that is truly zealous for Christ Jesus will not be ashamed. The trouble why sincere preachers and lay people that use the Name of Christ Jesus like He said to do is not because they lack faith, but because they have too much faith in themselves, and want so bad to show themselves to be something great in front of a congregation of unbelieving "Christians", and also they think because they are justified by confession of Christ Jesus, that they are qualified to use the Name, Christ Jesus. They are disillusioned because you have to have the old man that you were born with killed by Christ Jesus, and you have to put the old man off of you. "That you put off concerning the former conversation, the old man, which is corrupt according to the deceitful lusts, and be renewed in the spirit of your mind, and that you put on the new man, which after God is created in righteousness and true holiness." (Ephesians 4:22-24)

Before you are allowed to use the Name of Christ Jesus effectively, there has to be a true sanctified, Holy, and righteous vessel, free from all covetousness, envy, pride, wrath, all lying, which is the nature that you were born with, which is the fallen nature that we inherited from Adam and Eve. We were all born with the genes of Adam, and we have to put them off before we can be sanctified and Holy, and be baptized with the Holy Ghost and fire. The fire is what burns the sin nature out of you. You can believe in (*Jesus Christ*) (*King James*) until you join the rich man; but you will never be able to have the use of Jesus and His Power until you believe Him.

"At that day you shall know that <u>I Am</u> in My Father and you in Me and I in you." (John 14:20) You are lost if you believe in Jesus Christ. So do the devils. But on the other hand, you are a candidate for the Kingdom of God, if you believe Christ Jesus and have His Commandments and keep them, he it is that loves Him; "and he that loves Jesus shall be loved by His Father, and Jesus will love you and will manifest Himself to you." (John 14:21) But you are a liar if you say you keep His Commandments and have any covetousness, envy, pride, wrath, uncharitableness, evil speaking, anger, irritability, fear of man, lust and most of all doubt. So if you have any of the above works, you need to direct it toward Satan; and pray for God to kill the old man in you; and after God kills the old man in you, you have to get rid of the dead body and not carry a dead body around with you for the rest of your life. "Oh, wretched man that I am! Who shall deliver me from the body of this death." (Romans 7:24) The body of this death being the old man that God killed. The sin nature that you were born with is not sin that you committed, so you can ask God to forgive you, and He will tell you He cannot forgive you for something you did not do. The "Christians" have humbled themselves and asked Jesus to forgive them their sins, and He was crucified for this purpose. That made them justified; but they stopped seeking for sanctification, Holiness, and the Holy Ghost.

If we have died out to sins, then we have come out of the worldly things, the lust of the flesh, the lust of the eyes, and the pride of life. But if we are still in the worldly things, politics, *churches,* governments, heathen schools, idolatry, the world system, like voting, like competition with your neighbor, or any thing that offends, then you have not died with Christ. "For if we have been planted together in the likeness of His death, we shall be also in the likeness of His resurrection. Knowing this, that our old man is crucified with Him, that the body of sin might be destroyed, that henceforth we should not serve sin." (Romans 6:7,8) So you are still carrying that old man that is supposed to be crucified around, "O wretched man that I am, who shall deliver me from the body of this death." (Romans 7:24)

"Yea, and all that will live Godly in Christ Jesus shall suffer persecution." (II Timothy 3:12) To all these countries that are killing and persecuting "Christians", India, Turkey, Mali, Nigeria, Ethiopia, Colombia, Tanzania, Sri Lanka, Indonesia, Philippines, Iraq, Israel, you are accursed and all kinds of plagues have already come upon you, but get ready, more worse plagues are yet to come upon you. "It were better for you that a mill stone were hanged about your neck, and you cast into the sea, than that you should offend one of these little ones." (Luke 17:2)

"We have not yet resisted unto blood, striving against sin." (Hebrews 12:4) But I personally have resisted persecutions striving against sin, but that is because I am not politically correct, telling lies, calling evil good, and darkness light. None of the *churches* or any "Christians" that I know of in America are suffering any kind of persecution. Is it because they are not living Godly? I personally am persecuted because I do not buy anything black. Black signifies death and evil. God cursed Cain. God cursed Canaan. God turned Lucifer, the brilliant archangel, into a black angel. God turned Nimrod, which was black, into confusion. Everything in God's Word that is Godly is <u>white.</u> We have to be clothed in clean,<u> white,</u> fine linen. There will nothing black enter into the Bride of Christ. "Let us be glad and rejoice, and give honor to Him, for the Marriage of the Lamb is come, and His wife has made herself ready. And to her was granted that she should be arrayed in fine linen, clean and <u>white,</u> for the fine linen is the righteousness of the Holy Ones." (Revelation 19:7,8)

"And He said to me, write, blessed are they which are called unto the Marriage Supper of the Lamb, and He said unto me, these are the true sayings (Words) of God." (Revelation 19:9)

"And the armies which were in heaven followed Him upon <u>white</u> horses, clothed in fine linen, <u>white</u> and clean." (Revelation 19:14)

If you have a problem with you being a racist, take it up with God. He is a racist. He made the different races, and you can march and loud mouth God all you want, but you cannot change God, because He is the same yesterday, today and will be the same forever. Thank you, Lord Jesus. What you need to do is shut your mouth, quit talking, get off to yourself and let God talk to you. There are millions of things wrong with this untoward generation. (Acts 2:40) But the scriptures say old things are passed away, that does not keep me from remembering **"Corn Shelling Time"** and the double razor strop across my---butt. In that generation you did not see a bunch of gang-bangers raping <u>white</u> girls, aborting their babies, or the blacks rioting and wanting everything the rest of the people have, without working for it. They want everything the world has to offer given to them. They needed some of my daddy's hickory tea. But there was some guy from outer space, named Spock, I think, that was all deranged in his head, that said: "Do not spank a child." The world adopted that baloney, and all any older person has to do is look around him, and see the results.

I questioned God and asked Him. "Lord Jesus, if the heathen did not listen to you, and killed you, what makes you think they will listen to me, who is nothing!" His answer was: "Our job is to preach this good news to all the world. I finished my work, now you do your work. If you read in Matthew's gospel, (26:65) where the high priest rent his clothes at what I said, what do you think the world will do when they read **"Corn Shelling Time?" You have not chosen Me, but I have chosen you, and ordained you that you should go and bring forth fruit, and that your fruit should remain: That whatever you shall ask of the Father in My Name, He may give it you."** (John 15:16) **"Then shall they deliver you up to be afflicted, and shall kill you and you shall be hated of all nations for My Name's sake."** (Matthew 24:9)

The ones that have been given authority over flesh and blood, *(humans)*, always false charge someone that is Godly with some crime that is false and ungodly. They try them before a courtroom full of ungodly jurors, and ungodly lawyers, and an ungodly judge, and I can tell you the verdict before the accused ever goes to Court: Guilty! Just like Jesus, they had false witnesses, and found Him guilty of blaspheming God, and He was God. They do the same thing to a Godly person, and always find him guilty of some false charge of murder, rape, robbery, stealing or anything to extract money or time just to get one of Jesus' witnesses out of proclaiming their stealing, killing, or destroying. On the other hand if the defendant happens to be black, with a lot of money, and murders his wife and her friend, the police follow him down the highway until his Bronco runs out of gas. Then they take a long time to finally charge him. Then, because he is a gladiator in the sports world and famous, he hires a team of lawyers, but the main lawyer, being black, that cohorts with the Prosecuting Attorney and judge; and all during the trial, they call these huddles that have a politically correct name of a "side bar", *(just a big lie)*. So they can make up a new set of rules, as they go, and instead of trying him for murder, the game plan changed to whether a pair of gloves fit him or not. So the charge changed from murder to the fitting of a pair of gloves. The black lawyer told the black biased jury, quote, "If the gloves don't fit, you must acquit." And they let a murderer go free.

I cannot leave out the most horrendous, in my opinion, mass murder in the world, save of course, the Holocaust where the Nazis killed millions of Jews. The mass murders were the cremation of men, women, and children in the Koresh Home in Waco, Texas. These people were just like the Jews in WWII, innocent of any crime. The jack booted thugs in the government from the president on down to the lowest private in the military will be judged for murder, including the unqualified woman Attorney General of the USA, Janet Reno. she gave the order to shoot the gas into the house that burned all *76?* humans alive. Why was not all the participants, including the President, tried in a Court of Law for murder in the Nth degree. The only consolation is the plagues God will allow to come upon all of them, which is a part of "Her" that it is too late to come out of.

I wonder if anyone that was a party of that mass murder, can hear the little children, and the women, and the men crying at night, and cannot sleep for the crying out of those souls. The judge will tell you at the Great White Throne Judgment. "Just doing my job." Then Timothy McVeigh tried to justify himself when he bombed the O.K.C. Federal Building, which this writer was a victim of, but I only suffered loss of property. It did not take the government long to try him and commit murder on him when they killed him. All of these things are a part of Satan's plan to destroy God's people. That is why God said to "Come out of "Her", My people, that you be not partakers of "Her" sins, and that you receive not of "Her" plagues." (Revelation 18:4)

The last time I saw the woman, Attorney General, on television, she had a plague of shaking like a cold dog, *(s_itting peach seeds)* First you sin, and then after you sin, comes a plague, and then after the plague comes death. Then after death comes the second death. **(Hell)**

"But the fearful, and unbelieving, and the abominable, and murderers, and whore mongers, and sorcerers, and idolaters, and all liars shall have their part in the lake which burns with fire and brimstone, which is the second death." (Revelation 21:8)

This writer, I, have committed all of the above sins, but I will never die. Yes, I know all the scriptures about death. It is appointed unto men once to die." (Hebrews 9:27) But a believer, that is one that believes Him, not one that believes in Him, has better promises. "Behold I show you a mystery, we shall not all sleep; but we shall all be changed, in a moment, in the twinkling of an eye, at the last trump, for the trumpet shall sound, and the dead shall be raised incorruptible, and we shall be changed." (I Corinthians 15;51,52)

"And Jesus said unto her, I Am the resurrection and the life. He that believes me, though he were dead, yet shall

he live. And whosoever lives and believes me shall <u>never</u> die. Believe you this?" (John 11:25,26)

"He that overcomes shall inherit all things, and I will be his God and he shall be My Son." (Revelation 21:7)

"As far as the east is from the west, so far has He removed our transgressions from us." (Psalms 103:12)

If He was not a merciful, forgiving, God, this old sinful soul would not have any hope of the Kingdom of God; but since He is a merciful, forgiving God, I "Bless the Lord, O My Soul, and forget not His benefits, who forgives all your iniquities, who heals all your diseases, who redeems your life from destruction, who crowns you with loving kindness and tender mercies." (Psalms 103:2,3,4) After I sinned all those sins against Christ Jesus, the Son of the Living God, He extended all those benefits toward me; and there is no way I can repay Him for the kindness He showed to me while I was yet a sinner. The only slack I can take up, is to "Shell Down the Corn" to Him and quit sinning and do what I promised a long time ago, and live the rest of my life witnessing for Him. There is no sin that He cannot eradicate. "For if our heart condemns us, God is greater than our heart, and knows all things." (I John 3:20) You can have all His benefits if you will just "Shell Down the Corn" and (confess) to the Lord Jesus. Say, "Father God, I confess I am a sinner, and I ask you to save me in the Name of Jesus. Amen". If you just asked Jesus to save you and you believe He did save you, if you believe in your spirit, which is your heart that you shall be saved and Jesus will raise you up in the last day, then you are eligible to receive all the Lord"s benefits. "Bless the Lord O my soul, and forget not all His benefits. Who forgives all your iniquities, who heals all your diseases, who redeems your life from destruction, who covers you with loving kindness, and tender mercies, who satisfies your mouth with good things, *so* that your youth is renewed like the eagles. The Lord executes righteousness and judgment for all that are oppressed. The Lord is merciful and gracious, slow to anger, and plenteous in mercy." (Psalms 103:2-8) All these benefits belong to you if you believe Him. Father God, I agree with the one that just called on the name of Your Son, Christ Jesus and Your Word, which says anyone that calls on the name of Christ Jesus shall be saved and He will raise them up in the last day, and I believe and agree that we will be in the first resurrection and eat with Christ Jesus at the Marriage Supper of the Lamb, Amen and Amen.

This is an insert in the book, **"CORN SHELLING TIME"** and **MICHAEL DUISHKA** with some of his belief. Please understand Michael Duishka is not speaking for God as an APOSTLE, PROPHET, or any other title of importance. Duishka is only reiterating what the apostles, prophets, evangelists, pastors, teachers, BROTHERS in Christ JESUS said in THE WORD of GOD ALMIGHTY, (PANTAKRATOR), which is THE FATHER, THE SON, THE HOLY SPIRIT, which is ONE GOD. I (Michael Duishka) AM NOTHING! **Verily, verily I say unto you he that believes me, the works that I do shall he do also; and greater** *works* **than these shall he do; because I go unto my Father.** (JOHN 14:1). What is the reason this statement of our LORD is not happening? Could it be lack of faith? Could it be that Satan has deployed his seducing spirits to cause the "Christians" to believe false instructions, and lies from the seducing spirits? That seems more likely, that the preachers are proclaiming what the seducing, religious spirits are telling them to say, what organized religion, says, Who changed the truth of God into a lie, and worshipped and served the creature, more than the Creator, who is blessed forever, Amen. (Romans 1:25). Why has God given them over to a reprobate mind? Could it be because the preachers are possessed with seducing, religious spirits, sent from Satan, and cannot cast them out? How come the misled ones with infirm spirits, are leaving the *Churches* in a worse condition than when they were joined to the *harlot?* There are many preachers, and promotional experts that are possessed with lying demons, that say all the spiritual gifts are active and working in their *Church,* but you know what they say is, it is always a lie. How come in every

Church the demonic spirit of lust can be found in some manifestation or other like homosexuals, or fornicators, or adulterers, or many on narcotics, some on alcohol, some cannot break the smoking habit, or nicotine habit, many are slo-bellies, whose god is their belly, many nymphomaniacs? How come the spirit of pride, jealousy, covetous, greed has not been cast out by the hireling shepherds? Could it be that these are the wolves in sheep's clothing? I know there are a lot of just, wise ones, that are God's people still in the Babylonian system, because brother John was obeying Christ's command when He said to come out of her my people in Revelation 18:4. The question is why do these wise, just ones not cry out, the wolf? At least, should they not question the wolf that they hired to fleece them? **The SPIRIT of the LORD is upon me, because He has anointed me to preach the gospel to the poor; He has sent me to heal the broken hearted, to preach deliverance to the captives, and recovering of sight to the blind, to set at liberty them that are bruised,** (Luke 4:18) Are all the Harlots blind and cannot see that His ministry is not being carried out? YES, the *Harlot Churches* are the blind guides leading the blind and they have already fallen into the snare of the fowler, *(Satan)* they are the captives that need delivered. The only hope for those captives to be free is to read and do, **"CORN SHELLING TIME".**

Chapter 18

AMERICA; THE "OBOMANATION OF Desolation". "Ichabod" should be put on the "pseudoaphesis" statue. Explanation: Ichabod is Hebrew, meaning, "The glory has left Israel". "Pseudoaphesis", meaning in Greek, false liberty or false freedom. What the whole interpretation says: The sign Ichabod should be put on the statue of liberty to be interpreted: The glory of God has left America, which is a nation of false freedom. Almost all of the freedoms that this writer knew when he was a young man have been rescinded, mostly in the present Obama administration. I am not talking about this land of plenty, I am talking about the people that had pleasure in the destroyers of the earth. Mr. President Obama, God is not mocked. You can fool some of the idiot people, but you cannot fool God Almighty. He knows that you are not responsible for being a puppet, but you can only do what your string pullers make you do. Your string pullers being behind the curtain. But you sold your soul to the Devil, when you agreed to do what your string pullers told you to do to get elected President of these Divided States of America. It is too late for you to take the silver back to the chief Priests and Elders. And God only knows if it is too late for you to repent and cut the strings attached to you, and become a whistle blower on the pullers. Nevertheless I have done what the Lord Christ Jesus, called me to do and that is for you, Mr. President Obama, to repent and "Shell Down the Corn" to God, and come out of "Her". (Revelation 18:4) "**Corn Shelling Time**" is to reiterate (I John 1:9). "If we confess our sins, He is faithful and just to forgive." Every kingdom divided against itself is brought to desolation. (Matthew 12:25) I do not need to be very intelligent to know for a fact that America is divided; and if I believe Jesus, which I do, then it is just a matter of a short time until it is brought to complete desolation. Since Mr. Obama is the leader of this nation, that makes the USA an ObomaNation of Desolation.

Jesus called it "Blind guides. **"Let them alone: They be blind leaders of the blind. And if the blind lead the blind, both shall fall into the ditch."** (Matthew 15:14) The leaders of this country inherited a fruitful country; and since they were a failure and promised lies just to get elected, they laid the blame for their failure on to the previous administration. It is called "Passing the Buck". The former President George H. W. Bush called them Jack booted thugs. He apologized later, but that did not change the fact that He said it.

The Obama government has not contributed any asset, that I can see, to this country. On the other hand I can see where they have robbed the working class of people to give to the insurance companies, the big giant corporations, car builders, banks, all terrorist countries, all the lazy unemployed that do not want to be employed, the lazy welfare recipients, and most of all benefits for themselves. The hard working class has been supporting all the above give away programs, and the Obama Care has caused many many hard working people to have to quit their jobs, because they could not pay the insurance for contraceptives, abortions, *queer* dependencies, drug addicts, and pregnancies, and on and on and on. The working class is paying for all of this graft; and the Supreme Court Justices violated the Constitution; and just like the side bar, they make new game rules as they come upon a law that does not help the robbers of My people, they change the law to fit them. The Obama Care Insurance Bill was against the Constitution; and the biased Judges turned it into a tax, which whenever it was voted on in Congress, it was a law.

The string pullers tell Obama what to say; and when he says it, the congress does it.

They make it a law just like the law of Hammurabi that is on the walls of the Supreme Court, and The House of Representatives and Obama betrayed America, just like Judas betrayed Jesus. "His rewards and end shall be according to his works" (II Corinthians 11:15) One man stood and called his words a lie, but they threw that man out, never to be heard again.

"Fear them not therefore, for there is nothing covered that shall not be revealed, and hid that shall not be known." (Matthew 10:26)

This country is supposed to be a model for other uncivilized countries to learn how to keep the Commandments of God; but as it turns out, it is a model example of how to steal, kill, and destroy. So now, as God looks down upon His creation, there is no country that is keeping His Commandments. Only individual people that believe Christ Jesus. That is what **"Corn Shelling Time"** is supposed to accomplish, the uncovering of the evil that the heathen nations think they have hidden, which the greatest of all these nations that teach and do evil is the *NewNited States of America*, AKA "The Great Satan." The ObomaNation of Desolation. The model country for the entire world. Amen?

Whenever some patriot like Edward Snow den uncovers the government violating the Espionage Act by spying on it's own citizens, the government accuses the whistle blower of being a traitor, when all along it was the government committing treason, is what I believe. The Obama machine points the finger at anyone else, just to cover up their evil decrees. Like saying it was Bush that caused America to go in debt trillions of dollars, that will never be paid. Making America the borrower instead of the lender. Making America the tail, instead of the head. The only thing America is the head of is policing every other nation in the world. Only it will not work on China, or Russia. America could take some lessons from China on how to mind your own business, don't you think? Obama used America's money and military support for the rebel terrorists to overthrow Egypt, Libya, Palestinian Terrorists, and many Muslim, countries, which are mostly terrorist countries.

Just borrow more money, print more money, which has to come to a disappointing end for the "Christians" that voted. They gave their allegiance to the government, no matter who they voted for; and when the collapse comes, there will be weeping and gnashing of teeth, more than they already are. The Obama machine calls it spending, I call it giving America away to every evil cause and country on this planet.

My mama used to say: "Give him enough rope, and he will hang himself." There is another old saying: "What goes around, comes around."

This writer of **"Corn Shelling Time"** does not have insurance, does not go to doctors, does not have any sickness or plagues. Because, "I will say of the Lord, He is my refuge, and my fortress, My God, in Him will I trust." (Psalms 91:2) "Thus saith the Lord: Cursed is the man that trusts in man, and makes flesh his arm, and whose heart departs from the Lord." (Jeremiah 17:5)

Eighty million "Christians" that are joined to one of the Harlot Churches, reject repentance. This would be the Anglican Church, which is in the United Kingdom of England, Swingers; and they will not call anymore for repentance, as per the News Media.

This writer abstains from any type of medication, or any form of medicine, or pharmaceutical drugs. I would not know how someone hallucinating would act; but it seems as though the entire government and church are hallucinating, as if on some kind of drugs or medication. I do know that a poll showed that a large portion of society is on drugs. It is so very hard to write about the Church, without writing about the state, or the government, because they are allied together, both doing the will of Satan, which come to rob, kill, and destroy anything that belongs to God. They say there is a separation between *church* and state, but you know what they say is: "They say", is always a lie. The President and the Vice President of these *NewNited States of America* both attest to the title of a "Christian", and both agree that it is lawful for a man to be married to another man, that is to say it is alright for a man to lie with another man. So, because a heathen Babylonian "Christian" says right the opposite of what the Word (Christ Jesus) said, then the "Christians" vote for the heathen, which makes them allied with Satan, which is enmity against God.

The Pope, which puts himself in the stead of Christ, which is the head of the Great Mystery, Babylon, the Mother of Harlots and abominations of the earth, came out of the closet, and agreed that the gays, *(queers)* rights should be sanctioned in the Catholic world, which makes the Mother of Harlots allied with the government and the "Christians", which portrays there is no separation between *church* and state.

There are a lot of "Christians" that say: "I did not vote for this party". It does not make any difference, they did not cry out as they were being raped. There are a lot of politicians that say, "I did not vote for this law, or this bill." It does not make any difference. They did not cry out when the country was being raped. Poly, Poly, Bear, if you was not raping her, what was you doing there?

There was a church that this writer knows about that were Swingers. I use that word because I take it to mean wife swappers. This *Church (Harlot)* was swapping wives, and it was quite a large church, made up of whites, and blacks, swapping wives and girl friends. To say the least, it was a model of filth and abomination.

Another denomination said, "Oh, our *Church (Harlot)* are all "Christians". We would never do something like that; but if you watch on *Sunday* at 12:00 o'clock the service ends, and the doors open; and you can see couples of men and couples of women walking out together, getting in their cars and leaving. Still another large denomination hired a new preacher that lasted a few months before they fired him for committing adultery with a deacon's wife. Same song, second verse, "Could get better, but it is gonna get worse." You know who gonna is!

"And that servant which knew his Lord"s will, and prepared not himself, neither did according to His will, shall be beaten with many stripes (plagues)." (Luke 12:47) Those "Christians" in those Harlot Churches that you just read about do not have a cloak or covering for their sins, and the stripes they are receiving are plagues just like the ones the Mother of Harlots receives; and you, dear reader, will receive the many stripes (plagues) if you do not "Come out of "Her".(Revelation 18:4)

All of my old friends, the ones still breathing, are all just barely surviving with all their burdens of plagues. They have one foot in the grave and the other foot on a banana peeling, telling what a good doctor they have. This writer told them many years before they received the plagues how to "Shell Down the Corn" (confess) to Christ Jesus; and all I accomplished was to offend them and make them think I was self righteous; when, just like right now, I am warning you with the Word of God, and showing you God's way He has provided for you to escape. Some of my old friends take dialysis every other day, which is very painful; some take chemotherapy to try to control their disease (*plague).* All of them have their gall bladder removed. Some have had strokes, some with heart bypasses, from the wrong kind of cholesterol blocking their blood passage. All of them ate swine's flesh, which is an abomination to the Lord. But if you tell them about the split hoof and chewing of the cud, all they can remember is (Acts 10:10) "Where Peter fell into a trance, and saw a vessel descending down to earth with all manner of four footed beasts, and creeping things, and fowls of the air. And there came a voice to him, "Rise, Peter, kill and eat." But Peter said, "Not so, Lord, for I have never eaten anything that is common or unclean." And the voice spake unto him again the second time, "What God has cleansed, that call not you common." This was done thrice, and the vessel was received up again into heaven." My ignorant friends are compared to millions of unlearned "Christians" that do not know what a metaphor is, a figure of speech in which a word for one idea or thing is used in place of another to suggest a likeness between them. (As in **"Corn Shelling Time"**), meaning to confess your sins to Christ Jesus. So God spake to Peter with a metaphor that had nothing to do with eating unclean animals, but was sending Peter to a bunch of Gentiles, that God showed me were dogs in the vision of the devil filled woman. So Peter went and preached salvation to a bunch of Gentiles, which was the metaphor God was talking about, and not about eating unclean animals.

I have compassion on all people, not only my friends, that are being destroyed for lack of knowledge. (Hosea 4:6) "Because you have rejected knowledge, I will also reject you." Sin is what causes you to have diseases, disasters, plagues, troubles, sickness, infirmities, persecutions, and tribulations. This is knowledge from God. Are you going to reject this knowledge? **"Corn Shelling Time"** is a Word of knowledge from God. Will you confess or reject God's Word? Confess! Just in case you do not know about God's Word about what to eat. "God said: Whatsoever parts the hoof and is cloven footed and chews the cud, among the beasts, that shall you eat." (Leviticus 11:3) "And the swine, though he divide the hoof, and be cloven footed, yet he chews not the cud. He is unclean to you. Of their flesh shall you not eat, and their carcase shall you not touch. They are unclean to you." (Leviticus 11:7,8,9) They say it is not a sin to eat pork (swine, hog, pig); but you know what they say is: Always A Lie. "For this cause many are weak and sickly among you, and many sleep. For if we judge ourselves, we should not be judged; but when we are judged we are chastened of the Lord, that we should not be condemned with the world." (I Corinthians 11:30,31,32)   "These shall you eat that are in the waters, whatsoever has fins and scales in the waters, in the seas, and in the rivers, them shall you eat." (Leviticus 11:9) "And all that have not fins and scales in the seas, and in the rivers, of all that move in the waters, and of any living thing which is in the waters, they shall be an abomination unto you. You shall not eat of their flesh, but they shall be an abomination to you; but you shall have their carcases in abomination. Whatsoever has no fins nor scales in the waters that shall be an abomination to you." (Leviticus 11:9,10,11,12)

I do not like to burst some of your bubbles, but catfish are scavengers that do not have scales. My acquaintances go and waste their lives, what little they have left, waiting in waiting rooms to see a quack doctor; then after they get a script for some more dope, they go fill up on swine, or catfish. They are just adding fuel to the fire. They are hard headed, and God said they are headed for destruction. You, dear reader, be obedient to the Word of Christ Jesus; and if you do not understand, just trust Christ Jesus to send His Holy Spirit to you, "That will bring to your remembrance all the things He said, and will show you things to come. This is the anointing that will teach you, and you have no need of any man teaching you anything." (I John 2:27)

Remember, "Nothing covered that shall not be revealed. Nothing hid that shall not be known." If you are in the government in any capacity, you cannot hide the things you do from God. He knows you have an ulterior motive, to exalt yourself for personal gain by persecuting your neighbor. If you are joined to a Harlot (Church), He said to "Come out of "Her". If you are partaking in any form of politics, or any part of the Great Satan, or partakers in the ObomaNation of Desolation, you have already received some kind of sickness, disease, condition, disaster, or plague, because of your participation in "Her" sins.

The only hope you have is to "Shell Down the Corn", (confess your sins) to Christ Jesus, and do not be like the 80 million Anglicans that think they do not need to repent; but you repent for being a party to voting, supporting lying politicians, or supporting some *Harlot Church* with your tithe and offering, all for the plan of Satan.

The **Lord**, Christ Jesus said for you to feed Him, and clothe Him, and to give Him drink, and visit Him when He is sick, when He was a stranger, you took Him in, visited Him in prison. He never said in His Word anywhere to give to a *church*, and hope that they will minister to Him. He said for you to minister to Him personally, and not to give to some *Harlot Church*, so you can try to justify yourself. If you do, you will be judged on His left hand with the goats; and you know what (Matthew 25:41) says will be your judgment. Everlasting Fire.

If you have already been a partaker in all the sins of the world, and you think you have been too bad for Christ Jesus to save you, you are wrong. I can testify for a fact that Christ Jesus is a merciful God that will have mercy on you just like He did to the lowest sinner in the world, which was me. All you have to do is "Shell Down the Corn", which is confess your sins to Christ Jesus, and repent, and turn from your wicked ways, and humble yourself, and pray for Him to forgive you, and to save you, and to cleanse you from all unrighteousness; and most of all, believe Him. Amen.

What about the people who never step foot inside a *church*? These people are closer to the Kingdom of heaven than the "Christians", that know the will of God, but do it not. All you rank strangers that are sinners by nature, the Word is nigh you already. All you need to do is say it right now. Say, "Lord Jesus I am a sinner. Will you please forgive me? And He said He would, and your part is to simply believe Him.

If you are able to read, just open the Bible to any page, and read it for yourself. If you cannot read, on account of some infirmity, get anyone you see to read it for you. Anyone on the street, in a restaurant, grocery store, or a mission will read the Word of God to you, and who knows, you may be instrumental in the one reading to you being converted, and going to heaven with you. If they say they do not have time, you ask them when they will have time? Just tell them Jesus will give them time to read His Word. If they ask you where do you want them to read? You say the Book of John.

There are many levels of gifts from Christ Jesus. He never left anyone out, without giving them gifts of some kind. "Wherefore He says, when He ascended upon High. He led captivity captive, and gave gifts unto men." (Ephesians 4:8) "But everyone of us is given grace according to the measure of the gift of Christ." (Ephesians 4:7)

There are many preachers that say no one can be saved outside of a *church*; but what did Jesus say? I thought you would never ask. Jesus said: "Come unto Me, *(not Church)*." Anyone that calls on that Name, Jesus, shall be saved. (Romans 10:13) Lord, Lord. That is the measure of grace that Jesus gave to everyone, the ability to call on Jesus. Some people are at different levels of understanding than others. If you have been given a higher level of understanding than others, more will be required from you. If you have the ability to read and learn the Greek Scriptures and do not do it, you will receive more stripes than the ignorant, unlearned one. Jesus gave you many talents, and you buried them; and **"Corn Shelling Time"** is telling you to repent and confess, and go dig up the buried talents you have been given free gratis, no charge, and start exercising them. O.K.?

There are a multitude of readers of **"Corn Shelling Time"** that know exactly what it is talking about, because you are wise. Daniel said the wise ones will shine as the firmament and will lead many out of Mystery, Babylon, the Organized Religion, The Harlot, the Mother of Harlots; and since you, dear reader, have asked God for wisdom; and I know He kept His promise to give you wisdom, you read it for yourself and disregard the other gospel you have learned, other that the gospel that Paul preached, and do not be anathema, *(accursed)*. (Galatians 1:8) There are a great multitude of "Christians" that started the race running well; but on the road they became bewitched by the glory of the kingdoms of Satan; and "because iniquity, (lawlessness) abounded, the love of many waxed cold." (Matthew 24:12)

"Corn Shelling Time" says dig up your buried talent and read it for yourself, and "Come Out of "Her". (Revelation 18:4) Quit going to that *deep freeze church* where the love of many have waxed cold, and take the money you are giving to Satan, and spend it on Christ Jesus to feed Him, give Him drink, visit Him when He is sick, visit Him in Prison, find a stranger and take Him in. They said when did we do that to you, and He said: "And the *King* (Jesus) shall answer and say unto them. **Verily I say unto you, inasmuch as you have done it unto one of the least of these My brethren, you have done it to Me."** (Matthew 25:40) Do not give the children' bread to dogs. Do not give all your excess to the *Harlot Church*. Do not give your tithe and offering to the hireling preacher; but do like Jesus, seek for the family that is not bums, on welfare, but a hard working family man that needs a little help, and is not about to ask for any help. You open your eyes. Do not give anything to the lazy bums that stand on the street corners begging. "I have been young and now am old, yet have I not seen the righteous forsaken, nor his seed begging bread." (Psalms 37:25) So the so called homeless person is just a *scammer*, begging bread, too lazy to work; and Paul said; "If you do not work, you should not eat." (II Thessalonians 3:10) The so called homeless are falsely called homeless. They have a home on earth, just like Jesus had. The only difference is Jesus never had any missions or Salvation Armies for shelter like the bums do.

The schools proselyte all the children to be converted into the present belief of evolution. After they have converted them into fools like they are, they have made the child a twofold more a candidate for Hell than they are. The reason this generation and the former generation

| 201 |

are evil is not because they blatantly chose to be disobedient to the Word of God, but it is because they never were taught about creation; and never did eat the fruit of the tree to have knowledge of good and evil. The present and past generations were taught only evil, because their teachers were taught only evil. Oh, how I wish I had learned the knowledge of good earlier in my life; and I would have devoted my entire life to every one I ever came in contact with, that there was knowledge of good, also beside the knowledge of evil. "And Jesus said unto him, **"Why do you call me good? None is good, save one, that is God."** (Luke 18:19) The fruit of the tree of knowledge of good and evil only added knowledge of evil to Adam and Eve, because God had already said when He created man that it was good. So the knowledge they were increased with was God. (The Good One) and Satan (The Evil One). Not looking back at missed opportunities, but looking forward to the opportunity **"Corn Shelling Time"** has to relay the knowledge of good to a lost, untoward ignorant generation. This is my last opportunity to rescue you, dear reader, my loved ones, from the bondage you are bound with, and cause you to free yourself from the prison that you locked yourself in. I realize I can not do as good a job as Jesus did in His Holy Word, but maybe there is a slim chance, you may realize that you will never know the Truth unless you read it for yourself. You have tried all the fruit of Satan, the Evil One, and you are exposed to all the evil inventions and evil vices that the world has to offer; and all you have are *pseudomakariwv, (false blessings)*. So would you just think about the other way, and try the Good One, God? The way is simple, not complicated. Since you are being introduced to a King, a Deity of Royalty, take your hat, or your cap from off your head, "because every man praying or prophesying, having his head covered, dishonors His Head," ((I Corinthians 11:4) Christ Jesus being your Head. Even if you go before a heathen judge in a court of law, he orders every one to take their hat off. Next, Just look up and say, "Lord Jesus, you said to come unto you." (Matthew 11:28) Well, here I am with my hat in my hand, asking you to save me in the Name of Jesus. So Lord, what will you have me to do?" And believe the Lord will save you, and He, the Lord will save you; and He gave you an instruction book on salvation, so He will tell you what to do in the instruction book, (Bible). From that time on, if you meant what you said to the Lord, Christ Jesus, your life will be a continual war with Satan. But you just be steady in the traces, and do not look back; but just keep rebuking Satan and all his unclean spirits, in the Name of Jesus; and I will guarantee that the Lord Himself will be with you helping you until you overcome the Evil One in every battle, until the war is won by you and Christ Jesus. Amen. He will lead you and guide you by His Holy Spirit. As you read the bible, the Holy Spirit, which is the anointing, will make the Words in the Bible alive. So you do not need anyone to tell you what a scripture means. That is what is wrong with all the "Christians" and *church goers,* they had a justified, unsanctified preacher, or teacher, that will tell you the wrong meaning, because they got their meaning from the KJV or the Catholic Bibles, or from some commentary, or some false doctrine. But you get your teaching just like this writer did, from the horse's mouth, direct from the Teacher Himself, the Holy Spirit. (I John 2:26,27) Do not try to tune in Jesus by typing in Jesus. Com-Search, or sending Him an E-Mail, or Skype Him; but you call Him up by prayer; and He will answer you. "Call unto Me, and I will answer you, and show you great and mighty things, which you know not." (Jeremiah 33:3) (His Phone #). The way to build your faith is to bind the Devil, when you are in a situation that no man can help you; and you put your trust in Christ Jesus, either live or die, sink or swim; and when Christ Jesus delivers you and puts you back on dry ground, do not ever doubt Him again, because you are now into Christ Jesus; and "all of His promises are yea and amen." (II Corinthians 1:20) "Submit yourself to God, resist the Devil, and he will flee from you." (James 4:7)

Father God, in the Name of Your Only Begotten Son, Your Christ, Jesus, I pray for the ones that read **"Corn Shelling Time"**, and find an answer to their problems. The answer to any problem they have is to call on the Name of Christ Jesus. Father, I thank you for teaching me by your anointing, the Holy Spirit. I pray you will draw the readers of **"Corn Shelling Time"** to Christ Jesus, the One that has the answer for every problem, no matter if it is marital or drunkenness, suicide, dope, obesity, or any care or anxiety or worry of this life. Father cause them to trust Jesus for the promised answer, and Father I thank you for delivering me from all those above mentioned destruction, and thank you, Father, for satisfying my mouth with good things, and renewing my youth like the eagles, in the Name of Christ Jesus. Amen.

THIS is an insert in the book, **"CORN SHELLING TIME"** and **MICHAEL DUISHKA** with some of his belief. No matter where you are on God's earth, Satan is trying to murder you and your loved ones, and after he does kill, steal, or destroy one or more of your loved ones, you are so broken up that you have to lay the blame on to someone, and the first one you can think of is God. OH dear reader please listen to someone that has suffered more kinds of loss than anyone. There are a lot of people that would say to you, "I know what you are going through", and they do not know that your heart is being torn out of your body, because they have never been through what you are suffering. I want you to know that for double dog dead sure Mavis and Myself are having compassion for you and yours, and we are suffering with you. This is the truth and is no lie, I can truthfully say "I know what you are going through", because I do not believe there is any kind of loss that this old man has not suffered. You may say, how does that benefit me? Much, if you will listen and learn from someone that has been through any thing that you are suffering from. First of all God does not do any thing except GOOD. HE does not in no way, shape, form, or fashion take life from this earth, because He created all life, and HE gives life, and never, I say never does HE take back what HE has given. He is not an Indian giver. Even though He gets blamed from saddened people, suffering heart breaking loss. But please tell God you are sorry and let us learn what and who caused the problem. I have lost many flesh and blood children, which I know now after it is too late to save them, that it was Satan that comes to

Kill, Steal, and Destroy, but I have to shell the corn down, which means to confess. Satan could not take my loved ones lives if I had not sinned. Whenever I sinned I gave place to Satan, which I gave him the right to kill my precious little ones that CHRIST JESUS, GOD gave to me and though I was ignorant I gave Satan the right to kill my little loved ones. I will guarantee that Satan is laughing at my calamities and will never let up or have any compassion but is just waiting for the victim to give him place, or the legal right to kill, steal, or destroy God's Creation. But God had mercy and compassion and long suffering on me and taught me by the Holy Spirit of God what was the mystery of His will which is to overcome all the evil unclean spirits of Satan and to show the ones with broken hearts how Christ Jesus will come to them in the HOLY SPIRIT and heal their broken spirit just like He did for me. Not only did He heal my broken spirit (*heart*) but He set me free from the captivity of Satan, and taught me how to use His name to **say,** and bind and loose the unclean spirits by what is written in His WORD by using the promises He gave to the ones that belong to, and are INTO CHRIST JESUS. He made His loved ones this promise; **"I will not leave you comfortless, I will come to you".** (JOHN 14:18) If you ever read the book of JOB, you can see that is what happened to me. I confess I was not as strong as JOB. I lost faith and blasphemed God, I figured He would get revenge on me, but instead He just showed me more love than I could hold, until I broke so I fell upon the ROCK JESUS and was broken, I fell to my knees and shelled down the corn, (confessed how unclean I was and how I had sinned) I repented of my sins and THE LORD JESUS forgave me and now I know that I love Him and I keep His commandments. Like JOB I lost all my riches, which meant nothing to me. I was afflicted with deadly diseases, but I kept my faith in the promises He made me and through Christ Jesus I overcame the health problems. Seven times or more Satan has tried to take my life, but I remembered GOD told Satan, you cannot take JOB'S Life. He told Satan the same thing for you and me. AMEN

Chapter 19

THE REASON THIS COUNTRY boy is writing so much about the "Christians" and the *churches* is because of the staggering effect the ones that are supposed to be moral examples for Christ and His Holy Ones, has disillusioned the entire Body of Christ with their immorality and their deception of the naive decent people.

Just a short time ago, there were many people like myself that did not even know what the word *queer* or homosexual meant. Fornication was just a bad word for an act that was not supposed to be named, much less committed. Idolatry was thought of as some stone statue that people worshiped or cherished. But the more knowledge that is acquired about God's Laws and Commandments, the more wisdom one acquires about the effect that sodomy, fornication, and idolatry has upon the entire world. This country boy always thought that any wrong doing would have just punishment for only the one committing the sin. That is true, except when so many commit all those immoral acts, it not only causes the ones committing the acts to suffer diseases, sicknesses, plagues, and disasters; but it causes the entire earth to suffer disasters in this way.

I cannot use the politically correct word for homosexual, that the world uses, that would be a lie. Because they are not spunky, or vigorous people; but on the contrary, they are very unhappy, and dejected souls that are searching for the void of not knowing Christ Jesus, who fills all voids. That is the reason *queers* think "**Corn Shelling Time**" is using offensive words; when all along, they do not understand the meaning of words. "**Corn Shelling Time**" is only repeating God's Judgment on the ones that do such things, which He says is worthy of death. Not only do the homosexuals receive the plagues of AIDS, or other serious diseases; but they cause the population all around them to receive all kinds of disasters from God Almighty (PANTAKRATOR) for allowing the homosexuals to live in their community.

For an example, David the King sinned against God and numbered the people; and God caused a pestilence, a quickly spreading infectious disease, that killed 70,000 men in one day. David said: "What did these sheep *(children)* do? I was the one who sinned." So David "Shelled Down the Corn" to God, and God stayed the pestilence, because David confessed and repented.

If you are a *queer* person, or homosexual person or whatever you want to be called, God is calling you out loud to "Come Out of Mystery, Babylon", and confess your sins to God, and repent to Christ Jesus, which means quit being a homosexual, and go and sin no more, and God will forgive you just like He did the vilest sinner. Which was me, the author of this book.

If you think you were born with this sin nature, you are just like every one that is born with sin nature, the old man in you; "And that you put off concerning the former conversation, the old man, which is corrupt according to the deceitful lusts; and be renewed in the Spirit of your Mind." (Ephesians 4:22)

The example of David the King causing 70,000 people to die in one day, is what the churches and "Christians" are bringing upon the people all over the world, by not only committing homosexuality, fornication, idolatry, and greed; but they allow and have pleasure in those that do such things. That is why the doctor's offices are packed with infectious plagued people from 8:00 o'clock Monday morning until 5:00 o'clock Friday evening. All are claiming to be "Christians."

God's people are not sick, so they do not need a physician. They do not need to take any kind of drugs or medication, but only home remedies prescribed by Doctor Jesus. Amen.

Because the *Pope*, and the *churches*, and the governments are allowing homosexuals to marry each other is why natural disasters, such as whirlwinds, *(tornadoes)* tsunamis, earthquakes, death, famines, pestilences, diseases, wars, thefts, robberies, rapes and all kinds of plagues have come upon the people, destroying them. In 2011 the ObomaNation of Desolation started manifesting, causing birth pangs to come upon the whole world, which will keep escalating until the tribulation begins, which will affect the entire earth. The countries where the worst plagues will be in, will be the ones that have waxed cold toward God, lovers of themselves more than God.

I know real believers that have to congregate underground, and the only directions they have on where to go is the Holy Spirit. If the government informers *(snitches)* find out, they will betray them; and they will either be put in prison, or killed, or eventually both. But the Lord Jesus promised great is their reward. It is subtly becoming more manifest all over the world; and more so in America, because the *churches* conform to politically correct lies; and that is why the pure, Holy, sanctified, Holy Ghost filled believers have "Come Out of "Her", and are inconspicuously meeting with fellow believers, and God the Father, God the Son, and God the Holy Spirit.

"And I sought for a man among them that should make up the hedge, and stand in the gap before Me for the land, that I should not destroy it; but I found none. Therefore have I poured out Mine indignation upon them: I have consumed them with the fire of My wrath: Their own way have I recompensed upon their heads", saith the Lord God." (Ezekiel 22:30,31)

That is the reason Gabriel, the Messenger Angel of God, told Daniel to seal his book until now, which is getting close to the time of the end. A good many bible commentators and theologians have ignorantly deceived themselves, and the people that do not read for themselves, but just take the comments of someone else, into thinking the tribulation will be just for the nation of Israel. They could not be any more wrong, because the Word of God bears out that it will be from one end of the earth to the other end of the earth. Many commentators think that when the bible says: "All the world wondered after the beast" in Revelation 13:3, that that is a *synecdoche*, which is a term that says the whole world only means a part of the world. I believe it means what it says.

Pay attention: Listen: **"<u>Corn Shelling Time</u>"** is only reiterating Christ Jesus' Word. He is the one that made all these promises and penalties, and judgments. If you live in Europe, you are a subject of one of the 10 toes that are on the statue of the image the King Nebuchadnezzar dreamed of, and Daniel interpreted on this wise. All the image was smitten by a stone that was cut out without hands, which was the Rock Jesus. These 10 toes that were on the feet of the image were made of iron and clay, which represents a mingled people, which is not strong, but very weak. If you live in Europe, you have many things to overcome: One is the ten nations being formed in the future which will be ruled by the *Anti-Christ and the Roman Catholic Church,* which is part of "Her", which is Mystery, Babylon.

So you need to "Come Out of "Her" now. Until you come out of "Her", you share in the guiltiness of millions of slain Holy Ones that the Catholics caused to be martyrs for the Name of Christ Jesus. Because as long as you are joined to a Harlot, you are just as guilty as She is, by reason of association. If you need any more reason, there was the fact that She helped finance and gave "Her" support to Hitler, who murdered six million or more Jews, which She, the (*Catholic Church*) and (*the Pope*) at that time are just as guilty as Hitler, with all that innocent blood on their hands. So, if you live in Europe, you have been warned to Come Out of Mystery, Babylon before you share in "Her" plagues, that have already come in part upon you. Just go to Christ Jesus and "Shell Down the Corn" and confess and repent and let the Holy Spirit lead and guide you.

If you live in one of the Middle East Nations that are in Asia, or Asia Minor, and if you are a Muslim, you are guilty of denying Christ, the Messiah; and you are depending on Allah, or Mohammed to save you. There is no one that can give you salvation except the Christ, Messiah, called Jesus. "This is the stone which was set at naught of you builders, which is become the head of the corner. Neither is there salvation in any other, for there is none other name under heaven given among men, whereby we must be saved." (Acts 4:11,12)

"This is the same God that saves people the world over, which is called the Christ, the Son of the Living God." (Matthew 16:16) His Name is Jesus. The same one that was resurrected from the dead and is alive. Mohammed is dead. He cannot do anything for you; but Christ Jesus will save you if you will "Shell Down the Corn", and call on His Name. (confess you are a sinner)

If you live in Australia, you are living in Mystery, Babylon, because the majority of you belong to organized religion, with the biggest percent being Roman Catholic, and the next largest percent being Anglican, or the Church of England, and you have a membership of 80 million people with a leader that says there is no need of repentance when you are baptized in water. Where do you think your leader is leading you? Twenty percent of the people of Australia are of no religion at all, and they are closer to the Kingdom of God, than the Roman Catholics and the Anglican "Christians". There is very little difference between Roman Catholicism and the Church of England, (Anglican). They both have Holy blood on their hands.

To the Roman Catholics and the Anglicans, and any other church affiliated organization, you are a partaker of "Her" sins, and you will also be a receiver of the plagues that She has contracted, when She committed murders, robberies, and destruction of God's people. Your only hope is in Christ Jesus, and He said to "Come Out of "Her". (Revelation 18:4)

"Corn Shelling Time" is the official herald of God's last warning to "Come out from among them and be you separate, saith the Lord, and touch not the unclean thing, and I will receive you." (II Corinthians 6:17)

To all the ones in Australia that do not go to church, you are nigh the Kingdom of God. All you need to do is say "the word that is nigh you, even in your mouth, and in your heart, that is the Word of faith which we preach." (Romans 10:8) "That if you shall confess with your mouth the Lord Jesus, and shall believe in your heart that God has raised Him from the dead, you shall be saved. For with the heart man believes unto righteousness, and with the mouth confession is made unto salvation." (Romans 10:9,10) In other words, "Shell Down the Corn," (confess). You cannot go up any other way except though the door. **"Verily, verily, I am the door of the sheep."** (John 10:7)

To all the Muslims that believe in Allah. You are appeasing yourselves, because you think just like the "Christians" and Jews, which they all believe in God; but they do not believe Him. You Muslims believe God sent Gabriel to give Mohammed a revelation, and that is fine, except Mohammed did not tell you how to be saved, you must believe God, not believe in Him. If you would believe God, or Allah, you would do what God said for you to do. You believe in the prophets of God, such as Moses, Abraham, Zechariah, and even Jesus; but you do not believe what they all prophesied, because they all spoke of God sending a savior to earth to pay the debt you owe, on account of the condemnation that Adam put on all mankind, including all you Muslims, Jews, "Christians", and every human being that breathes the breath of life. You cannot just believe in God, or Allah, but it is imperative, necessary, mandatory, obligatory, that you believe God's Word. God, Allah, said that. This writer did not just make it up. "In the beginning was the Word. And the Word was with God. And the Word was God." (John 1:1) Mohammed failed to tell you the Truth about God. Some of you Muslims are good people, but everything that pertains to everlasting life, Mohammed failed to tell you, because God's Word said, "There is none that is good, except God." God's Word said that He would send you another Comforter, even the Spirit of Truth, which you Muslims, Jews, "Christians", pagans, and heathen do not have because the world cannot receive Him, because it sees Him not, neither knows Him not, because Mohammed and the Quran failed to tell you about Him; and without Him, (The Spirit of Truth), the Word of God says you will not enter into the Kingdom of heaven. So when you are praying to Allah, ask Him about the Spirit of Truth; and see if Allah will answer you, or see if the Quran will appease, satisfy you, or even answer you. Mohammed was a natural man, and the words that are in the Quran are all hearsay. Some of his friends say they heard Mohammed say he was talked to by Gabriel, the messenger from Allah, and that is rumor that his friends testified to. But give all that to the Quran, and it is still just some good words that supposedly came from God, Allah, to Mohammed, to his friends, to the writer of the Quran; but they do not contain the Word of the Spirit of Truth that God's Word said you could not receive, because you are natural and do not have the Holy Spirit, and neither can you receive Him; unless you do what **"Corn Shelling Time"** witnesses to you about; and that is "Shell Down the Corn" to Allah, (confess to Allah, God, that you are a sinner; and ask Jesus, the Christ, Messiah, to save you from eternal damnation.) If you say you believe God, or Allah, then this is what the Word of God says for you to do. Whether you are a Muslim, Jew, "Christian", heathen, pagan, unbeliever, atheist, agnostic, or any organized religion, and you cannot receive eternal life without doing this: Confess "I am a sinner, and I ask you God, Allah, to save me, and I believe you sent your Word, Jesus, to sacrifice His life, and shed His blood to pay the debt I owed, and I thank you for saving me. I believe you when you said by your Word that you are faithful and just to forgive me of my sins and cleanse me from all unrighteousness. I repent of all my sins, and I renounce the deceiving word of Satan, and ask you, God, to send me the Spirit of Truth, in the Name of Jesus. Amen."

Mohammed cannot send a comforter back to the Muslims. The Quran cannot bring the spirit of life to the Arabs. It does not matter if they are Sunni or Shia, they cannot receive the Holy Spirit, because they are natural flesh, and they do not believe that Jesus is the Christ of God. They do not believe that Jesus is the only begotten Son of God, and no one can enter into the Kingdom of God that is an unbeliever.

"Prove all things. Hold fast that which is good. Abstain from all appearance of evil, and the very God sanctify you wholly, and your whole Spirit and Soul and body be preserved blameless unto the coming of our Lord Christ Jesus." (I Thessalonians 5:21,22,23) "You cannot see the Lord without holiness." (Hebrews 12:14)

You cannot be holy without sanctification. You cannot be sanctified without the Holy Spirit. You cannot receive the Holy Spirit unless you are pure in heart, (which is Spirit). That is where "Christians" come short. They do not pursue the second work of faith, which is sanctification. They receive justification and stop seeking the Kingdom of God, thinking that justification is being set apart for God's use. Wrong! You just read I Thessalonians 5:23, where the Apostle prayed for you to be sanctified wholly, not just part of you, but wholly, which is Spirit, and Soul, and Body, which is the whole of a human. "Christians" are justified by faith. Believers are sanctified by God, which without sanctification you cannot receive a glorified body, spirit, soul. Sanctification is a pure heart, holiness, and baptized with the Holy Ghost.

"Jesus is the Word of God; and He said He was the Door; and if any man tried to go up except through the Door, he was a thief and a robber." (John 10:1) "Jesus said, "I Am the Way, the Truth, and the Life; and No Man can come to the Father, except through Me." (John 14:6) So you cannot get to God by Allah. You cannot come to God without using the Name of Jesus. The Jews have been praying to God for two thousand years without using the Name of Jesus, and God has not heard them, and will not ever hear them until they pray in the Name of Christ Jesus. **"Corn Shelling Time"** is reiterating the living Word of Almighty God, (PANTAKRATOR); and nothing shall enter into the Kingdom of heaven that is not pure, and holy, and sanctified.

Father God, in the Name of your only begotten Son, Christ Jesus, I pray for the Europeans that have the seat of Satan in the Great Whore that sits upon many waters, that has the name written upon "Her" forehead, Mystery, Babylon the Great, the Mother of Harlots, and abominations of the earth, that they would "Come Out of "Her"", and be Holy, Pure, and Sanctified. Also for the leaders of 80 million Anglicans that you would draw them to Christ Jesus, and they would do what He said to do. Repent! And "Shell Down the Corn", (confess Christ Jesus); and I pray for the so called "Christians" all over the world that they would come out and be separate, and touch not the unclean thing. I pray for the prisoners of the great Satan, America, the ObomaNation of Desolation, Lord that you would set the captives free from the yoke of tyranny of a tyrant government and cause subjects to take your yoke upon them, which your yoke is easy, and your burden is light. I pray Father for the Australians, that they would recognize that the plagues that have come upon them and the disasters that have come on their land is because of their transgressions against you; and they would repent, and "Shell Down the Corn" to you, (confess their sins); and the Lord Jesus would save them. Father, I pray for the misled Muslims, that they would know that there is no other Name except Christ Jesus, whereby men must be saved. Father, I pray for your chosen people, the Jews, that after two thousand years of praying in vain, that they would repent for killing their savior and pray in the Name of Jesus. I ask you for this in the Name of Jesus. Amen.

This is an insert in the book, **"CORN SHELLING TIME"** and **MICHAEL DUISHKA** with some of his belief. The life of the natural man is in the blood. The life of the flesh is in the blood. (Leviticus 17:1) The blood holds the physical body together until the body is dead. But there is a new life given to a very few of us, by the giver of this new life, who is Christ Jesus. The reason there only be a very few of us to receive this gift of new life, which is life forever, is because the majority of God's creatures love this present sinful life, which is temporal, very short, more than the Holy, new life which will never end. The "Christians" in all churches have been led astray (*seduced*) by the god of this world, AKA Satan, that has blinded their minds by **THE LIE,** the same lie he seduced eve with, which was, "you will not surely die". But God said you would. The biggest fallacy is the baptism in water, thinking that will save the sinner. The greater cult of this belief is the Baptist Church. Many of this division of the body of Christ think that just because they are submerged in water, that they are automatically baptized into the HOLY Spirit of CHRIST. (WRONG) In the 8th chapter of acts, Phillip baptized many in the name of Christ Jesus, including Simon Magus. Then Simon himself believed also: ACTS 8:13 When the Apostles heard they had heard the word they sent Peter and John down to lay hands on them and they received the HOLY GHOST, because HE had not fallen on them. So the old man, which is the sin nature that our Father Adam left every human, was not dead in Simon, he was not saved, much less baptized with the HOLY GHOST, which is synonymous with all the cult Churches. Knowing this that our old man is crucified with him, that the body of sin **MIGHT** be destroyed, that henceforth we should not serve sin.(Romans 6:6). Brother Paul used the words might, and should, which is the way it should be, but just because you are baptized, submerged, sprinkled, or any other way does not mean you are saved and not serve sin as all churches do. If millions of "Christians" were baptized in the HOLY SPIRIT like they profess or if they even possessed a measure of the HOLY SPIRIT like every "Christian" I ever talked to professed to have the HOLY SPIRIT, how is it that evil spirits are overcoming government rulers of this world? How come we believers do not have any help wrestling against the Powers of the air? How come all the millions of so called spirit filled "Christians" cannot agree with us believers to even put ten to flight, much less ten thousand? Every Church says they are in the body of CHRIST, but you know what they say is? Always a lie. The body of Christ is held together by the Holy Spirit. We of the body of CHRIST are baptized into one Spirit, which Spirit is the Spirit of Love, which is pure and HOLY, believing and saying the same thing. Believing and doing the ONE doctrine (TEACHING) of CHRIST. Now I beseech you brethren mark those which cause divisions and offenses contrary to the doctrine we have learned: And avoid them. (Romans 16:17). We believers have done what the WORD said, and we marked all Churches as divided and offensive because they vote for politicians that are anti-Christs. The Churches are all Apostate; Departed from the faith, giving heed to seducing spirits, teaching doctrine of devils, speaking lies in hypocrisy, worshipers of idols, such as Christmas trees, Santa Claus, Easter, witches, Halloween, Silence is assent to homosexuality, fornication, blacks marching, rioting, looting, killing, abortion, wars, capitol punishment,(Murder) teach your children in public schools which have heathen teachers, and councilors that subject your children to every kind of filth and abominable lawlessness of MY GOD, Then profess to be in the body of CHRIST, sanctified and Holy GHOST filled. OH ME, I trow not. Shell down the corn, confess to God, REPENT, BELIEVE, COME OUT OF HER.(REV. 18:4)

Chapter 20

"CORN SHELLING TIME" CANNOT get to the heart of the written Word until the misinterpretation of the KJV has been corrected to know the Truth, Truth being the correct Word of the Lord God, which was the Truth. The "Christians" have been misled for 400 years from 1611 A.D. to 2011 A.D. by the King James Bible, which is a derivative of the Latin Catholic Bible, which is Pagan Babylonian Idolatry; and the words are man made words and not God spoken inspired words. Learn how to pray!

"For the Lord has a controversy with the inhabitants of the land, because there is no Truth, nor mercy, nor knowledge in the land (*world wide*)." (Hosea 4:1)

"Woe unto them that call evil good, and good evil, that put darkness for light, and light for darkness, that put bitter for sweet, and sweet for bitter." (Isaiah 5:20)

"My people are destroyed for lack of knowledge. Because you have rejected knowledge, I will also reject you." (Hosea 4:6)

God called it lack of knowledge. Paul, the Apostle, called it ignorance. The reason this scripture is being repeated is to impress on the worldly intelligent, how ignorant they really are, when they cannot discern *(judge)* the difference in the most original Greek scriptures that our Lord spoke in, from the pagan heathen words of idolatry.

In (Revelation 1:1) the Word does not say, "The Revelation of Jesus Christ." The correct Word is "The Revelation of Christ Jesus. Christ is not Jesus' last name. Then the Word continues with; which God gave unto Him, to show unto His doulos *(slaves)*, not servants. Ask any black person if their ancestors were slaves or servants. There is a difference.

Then in (Revelation 1:4), the Word does not say:"John to the seven *churches*", which is another man made word. The true Word says: "John to the seven Ekklesia, which means to seven cities that have a meeting in each city of Called Out Ones, ones that have been called out of organized religion and have been called out loud to repent and believe Christ, not believe in Christ. The Muslims, Buddhists, "Christians", and devils all believe in Jesus Christ; but only sanctified, blood bought believers believe Christ Jesus. Believers have come out of the world and do not love the things that are in the world, because the love of God is in them. The believers are separate from unbelievers, unrighteousness, darkness, Belial, infidels, and idols. (II Corinthians 6:14,15,16,17) Believers are baptized into the Holy Spirit, not just say they have the Holy Spirit.

The seven cities that Christ Jesus sent His angel to His slave John to signify to, these seven cities are all in Asia, which were in the part of Asia that is now known as Turkey. These seven cities had congregations of different types of Called Out Ones that had been preached to by Paul and John, Apollos, and other Apostles; but they were just Called Out Ones, and only a few were chosen. These seven cities were evangelized by Apostles and teachers that were sent to the Called Out Ones to make witnesses for Christ Jesus to testify to the known world at that time. But some of the seeds fell by the wayside, some fell on stony places, and some fell among thorns; but some of the seed, which was the true Word of God, fell into good ground.

The seven cities had all different doctrines, just like the modern "Christians" in this present time that are being warned to come together and be one with the Lord Jesus, and not be divided, which the Angel of the Lord said were lost, except the ones (*seed*) that fell on good ground.

The Apostle, John, said: "They went out from us; but they were not of us; for if they had been of us, they would no doubt have continued with us; but they went out that they might be made manifest that they were not all of us." (I John 2:19)

So the Apostle, John, was talking to the Called Out Ones and about the Called Out Ones in the seven cities of Asia.

Paul told the elders of the Called Out Ones in the City of Ephesus: "For I know this, that after my departing, shall grievous wolves enter in among you, not sparing the flock. Also of your own selves shall men arise speaking perverse things to draw away disciples after them." (Acts 20:29,30)

After the apostles said these things, their words came to pass; and John was exiled from the part of Asia that had the seven cities; and the angel of Christ had John to write to the seven congregations in the seven cities warning them about their *backslidden* condition, except the city of Philadelphia and the called Out Ones in Smyrna.

The King James Bible calls these cities the seven *churches*. The word, *church*, was not created in those days; and the Greek language that believers spoke and our Lord Jesus spoke did not have any "C" or "CH", but only "X" and "K", so that is the reason so many "Christians" are misled and teaching doctrines of devils, no *church*. (I Timothy 4:1)

There are a lot of professors that try to interpret the parables of the bible; but they are only professors, not possessors; which is the mystery that the Angel of Christ Jesus is telling John to write to the angel that has been appointed over the seven different groups of Called Out Ones in the seven different cities of Asia.

Jesus told John and the other eleven disciples that it had been given to them to understand and know the mysteries of the Kingdom of heaven, which John was a possessor of the Kingdom and understood what he was writing to the seven angels of the Called Out Ones. John was remembering the mystery of the Kingdom of God that Jesus revealed to him of the sower of seed in the 13th Chapter of Matthew's gospel. It is the same warning to the seven congregations in Asia, that the seed, (the Word of God), had been sown in: Some fell on stony places, which they received it gladly for a while; yet they had not root in themselves; and the Word dureth for a while; for when tribulation or persecution arises because of the Word, by and by they were offended. Which means they stumbled and fell. When anyone hears the Word of the Kingdom, and understands it not, then comes the wicked one, and catches away that which was sown in his heart. This is what happened in Asia, and continued, and spread to every continent of the world, even up to this present time.

The cities of Philadelphia and Smyrna are examples of the seed falling into good ground and producing fruit, which is happening in every **believer** in the world, even in this present time. The Word of God is not just sown in different ages, or eras of time, and not just sown in churches, or synagogues; but Christ Jesus has a lot of believers sowing the Word of the Kingdom in every continent of the world, that would not enter into a Satanic Church.

Then there are a lot of God's people in those *harlot churches* that know something is not right; and they are either coming out of them; or they are not God's people, and cannot feel the pull of the Holy Spirit. Some of those people have their conscience seared with a hot iron. "Departing from the Faith, giving heed to seducing spirits, and doctrines of devils, speaking lies in hypocrisy, having their conscience seared with a hot iron." (I Timothy 4:1) This was the example of the ones in Asia in Revelation Chapters 2 and 3 (two and three).

Those people that have their conscience seared with doctrines of devils, that are joined to one of those *harlot churches,* that call themselves "Christians", no matter which part of the world you are in, can do what Jesus said to do; and that is to repent, and come out of "Her", and come to Jesus for refreshing of safety.

"Corn Shelling Time" is just a reminder to do what Christ Jesus said to do; and that is to repent, and confess, and possess the Kingdom of God; instead of professing to be a believer, and not doing what He said, "And why call you Me, Lord, Lord, and do not the things which I say?" (Luke 6:46)

The entire bible is the Mystery of God Almighty (PANTAKRATOR), pleading with you to come out of Mystery Babylon, and come to the Marriage Supper of the Lamb.

Signs are being put up in front yards, and right of ways, and easements, and on signboards, and anywhere people will give permission to put up a sign that says, *"Come to Church",* or *"Go to Church on Sunday".* The churches are proselyting many new converts to their doctrines. **"Woe unto you scribes and pharisees, hypocrites! For you compass sea and land to make one proselyte; and when he is made, you make him twofold more the child of hell than yourselves."** (Matthew 23:15) The signs never say or read, "Come to Jesus". If they, the "Christians" ever use the word, "Christ", or "Jesus", they look around to see if the devil hears them whisper that name. The same way with the blood of Jesus. It is not confessed anymore; and that is the only way your sins can be blotted out, is by "the blood of Jesus, and your testimony of the Word." (Revelation 12:11)

One doctrine of devils is: It used to be a sin to profane the sabbath day, which is the seventh day of the week, AKA *Saturday.* It still is a sin to profane the Sabbath; but Satan told man it was O.K. For him to choose any day of the week for the Sabbath. So most "Christians" chose the man made first day of the week, which is the day of the pagan god *Sunday*. Now it is a doctrine of the devil to disobey God and obey man and the devils. It used to be a sacred day called "Passover". Now it is a doctrine of devils called *"Easter"*. It used to be a law of the land to not celebrate *"Christ-mass"*. Now it has become another doctrine of devils. It used to be an abomination to be a Sodomite *(Queer)*. Now they get married in the ObomaNation of Desolation of America, "the habitation of devils, and the hold of every foul spirit, and a cage of every unclean and hateful bird, *(blackbirds and crows)*, and by "Her" sorceries all nations were deceived." (Revelation 18:2-23)

In God's judgment, it is still an abomination for a man to lie with man, but that is just another doctrine of devils. Even the *Pope,* the one that usurps the power of Christ, condones homosexuality, because there are so many of his priests that are *queers* and pedophiles, which is still yet doctrines of devils.

One of the biggest doctrines of devils is hiding and covering up possession of unclean spirits, calling them by a name of a medical disorder, or a psychiatric disorder, or a neurological disorder. There was a man that brought his son to Jesus that had the symptoms of *epilepsy*; but Jesus cast the devil out of the boy. The bible called the boy a lunatic, when that is what the rulers of the world governments should be called, is lunatics, which means they are moonstruck. But Jesus just rebuked the devil and he departed out of him. (Matthew 17:18)

That is the way God cured neurological disorders, but it is not politically correct to cast out devils anymore, that is why *churches* are full of devils and dope heads. Now they go to doctors to get dope to soothe the devils, and then go to *church* to try to cover up their sin. Another neurological disorder is ADHD *(Attention Deficit Hyper-activity Disorder),* which is a psychiatric disorder that they give dope to little children that they call medication that gives that child a disorder for the rest of his or her life, addiction to drugs. That is just another kind of demon. I just told you how Jesus cured the disorder. Now let **"Corn Shelling Time"** tell you a tested, and tried, sure fire remedy for ADHD. My daddy used a method called S.P.A., which is Seize, Possess, Afflict. Daddy would go get the double razor strop off the nail, and **S**eize me with his left hand, and **P**ossess the razor strop in his right hand, and **A**fflict my butt till the ADHD was eradicated. Another remedy my daddy used for multiple disorders was called hickory tea. My daddy would have us kids working with him in the woods or a field nearby the woods; and he would warn me and rebuke me one time for one of my attention disorders; and if I thought he was not looking, and I did it again, dad would put down his tool, and go over to a hickory tree, and break off a keen limb, and come back to me, and use S.P.A., (**S**eize me, and **P**ossess the hickory switch, and **A**fflict my bottom) until the disorder was gone. Sometimes we would be in a cotton patch picking cotton, or pulling bolls, when we required some attention; and dad would go pull up a cotton stalk, strip off the leaves, and the small branches, and tell us we needed some hickory tea, which he called any kind of S.P.A., (Seize, Possess, Afflict) hickory tea. Then he would wear me out with the cotton stalk. But this is exactly what the problem with the world is today, is because fools spared the rod and spoiled the child, and turned out a world full of criminals; and some of you have not been caught yet.

"Corn Shelling Time" is telling you that God sees everything you do, and He is not mocked. "For whatsoever a man sows, that shall he reap." (Galatians 6:7) Just "Shell Down the Corn" to God, (confess). God gave a child to a man for a possession to be corrected and raised up in the way the child should go. But man let the devil enter in and usurp authority over the authority God gave the man to correct his child anyway he chooses. My daddy chose his way, which happened to be God's way, which would have conflicted with the heathen devil filled laws of the land that are appointing any unqualified heathen to judge God's people; and the lawyers, which make the laws, always make the law for themselves to make *mammon;* and it always disobeys God's law. "Apply your heart unto instruction and your ears to words of knowledge. Withhold not correction from the child; for if you beat him with the rod, he shall not die. You shall beat him with the rod, and shall deliver his soul from Hell." (Proverbs 23:12,13,14)

All these words are wisdom God is giving mankind; but the ignorant heathen judges are sold out to Satan and the kingdoms of this world for the glory of the kingdoms of this world, and have made a covenant with death and Hell.

"Because you have said we have made a covenant with death, and with Hell are we at agreement, when the overflowing scourge shall pass through, it shall not come unto us, for we have made lies our refuge, and under falsehood have we hid ourselves." (Isaiah 28:15)

The heathen judges would have sent my daddy to the penitentiary for child abuse, and turned us kids over to some foster pervert to rape us or sexually abuse us, and pay the foster pervert for doing it. Thank you, Father God in the Name of Jesus for my daddy and S.P.A. Amen and Amen. Our forefathers set up the rules and regulations to agree with the law of God Almighty (PANTAKRATOR); and the heathen judges twisted the Constitution to fit the Anti-Christs, and escalate the destruction of God's people and God's earth. The only hope for God's people is to carefully read **"Corn Shelling Time"** to know the Truth, and to come unto Jesus, and read (I John 2:26,27), and let the anointing (Holy Ghost) teach you how to possess instead of just professing. He (the Holy Spirit) will teach you how to overcome the world and the things that are idolatry and whosoever loves idolatry and makes a lie. (Revelation 22:15) God sent **"Corn Shelling Time"** to the world to get the children that are in darkness and profess to be in light to read the Truth for themselves and repent and "Shell Down the Corn" (confess) to Jesus and let Jesus shine His light on you, because Jesus is light. It does not matter what part of the world you are in. It is imperative that **"Corn Shelling Time"** preach what the three angels are going to preach to the whole world. "To every nation, kindred, and tongue and people; Fear God and give glory to Him, for the hour of His judgment is come, and worship Him that made heaven and earth, and the sea, and the fountains of waters." (Revelation 14:7)

You, dear reader, do not have to wait for the angel to tell you to fear God, give God glory, and worship Him. You can come to Him now. Just confess to God that you are sorry for your sins; and would He please forgive you in the Name of Jesus; and He will save you from the enemy, which is the ruler of this world, which is Satan, the Devil, the Dragon. Do you believe that? You must believe Him.

Father God, the one in heaven, the one that created the heavens and the earth, and the sea, and all the things that are in them, I humbly come before you on your throne of Grace, in the Name of Christ Jesus; and I am "Shelling Down the Corn" to you, and that is confessing to you that I have sinned; and not only do I confess, but I confess that all your people have sinned all over the earth; and we, the people, did not listen to you, or your Son, or your Holy Spirit, or listen to your servants the prophets, or even to your written Word; but Merciful Father in the Name of Christ Jesus will you forgive us, because we are too ignorant to listen to your Word and to come unto Jesus, and learn of you.

I pray for all the Japhethites that are in Russia and Germany, and in all the Continent of Europe, and my brothers the Japhethites all over the world that they would comply with their role to enlarge themselves and dwell in the tents of Shem. (Genesis 9:27). Because, Lord God, Noah said you would do that; and not only do I pray for all my brothers the Japhethites, but also for my brothers the Shemites that Noah said, "You would bless them and cause us to dwell in his tents." (Genesis 9:27) Father, I agree with Noah that you will bless all the Japhethites and the Shemites; but I cannot pray for Ham and his son Canaan, because Ham sinned a bad sin, and Canaan received a curse from you, and I cannot pray against you and your Word. But, Father, I pray for all the descendents of Japheth and Shem that they would come out of Mystery, Babylon and be not a partaker of "Her" sins, and that they will get the opportunity to read **"Corn Shelling Time"**, and repent from their murders and their sorceries, fornication, and thefts. Father, I pray for my Japhethite brother, Vladimir Putin; and Father, I ask you to bless brother Putin, because he helped another brother, Edward Snow den, who was persecuted by the President and leaders of his native country, and by America, the ObomaNation of Desolation. I thank you, Father, in the Name of Christ Jesus, for brothers like Vladimir Putin, and Edward Snowden, and I pray they will get to read **"Corn Shelling Time"** and do like their ancestors, Noah and Japheth, and Shem, and trust in Christ Jesus, who was your Word, who was God. (John 1:1) And, Father, save them and not only them, Lord, but every Japhethite and Shemite that reads **"Corn Shelling Time"**.

Lord, I shell down the corn and confess that we have sinned, and we have committe**d** iniquity, and we have rebelled, and we have done wickedly by departing from your precepts and from your judgments, and confusion *(Babylon)* belongs to us; and that is why, Father, I depend on you, and trust in Christ Jesus to sow this Word, **"Corn Shelling Time",** in every nation and kingdom and tongue of the earth.

I pray for all the leaders of all countries to take the blinders off their minds and pray to you, Father, to give them the power to overcome the spirits of the wicked one, and receiv**e** the Spirit of Christ Jesus **to** teach them, and lead them, and guide them to peace.

I ask all this, believing you, Christ Jesus, have anointed **"Corn Shelling Time".** Amen!

"There is a sin unto death. I do not say that he shall pray for it." (I John 5:16) Brother, John, did not say what the sin unto death was, but **"Corn Shelling Time"** will expound on the sin unto death.

"Wherefore, I say unto you, all manner of sin and blasphemy shall be forgiven unto men; but the blasphemy against the Holy Ghost, it shall not be forgiven him, neither in this age *(world)*, neither in the *world* (age) to come." (Matthew 12:31,32)

So, if a man sins a sin unto death, there is only one sin that will never be forgiven, and that is called the unforgivable sin, which is blasphemy against the Holy Ghost. The Greek word for Ghost is Pneuma, which is the same word for spirit. So to clarify the meaning of Holy Ghost and Holy Spirit, they have the same meaning. So, blasphemy means attributing anything done by the Holy Spirit to the Spirit of Satan. For example, just before Jesus told about blaspheming the Holy Ghost in (Matthew 12:24), the Pharisees heard it. They said: "This fellow does not cast out devils, but *(except)* by Beelzebub, the Prince of the Devils." Which is blasphemy of the Holy Ghost, which is the unforgivable, or unpardonable sin. (Matthew 12:24)

So, as has been referenced before in (Hebrews 6:4-9). It is plainly discerned that "Christians" have not been partakers in the Holy Spirit *(Ghost)*, or they would be pure, Holy, and led into Truth. "He that believes on Him is not condemned; but he that believes not is condemned already, because he has not believed in the Name of the only begotten Son of God." (John 3:18)

So, that is the unpardonable sin: "Not believing Christ Jesus". To shorten it down, "Unbelief". It makes no difference what race or kindred, or tongue, you are of, you can be assured that you will inherit the Kingdom of God and heaven if you believe Christ Jesus. Even the Hamites and the Canaanites that have been cursed can be redeemed from the curse if you believe Christ Jesus, and "Shell Down The Corn", which is to confess your sins to God Almighty (PANTAKRATOR), and believe Christ Jesus will save you.

"Corn Shelling Time" is going to make every effort to reveal the Mystery of God to the whole world; and whosoever believes can renounce the curse that Satan put on man. The black race, which are descendants of Ham, Noah's youngest son, which sinned a sin unto death; and his son, Canaan, was cursed and all his descendents from that time until the end of this age. They were sold into slavery by their own race; and they are racist, because they use their misfortune to blame the white race for their own curse that God put on them. As a result of the hate that Satan has filled their heart (spirit) with, they think they have the right to steal, kill, and destroy the country that gave them a place to live and prosper, at the expense of the white race. This generation of white people had no part in their ancestors selling them into slavery over a century ago. This country boy does not owe anything to anyone, except my love; and I love the spirit of every race, kindred, tongue, and people, including the blacks. I do not condone the sins and the acts of the blacks that yell discrimination every time they get caught stealing, murdering, or destroying God's people and God's earth. Then when one of them gets killed for his evil act, the other loud mouthed ones yell racism and discrimination. They do not seem to know that the white people were created by God, and God gave life to every human being, and they do not have the right to take a life that does not belong to them. The prisons are more a percentage of blacks than all other races; and the blacks say they are there because of discrimination. They yell, they want justice; and little do they know that at the Great White Throne of Judgment, they will get justice.

The blacks are blessed above all people of all races, because they have been given all the things that pertain to life without working for it. Through the past years, the government has spent billions, and billions, of taxpayers' money to build them a free place to live in houses and apartments; and they just destroy the millions of houses and apartments, and the government just rebuilds and gives the blacks free access to live there until they destroy them again, and again, and again.

The government never gave this white boy anything. Then the government passed a law that it was mandatory to put so many blacks in a position of work that they were not qualified to have that position, except they were black. Then when that company folded and went belly up, because they had unqualified personnel to do the work, the unemployed blacks laid around drawing unemployment benefits and using the money to do vice and criminal activity, while their girlfriend was having illegitimate babies drawing welfare checks and food stamps to feed them. This is all documented in the history of these *NewNited States of America*.

Then, whenever you catch one of them stealing or destroying your property and call the police, the police threaten to arrest you for being a racist. The police have beat this white boy unmercifully several times, and there is no way a lawyer will sue the city, state, or federal government for beating me; but let a black man get beat by the police, and he gets thousands of dollars for police brutality.

And the story gets worse and worse; but this is what **"Corn Shelling Time"** believes. I believe the black president of these NewNited States of America is the most unqualified person for that job that was given that position. The proof is in the pudding, if you will just try to find one good thing he has done for this country. I believe he has given the country away to his race, and the stimulus money to the rich ones that helped get him elected to a position that I believe the most uneducated farm boy in America would be more qualified to run this country than him. Just look at the trillions of dollars he has put the country into debt, just to flatter his supporters. "And in his estate shall stand up a vile person to whom they shall not give the honor of the kingdom, but he shall come in peaceably and obtain the kingdom by flattery." (Daniel 11:21) America, the ObomaNation of Desolation.

Father God, in the Name of Jesus, I pray for your believers that they will "Come out of Mystery, Babylon," which is the *Catholic Church*, as the Mother, and all the *churches*, which are the harlots, and daughters of the Mother, and the governments of the world, and the world itself. I pray that every one in the world that reads **"Corn Shelling Time"** will apply himself to read (I John 2:26,27) in the bible for himself, and come out of every fornication, idolatry, and theft in the world. I pray for the ones that have not committed the unpardonable sin, which is unbelief, that they will start believing Christ Jesus. He said; "Whose end shall be according to their works." (II Corinthians 11:15); and Father, I ask you to keep the believers in your protection, and deliver every believer from the hour of temptation. Amen.

THIS is an insert in the book, **"CORN SHELLING TIME"** and **MICHAEL DUISHKA** with some of his belief. For there is no power but of God: the powers that be, are ordained of God. (Romans 13:1). It goes against my grain to be a subject to an evil power that kills, steals, and destroys, my brothers, and my people, even though I must be obedient to my master, Christ Jesus, who is God. The only consolation a believer has is that he has put his trust in Christ Jesus. Knowing this that God's ways are above my ways, and His ways are past finding out. So I will subject myself to the office and the place the power comes from. We, believers know that God raises up evil rulers for His different purposes, like HE told pharaoh ; And in very deed for this *cause* have I raised you up, for to show *in* you my power: And that my name may be declared through out all the earth. (Exodus 9:16). We, believers, also know that God also puts down rulers. God raised Nebuchadnezzar up for the purpose to take His people, Judah, into captivity for Seventy years. In my opinion, since DUISHKA is not an Apostle, Prophet, or Seer, that He raised Oboma up to destroy the land of beauty, the land flowing with milk and honey. All this country boy can see is all the freedoms that I have enjoyed in my four score plus times he has destroyed. But God ordained him to that power to show God's power in him. In my opinion he has destroyed the beauty of hard work to achieve promotions, but rather give the goals of hard work and skillful mechanical technology to his people that are not qualified with knowledge to do the job because of their race. **"CORN SHELLING TIME"** believes God is pleading to His people to come out of her, (MYSTERY, BABYLON) before they are destroyed by the destroyer. All the lands from sea to sea is filled with filth and corruption, and the literal BABYLON, *NEW UNITED STATES* is the leader of all ABOMINATIONS of the world. It is just a short time till terrorist find a way to infiltrate the divided country. Obama has let the Muslim, and Mexican immigrants set up their workshop to take it on down to destruction. Just like Noah told the people it was going to rain, they were deaf and did not believe him, until they missed the boat and were destroyed. Just like LOT tried to get his sons in law to come out of Sodom and Gomorrah before the cities were destroyed with fire and brimstone and they would not. The Angels took LOT, his Wife, and two daughters by the hand and led them to safety. But it is not likely that an Angel will lead you out of BABYLON before it is destroyed the same way, with fire and brimstone. (Nuclear Bomb). Just like Isaiah, and Jeremiah warned Judah that BABYLON was going to carry them away, and they did not believe the Men of God until the king had to watch his sons eyes get pulled out, then they, the BABYLONIANS killed him. DUISHKA is not prophesying, just iterating God, He is the one begging you to come out of her, my people, that you be not partakers of her sins, that you receive not of her plagues. (Revelation 18:4) The reason the gate and way to eternal life is strait and narrow, and few there be that enter in, is simply because of unbelief. So called "Christians" say they are believers, but when it comes down to where the rubber meets the road, they fail miserably. They straddle the fence and obey the laws of the land,while saying they are obeying God, and use the 13th chapter of Romans to **_try_** to justify their sin. Brother Peter said; should we obey God or man? Brother James lost his head to the guillotine by obeying God instead of the man made law. The Apostles,Disciples, Believers, all got killed for not obeying man made law. It is a paradox to say you obey man and God, it is impossible. **No man can serve two Masters;for either he will hate the one, and love the other; or else he will hold to the one and despise the other. You cannot serve God and Mammon.** (Matthew 6:24) Which gate will you enter, destruction or Life?

Chapter 21

As **"CORN SHELLING TIME"** continues with the opening up of Daniel's sealed book, the Lord Jesus is opening the seals of not only Daniel's book but also the book that was taken from the hand of Him that sat on the Throne. The Lamb, (Jesus), was the only one that was found, that was worthy, to open the book, because it was Holy, and Jesus, (The Lamb), that was slain and by His blood has redeemed some of us out of every kindred, and tongue, and people, and nation. He was Holy and therefore worthy to open the Holy book that had seven seals that had the book sealed. Daniel's book had been incorporated into this book that had the seven seals, and also events that all the former prophets had prophesied would occur.

"Corn Shelling Time" has reiterated in previous chapters about the four horsemen and the four horses they rode when the Lamb opened the first four seals, and also when the Lamb opened the other three seals, which was the Menu of the whole book; but now we will look at the contents that are in the Menu. There are plagues that will come specifically to Daniel's people, the Israelites, the Jews, and the converted Gentiles, which are spiritual Jews, that have been grafted into the Olive Tree. These Believers know, and God knows who they are. They are not "Christians", they are Believers.

The contents of the book with the seven seals that are broken are also revealing in the Mystery of God the plagues that will come upon the whole Gentile world. These plagues have already started and will escalate in extent, volume, number, intensity, and scope, until iniquity is destroyed.

Daniel wrote in his book what the angel Gabriel told him: "That the last of the seventy weeks that had been determined upon Daniel's people would finish the transgression and make an end of sins and to make reconciliation for iniquity and to bring in everlasting righteousness, and to seal up the vision and prophecy and to anoint the Most Holy." (Daniel 9:24)

In the last week of the seventy weeks, which is the last seven years of this age that we are almost in at this present time, this game is for keeps. This is for all the marbles. When I was a young kid, some of the sissy kids would cry and want their marbles back after some other kid had won them. So the rules were; A game of marbles was for keeps, and the winner took all the other kids marbles home.

So Daniel's book is being opened as the Lamb is opening the seven seals of the book that was taken out of the One's Hand that sat on the Throne.

The beginning of sorrows became more frequent and more fervent. I believe the sorrows will intensify until 2018, when they will turn into the last plagues to come upon the earth. The last plagues being the fall of Mystery, Babylon. **"Corn Shelling Time"** is revealing what Christ Jesus revealed to brother John. The revelation of Babylon and Mystery, Babylon is the culmination of the sins of the entire world, which includes all organized religion, all world governments, and all people that love the world and all the idols of the world, which are the things of the world. First is the organized religion, which commits fornication, which is revealed as spiritual adultery, or fornication against God, with not only the kings of the earth, but also caused the people who are in organized religion to commit spiritual adultery and fornication against God Almighty, (PANTAKRATOR).

"And there came one of the seven angels, which had the seven vials, and talked with me, saying to me, Come here, I will show unto you the judgment of the Great Whore that sits upon many waters, with whom the kings of the earth have committed fornication, and the inhabitants of the earth have been made drunk with the wine of "Her" fornication." (Revelation 17:1,2)

The words, many waters, refers to many branches of organizations that are false religions called churches, synagogues, temples, mosques, and any other place of religion. The fornication that She causes the inhabitants of the earth, and the rulers of world governments to commit with "Her" is the worship of idols, called idolatry. The spiritual fornication, which includes literal fornication, is not only committed by the Great Whore Herself, but She is influential to the whole world by "Her" beauty and riches to commit abominations. The head, *(Pope)*, of the Great Whore, the Mother of Harlots, condones adultery, fornication, *(men lying with men)*, called homosexuality, which is called *queers*, and all kinds of idolatry, which is all filth and abomination. Not only does the Mother Whore, which is the Roman Catholic Church, commit sins by worship of *images, the cross, Christmas, Easter, Saints, necromancy (worship and talking to the dead) like the Virgin Mary, or the ones supposed to be in purgatory,* and many, many, other rituals; but She is influential in all the Harlots, the branches AKA the Daughters of the Mother Whore to commit the same abominations of mixed religion with paganism, called heathenism, AKA "Christians"

The *churches* claim to be the Bride of Christ; but it is impossible for the Lamb to be married to a Whore. The churches say: "The Good man of the house is not at home. He is gone, (Christ Jesus), on a long journey. Come, let us take our fill of love. I have peace offerings with me. I have paid my vows." (Proverbs 7:19) "And behold there he met a woman with the attire of a Harlot, and the woman *(church)* was arrayed in purple and scarlet color, and decked with gold and precious stones and pearls, having a golden cup in Her hand full of abominations and filthiness of Her fornication." (Revelation 17:4)

GOLDEN CUP OF ABOMINATIONS

Christmas – Easter – Sunday – Saints – Necromancy – Cross – Church – Images – Icons – Pictures of Mary or Jesus – Theatrical Shows – Murders - House of Thieves – Adulterers – Queers – Homosexuals – Lizzies – Witches – Wizards – and every kind of Idolatry – Celebrity Worship – New agers – Fornicators – Proselytes converted to doctrines of devils that are twofold more a child of Hell than the *Church.*

The *church* is the woman saying "Come in to me, because the Good Man of the house is gone on a long journey"; but the Good Man, (Christ Jesus), is saying: "Come out of "Her", My people, that you be not partakers of "Her" sins, and that you receive not of "Her" plagues." (Revelation 18:4), of which you are already receiving of "Her" plagues: Sickness of all kinds, diseases of all kinds, aids, cancer (a malignant tumor), diabetes, dropsy, palsy, arthritis, *(that big democrat from Dallas)*, Parkinson's Disease, Alzheimer's Disease, gall stones, kidney stones, osteoporosis, obesity, (which causes many other infirmities), itch, and many, many diseases that cannot be diagnosed. Plus the plagues of insects, lice, fleas, mosquitoes, ticks, parasites, *(some DHS recipients)*, all kinds of disasters, such as tsunamis, tornadoes, cyclones, earthquakes, volcanoes, floods, famines, wild beasts, snakes, politicians, dogs, crocodiles, rabid animals, rats, skunks, *(politicians)*, and many other plagues too numerous to mention, all because you disobeyed the Commandments of God, and did not come out of Mystery, Babylon, the world, and the things that belong to Satan, churches *(organized religion)*, governments, *(laws of the land)*, worship of Idols, and any sinful act of fornication or blasphemy of any Holy One.

"Corn Shelling Time" is reminding you that none of these plagues will come on God's people; and if you just now learned that your sins

Michael Duishka

caused these plagues to come on you, the remedy to heal you of these diseases and sicknesses, and disasters, is very simple. Do what I did to my daddy and to God. Cry out to Jesus and "Shell Down the Corn", (confess that you sinned, and you are sorry, and you repent, and do like Peter did when he was sinking, which was say, "Lord Jesus, Will you save me." Jesus cannot lie, and He said He would do anything you ask in His Name. So, if you come to Him with a broken heart and a contrite spirit, He will save you if you believe Him. Every heathen and Devil believes in Jesus; but that will not feed the bull-dog. You must **believe Him.** "Jesus told the rich young ruler to keep the Commandments of God and follow Him". (Matthew 19:21) Maybe your false teacher has told you the Commandments of God have been done away with. That is just not so. He or she has added plagues to themselves by false teaching. The Commandments of God are from everlasting to everlasting. Because I keep the ordinances of God is the reason I do not have any of the plagues mentioned above. I do not have Obama Insurance, and I never will. I do not need a physician, because I am never sick. I do not eat any kind of animal that does not have a split hoof and chew a cud. I do not eat any kind of fish that does not have scales and fins. No catfish, because they are scavengers. I do not eat any fat, because God said give the fat to Him. I do not eat any sweets excessively. I do not eat grease, only food cooked with Olive Oil. I eat what John the Baptizer ate, wild honey. I eat what Daniel ate, pulse, (vegetables). I eat bread like Ezekiel made. I eat raisins like King David ate. I eat birds like Moses said that are not webfooted and have a craw. I drink water that is boiled and purified. I work every day except the seventh day, which is the sabbath, which I keep Holy. By faith in the grace of God, I am saved, and I love Jesus, and I keep His Commandments. (John 14:15) I told you all these things about me, in order to praise God and give Him glory, because He is the source of my health and my soul's prosperity. I cannot do anything of myself, but it is all done by Christ Jesus that dwells in me, and He is no respecter of persons, He will do the same for you. If you would quit eating swine flesh, and all manner of sweets, such as candy, cake, pies, sweet rolls, chocolate, sugar, soft drinks, catfish, oysters, shrimp, eels and snakes, and any kind of unclean fish, bird, fowl, or animal. Give up T.V., computers, sports, Hollywood, laws against God's people, police, politics, governments, voting, stealing, killing, and destroying. That is just some of the things a blessed person does not participate in. I do not believe two wrongs make a right. I believe God is the One that had mercy on me, instead of justice. If I had received justice, I would be in Hell.

All these Commandments and many many more are all written for your good. If you believed Jesus, you would do them and have life and life more abundantly. All this life more abundantly is a gift of Christ Jesus; and I do not brag, *(boast)*, anything of myself; but I give all the praise and glory to God through Christ Jesus, who is God! Thank you, Jesus.

This Mystery of Iniquity, being the organized religion of the world, that professes to be married to Christ Jesus, or God, but commits fornication with the world and Satan, and receives all the glories of the Kingdoms of the World that Satan gives them for their soul. When you receive the gifts of the devil, which are the things of this world, you are committing spiritual fornication against God. But this just covers part of the Mystery, Babylon, which is the religion of the whole world, that has it's head, *(the Pope)* in the Mother of Harlots, which is the Mother, *Roman Catholic Church,* with headquarters in Rome. Their creed and doctrines come from their pagan bible and their pagan gods, which are the filth and abominations of the earth. All the Harlots are the branches that have sprung up over the world that have been influenced by the Mother to commit whoredom and fornication by worshiping idols and false gods. No matter what they call themselves, if it be protestant, "Christian", *church,* reformation, or any other name, they are still Harlots. They worship idolatry, *church, Sunday, Easter, Christmas, Saints,* and many, many other things that are idolatry, which classifies them as Harlots. Their English Bible is only a sequel of the false Catholic Bible, which has the readers thinking it is the Word of God. That is exactly what Satan wanted them to believe, and he started his lies in the Garden and also with the attempt to deceive Jesus with his lies. He could not seduce Jesus, but he has succeeded in causing many to believe The Lie and be damned. (II Thessalonians 2:12)

"And for this cause God shall send them strong delusions, that they should believe THE Lie that they might be damned, who believe not the Truth, (Jesus), but had pleasure in unrighteousness." (II Thessalonians 2:11,12)

All the English and Latin translations of the Greek Scriptures have enough Truth to deceive many, but Satan caused the interpreters to put lies and false words that would fool the very elect, if it were possible. (Matthew 24:24) The very elect are the Chosen Ones. The Chosen Ones are the believers that possess the Holy Spirit of Christ Jesus, the ones that are consecrated to God and sanctified, pure, and Holy. The ones that are chosen are the ones that have "Shelled Down the Corn", (Confessed) their sins to Christ Jesus and had His blood applied to their hearts, and keep His Commandments. They are the ones that are not unequally yoked to Harlot Churches and to other false religions, and gods of this world, and have "Come out from among them and be you separate, says the Lord, and touch not the unclean thing, and I will receive you."(II Corinthians 6:17) **"Come unto Me"** (Christ Jesus) (Matthew 11:28) **"Corn Shelling Time"** has warned you about the organized religion of the Whore and "Her" Harlot Daughters.

"John answered and said, a man can receive nothing, except it be given him from heaven." (John 3:27). This John is John the baptizer.

Mystery, Babylon includes three parts, the religion, the literal, and the world Satan led system. The religious system including all religions will be done away with for the one world worship order, which will be the image of the Beast. (Revelation 13:14)

The Mother of Harlots, which is the Whore, will be destroyed by the ten horns, which are ten kings that have given themselves to the Beast. "And the ten horns which you saw upon the Beast, these shall hate the Whore, and shall make "Her" desolate and naked, and shall eat "Her" flesh, and burn "Her" with fire." (Revelation 17:16) This includes all churches, which are Harlots, because by the time the Beast comes, all the *protestant churches* will have went back to their Mother, the universal Whore. This is where the wise ones that have come out of "Her" shall shine. "And they that be wise shall shine as the brightness of the firmament, and they that turn many to righteousness as the stars forever and ever." (Daniel 12:3)

This will be the separation time of the believers from the "Christians", separating the sanctified ones from the justified ones; dividing the professors from the possessors, separating the Holy Ones from the "Saints". Dividing the Ekklesia from the *churches*.

"And it was given unto him, (the Beast), to make war with the Holy Ones (*Not Saints*), and to overcome them, and power was given him over all kindreds and tongues, and nations; and all that dwell upon the earth shall worship him, whose names are not written in the Book of Life of the Lamb slain from the foundation of the world." (Revelation 13:7,8) "If any man have an ear, let him hear." (Revelation 13:9) Pay attention!

This will be the time when the hireling preachers will cut a *chogie* and run and leave the sheep. "But he that is an hireling and not the shepherd, whose own the sheep are not, sees the wolf coming, and leaves the sheep, and flees; and the wolf catches them, and scatters the sheep. The hireling flees, because he is an hireling, and cares not for the sheep." (John 10:12,13) Is your preacher a hireling? If he was sent by God, he would no doubt warn you like the Apostles did, to "Come out of "Her", My people", God doing the the talking.

"Corn Shelling Time" is telling you before it is too late to learn to dance on one foot and then the other before God, and say, "Father I'll be good. I will not do it any more. Give me another chance. I have had *enuff* stripes. I repent, and in the Name of Jesus, I am sorry. Please forgive me.

The Mystery, Babylon includes literal Babylon, which is a culmination of all "Her" sins from the time of Nimrod, and Hammurabi, to Tammuz and Molech, Ishtar, and all "Her" sins that were glued together (Ekollethesan) (*Greek for glued together, that KJ omits*) until they reached heaven; and God has called to mind all "Her"unjust acts. (Revelation 18:5), which are so many they cannot be named for lack of space.

Some theologians and commentaries think that literal Babylon will be rebuilt in what is now the country of Iraq. The Lord said through (Jeremiah 51:29) that it would be a desolation without an inhabitant, which came to pass with the Medes and Persians. But the Mystery, Babylon is so difficult for someone that understands all mysteries to explain the word Babylon to the natural person, when it can only be understood by the spiritual man. "Her" sins, which are transgressions against God, have been glued together (Ekollethesan) ever since all the Babylonian gods have enticed God's people to commit fornication with "Her", which is all kinds of idolatry, which are the glories of the kingdoms of this world, which belong to Satan. Satan is the ruler of Babylon, which means confusion, which is a state that the entire world is in, because the confused people are natural; and Satan has deceived them into thinking, because they go to a church, or to a synagogue, or a shrine of any kind, and put on a facade of being spiritual, they are spiritual; granted, but it is the wrong spirit that leads them into worship of all kinds of Satan's dead idols of gold, silver, wood, and witchcraft, and things that leads to destruction and spiritual death, which is the second death.

Babylon started with Nimrod, a son of Cush, a son of Ham, that was the king of the Tower of Babel, whose kingdom was Babylon. (Genesis 10:10) Even at that time the spirit of Satan entered into Nimrod and caused him to deny the Word God, and be a killer, a mighty hunter of men. God in the days of Peleg caused the earth to be divided and caused confusion to come upon the Babylonians until this present time. God divided the earth and separated all kindreds, tongues (languages), and even foodstuff, and put boundaries on all nations. The greedy tyrants that were natural men wanted to expand their boundaries and possess the Kingdoms of Satan with hands that shed innocent blood. Which escalated for thousands of years and is still increasing and will continue until Babylon comes into God's remembrance. God started pleading with His people thousands of years ago, even in the days of Isaiah and Jeremiah "To Come out of "Her"; but they would not. Thousands of years have passed, and God is pleading with you, dear reader, of **"Corn Shelling Time"** to come out of "Her" and separate yourself from the unclean thing, which is connected to Mystery, Babylon.

It does not make any difference if you are the most faithful member of the Harlot deep freeze church, you are in Babylon. If you are a voter in the political process that elects any kind of politician, you are in Babylon. If you work for any organization that passes laws of the land, you are in Babylon. If you are a teacher of anything, except teaching to keep God's Commandments and His Statutes, you are in Babylon. If you send your children to a public government funded school, you are in Babylon. If you have any idol in front of you that takes more of your time than you give to worship God Almighty, (PANTAKRATOR), you are in Babylon. If you are in a mosque paying homage to Allah or Mohammed, you are in Babylon. If you are a policeman, you are in Babylon. God did not command any of the above things, except "Keep My Commandments. God added another Commandment to anyone of the above deceived and deceivers, and that is to "Come Out of "Her", (Babylon), My people."

Michael Duishka

Anyone or anything that is not Holy will not inherit the Kingdom of God. Satan has deceived the people on this earth ever since Adam and Eve, until they think it is O.K. If they sin, because everybody does it. Sin is a weapon of mass destruction. W.M.D. **"You, enter in at the strait gate, for wide is the gate and broad is the way that leads to destruction, and many there be which go in thereat."** (Matthew 7:13)

You, dear reader, are in Babylon if you participate in any kind of organized religion, governments, or the glories of Satan's Kingdoms of this world. When God divided the earth and divided the people, they were of one language, and one culture, and one custom at the Tower of Babel. In the days of Peleg the earth was divided. (Genesis 10:25)

Literal Babylon was destroyed, never to be rebuilt again; but Mystery, Babylon seeped into the entire world, and became a festering boil, filled with corruption, which will keep on festering up, until God remembers all the blood She has shed of His Holy Ones, The Prophets, Apostles, Disciples and His Holy Ones, that came out of "Her" and did not partake of "Her" sins. The Unholy Roman Catholic Church, the Whore, killed millions on top of millions from the First Century on until the present time. The Church of England slaughtered millions of people that disagreed with them. All of this is Mystery, Babylon. The Spanish Inquisition was a blood bath from Mystery, Babylon; and Mystery, Babylon just kept spreading all over the earth, until God gave his people a refuge to "Come Out of "Her"", which was a newly discovered land called North America. But just like the land of Israel had to have the Canaanites driven out, North America had to have the natives subdued and driven out, and America was blessed by God and became a Holy Nation that worshiped the One God, the Father, the Son and the Holy Spirit, until the Holy Ones let the greedy tyrants spread like a festering boil until the corruption of the world has spread into a cancer; and America has become an ObomaNation of Desolation that took on the works of the thief that comes not except to kill (murder), rob (steal), and destroy the once Holy Nation, the one time nation under God, the last Holy refuge for Holy Ones to worship Almighty God, (PANTAKRATOR); and the Holy Ones let it be turned into a den of thieves and destroyers.

The Holy Ones allowed the descendants of Nimrod and Ham and Canaan to overtake them; and the sinful Hamites have become the head, and the Holy Ones have become the tail, because they waxed fat and forgat God. Now the boil is festering up and coming to a head, and soon the corruption will be squeezed out when Mystery, Babylon is paid back double for "Her" sins against the Holy Ones of God. The writer of **"Corn Shelling Time"** believes that Mystery, Babylon is the culmination of all the pagan gods of worship of idolatry that covers the entire earth, with the United States of America being the Head of Babylon the Great, and New York City being the Great City, Babylon, that mighty city! "For in one hour is your judgment come." (Revelation 18:10)

The world system, including every nation, kingdom, government, every shrine and worship center, churches, synagogues, mosques, temples, or any arena, theater, or any worldly thing is Mystery, Babylon; and it belongs to the ruler of this world, which is Satan. The Ekklesia (Called Out Ones) that have come out of Mystery, Babylon and do not participate in any of the above mentioned institutions are God's people. God's people have come out of Satan's Kingdoms, and they are the property of Christ Jesus, who is soon to be the Ruler of the heavens, earth, sea, and all the things in them. But while we, the Called Out Ones, and the Ekklektos, (Chosen Ones) are waiting for Christ Jesus, we must be sealed with the seal of God in our foreheads.

"And I saw another angel ascending from the east having the seal of the Living God, and he cried with a loud voice to the four angels, to whom it was given to hurt the earth and the sea, saying hurt not the earth, neither the sea, nor the trees till we have sealed the doulos *(slaves)* of our God in their foreheads." (Revelation 7:2,3). How do we qualify to receive the seal of God in our foreheads? "Here are the things that will disqualify you. All of the things mentioned above previously. You cannot belong to anything that is in the Great Harlot, Mystery, Babylon. You must come out of any unclean thing, such as the *Harlot Church* that profanes the Sabbath Day and does not keep it Holy. The *Harlot Church* that has pagan gods for their idols of worship, *Sunday, Easter, Christmas, Saints, Saint Valentine, Saint Patrick, All Saints Day, (Halloween), Martin Luther King Jr., Saint Mary, the Crux (Cross) (Tammuz), vote for any politician or government worker, do not send your children to a government funded public school, that teaches rebellion against God's law, the Ten Commandments, and the over one thousand commands in the New Covenant.* "Christians"already have the mark! Believers already have the seal of God. "Christians" profess the Holy Spirit! Believers possess the Holy Spirit! You cannot make God hire you in His Kingdom just because you are black. NO,NO,NO.

The Tower that Nimrod tried to build to heaven, (*The Tower of Babel*), was destroyed. So after all these years New York City built twin towers that reached into the first heaven, called skyscrapers. This writer never understood the works of the Devil, but it is my belief that these twin towers held all the merchandise that (Revelation 18:12) mentions, which was gold, silver, precious things, etc. But up jumped the Devil and caused these Trade Towers to come to naught on 9-ll; but that was just a small obstacle for a Woman with so many riches, that sits as a Queen, and lived deliciously, and am no widow. So She just sucks it up and builds a One World Trade Center with a tower in the heaven that is the tallest tower in the western half of the earth. The terrorists only destroyed the Twin Towers on 9-11; but the bible predicts the entire city will meet "Her" waterloo. "Therefore shall "Her" plagues come in one day, death, and mourning, and famine, and She shall be utterly burned with fire, for strong is the Lord God who judges "Her." (Revelation 18:8) The Muslim terrorists had bombed the towers once before 9-11, and 9-11-2001 was the second time; and they *(Muslim terrorists)* are working at the present time to destroy the entire city of New York City, the third time. The city is the home of the United Nations, which rules the whole world. The One World Trade Center has made the kings of the earth to commit fornication with "Her"; and all the merchants of the world shall weep and mourn, because no man buys their merchandise anymore. That great city, Babylon, that mighty city, for in one hour has your judgment come. (Revelation 18:10)

The evidence and clues that New York City is the great city, Babylon, is because it is the only city in the entire world that has so many different riches to buy and sell and trade. It has made the kings of the whole world rich with "Her" generosity with the working class of Americans footing the bill, and supporting the flattery of the President. "Spread it (*the wealth of America*) around." New York City is the home of the United Nations. New York City is the home of the World Trade Center, not to mention the New York Stock Exchange. The Big Banks are in New York City. New York City is the city of the Great Satan, the head of that old serpent. If you cut the head off, the serpent dies. And when they saw the smoke of "Her" burning, saying what city *is* like unto this great city? What they cried. (Revelation 18:18) God's judgment.

Keep in mind there are three factions to Mystery, Babylon. One is the religious sect, which is a dissenting body of so called "Christians" adhering to a doctrine of devils; and their leader is the False Prophet, which has deceived the Whore, (*Catholic Church),* and "Her" daughters, (Harlots) into believing **The Lie.** Another faction is the political group of rulers of the Kingdoms of Satan's world, which are against God's Kingdom and His Government of Theocracy. This group is forming now at this present time in New York City in the United Nations. The members of the United Nations are not in agreement on the One World order at the present time; but when their leader shows them all of his glories of his kingdoms of this world, then they, (*the United Nations)* will become an inclusive faction, giving their power and worship to their leader, the Beast and Anti-Christ. At this present time, the Whore and "Her" Harlots are stuck together with the United Nations, and the only separation of church and state is lip service. A propaganda to deceive the third faction of Mystery Babylon, which are the unlearned, ungodly, agnostics that really do not care, one way or the other. This people are the ones that have never heard the gospel of Christ Jesus, and the so called "Christians" did not obey the Commandment of Christ to go you therefore and teach all nations, baptizing them into (eis) the name of the Father, and of the Son, and of the (tou) Holy Ghost. *(Clearly the trinity)* (Matthew 28:19) this ignorant and unlearned faction of Mystery, Babylon will get their opportunity to hear the everlasting gospel when God sends His Angel to this third faction of Mystery, Babylon in this manner. "And I saw another angel fly in the midst of heaven, having the everlasting gospel to preach unto them that dwell on the earth, and to every nation, and kindred, and tongue, and people, saying with a loud voice **"Fear God and give glory to Him, for the hour of His judgment is come, and worship Him that made heaven, and earth, and the sea, and the fountains of waters."** (Revelation 14:6,7) Now the first faction, the Whore, and "Her" Daughters, *(Harlots)*, branches of the Mother of Harlots *(churches)* will adhere to the second faction of Mystery, Babylon, the political government faction until: "And the ten horns *(kings)*, which you saw upon the Beast, these shall hate the Whore, (the religious faction), and shall make "Her" desolate, and naked, and shall eat "Her" flesh, and burn "Her" with fire; for God has put in their hearts to fulfill His will, and agree and give their kingdom to the Beast, until the Words of God shall be fulfilled." (Revelation 17:16,17)

Then the Mystery, Babylon will be inclusive, all factions in agreement to fight against God. And then at that time the Woman will be That Great City, which reigns over the kings of the earth. (Revelation 17:18) And I believe That Great City is *New York City, USA*, and the home of the United Nations, and the Trade Center of the World. And the destruction of Mystery, Babylon will not come until the last days of the tribulation, which affects every nation, kindred, tongue, and race; and since the Ekklesia (Called Out Ones) did not preach the gospel to every creature on earth, God's angels will. (Revelation 14:6,7) God's Commandment that they did not do was: "Go you into all the world and preach the gospel to every creature." (Mark 16:15) Then comes destruction.

The misled Harlot churches think they are going to be *raptured* out of the world before the tribulation. It will never happen. That is why God is calling out loud for His people to come out of "Her", before She receives "Her" plagues of sorrow and destruction in one hour. (Revelation 18:10) Rome is the number one choice of commentaries for the physical manifestation of Babylon, and some think the Babylonian City itself is going to be rebuilt; but **"Corn Shelling Time"** believes She is glorified and living too deliciously to ever be as ignoble as those desolate places to be, the city. New York City, USA, is the commercial center of the whole world and is the one city, that has made all the merchants of the world rich with buying, selling, and trading of every kind of merchandise that can be named. "She says in "Her" heart, I sit a queen and am no widow, and shall see no sorrow." (Revelation 18:7)

The City of Babylon was the leading city of the world when Nimrod was the king. That was then, and this is now. The leading city of the entire world at this present time is New York City, AKA "Mystery, Babylon City." She is the leading city in causing the kings of the earth to commit fornication, and the inhabitants of the earth have been made drunk with the wine of "Her" fornication. (Revelation 17:2) "And all the nations have drunk of the wine of the wrath of "Her" fornication, and the kings of the earth have committed fornication with "Her", and the merchants of the earth are waxed rich through the abundance of "Her" delicacies." (Revelation 18:3)

Because of the fact that New York City is the One World Trade Center, the prophet describes New York City as the City of Babylon at this present time. Wall Street in New York City is the world's leading financial center, leading the world in economic power with a large port, She is groomed for trade; and that is why "the shipmasters and all the company in ships and sailors, and as many as trade by sea, stood afar off and cried when they saw the smoke of "Her" burning, saying "What city *is* like unto this great city. For in one hour so great riches is come to naught." (Revelation 18:17,18) **"Corn Shelling Time"** is pleading with you, dear reader, to not wait until the manifestation of "Her" destruction to come out of "Her", because you are in Babylon now at this present time, and She is causing you to be drunk with the wine of "Her" fornication, which She provides you with so many sorceries,*(dope)* and delicious idols to commit fornication with. Mystery, Babylon is not just New York City, but rather is prevalent in the entire world, and New York City is the Great City that will be destroyed in one hour. Some commentaries believe She will be destroyed by a natural disaster, even by a great earthquake; but this writer believes the bible when the angel said to pay "Her" back double, so She will be destroyed by violence and natural causes. Some kind of a bomb will explode causing a tsunami and an earthquake, and a burning. The Great City of New York City is in Babylon, the part called America; but the United Nations causes the whole earth to be affected by its overbearing domineering power to dictate to every country how they should conduct their business. America and her president are busybodies causing unrest in every country that allows loud mouth threats and cutting of sanctions. The president of the USA has already turned America into an ObomaNation of desolation, and desires to do the same to all the nations, and create a One World Dictatorship, a One World Government. And that is what the Beast and the Anti-Christ will do until Mystery Babylon is judged and destroyed, and Christ Jesus destroys all the armies of Anti-Christ at **Armageddon.** (Revelation 16:16) America is the leading nation of Mystery, Babylon, and New York City is that Great City; and the angel has already told the end of "Her", which will be according to "Her" works. All of "Her" delicacies are being sold and given to heathen nations to flatter them and be "Her" lovers.

The King of Babylon will rule the nations out of New York City, because the United Nations is headquartered in New York City; and the King of Babylon will influence the majority of the nations to follow him. This writer believes that Obama, the President of the USA, does not have the mental capacity to rule any city, or nation, himself; but he has some behind the scenes, string pullers, that make it obvious they want to destroy the *NewNited States of America,* and turn it into an ObomaNation of Desolation.

When the Anti-Christ comes on the scene, he will rule the Old Roman Empire from Babylon for the first half of Daniel's 70th week, or the first three and one-half years of the 7 year covenant that Israel will make with the Anti-Christ. Then the last three and one-half years of the Covenant, the Anti-Christ will move into the Holy Place in Israel, and declare that he is God, and believe he is God his own self. (II Thessalonians 2:4) This writer is of the opinion that the Anti-Christ will sit in America, which is Mystery, Babylon, and cause many nations to fall, until he moves into Israel and causes the sacrifice to be taken away; and the False Prophet will make an image of the Beast, and cause the mark of the Beast to be on all the people whose names were not in the Book of Life of the Lamb slain from the foundation of the world. (Revelation 13:8) The Lord has put it in their hearts to fulfill His will, and agree, and give their Kingdom unto the Beast, until the Words of God be fulfilled. (Talking about the ten kings that destroy the Whore) (Revelation 17:17)

"Then God tells Ezekiel to prophesy to "Gog", which is the fallen angel that rules in the heavenlies over Meshech and Tubal, which came out victorious over Persia, Ethiopia, and Libya, (talking about modern day Iran, Ethiopia, in Africa, and Libya). Also Gomer and all his bands, which is Germany and the nations of the European Union, the house of Togarmah, which is modern day Turkey. Gog is the spiritual ruler over these countries that has been appointed by the Dragon, which is Satan, to bring all these kings and their armies to the Valley of Decision., AKA **Armageddon.** (Revelation 16:16) "And you, son of man, set your face against "Gog", the land of Magog, the Chief Prince of Meshech and Tubal, and prophesy against him; and I will turn you back and put hooks into your jaws; and I will bring you forth." (Ezekiel 38:4) Forth to *"GOD'S SUPER BOWL ON A SUNDAY"* (**Armageddon)**

"And I saw three unclean spirits like frogs come out of the mouth of the Dragon, and out of the mouth of the Beast, and out of the mouth of the False Prophet, for they are the spirits of devils, working miracles, *which* go forth unto the kings of the earth, and of the whole world, to gather them to the battle of that Great Day of God Almighty (PANTAKRATOR)." (Revelation 16:13)

This is how He put it into their hearts to fulfill His will. (Revelation 17:17) "He put hooks in their jaws". (Ezekiel 38:4) "And three spirits like frogs from the dragon, and the Beast, and the False Prophet to draw all the kings of the world to put an end to all transgressions and end all sin."

"Behold I come as a thief. Blessed is he that watches, and keeps his garments, lest he walk naked, and they see his shame." (Revelation 16:15)

"And He gathered them together into a place called, in the Hebrew tongue, **"Armageddon."** (Revelation 16:16) "And the wine press was trodden without the city; and blood came out of the wine press, even unto the horses' bridles, by the space of a thousand and six hundred furlongs." (Revelation 14:20) *"GOD'S SUPER BOWL ON A SUNDAY"* (**Armageddon)**

"And every island fled away, and the mountains were not found. And the Great City *(New York City, USA)* was divided into three parts; and the cities of the nations fell; and Great Babylon came in remembrance before God, to give unto "Her" the cup of the wine of the fierceness of His wrath." (Revelation 16:19) "For in one hour, so great riches has come to naught." (Revelation 18:17) There is not any need to itemize all "Her" riches, because you cannot name anything that she did not have.

"So all the shipmasters, and all the ship companies, and sailors, and as many as trade by sea stood afar off, and cried when they saw the smoke of "Her" burning, saying "What City is like unto this Great City." (Revelation 18:17,18)

The reason this writer believes New York City is the Great City of Mystery, Babylon is because, as stated earlier, it is the leading Trade Center of the world; and She has all this merchandise that made all the kings of the world rich. It has harbors and waterways that Rome and Babylon does not have, places for large ships to unload and load their merchandise in the New York Harbor. That is why the mariners cried when they saw "Her" burning. Not only was the city destroyed, but also all of America was made desolate on account of "Her" fornication, which is idolatry.

"And the seventh angel poured out his bowl into the air; and there came a great voice out of the temple of heaven from the throne, saying, "It is done", and there were voices, and thunders, and lightnings, and there was a great earthquake, such as was not since men were upon the earth, so mighty an earthquake, and so great; and the great city was divided into three parts." (Revelation 16:17,18,19) (We will insert a parenthetical injunction to ad lib on the three parts. Most learned commentaries believe this is the city of Jerusalem, others believe it is Rome. Some believe it is the ancient City Babylon, and believe it is divided into three physical parts, or into sects, like Jews, Samaritans, or "Christians", which is the way Babylon will be divided into factions, but not physical. The literal city itself will be destroyed all at once in one hour, (Revelation 18:10), and the dividing into three parts is the religious people, and the literal, physical, and the agnostics, the Mystical Babylon being the Mother Harlot; and the literal Babylon being the commercial part, and the third part of Babylon being the ignorant unlearned agnostics that do not have sense enough to believe in anything except themselves.)

The Mystery, Babylon the Great is New York City, because She is all the adjectives that God used to describe "Her" as being haughty, and rude, and an oppressive bully to all the other nations of the world. How She glorified Herself in all idolatry; and She was the leader in all pagan rituals, such as *Christmas, Easter, Saint Patrick, Saint Valentine, Martin Luther King, Halloween, or witches, and wizards, and New Year, and many, many more idolatrous abominations.* "She caused all nations to drink of the wine of the fierceness of the wrath of God." (Revelation 14:8)

"Thus with violence shall that Great City Babylon be thrown down and shall be found no more at all." (Revelation 18:21)

I believe that the rulers of these *NewNited States of America,* most especially the current one, have been overbearing and domineering over all of the countries that would not stand up for themselves, even to the point of stirring up riots and being instrumental in the overthrowing of governments, and presidents, and kings by exercising the power that God gave to this once God fearing nation. That was then, and this is now an ObomaNation of Desolation. All the merchandise of this great country is being squandered for the greediness of the politicians through the One World Trade Center, which is Mystery, Babylon The Great, the Mother of Harlots and abomination of the earth, *New York City,USA.*

"Come out of "Her", My people, that you be not partakers of "Her" sins, and that you receive not of "Her" plagues". Millions of you are already receiving of "Her" plagues. (Revelation 18:4) The reason you are crippled, sickly, diseased, infirm, unhappy, sorrowful, sad, disappointed, divorced, addicted, lonely, or contemplating suicide is simply because you participated in "Her" (*Babylon's*) sins. You cannot come out of "Her" by yourself. Just as you cannot quit sinning by yourself. Here is a sure fired way, that has been tested and sealed with God's stamp of approval. The first step is to pray to God in the Name of Jesus for Him to help you to quit sinning. "Shell Down the Corn" to Him and confess that you are a sinner. Do not try to cover up your sins with being good or going to *church*, because you have tried that already, and that is why you are in the condition you are in. Do not go to any man for help, no preacher, no doctor, no lawyer, no teacher, no friend, no spouse or loved one; but go to Jesus, because He is all of these; and He can do more for you than all of these put together. Amen.

You have already put your trust in all of the above, and that is the reason you are cursed. "Cursed be the man that trusts in man, and makes flesh his arm, and whose heart departs from the Lord. Thus saith the Lord." (Jeremiah 17:5).

If you have read **"Corn Shelling Time"**, then you know the end results of Mystery, Babylon; but your end is coming before the manifestation of the destruction of Mystery, Babylon. You are already cursed with "Her" plagues. If you are a church goer, you are smart enough to know the Whore has not worked for you. If you do not know how to come out of the world, (John 2:15,16), and be separated from the unclean thing (II Corinthians 6:17), then read (I John 2:26,27), and let the Holy Spirit teach you how to be saved. If you do not understand, just do what the writer of **"Corn Shelling Time"** has done. Come out of Babylon, *(sin)*, confess, "Shell Down the Corn" to Christ Jesus, and ask Him to help you, and He will. This old country boy has done all the above things and more, but he asked Jesus for help, and Jesus stayed the plague, and this writer has had the death angel to pass over him seven times and more. Read the book, "Please Do Not Call Me a "Christian", by Michael Duishka. **"Corn Shelling Time** has told you at the beginning to keep God's Commandments, or be destroyed like Mystery, Babylon will be destroyed. If you don't understand anything, "the same anointing which you have received of Him, (the Holy Ghost) abides in you, and you need not that any man teach you; but as the same anointing teaches you of All things, and is Truth and is no lie, and even as He has taught you, you shall abide in Him." (I John 2:27)

If you forget what the Holy Ghost teaches, read **"Corn Shelling Time"** over, and over, and over, and just "Shell Down the Corn", (confess) to Christ Jesus; and He will raise you up in the last day. (John 6:44) But if you do not want to be saved, and healed, and have power over sin, sickness, and the devil. "He that is unjust, let him be unjust still, and he which is filthy, let him be filthy still, and he that is righteous, let him be righteous still, and he that is Holy, let him be Holy still." (Revelation 22:11)

THIS is an insert in the book, **"CORN SHELLING TIME"** and **MICHAEL DUISHKA** with some of his belief. If you have ever been the victim of a tornado and survived you will know the swiftness without warning it is suddenly upon you, and there is nothing you can do except pray. In this book Duishka told about the great typhonic storm that brother Paul called Euroaquilo in the book of Acts 27:14, But Duishka related the great Noreastor storm that came upon brother Paul to a great storm that was twisting the heart right out of him without any warning. But unlike that storm, and unlike a tornado, Christ Jesus told us about a storm that is coming upon the whole world, that will be worse than all the storms that has ever happened. The difference is Jesus sent His Apostles, Prophets, Evangelist, and witnesses to warn the entire world about the oncoming storm so it will not come upon anyone unaware. Christ Jesus sent Duishka, who is nothing, but a slave *(doulos)* to reiterate that warning,which is indubitably going to come, because God cannot lie. But just like in the days of Noah the people were eating and drinking, marrying and giving in marriage, planting and building until the flood came and drowned every living creature on the whole earth. Just like Noah warned the people for 120 years and they would not listen. This storm that God is warning you about is going to be worse than words can describe. The sword, nuclear warfare, beheading, your children slaughtered before your eyes, tornadoes, rape of girls, and boys,floods, starvation, diseases, being burned at the stake, die of thirst, no water, all kinds of torture that you cannot imagine. You have been warned more so than in the days of Noah. All you need to do is confess to God, Repent of your sins, ask Jesus to save you, **believe** He will.

Chapter 22

BABYLON IS AN ARMY of rebels fighting against God and His Son, Christ Jesus, and the Holy Spirit. They are the ones living deliciously, and the ones that have drunk of the wine of the wrath of "Her" fornication, and the ones that say, "I am rich and increased with goods and have need of nothing; but these are the ones that know not that they are wretched, and miserable, and poor, and blind, and naked, and lukewarm; and "I will spue you out of My Mouth," thus saith the Lord." (Revelation 3:16,17,18)

The biggest portion of these world wide rebels are educated fools that read the Bible, and the Quran, and other religions, only as a requisite to obtain some kind of degree. Others know to obey God, but do not do it. "To him that knows to do good, and does it not, to him it is sin." (James 4:17); but that is another problem. Some do not know what is good. Those that do not know what is good are fighting to destroy themselves. For instance, all the people that are campaigning for a politician that votes for a law that allows women and men to commit murder. One example being a woman having a doctor to murder her baby. It is just like who killed the baby, the mother or the doctor? They are both guilty of murder. Not only the mother and the doctor, but also all the voters that voted for that murdering politician that passed a law allowing murder, and also all the Supreme Court Judges that ruled against the Law of God, and made it a law of the land. Woe be unto all the people involved. They all are in Babylon, just waiting to be destroyed by fire. Those people that voted think they did good, voting for murder.

That is the reason this writer of **"Corn Shelling Time"** is sad to see a fruitful, God given land, that once was flowing with milk and honey, turn into Babylon, ruled by Satan and his demons. Blatantly passing mandatory laws that takes away every freedom that Christ Jesus gave to mankind. If the government could, they would put a charge on breathing God's air, which is His Spirit. It is my belief that I have the freedom to not participate in sinful mandatory insurance of any kind. It is my belief God gave me command to not trust in man. If you do not go to a doctor, or do not take a member of your family to a doctor, or do not have the tax of insurance, you have broken the law of the land; and if you do trust in doctors and insurance, you are cursed, because you put your trust in man, and broke God's Command."Thus saith the Lord, "Cursed be the man that trusts in man, and makes flesh his arm, and whose heart departs from the Lord." (Jeremiah 17:5) It is a matter of coming out of Babylon and trusting the Lord, or staying in Babylon and being destroyed by fire. (Revelation 18:4,5)

The laws of the land make it mandatory to send your children to a government subsidized school; or in order to home school them, the government puts strict worldly qualifications on the parents, so they will have to break God's Commandment that requires the parent to teach their children about God and His Commandments, statutes, and laws. If you do what God commanded, the parents will go to jail, or be fined, or both. If you send your children to a public school, you are sending your child to destruction. In the public school, they will teach the child Babylonian, "Christian", pagan, heathen rituals of humanistic ways, which are to observe all kinds of socialistic ways of the god of this world, which is the wide and broad way to destruction; and many there be that enters.

The lost "Christians" say there is another option, send your child to *church* for one hour a week and let the *Sunday* School Teacher make them a two fold child of Hell that is more than he or she is. How many adults are there that teach their children what will cover their sins, when the adults do not know? How many adults teach their children to come out of Babylon, when the adults do not know how? How many adults know what the Mystery of Godliness is? How could they teach their children? How many adults know what the Mystery of Iniquity is, and how could they teach their children? How many adults know how to pray? How could they teach their children?

A historian that is very fluent in worldly knowledge told me, "You do not have to use the Name of Jesus to pray." Oh Me! "You believe in God, believe into me also." (John 14:1)

There was once a wealthy family that had a precious young son that got hit in the head with a baseball. The boy was rushed to a large denominational hospital, where he lay in a coma for three days. The Lord Jesus sent His Holy Spirit to me and told me to go and lay hands on the young boy and pray for him. I took off my work and went to the hospital. The young boy's sister went and told the boy's father I was there and would he come and talk to me? The father came and told me he was the boy's father. I told the father that God had sent me to pray for his son. The father said, "Oh no, we have a large *church* that knows how to pray, praying for him." I told the man that God sent me to pray for his son. The father rejected me, and refused to let me minister to his son. The boy died that night. There are people that are too busy with the cares of this life to hear the still small voice of the Holy Spirit. These people are living deliciously in Babylon, receiving their rewards in this life only.

There was another man that had 3 sons. Two of the boys were twins born prematurely that weighed less than 3 pounds a piece. These twins were given up to die, because they had jaundice, collapsed lungs, hives, and many other maladies; but God heard the father's prayers and caused the twins to live. For the first year the father would have to be very attentive to the babies, because they would become choked on the mucous that stuck in their throats. A syringe was kept by the boys' baby beds to suck the phlegm out of their noses and throats. Sometimes the father would take the boys by the heels and shake the phlegm out of them, praying and saying to God, "Live, boy, in the Name of Jesus", and they lived. The third boy was a preemie also, with asthma and other infirmities and infection of allergies. Many times the boy would stop breathing completely, and the father would shake him, and pound on his chest, and pray, and say, "Live in the Name of Jesus", and he did. The father of those boys fought the devil and the laws of the land, that tried the father for child abuse and anything they could conjure up; but God is greater than the devil and the laws of the land, and that father is praising and thanking God even to this day that He, (God), chose to let those boys live and have life more abundantly. That father came out of Babylon, and does not receive "Her" plagues, and does not partake of "Her" sins.

You, dear reader, can overcome your sins and maladies, if you will "Shell Down the Corn", (confess) to God Almighty, (PANTAKRATOR); and let God rule your life instead of you trying to rule it. Look at the mess you made of your life. Quit trying to help God solve your problems; and just give up helping yourself, and completely turn your life over to God; and He is bigger than all your problems; and remember, "If your heart condemns you, God is bigger than your heart." (I John 3:20) Dear reader, please understand, you will never get any help from the *church,* or the doctor, or the police, or an institute of learning, or any other source to solve your problems, except get off in a quiet place, and do not talk, but listen for the small still voice to direct you, and guide you, and stay away from people. Stay off to yourself and listen. Read (I John 2:27) and (I John 2:15,16)

This writer had more problems than anyone in the world; but when he quit talking and started listening to the Holy Spirit, God helped him overcome all of his problems. Amen.

The writer of **"Corn Shelling Time"** knows there are many millions of God's people that have prayed over and over, begging God to answer them; and they just do not have the patience to wait until they have the knowledge that God has given them in the Manufacturer's Manual, the Handbook that holds all the secrets of how to activate God's promises that are always "Yea and Amen" to those that are into Christ Jesus. (2 Corinthians 1: 20). I wish I could have some, one on one time with you millions that are hurting and have grown weary from waiting on an answer from God. Please do not give up; but just apply yourself more into the handbook until you have studied enough for God to approve you. "Study to show yourself approved unto God, a workman that needs not to be ashamed, rightly dividing the Word of Truth."(II Timothy 2:15) All the time you spend searching for an answer will not go unrewarded, if you will rely on (I John 2:27), and "Let the anointing, which is the Holy Spirit, teach you," in your quiet time. The answer to all your problems is Christ Jesus. You will find Him, if you will just seek, and keep on seeking. An awful lot of you people have turned to addictive substances prematurely, when the answer was nigh you, even in your mouth, and on your tongue. All you had to do was **say** whatever you desired.

Peter and John at the Gate Beautiful did not pray to the Father for Jesus to heal the man; but Peter commanded, and said; "In the Name of Jesus, rise up and walk." (Acts 3:6) That was one of the good promises Jesus gave His disciples. They could have whatever they said. (Mark 11:23) All of the promises of God in Him (Christ Jesus) are Yea and in Him (Christ Jesus) Amen. (II Corinthians 1:20)

But, dear reader, please understand that all of His promises were to be Yea and Amen, no matter if the promise was good, or if the promise was chastisement. God promised punishment for His people that are still in Babylon, which is the state of sin. God would not be a just God if He did not keep His promises of castigation, or "are you bastards?" (Hebrews 12:8) "If you endure chastening, God deals with you, as with sons; for what son is he whom the father chastens not? (Hebrews 12:7) "But, if you be without chastisement, whereof all are partakers, then are you bastards, and not sons?" (Hebrews 12:8) "Furthermore, we have had fathers of our flesh which corrected us; and we gave them reverence. Shall we not much rather be in subjection unto the Father of Spirits and live?" (Hebrews 12:9)

I asked the Lord Jesus, "If these people here on earth would not listen to you, do you think they will listen to an unlearned country boy like me? And Lord Jesus, how will I ever get this book published?" He answered, "I have people in the publishing business that love Me and are anxious to do my will; and, furthermore, do not call yourself unlearned, because I commanded you to take my yoke upon you and learn of Me in (Matthew 11:29); and you did, so do not call someone that I taught unlearned." Jesus doing the talking! Furthermore, He told me I was wise to Come out of Babylon and not partake of "Her" sins, and receive not "Her" plagues, *(chastisement, castigation)*. Thus saith the Lord God of Israel unto me, take the wine cup of this fury at my hand and cause all the nations to whom I send you to drink it. Just because I live in America, the ObomaNation of Desolation, does not mean that the Lord Jesus just sent me to them; but rather He sent me to all nations, from one end of the earth to the extremities. OH, that the Europeans, Russians, all Asians, all Spanish, all Muslim Arabs would **read.**

"And it shall be, if they refuse to take the cup at your hand to drink, then you shall say unto them, thus saith the Lord of Hosts, you shall certainly drink." (Jeremiah 25:15,28) This is one of God's promises that is not (Name it and claim it) (gab it and grab it), but rather a promise of condemnation and judgment. "For lo, I begin to bring evil on the city which is called by My Name, and should you be utterly unpunished? You shall not be unpunished, for I will call for a sword upon **all** the inhabitants of the earth, saith the Lord of Hosts." (Jeremiah 25:29)

This is one of the promises and prophesies that God told Jeremiah to promise all the inhabitants of the earth would occur. "The Lord shall roar from on high, and utter His voice from His Holy Habitation. He shall mightily roar upon His habitation. He shall give a shout, as they tread the grapes against all the inhabitants of the earth. A noise shall come even to the ends of the earth, for the Lord has a controversy with the nations. He will plead with all flesh. He will give them *t*hat are wicked to the sword, saith the Lord. Thus saith the Lord of Hosts, behold evil shall go forth from nation to nation; and a great whirlwind shall be raised up from the coasts of the earth. And the slain of the Lord shall be at that day from one end of the earth, even unto the other end of the earth. They shall not be lamented, neither gathered, nor buried. They shall be dung upon the ground." (Jeremiah 25:30,31,32,33)

This is also one of His promises to those that are into Christ Jesus, which is yea, and into Him Amen. This sword, or whirlwind (Tornado, tsunami, hurricane, cyclone) will not harm you if you come out of Mystery, Babylon and quit partaking of "Her" sins. God has given this book, **"Corn Shelling Time"** to benefit all the inhabitants of the earth that will take the time to read all the Words of this book, because it will bring to your remembrance the things the Lord Christ Jesus has said. Also some things the Holy Spirit has taught this writer; and he will pass it on to you. Not one word of this book will fail, because it is God inspired. Amen.

"But when you shall hear of wars and commotions, be not frightened (*terrified*)**, for these things must first come to pass; but the end is not by and by."** (Luke 21:9) This writer cannot help but feel compassion for the educated fools that voluntarily join up with Satanic forces to kill in the name of patriotism, because they have increased knowledge, running to and fro. (Daniel 12:4) The knowledge they are increased with came from Satanic forces on how to use evil inventions, such as computers or explosives, or any kind of device that kills or destroys their brothers. Sometimes the innocent ones are drafted by the Satanic rulers of the land.

If they hide or dodge the draft, they are called DD, Draft Dodgers; but these can be presidents of the United States of America and cause thousands of young men to die to fill their greedy pockets with riches, causing wars and commotions, and causing the arenas of war to run red with the blood of young fools that turn out to be dead heroes that gave their lives in vanity, all for the war mongers that brainwashed the tender minds to believe The Lie of Satan. These greedy war mongers that keep the unrest and commotions going without ceasing will come to an end according to their works.

But you, dear reader, can come out of sin, and miss God's promise to destroy you, if you will just "Shell Down the Corn" to God, (confess) the same way this writer "Shelled Down the Corn" to not only my daddy, but also to Christ Jesus, and quit sinning, and started to apply for a job in the Kingdom of God with Christ Jesus as my ruler and my head. If you, dear reader, want to work for Christ Jesus, here are the qualifications. You cannot be a bum on welfare. You cannot be a liar. You cannot be a politician. You cannot be a voter that votes for a lying politician. You cannot work for Christ on the Sabbath. Remember the Sabbath day to keep it holy. You cannot be a church going "Christian" that blasphemes God's Holy Days and desecrates the Passover, calling it *Easter Sunday*. God will not hire you if you are a *Sunday* worshiper. You are in Babylon if you celebrate *church, saints, cross (Tammuz), Easter, Christmas, Halloween, witches, Sunday, Martin Luther King, Obama, Elvis, Michael Jackson, Ophra, Hollywood, sports, lethal injection, abortion, welfare, insurance, laws of the land, organized religion, schools, works of the flesh.* (Galatians 5:19,20) To work in God's Theocracy, you have to be pure, holy, clothed with a white robe, and shuck off anything black. If you have any of the above mentioned traits, "Shell Down the Corn" to God and repent, and perhaps Christ will forgive you. God told you repetitiously to obey Him more subtly than this country boy can tell you, but the command is the same no matter who tells you to come out of Babylon (sin).

The word "Christianity" used to be a holy, pure, word for God's people; but that was then, and this is now. The word "Christian" causes people to shy away and be skeptical of everyone that calls himself a "Christian", the same way people are dubious of blacks, because of the stigma of their past actions. So "Christians" are marked with the stigma of hypocrisy of the Pharisees or the heathen Catholic Church. Ask any one you meet if they are a "Christian"; and they will answer, yes, because they went to *church on Easter Sunday*. They think that makes them a "Christian" by association with a *harlot church*. They say, "I am a "Christian"; but "they say" is always a lie.

All of the ways God told His prophets to warn His people of their destruction is relayed to you, dear reader, through every book of the Bible and by every prophet. This writer of **"Corn Shelling Time"** wants you to know that he is not a prophet; but God has anointed him with the Holy Spirit to tell you in his crude way to "Shell Down the Corn", (confess), to God Almighty, (PANTAKRATOR), and repent, and "come out of "Her", (Babylon) *(sinning)*. (Revelation 18:4) God has given this writer an exclusive revelation of the Mystery of Godliness and the Mystery of Iniquity, and also the Mystery, Babylon: and Babylon is no longer a mystery; but continue reading **"Corn Shelling Time"** for the revealing of who "Her" is, and who is Mystery, Babylon, and also literal Great Babylon.

"A noise shall come to the ends of the earth, for the Lord has a controversy with the nations. He will plead with all flesh. He will give them that are wicked to the sword, saith the Lord." (Jeremiah 25:31) This is what God is doing with you, dear reader, pleading with you through **"Corn Shelling Time"** before you are destroyed from the earth. There are so many ways you are being destroyed: By the sword, or pestilence, or disease, or by: "A great whirlwind, (tornado, tsunami, hurricane, cyclone) shall be raised up from the coasts of the earth; and the slain of the Lord shall be at that day, from one end of the earth even to the other end of the earth. They shall not be lamented, neither gathered, nor buried. They shall be dung upon the ground." (Jeremiah 25:32,33)

So God is pleading with you, dear reader, at this moment. He is passing by you at this present time with His Holy Spirit, calling out loud for you to be "Called Out", (Ekklesia), (Not church); but He is calling you out of Mystery, Babylon, which is sin; and God is telling you to not be be a partaker of "Her" sin, so you will not be destroyed with the plagues of the world. (Revelation 18:4,5) – Disasters, diseases, accidents, heart attacks, famines, sword, war, lethal injection, drowning, airplane disappearance, car wrecks, etc. Which one of the above plagues has Satan put on you? Call CHRIST JESUS FOR DELIVERENCE! Christ's phone number; Jeremiah 33;3. "Call unto me"

To some of you there are places in this book that are repetitious and to some very boring. The writer wants to emphasize how important it is that you be *(attentive)* to the prophecy that God has inspired His prophets to warn you of the way God is pleading with all flesh. God has many armies here on earth, as well as the armies in heaven. Four of God's armies are the wind, fire, water, and the earth. These are called elements; but please understand that God is the fifth element over these four elements; and He (God) is called Pemptos Ousa, which means the fifth element, or the fifth Being. In Modern Greek (*Pembte Ousa);* but Jeremiah talked about the whirlwind, that is manifesting in the world today with many tornadoes, hurricanes. Paul wrote about a typhonic wind storm called Euroaquilo, which the KJV called Euroclydon, meaning an East Wind that is called a Noreastor. But God sent an angel to Paul to reassure him that Pembte Ousa was still in control of His elements. At this present time the news media is full of talk about global warming. "And the fourth angel with the bowls, or vials, when he poured out his bowl on the sun, and power was given him to scorch men with fire." (Revelation 16:8)   " A n d the serpent cast out of his mouth water as a flood, after the woman (God's people) that he might cause her to be carried away by the flood; and the earth helped the woman; and the earth opened her mouth and swallowed up the flood which the dragon cast out of his mouth." (Revelation 12:15,16) The fourth element is the earth, which is the volcano, and the earthquake, and pestilence.

At this present time, the beginning of sorrows has grown more fervent and intense. The whirlwinds (tornadoes and hurricanes) are killing people all over the world, and destroying billions of dollars in property damage. Fires are burning up the vegetation that animals need to survive, and mankind needs the animals to survive. The water is either drying up or flooding the crops out, and causing a worldwide famine. Tsunamis are causing entire cities to be washed away by the tidal waves. All of these elements, the wind, fire, water, and earth are being used by God to bring His people out of Mystery, Babylon; and the fifth being is pleading with all flesh that is upon the face of the earth. Pembte Ousa has many, many more ways to plead with you; and **"Corn Shelling Time"** is one of those ways God is pleading with you, dear reader, to quit listening to those words that are dressed up by the politically correct liars that are increased with worldly knowledge; but they are destitute of spiritual wisdom. They seduce you by turning Truth into lies. They trade the goodly pearl for temporal mammon that will perish with them in the fire. Whichever part of the world you may live in, you are living in Babylon, the place of destruction. The whore has caused you to commit fornication against God; and God has anointed the writer of **"Corn Shelling Time"** to plead with all flesh to "Come Out of Mystery, Babylon" and not receive "Her" plagues." And to Jesus, the mediator of the New Covenant, and to the blood of sprinkling, that speaks better things than that of Abel. See that you refuse not Him that speaks. For if they escaped not who refused him that spake on earth, much more shall not we escape, if we turn away from Him that speaks from heaven." (Hebrews 12:24,25) This writer put out a feeler to his acquaintances, and asked them if he should write it; and all answered negatively, emphatically: "No!" The only affirmative, "Yes", answers came from his wife and his head, Christ Jesus, which makes a majority. The laws of the land are written for the politicians; and they steal, kill, and destroy. You cannot show me a man made law that does not steal, kill, or destroy life that God gave. "But I Am come that they might have life, and that they might have life more abundantly." (John 10:10) There is life more abundantly in this book, **"Corn Shelling Time"**.

THIS is an insert in the book, **"CORN SHELLING TIME"** and **MICHAEL DUISHKA** with some of his belief. It is my belief at this time before all my constitutional rights are taken away by the President and the congress and the Anti-Christ, Supreme Court, that Duishka is afforded a right to have an opinion and believe what he wills, without getting charged with a crime of treason for my belief. In my opinion since Obama took office in 2008, this country of mine,(at present time) has diminished in every good thing that was here when he was forced into office by the lying News Media. To God fearing wise people of this land there is no way Jose he could have been elected except by falsifying illegal qualifications that is required to be a legal registered voter and falsifying the qualifications required to be President of THE UNITED STATES OF AMERICA back in 2008. Nevertheless, Duisha concedes that there is not sufficient proof to substantiate his agreement with the Holy Spirit. Since he took office all the surplus of that we had laid in store has been depleted. The health care of Americans is no longer available. The monetary system is gone belly up. The national debt is so much till we are in pawn to other countries, The God founded Constitution and Bill of Rights are twisted into Hammurabbi, Sharia, Islamic, and every humanist, heathen belief imaginable. In GOD We Trust has turned into trusting every black heart evil spirit of Satan that the pagans worship. The good pure foodstuff that is home grown is being bought with taxpayer money, and resold, given away to foreign terrorist that hate Americans. Our freedoms have been compromised to give the heathen our freedom. Obama and his perverted, democratic, anti-American constituents, have succeeded in making this Nation an OBOMANATION OF DESOLATION. Trying to lay it on to Bush. Every democrat from Truman getting defeated in Korea, to Kennedy and the Bay of Pigs, and Johnson stealing our SS to finance the war with Vietnam, which was a bloodbath and a disaster, Then Carter gave America's Sea gates away with the Panama Canal, on up to the jack booted thugs, as per George Herbert Bush, that included the murdering, fornication, Bill Clinton, that to my belief sold the WH to China, that said the buck stopped with him in THE WACO MURDERS, all Americans, and now Obama and his army of destroyers, is finishing the preparation of the fall of Babylon, (*The NewNited States of America)* BABYLON is fallen, is fallen. It seems that the countries that were our allies have turned into our enemies. The ones that say they are our allies are just after the fishes and loaves, and you know what they say is, always a lie. And now the thieves are trying to get Bill back into the WH via his wife Hillary that has lied and is still lying about her email coverups among hundreds of other adverse accusations. But now there are so many # "Americans" and # "Christians", not counting the dead people, dogs, and other illegal voters. How does some unqualified, illiterate, Muslim allied, person even get their name on the ballot? GOD raises up rulers to show his power when He destroys them. Mister Obama, Ms. Nancy Pelosi, All you Democrats, and Republicans,all Supreme Judges, I believe it is too late for you to shell down the corn, but I am not your Judge, but I would not be in your shoes, and have all the blood of the fallen soldiers, both foreign and domestic, all the blood of murdered, aborted babies, the blood of murdered capitol punishment victims on my hands for all the riches you have amassed, Whose end shall be according to your works. (2 Corinthians 11:15) Duishka believes you are "HER" (Revelation 18: 4).

Chapter 23

GOD'S SUPER BOWL ON A Sunday is being prepared at this present time. This will be the last Super Bowl forever. Dear reader, please understand that just like you read in the previous chapter of this book how the writer "Shelled Down the Corn", (confessed), to my daddy and received stripes across my butt from daddy's razor strop; and later how this metaphor portrayed the grand event of "Shelling Down the Corn" to God Almighty, (PANTAKRATOR), and confessing my sins to Him, and still received more stripes, (*plagues*), from Christ Jesus, which this writer welcomed the stripes from Jesus, which was confirmation that I was a Son of God, and not a bastard. (Hebrews 12:8) After God gave me power to be called a Son of God, He gave me another gift of the Holy Ghost, which is the Spirit of Jesus. (Acts 2:38) The Holy Ghost was the promise made to Joel in (Joel 2:28). "And it shall come to pass afterward, that I will pour out My Spirit upon all flesh."

After this writer received the Holy Spirit, yes with evidence of speaking in other tongues, (*languages*), He, (The Holy Spirit), (*not an it*), led me to read (I John 2:26,27). "These things have I written unto you concerning them that seduce you. But the anointing which you have received of Him abides in you; and you need not that any man should teach you; but as the same anointing (Holy Ghost) teaches you of all things, and is Truth, and is no lie; and even as He has taught you, you shall abide in Him."

Do not touch that dial, or the remote, or click the mouse. You are going to learn more knowledge from God through **"Corn Shelling Time"** than all the **P**ost **H**ole **D**iggers and professors from all (*cemetaries*) seminaries. You will know more Truth than the most learned theologians, because no man taught this writer; but the anointing of God, which is the gift of the Holy Ghost, taught this Saint Vitus Dancing, overall wearing, corn shelling, confessing, country boy things that He knew not of. (Jeremiah 33:3) If you, dear reader, will read **"Corn Shelling Time"** slowly and not skip any words, you will know to do good; and if you do not do good after you have read the book, it will be accounted to you as sin. (James 4:17). Listen! Pay Attention! Before we can broadcast *"God's Super Bowl On A Sunday,"* we have to go through the elimination process, since this event involves the entire population of the earth, including you, dear reader; and you will either be eliminated before the main event, or else you will be buzzard bait at the Super Bowl. If you exercise the skill the Lord has taught you, you will be eliminated by way of escape of these things that are coming upon all that dwell upon the face of the earth. (Luke 21:35,36)

Father God, I pray that everyone that reads **"Corn Shelling Time"** will be eliminated from the wine press of the wrath of God, by being "the ones that have kept the Word of My patience, I also will keep you from the hour of temptation, which shall come upon all the world, to test them that dwell upon the earth." (Revelation 3:10) In the Name of Jesus. Amen.

The preliminaries have already begun; and many will be eliminated by the four elements, wind, fire, water, and earth. Before you get through reading **"Corn Shelling Time"**, you will hear of a tornado, or hurricane, or a tsunami, or a volcano erupting, or a mudslide from a flood, or a fire that destroys many acres of trees or vegetation, or an earthquake that Jesus called "the beginning of sorrows". (Matthew 24:8) This writer calls these disasters the preliminaries of elimination to *"God's Super Bowl On A Sunday"*. I believe by 2018 the beginning of sorrows will escalate into the last plagues.

But you, dear reader, I just prayed for you, because you are still in Babylon (sin). If you do not repent, and"Shell Down the Corn" to Christ Jesus, and Come Out of "Her", *(the church)*, the Babylon, (the world system), you will be eliminated by the four elements, or by a disease, or by an accident, or by violence, or by the government laws of the land, or some other plague related to your sinning. "If you do not believe Jesus to keep His Commandments, you are condemned already." (John 3:18)

There are no such words as *churches, saints, cross* in the most original New Testament Greek Scriptures; and this writer cannot print a lie. So, as the participants for God's Super Bowl are being chosen, pure, Holy words are used, not cognate or substituted, or false words will be used. Christ Jesus uses the word Ekklesia, which has the definition in the Greek tongue, "Called Out Ones", and has the inference of "Called Out Loud". So in God's Super Bowl God's Quarterback, or Captain, will be God's only Begotten Son. So Christ Jesus is calling you and everyone that obeys Him, out loud to "Come Out" (Ekklesia) of Mystery, Babylon, the Whore, "Her" Daughters *(the Churches)*, and the world system. Then, if you "Come Out of Sin", there is a possibility Christ Jesus will choose you to be on His team. "So the last shall be first, and the first last: For many be called, but few chosen." (Matthew 20:16)

On the other team, the Captain is the Dragon, the Beast, and the Anti-Christ; and you are the one that chooses which team you want to be on. The winner of the contest has already been decided; and Christ Jesus and His armies are the winners.

Before the main event, the sinners, *church goers,* "Christians" pagans, heathen, and lovers of the world and the things of the world will all be eliminated by destruction, if they do not repent of their sins and "Shell Down the Corn", (confess to Christ) their sins. They will all die by the sword, (violence), or pestilence, (diseases), famine, disaster, or an accident. The only way to be on Christ Jesus' team is to hear Him "Calling You Out of "Her". (Revelation 18:4)

So that faction of Mystery, Babylon will be eliminated, "Because they are lukewarm, neither hot nor cold; because you say you are rich, and increased with goods, and have need of nothing; and you do not know that you are wretched, and miserable, and poor, and blind, and naked; and except you repent, Jesus will spue you out of His mouth." (Revelation 3:17)

Besides Jesus cannot heal you of your infirmities as long as you are in sin, because sin is the reason you have AIDS, hepatitis C, heart trouble, STD, cancer, emphysema, no gall bladder, shingles, gout, schizophrenia, paranoia, prostate, kidneys, liver, *(cirrhosis)*, epilepsy (devil possession). So you are losing your members, because you are a diabetic, you enjoyed too many delicacies when you were able to get down on your knees and pray, you did not; now you have arthritis, or your joints have deteriorated to where you cannot humble yourself before the Living God. The answer is Jesus. "Shell Down the Corn", (confess), tell Him you are sorry for your sins, repent, and ask Him to have mercy on you, a sinner, in the Name of Jesus.

Those that refuse to "Come Out of Babylon", *(church, government, worldly system, laws of the land),* will be eliminated from the Super Bowl Contest by reason of destruction. If you repent and "Shell Down the Corn", (confess to Jesus), you will be one of His army that mounts up on white horses and rides to *"God's Super Bowl On A Sunday".* (Revelation 19:14) The elimination process continues on to the organized religion, which is the Great Whore the Mother of Harlots *(churches)* ("Christians") (Revelation 17:5) "And the ten horns which you saw upon the Beast, these shall hate the Whore, *(churches),* and shall make "Her" desolate, and naked, and shall eat "Her" flesh, and burn "Her" with fire." (Revelation 17:16) The ten horns are a symbol of the wolf in (John 10:11,12). **"I Am the Good Shepherd, the Good Shepherd gives His life for the sheep; but he that is a hireling, and not the Shepherd, whose own the sheep are not, sees the wolf coming, and leaves the sheep, and flees; and the wolf catches them, and scatters the sheep."** (John 10:11,12) **"The hireling flees, because he is a hireling, and cares not for the sheep. I Am the Good Shepherd, and know My sheep, and am known of Mine." (John 10:13,14)**

"Take heed therefore to yourselves, and to all the flock, over the which the Holy Ghost has made you overseers, to feed the Ekklesia (Called Out Ones) of God, which He has purchased with His own blood. For I know this that after my departing, grievous wolves shall enter in among you, not sparing the flock. Also of your own selves shall men arise speaking perverse things to draw away disciples after them." (Acts 20:28,29,30). This is Paul the Apostle doing the talking, which is Jesus speaking to the Called Out Ones at Ephesus through Paul. Paul had departed, and they did just what he said, they let grievous wolves come in; and they are still among you in the perverted churches. Jesus' angel told John to write to you and say: "Never the less I have somewhat against you, because you have left your first love. Remember therefore from where you are fallen, and repent, and do the first works." (Revelation 2:4,5)

"And the third angel sounded *(blew his trumpet)* and there fell a great star from heaven, burning as it were a lamp; and it fell upon the third part of the rivers, and upon the fountains of waters; and the name of the star is called wormwood, and many men died of the waters, because they were made bitter." (Revelation 8:10,11) Elimination of the "Christians" that did not "Come Out of "Her". More to come. Same song, second verse, could get better, but it's gonna git worse.

"But it shall come to pass, if you will not hearken unto the voice of the Lord your God, to observe, to do all His Commandments and

His statutes, which I command you this day, that all these curses shall come upon you and overtake you." (Deuteronomy 28:15) "The Lord shall send upon you cursing, vexation, and rebuke in all you set your hand unto for to do until you be destroyed and until you perish quickly, because of the wickedness of your doings, whereby you have forsaken Me". (Deuteronomy 28:20)

"And the Kings of the earth, and the great men, and the rich men, and the chief captains, and the mighty men, and every bondman, and every freeman hid themselves in the dens and in the rocks of the mountains, and said to the rocks and the mountains, "fall on us and hide us from the face of Him that sits on the throne, and from the wrath of the Lamb." (Revelation 6:15,16)

"And the fifth angel sounded, and he opened the bottomless pit and locusts came out that had power as scorpions; and it was commanded them to hurt only those men, which have not the seal of God in their foreheads. And to them it was given that they should not kill them; but just torment them for five months." (Revelation 9:1,2,3,4,5) Observe, these are only the men that did not "Come Out of "Her" and be sealed with God's seal in their foreheads. "These men shall seek death in those days and shall not find it." (Revelation 9:6)

Dear reader, all you have to do to avoid this plague and all the other plagues of the Great Whore and Babylon is to "Shell Down the Corn" to Christ Jesus (confess you are a sinner), repent, and Come Out of association with unbelievers, ("Christians"), pagans, heathen, and fornication, which is idolatry.

"Moreover He (The Lord), will bring upon you all the diseases of Egypt, which you were afraid of; and they shall cleave unto you, also every sickness, every plague, which is not written in the book of the law, them will the Lord bring upon you, until you be destroyed." (Deuteronomy 28:60,61)

"And the first angel went and poured out his vial (bowl) upon the earth; and there fell a noisome and grievous sore upon the men which had the mark of the Beast, and upon them which worshiped his image." (Revelation 16:2)

"Christians", and pagans, and heathen already have the mark of the Beast, *ObamaCare, welfare, stimulus, Section 8, extended unemployment benefits, ALGII, National Health Fund, revenue de solidarite active, social assistance, Nation Assistance Act 1948, AFDC, food stamps, SNAP, TANF, any government subsidy, Christmas, Easter, Halloween, any saint day, Sunday, Good Friday, Lent, Armed Forces, Police, Politicians, and many, many more that have any kind of organization that is influenced by the devil.* On the other hand believers have Come Out of "Her", and they have the seal of God in their foreheads.

All of the ones with the plagues mentioned above will miss the contest of God's Super Bowl, because they are being eliminated with these plagues of the Whore. Someone asked if this was just my opinion. I answered: "Yes, but it is also God's opinion, because He said these things before He called this writer to tell all the benefits the readers of **"Corn Shelling Time"** would enjoy if they obeyed God and believed Jesus, instead of believing in Jesus. The proof is in the pudding. Look at the plagues that have attacked you; and you have put your trust in man, *(doctors and drugs, and insurance)*. That is God's chastisement for being in sin, (Babylon). Those previous sores have already come upon you in the lungs, in the pancreas, in the prostate, on your skin; and the tribulation has not started yet. All of the things that caused these sores are called sins. The sores are called cancer. Some one asked some one to sing the other day, and he replied, "Can't sir." Get it, cancer.

Some stupid fool that was dying from the plague was told what God said: "The reason he had the plague was because God said he would be destroyed because he did not keep God's laws and commandments and statutes." The fool argued; "God only told that to the Jews."

Someone said: "Is God only the God of the Jews? Then why are you dying?" Another fool said; "God's laws and Commandments have been done away with", and he was asked; "Why are all these plagues come upon you?" Listen! Understand! God's laws and Commandments cannot save you. You are being saved by the gift of God, called the law of grace; but you stay saved by obeying God's Commandments; or else you receive the plagues that have come upon you already by sinning.

You voted for a heathen that told you he was a "Christian" just like you, so the blind is leading the blind; and both you and the one you voted for will fall into the ditch of destruction.

Jesus sent me, the writer of **"Corn Shelling Time"** to plead with all flesh to repent and "Shell Down the Corn", (confess), to Christ Jesus; and perhaps He will raise you up in the last day. The hospital and doctors sent a veteran of foreign wars home for Hospice to come in and help him die without so much pain. He will get the 21 Gun Salute. His wife will get a flag and a lot of debt to pay off; but what are the rewards of his patriotism? He is dead, you know. "Whose end shall be according to their works." (II Corinthians 11:15) He let the Whore, the Mother of Harlots, cause him to commit fornication with the world, and the things that are in the world; but he lived deliciously until he died; but now comes the judgment. He lies asleep until he is resurrected to stand before the throne where the Judge sits. David said: "For in death there is no remembrance of you in the grave who shall give you thanks?" (Psalms 6:5) Do you think God will save the veteran of war for his patriotism? What about you? Do you think God will save you for doing your civic duty, and voting for a lying, stealing, murdering politician? You answer that question, please. You, young man, whichever country you live in. Do you not know that when you do service with weapons that kill your neighbor, you are doing service for the Kaiser and Satan? Even if you are doing K.P., you are just as guilty as the soldier on the front line, because you are an ally with a murderer, that is a child of Satan. Your patriotism to Satan will not save you. If you do not get destroyed before you become buzzard bait of God's Super Bowl, if you take the mark of the Beast in your right hand or in your forehead, you will be a soldier in the army of the Beast, Anti-Christ. (Revelation 13); and you will be a contestant in *"God's Super Bowl On A Sunday"*; but you will be the main entree in God's great supper for the eagles, AKA buzzard bait. (Revelation 19:17)

It is so sad for this writer, because I am a Japhethite, a son of Japheth; and the Germans, Russians, Scandinavians, Greeks, and other Europeans are Japhethites, the most beautiful people that God created. They will be in the army of Gog at *"God's Super Bowl On A Sunday,"* if they do not "Shell Down the Corn", (confess), to Christ Jesus and repent, and Come Out of "Her", Mystery, Babylon, The Whore. The Japhethites are the light complected humans that God created to be the separated beauty of His creation. It turns God's stomach to see a beautiful blonde headed, light skinned, daughter of Japheth letting a Canaanite, a son of Ham, spill his seed into her belly to produce an innocent mixed breed child. *(if she does not murder the baby)*

"And you shall not let any of your seed pass through the fire to Molech." (Leviticus 18:21) Molech was a heathen god of the Ammonites. "You shall not sow your field with mingled seed." (Leviticus 19:19)

The pure seed of Japheth will follow Gog to *"God's Super Bowl On A Sunday"* and be wiped out, to be buzzard bait. "Land of Magog, Meshech, Tubal, Gomer, Togarmah (all Japhethites)." (Ezekiel 38:2) **"Corn Shelling Time"** is pleading with my brothers, the sons of Japheth, Germans, Russians, Scandinavians, Greeks, to Come Out of "Her". Repent and "Shell Down the Corn" to Christ Jesus, and be riding on a <u>white</u> horse, following Jesus, at *"God's Super Bowl On A Sunday"* of God Almighty (PANTAKRATOR).

Wars and earthquakes, tornadoes, floods, and fire are taking my loved ones, even as I speak, because the sorrows started to escalate in 2011, and are growing more intense as I write this. Disasters are happening where ever you are. Some of my dear loved ones are dwellers in the Phillipines, where they recently suffered a deadly tropical cyclone *(typhoon)* that hit the central Phillipines, killing thousands, because of sin. Another typhoon is on the way to the Phillipines as I write these words.

Earthquakes, hurricanes, floods and many other events have taken their toll in Europe, killing many and destroying property, as a result of not keeping God's Commandments, which is sin. This is all an elimination process to end all transgressions and sin. (Daniel 9:24)

Listen! Pay attention! Dear reader. This writer cannot give you a full testimony, and tell every detail of every event of salvation the Lord Jesus has helped this ignorant, revelrouser, killer, thief, destroyer to go and sin no more. The same Light that came suddenly on Brother Paul, on his road to destruction, came differently to me. Instead of the Light coming to me, I went to the Light. Instead of the Light causing me to be blind, the Light caused me to see, because I was already blind. Just like you, "Christian", sin had me blinded. Since I have gotten the beam, *(log)*, out of my eye, I can show you how to get the mote out of your eye, if you will to be healed and saved from ultimate destruction. This world's worst sinner was dying with one of those sores, called cancer; and I made a deal with Christ Jesus. He did not shake my hand and agree with me that it was a deal. But here is what happened. First I remembered telling my daddy a lie and denying my wrong. I remembered my daddy telling me if I would have "Shelled Down the Corn", (confessed), he would not have put stripes on me with his razor strop. I remembered I tested him to see if he would do what he said, and he did. So I know God, (Christ Jesus) is bigger than my daddy, but He is My Father. So the First thing I did was to "Shell Down Down the Corn" to Christ Jesus, which took a long time to confess that I had broken every commandment and law and statute of God, by cursing and using the Lord"s name in vain, and having all kinds of worldly gods *(idols)* before the Almighty God (PANTAKRATOR). Instead of the Word of God coming out of my mouth, I invented some of the most filthy words that Webster never heard of. I profaned the Sabbath Day. Instead of working 6 days, I worked seven days and nights also in revelings, fighting, drunkenness, and committing whoredom. I had two of the most virtuous, chaste, loving, parents that I dishonored, instead of honoring them. I killed people in many different ways with my words of death and blasphemy, and derogatory words to my loved ones and enemies also. I committed adultery and stole my neighbors' wives, and anything else he had. Since I was dying anyway, I took the time to go into detail with the Lord on each one of these broken commandments. I confessed to Christ Jesus that all the illegal gains I had acquired in life I would pay back. I asked Christ Jesus to forgive me of all those sins of disobedience to His Commandments and to save me from Hell. I told the Lord that whether I lived or died I repented of all my sins; and I was sorry. I said, "Lord, you are the giver of life; and if you will let me live and heal me, I will live the rest of my life for you, in the Name of Jesus." That was the vow, *(deal)*, I made to Christ Jesus; and He did not answer me that I could tell; but I just kept believing that He would do what I asked Him to do, if I would go and sin no more. By faith I kept believing Him (the Word). I did what I said I would do, and He did what I asked Him to do; but I believe that He made my salvation contingent upon my keeping my promise I made to Him. When I "Shelled Down the Corn" to Christ Jesus, (confessed), the Light that blinded Brother Paul, kept getting brighter to me each day; and my blinded eyes began to open; and I see more clearly each day. But not only did the Lord Jesus heal me and promised to save me if I endured to the end, I shall be saved. (Matthew 24:13) But He prayed to Father God to send me the gift of His Holy Spirit; and He did; and He is what taught me. So (I John 2:27) taught me that I had no need of any man teaching me anything. I trust no man for my Life. I Am doing what I promised Jesus, (God), I would do; and that is to tell you to repent, for it is **"Corn Shelling Time"**. If you, dear reader, will "Shell Down the Corn", (confess), and repent of your living in sin, (Babylon), and Come Out of "Her", and come to Jesus, (Matthew 11;28), and tell Him what you will do, and do it, Christ Jesus is merciful, and His promises are conditional on your promise to go and sin no more. But Jesus is not a respecter of persons, what He did for me, He will do for you, **if** you will do what I did, "Shell Down the Corn", (confess to Jesus). Quit worshiping Idols, sports,church, TV, family, food, Hollywood, etc.

The major events that are happening are occurring so fast this writer cannot write them fast enough to go into detail of all the sorrows that are taking place at breakneck speed over all the world. Even before the Great Tribulation arrives, tribulations of great magnitude are visible in all nations; and the nations that are Anti-Christ are cursed above all the other nations. "To the Jew first, and the Gentile." The Lord said whoever blesses Israel, He will bless them; and whoever curses Israel, He will curse them; and at this present time, every nation on earth is cursing Israel, except the USA and the U.K. Israel is cursed already because God cursed them for not keeping His Commandments; but so are the other nations cursed; but God wants to be the one to punish His chosen people. So as the Lamb is opening the Book of Daniel that was sealed up, we behold the plagues that are coming on the entire world, the Jew first, and the Gentiles.

This writer is being obedient to the calling of Christ Jesus to remind the whole world of the last warning, and all of the warnings in the scriptures, which are Holy, to Come Out of Mystery, Babylon, and to reveal the Mystery of God to the ones that hunger and thirst after righteousness. Just like God commissioned Noah to warn all the inhabitants of the earth that it was going to rain and come a flood over the whole earth. Because the people of the earth had never seen any rain, because it had never rained before. "But there went up a mist from the earth and watered the whole face of the ground." (Genesis 2:6) Just like Noah worked over 100 years building an ark, (*boat*), and preaching "Repent". Not any believed him, until God said "Come In Out of the Rain, Noah," and Noah took his wife, and 3 sons, and their wives out of the rain and into the ark; and God shut the door. (Genesis 7:16)

In like manner, God told Brother John to warn the people to Come Out of the Church (Whore), Come Out of the Mystery, Babylon (Idolatry), Come Out of the World, (lust of eyes, flesh, pride). Brother John is revealing to you what the Lord showed to him, all the plagues that you must suffer until you be destroyed from off the earth, if you do not repent. God has four angels holding the four winds of the earth, so you do not get destroyed by the hurricanes, tornadoes, or typhoons until you Come Out of "Her", and God's angels will put His seal upon your forehead. (Revelation 7:2,3)

The elimination process has already started; and millions are being destroyed, because they do not believe the Bible or **"Corn Shelling Time".** God prepared an Arena for His Grand Finale Event, the last Super Bowl On A *Sunday* of God. God made Himself a mountain to exercise His Title, the King of the Hill. The mountain God, (Christ Jesus), will stand on and direct His Army, is called Mount Megiddo; and all around this mountain is a large valley that makes a Bowl that covers miles and miles. This Valley of Megiddo is the Arena where the Last Event will be performed, which this writer calls *"God's Super Bowl On A Sunday"*, and since all the *churches* and big contests believe in practicing their Idolatry on the *Sun God Day, (Sunday)*, I believe God will bring His apex of destruction on a *Sunday*. Correction! Not all churches practice Idolatry on *Sunday*, only 99% of them. This mountain and this valley called Megiddo, have been prepared for this big Super Bowl Contest for thousands of years, and is soon to come to pass.

"A noise shall come even unto the ends of the earth, for the Lord has a controversy with the nations *(Gentiles)*. He will plead with all flesh. He will give them that are wicked to the sword, saith the Lord. Thus saith the Lord of Hosts, "Behold evil shall go forth from nation to nation, and a great whirlwind shall be raised up from the coasts of the earth; and the slain of the Lord shall be at that day from one end of the earth, even unto the other end of the earth: They shall not be lamented, neither gathered, nor buried. They shall be dung upon the ground." (Jeremiah 25:31,32,33) This is when the four angels loose the four winds they are holding back. This is a controversy God has against all flesh; and He is pleading with you at this present time to Come Out of "Her", and escape the plagues that are already upon you.

You, dear readers, are living in the time when God is pleading with all flesh, including you. You are more blessed than a lot of other people that do not have the opportunity to read **"Corn Shelling Time"**, because this book is the way God is pleading with you. If you will read the many scriptures in **"Corn Shelling Time"**, and do them, you will find your way of escape that Christ Jesus has provided for you; and you will be at the Super Bowl of God mounted upon <u>white</u> horses, following the Lord of lords and the King of kings; and you will not be on the losing side of the contest, and become a meal for the eagles. God is pleading with you at this moment to Come into His Ark of Safety and live, instead of dying in sin, (Mystery, Babylon), and being destroyed. Right now, do not put it off any longer, "Shell Down the Corn" to Christ Jesus and (confess) to Him, and say: Father, God, I confess I am a sinner, and I ask you to forgive me, because I repent; and I need Christ Jesus to save me. I renounce Satan and the sinful things in this world; and I will go and sin no more. I plead the blood of Christ Jesus to wash me and cleanse me from all unrighteousness; and I thank You Father in the Name of Jesus for saving me; and I believe Christ Jesus, when He said He would not turn me away. I believe Jesus is the Son of the Living God; and I believe I am being saved in the Name of Jesus. Amen.

Now that you have come unto Christ Jesus, start shucking off the old garments that are filthy from sin and know that you are a new creature, because you are in Christ. "So, do not remember the things that are passed away; but look! All things are become new." (II

Corinthians 5:17) So do not go back to the acquaintances you were fellow shipping with, because you are in the Light and want no part of darkness; and you have no part with an infidel, ("Christian"). Now you are the temple that God dwells in, and you cannot agree with Idolatry of any kind. You are the temple of the Living God, because God has said, "I will dwell in them and walk in them; and I will be their God; and they shall be My people. Wherefore Come Out from among them *(churches* and "Christians"), and be you separate." saith the Lord, "and touch not the unclean thing; and I will receive you; and will be a Father unto you; and you shall be My Sons and Daughters, saith the Lord Almighty, (PANTAKRATOR)" (II Corinthians 6:14,15,16,17,18)

"What? Know you not that your bodies are members of Christ? Shall I take the members of Christ (believers) and make them members of an Harlot? *(church)*. God forbid: What? Know you not that he which is joined to an Harlot *(church)* is one body? For two saith He shall be one flesh." (I Corinthians6:15,16).

So **"Corn Shelling Time"** is pleading for you to Come Out of "Her"; and He called you My people, which you are; and be not partakers of "Her" sins; and you receive not of "Her" plagues." (Revelation 18:4) Now, you have enough sense to come in out of the rain. The people in the days of Noah did not have have sense enough to come in out of the rain, they were destroyed. The people from Jesus' day until now do not have enough sense to come out of Mystery, Babylon, AKA, also known as sin. Those people were destroyed and are being destroyed and will continue to be destroyed, because they are ignorant unbelievers and are already condemned, because they did not believe Jesus or the ones Jesus sent to warn them how to come out of destruction. But you, dear reader, have read **"Corn Shelling Time"** and you have sense enough to come in out of the rain, also you have enough sense to come out of sin, which is Mystery, Babylon, which is "Her". The plagues will go away when you go and sin no more! In the name of Jesus, Amen and Amen.

THIS is an insert in the book, **"CORN SHELLING TIME"** and **MICHAEL DUISHKA** with some of his belief. They meet and they love and he makes her his wife, while both are young and both are sinners, and both are ignorant about the mystery of Godliness, because both were raised up by hard working, good, honest parents that were destitute of the knowledge of their creator. As the man and his young wife starts the journey through their life here on this earth, little do they know that they are groping around in total darkness without the light of Christ Jesus to guide them. Then the enemy, Satan starts his campaign to cause the death sentence that every human being is under to be carried out. The couple starts to have one catastrophe, one right after the other, which they call a streak of bad luck, which is so wrong, but just what the enemy wants them to believe. It starts with Satan taking their babies, while both parents are doing what they can to hold the other up and comfort each other. Then comes doctor bills, and hospital bills, utilities, rent, mechanical bills on an old junk car or truck, along with necessary medicine, with many miscellaneous things. The man gets a second job, working day and most of the night then the wife has more children and they live. But Satan is having his way and never lets up. The family keeps saying, things will get better, but without Christ Jesus, they never will. With all the loss of sleep and the extra vigor it takes out of the man working many hours, he hunted for a crutch and found one in alcohol, and dope to stay awake. In the places where the wine and whiskey flowed he found sympathy from loose women and went on into deep sin. But God knowing that the man or woman neither one had never heard about His Son, Christ Jesus, intervened in their lives and caused some of His witnesses to tell the couple about THE SAVIOR. The couple started going to a little *church* and things changed, not for the better but for the worse. **"Think not that I am come to send peace on earth: I came not to send peace, but a sword. And a man's foes** *shall be* **they of his own household.** (MATTHEW 10:34,36) The sword of the LORD, which is the word of God fell into some good ground with the man, but the woman could not forgive or forget all the trespasses her husband had committed against her so she developed a root of bitterness. Being saved is a progressive work that takes a lifetime to be perfect. The more the man put off the former conversation, the old man, which is corrupt according to deceitful lusts. (Ephesians 4:22), The more distant and hostile the wife became until no favor at all was to be found for her husband. Satan filled her heart with hate so much till Murder and Suicide demons entered into her after she won a divorce in the heathen courts, with the laws of the land. The children forsook all their up bringing in the way they should go and went with the liberal one that permitted them to commit fornication in her new home. Many years have passed without any communication of any kind between the man and what used to be his family. But the man believes Christ Jesus when He said through brother Paul: Believe the LORD CHRIST JESUS and you shall be saved and your house. (Acts 16:31). In the meantime the man is going through the land sowing the seed and praying to the LORD of the harvest that He will send some workers into the land where ever his loved ones are to sow some seed, the Word of God. Listen dear reader; does this story fit you or at least have some similarities that has befallen you. **"CORN SHELLING TIME"** and **MICHAEL DUISHKA** wants to encourage you with the WORD that the Master said: **"Have faith of GOD, Whosoever shall say unto this mountain, be thou removed, be thou cast into the sea; and shall not doubt in his heart, but shall believe that those things which he says shall come to pass; he shall have whatsoever he says"** (Mark 11:22,23) Just to make double dog dead sure your name is written in the Lamb's book of life, appease DUISHKA and SHELL DOWN THE CORN with me. If you can get down on your knees, do it and say with me; LORD GOD I confess I am a sinner, and I am so sorry, but I Repent of my sins and plead the blood of CHRIST JESUS to cover me and wash away my sins and cleanse me from all unrighteousness. I renounce the works of Satan and I will go and sin no more and I ask you LORD JESUS to save me, and I believe you will in the name of CHRIST JESUS: AMEN

Chapter 24

SO MANY THOUSANDS OF God's people are being destroyed, (eliminated), from *"God's Super Bowl On A Sunday,"* because they did not come out of "Her". They received "Her" plagues before the contest started; and thousands are being eliminated by the four elements, the wind, the water, the fire, and the earth, by tornadoes, hurricanes, typhoons, floods, mudslides, volcanoes, tsunamis, earthquakes, and wild beasts. This is not to mention infirmities, pestilences, including infectious diseases like AIDS, gonorrhea, syphilis, meningitis, smallpox, bubonic plague and many, many more ways to be destroyed for not keeping God's Commandments.

"Let us hear the conclusion of the whole matter, fear God, and keep His Commandments, for this is the whole *duty* of man." (Ecclesiastes 12:13) All these multiplied millions are being eliminated from the contest of *"God's Super Bowl On A Sunday"*, because they will not keep His Commandments.

Dear reader, what kind of plague are you going to the doctor for? What kind of dope (*medication*) are you addicted to? Are your children on drugs for Attention Deficit Hyperactivity Disorder? Did your child inherit devils from his parents or grandparents, such as hearing voices, thinking it is God talking? All these hallucinations are devils, and the more drugs the captive of Satan takes, the more the devils require, until a Columbine, or New Town, Connecticut, or suicide. Any way you slice it, it is caused from devils; and more than likely they were acquired at *church,* or school, or at home from parents. My daddy used SPA (seize, possess, afflict), **S**eize me, **P**ossess the razor strop, **A**fflict my butt; and magically the devils were gone. None of the children of darkness that enacted these massacres ever had any SPA. These children will miss *"God's Super Bowl On A Sunday."*

Very few of God's people understand spiritual warfare. People here on earth are ruled by spirits. The evil spirits in the heavens war against each other to gain possession of principalities, powers of which Satan is the ruler of the powers of the air. They (evil spirits) fight each other to gain control of the rulers of darkness (sin) of this world and spiritual wickedness in high places. (Ephesians 6:12)

The angels of God fight the evil angels of Satan to help God's people to overcome the fiery darts (wiles) of the devil. "God is spirit." (John 4:24), misquoted in KJV to read, "God is a spirit." The Greek does not have God as a spirit, but rather God is all spirit.

One of the reasons why *church* people cannot worship God in spirit and Truth is because they profane the Sabbath Day, and *Sunday* worship is a lie and is not Truth. That is the reason *church* "Christians" cannot overcome the evil spirits that oppress them and possess some of them, or else they would not go to a physician.

"But when Jesus heard that, He said unto them; **"They that be whole need not a physician, but they that are sick."** (Matthew 9:12| Believers know how to cast out the unclean spirits that believers wrestle against. (Ephesians 6:12)

Gabriel the archangel, which is spirit, told Daniel, "The Prince of Persia, *(the spirit that ruled from the air over the King of Persia),* withstood me twenty one days; but Michael, (another archangel), came to help me." (Daniel 10:13) "And now I will return to fight with the Prince of Persia: And when I am gone forth, lo, the Prince of Grecia shall come." (Daniel 10:20) Pay attention! This is not flesh and blood the angels of God are fighting against; but they are spirits. The Prince of Grecia is very significant in *"God's Super Bowl On A Sunday".* This angel, that ruled the flesh and blood King of Greece, (Daniel 10:20), was Abaddon; which means a bad son, which later will be manifest in (Revelation 9:12) under the name in Greek, Apollyon. But back to (Daniel 10:20), Gabriel and Michael. The angels over God's army, went to fight the spirits that ruled the King of Greece *(Grecia).* Guess who was the King of Greece. None other than Alexander the Great, which conquered the world; and it has been said he sat down and cried because there was not anything left to conquer. Alexander was ruled by the angel spirit that ranked next to Satan himself. Remember Gabriel said he must go and fight against this Prince of Grecia, which is none other than Apollyon, which means destruction or perdition. Michael and Gabriel bound this angel in the bottomless pit until the time of the end, when the angel with the key to the bottomless pit opens it and lets the locust out of the pit. (Revelation 9:3) "And, lo, behold, these locusts had a king over them, which was the angel that ruled over Greece, named in Hebrew, A-bad-don, but in Greek Apollyon." (Revelation 9:11)

"The beast which you saw, was, and is not, and shall ascend out of the bottomless pit, and go into perdition, (destruction)." (Revelation 17:8). This is talking about the beast that has not come on the scene yet, because Michael and Gabriel, the archangels of God bound this angel and locked him up in the bottomless pit until the last three and one half years of Daniel's 70th week. This is the Quarterback for the Dragon (Satan) that directs Satan's team into destruction at *"God's Super Bowl On A Sunday".* Pay attention:If you are interested in living forever. "The beast goes into perdition, and they that dwell on earth shall wonder, whose names were not written in the Book of Life from the foundation of the world, when they behold the beast, that was, and is not, and yet is." (Revelation 17:8)

If your name is written in the Book of Life, do not do anything to cause it to be blotted out of the Book of Life. If your name is not written in the Book of Life, you need to come out of sin (Mystery, Babylon) and "Shell Down the Corn", (confess) to Jesus. Repent from all your works of the flesh and get the blood of Jesus applied to your heart; and God's angel, the scribe, will write your name in the Book of Life. If you are not interested, you never will read this anyway; and you will be joined to the beast with his number, or his name, or his mark on your forehead, or on your right hand; and you will be destroyed forever. (Revelation 13:16,17)

"And here is the mind which has wisdom, the seven heads are seven mountains on which the woman sits." (Revelation 17:9) The Mountains are seven kingdoms. The seven kingdoms are Egypt, Assyria, Babylon, Media and Persia, Greece, Rome, the Anti-Christ. And there are seven kings, five are fallen and one is, and the other is not yet come. These are Pharaoh, Ashurbanipal, Nebuchadnezzar, Darius, and Alexander the Great. These are the five kings that are fallen. Kaiser *(Caesar)* is the one that is, and Anti-Christ is the one to come. The beast that ascends out of the bottomless pit, he is the eighth king. And he is of the seven. He is the spirit that ruled Alexander the Great until Alexander died, and Michael and Gabriel, the archangels of God bound the spiritual King of Grecia, and locked him in the bottomless pit, until the angel with the key to the pit opens it, and lets out the locusts and their King Apollyon. (Revelation 9:11) Brother John at that time was being ruled by the king that is, which is the Kaiser, or KJV says *Caesar.* The seventh king will be the Anti-Christ that rules the old Roman empire, which is being formed at this present time, AKA the E.U. Or European Union, which includes Greece, where the beast of the old spirit, that ruled Alexander the Great, which is the king that was, but will be of the seven, which will be the eighth, and will go into perdition, which will be the Anti-Christ. (Revelation 17:11).

The ten horns which you saw are the ten nations that will condense down to ten in the European Union, which at this present time, the union has twenty some nations. This is a very hard subject, as is all the bible, to a natural person. The bible is written by the spiritual man, and the natural man does not know what is being said. Jesus said, "The Words that I speak unto you, they are Spirit and they are Life." (John 6:63) "They, (*the words of the bible*), are alive to those that are spiritual, but darkness to the natural man. Howbeit, we speak wisdom among them that are perfect: Yet not the wisdom of this world, nor of the rulers of this world, that come to naught." (I Corinthians 2:6) "Which things also we speak, not in the words which man's wisdom teaches, but which the Holy Ghost teaches, comparing spiritual things with spiritual. But the natural man (*which is you that reads this*) receives not the things of the Spirit of God." (I Corinthians 2:13,14) "For they are foolishness unto him, (*you that are reading this book*), neither can he (*the one reading this book*) know them, because they are spiritually discerned." (I Corinthians 2:14) "But he that is spiritual judges all things, yet he himself is judged of no man." (I Corinthians 2:15) Not possessing the Holy Spirit in His fulness is the reason a critic cannot evaluate the contents and the context of this book, because to evaluate this book and be a critic of this book, the one that reads and understands has to have the Wisdom of God, and be baptized into Christ Jesus, and be submerged into the Holy Spirit of God. This writer can judge that you are not qualified to be a critic, or to be an evaluator of this book, because you are not spiritual. The reason this writer judges all things is because he is spiritual. (I Corinthians 2:15). If you were spiritual, you would not still be in Mystery, Babylon, or love the things of this world. (I John 2:15,16). If you, the reader, were spiritual and qualified to judge righteously, you would know the difference between Mystery, Babylon and Babylon itself. "You cannot receive the things of God, because they are spiritually discerned (*judged*) and are foolishness to you." (I Corinthians 2:14)

That is why the words of this book are so hard for a natural person to understand, because these words are spirit and they are life. (John 6:63) These words are patterned from the words that Jesus spoke, and "they are just like the wind blows where it wills, *(or wants to)*, and you hear the sound thereof, but cannot tell from where it comes and where it goes, so is everyone that is generated of the spirit." (John 3:8). "Verily, verily, I say unto you, except a man be generated of water and of the spirit, he cannot enter into the Kingdom of God. That which is generated of flesh is flesh, and that which is generated of the spirit is spirit." (John 3:6,7). The only way you can be qualified to receive this anointing from above is to "Shell Down the Corn" to Christ Jesus, (confess to God that you are a sinner). (Romans 10:9) "That if you shall confess with your mouth that Christ Jesus is Lord, and shall believe in your heart that God raised Him from the dead, you shall be saved." (Romans 10:9)

Listen! Pay attention! **<u>Corn Shelling Time</u>** is preparing you for the last great event that will happen in your time, which is *"God's Super Bowl On A Sunday."* If you are a participant, you will either be generated of the flesh and be destroyed and eaten by the eagles, *(buzzards)*, or you will be generated of the spirit from above and live forever. Since this generation is a generation of choice, you can choose which one you desire, either life or death, flesh, or spirit. God is preparing the arena, the Super Bowl, for the *Sunday* event. "And He gathered them together into a place called in the Hebrew tongue, **Armageddon.**" (Revelation 16:16)

This is how God calls and gathers them to come to the great event, *"God's Super Bowl On A Sunday"*. "And I saw three unclean spirits, like frogs come out of the mouth of the dragon, and out of the mouth of the beast, and out of the mouth of the false prophet." (Revelation 16:15) This is the hooks that God puts into the jaw of Gog to turn him back to the Super Bowl. (Ezekiel 38:4) The other way God gathers all of the kings of the world to His Super Bowl, is "God has put it into their hearts to fulfill His will, and to agree, and give their kingdom to the beast, until the words of God be fulfilled." (Revelation 17:17)

"And the fifth angel poured out his vial upon the seat of the beast, and his kingdom was full of darkness, and they gnawed their tongues for pain, and blasphemed the God of heaven because of their pains, and their sores, and repented not of their deeds." (Revelation 16:10,11)

God has put it into their hearts to come and do battle against Jesus and his armies, and the Holy Ones, which are the ones that were generated of the spirit from above, that were sanctified and now they will be glorified to mount upon white horses and follow the King of kings and Lord of lords to the Super Bowl. Since there will not be any fuel to power vehicles at that time, God has to prepare a way for the armies of the beast, that is the spirit that rules the Anti-Christ to travel to the Super Bowl. "The sixth angel poured out his vial upon the great river Euphrates, and the water thereof was dried up, that the way of the kings of the east might be prepared." (Revelation 16:12)

The prophesy has already been made that God will draw all the armies of the beast to the Valley of Decision, which is a valley that surrounds a hill, or mountain, called Tel Migeddo. God created this valley and hill, which is the arena, where *"God's Super Bowl On A Sunday"*, will be performed.

The elimination process, that is action happening as we speak, is so sad on one hand, but very exciting on the other hand. One of my acquaintances was just eliminated before he had the opportunity to read **"Corn Shelling Time"**. Millions are being eliminated from participating in *"God's Super Bowl On A Sunday"* for different reasons. You, dear reader, can be a participant on the spiritual winning team if you choose to believe the Lord of lords and the King of kings and the Word of Christ Jesus, and do what He says.

"Come out of "Her", My people, which is Mystery, Babylon, the culmination of abominations of filth, fornication, idolatry, and all sins of the flesh of this world. "For true and righteous are His judgments: for He has judged the Great Whore, which did corrupt the earth with

"Her" fornication, and has avenged the blood of His slaves at "Her" hand." (Revelation 19:2) "And again they said "Alleluia", and "Her" smoke rose up forever and ever." (Revelation 19:3) This should be an incentive for all of God's people to come out of " the Great Whore, the *Roman Catholic Church* and all the protestant *churches,* or any *church,* and also the world and all the things in the world.

"And He said unto me, write; "blessed are they which are called unto the Marriage Supper of the Lamb;" and He said unto me, these are the true sayings of God." (Revelation 19:9) This is the award banquet of God, where He rewards all of His believers with their crowns and jewels, awards, and rewards, including Jesus, who receives His Kingship and Lordship, and His new name. The two witnesses are the last people that are Holy to be taken from the earth. They will complete the first resurrection; and there will be millions of "Christians" that will be disappointed when they wake up at the Great White Throne Judgment, and realize they did not get *raptured.* Nothing sinful or unholy will enter the Kingdom of God. "And whosoever was not found written in the Book of Life was cast into the Lake of Fire." (Revelation 20:15)

Listen! There are so many false perceptions that have been taught to you that we have to leave the subject of *"God's Super Bowl On A Sunday"* to address another matter that will burst your bubble. There is not going to be any *rapture.* The only catching away that will ever happen is the first resurrection that Jesus plainly told you about: The ones that have done good unto the resurrection of life, which will be at the end of the age, or at the end of the dispensation of the Gentiles. (John 5:29) The rest of the verse said: "and they that have done evil, unto the resurrection of damnation." So, Jesus here is talking about the two resurrections, the first resurrection for those that have done good and obeyed His Commandments, and the second resurrection for the ones that have done evil, and disobeyed His Commandments, who will be judged by the righteous ones at the Great White Throne Judgment of God. All bodies die and go to sleep. The soul and the spirit cannot die, but they separate and leave the body; and when the soul and spirit leave the body, the body goes to sleep until the voice of God calls the ones that are in the graves to come and join their body, soul, and spirit together to be judged." (John 5:28) The first fruits of the first resurrection has already started when Jesus was resurrected, and He led captivity captive. The ones that were prisoners in Paradise are still prisoners in Paradise. Paradise was a section or a compartment of Hell; but Paradise was moved and the prisoners are still prisoners in Paradise in the section, or compartment of heaven called the third heaven. Every body that died after Jesus was resurrected is asleep in the grave, and their body has turned back into dust that it (*the body*) was formed, or made with. "But at the voice of God, which will be a shout, with the voice of the archangel, and only those that are asleep into Christ Jesus, will God bring their soul and spirit with Him and call the body to meet up again with it's soul and spirit; and the three, body, soul, spirit will rise, or be caught up and be forever with the Lord, Christ Jesus," forever. (I Thessalonians 4:13-17) This will be the culmination of the first resurrection.

All the wicked spirits go to another compartment of Hell to stay until they are resurrected, and their wicked spirits join with their bodies 1,000 years after the first resurrection to stand in front of the Great White Throne Judgment, which is called the second resurrection. The wicked ones that did not keep God's Commandments and their name was not found written in the Book of Life will be judged to go back to Hell, to the Lake of Fire.

There are going to be five groups of people in the first resurrection. The first group will be the first fruits made up of Jesus and the ones that were raised from the dead with Jesus. (Matthew 27:52,53) "And the graves were opened, and many bodies of the Holy ones, which slept arose, and came out of the graves after His resurrection, and went into the Holy City, and appeared unto many." (Matthew 27:52,53). "Then Brother John saw another angel that asked him, "who are these people of every nation, kindred, and people and tongues that stood before the throne and where did they come from?" And John said, "Sir, you know," and he said to John, "these are they which came out of Great Tribulation, and have washed their robes, and have made them white in the blood of the Lamb." (Revelation 7:9,13,14) This multitude that John saw are in the future, but will be in the general resurrection, when God brings their spirits back with Him to reunite with their bodies. (I Thessalonians 4:13-18) Next John saw the 144,000 that were redeemed from the earth, that had God's name written in their foreheads and had been sealed by the angel of God. These virgins are the man child that the sun clothed woman had in Revelation 12:5. This man child, which are 144,000 that will follow the Lamb night and day, and were caught up to God and to His throne to be prepared to rule all nations with a rod of iron. (Revelation 12:5) Comment: We know this will not be any *church* people, because <u>all</u> *churches* are harlots, not virgins. These pure and Holy Ones have been redeemed from the earth and are being taught and prepared to rule all nations with Jesus during the 1,000 years of peace until after Satan has been released, or loosed from where he was bound in chains, and will make war with the Holy Ones of God. But, he, Satan, will be defeated and fire will come down from heaven and devour them; and, Satan, the Devil, that old Serpent, which is the Dragon, will be cast into the lake of fire and brimstone, where the beast and false prophet are, and shall be tormented day and night for ever and ever. (Revelation 20:9,10)

"And when he had opened the fifth seal, I saw under the altar the souls of them that were slain for the Word of God, and for the testimony which they held, and they cried with a loud voice saying, "How long, O Lord, Holy and True, do you not judge and avenge our blood on them that dwell on the earth? And white robes were given unto every one of them, and it was said unto them, that they should rest yet for a little season until their fellow slaves also and their brethren that should be killed as they were should be fulfilled." (Revelation 6:9,10,11) These were only souls and spirits that go back to God that gave them, and they were killed and did not escape the persecution and tribulation, and were not *raptured*, but must rest until God brings their souls and spirits back with Him to be rejoined with their bodies in the first resurrection. (I Thessalonians 4:13-18)

The last of the believers on this planet earth will be the two witnesses that prophesy their testimony until they finish for the time of one thousand two hundred and three score days, which is 1260 days, or equal to three and one half years, when the beast, (Apollyon), will make war with them and kill them. Immediately their souls and spirits go up to God, and "their dead bodies lie in the street of the Great City, which spiritually is called Sodom and Egypt, where also our Lord was crucified. And they of the people and kindreds and tongues and nations shall see their dead bodies three days and an half *(the same amount of time Jesus' body was dead)*, and shall not suffer *(let)* their dead bodies to be put into graves. And after three days and an half, the spirit of life from God entered into them, and they stood upon their feet, and great fear fell upon them which saw them, and they heard a great voice from heaven saying unto them, You step up here, and they stepped into heaven in a cloud." (Revelation 11:3,7,8,9)

Pay attention! When these two witnesses are raised from the dead, the general or whole first resurrection of dead bodies, or bodies that are asleep in Jesus happens at the same time. The resurrection in (I Thessalonians 4:13 to 18) happens simultaneously with the two witnesses, and the great multitude, and the ones that were killed because they did not take the mark of the beast, but took the seal of God's name in their forehead, instead of the number of the beast, which will be 666. This will be the first presence of Jesus called in the Greek tongue, Parousia (Par-oo-see-ah). When Jesus brings all the spirits that are baptized into Him back in the air, He will not set foot on the earth, but will be only in the air, and will shout with a loud voice to everybody in their graves, "Step up here". And the bodies all over the earth will rise to meet their souls and spirits in the air, and we which are alive shall be caught up (resurrected) together with them in the clouds to meet the Lord in the air; and so shall we ever be with the Lord. (I Thessalonians 4:17)

So all the so-called "Christians" will be in the *dead churches* waiting for the *pretrib rapture* that will never happen. They will be resurrected to stand for judgment at the Great White Throne and wonder why their names were not written in the Lamb's Book of Life. Remember the Sabbath Day to keep it holy. The Sabbath does not mean man made sabbath, *(Sunday)* but the Seventh Day, God's Sabbath. Some believe they will be *raptured* before the tribulation begins. Some believe they will be raptured in the middle of the tribulation. Some believe they will be raptured after the tribulation is over. They are all disillusioned because the first resurrection happens all at the same time, just after the middle of the Great Tribulation, and just before the end of the Great Tribulation. The first parousia, or presence, of Christ Jesus happens in the air and no one will see him except the ones that are glorified, and the ones that are into *(eis)* Christ Jesus. Jesus at that time will not come back to touch the earth, but will call all the ones that are into *(eis)* Christ Jesus to the Marriage Supper of the Lamb, including those that are alive that will be changed in a moment in the twinkling of an eye, which will end the first resurrection.

After the first resurrection is complete, everyone in the first resurrection will be at the Marriage Banquet, where awards and rewards, diadems and crowns and jewels will be given; but the most spectacular event will be our now High Priest being awarded a name that no one knows, except the Lord Himself. His name is called The Word of God. He was seen by Brother John sitting upon a <u>white</u> horse, and He was called Faithful and True. His eyes were as a flame of fire, and on His head were many crowns. And the armies in heaven followed Him on <u>white</u> horses clothed in fine linen, <u>white</u> and clean. And out of His mouth goes a sharp sword, that with it He should smite the nations, (Gentiles); and He shall rule them with a rod of iron; and He had on His vesture and on His thigh a name written,

"King of kings and Lord of lords." Please notice nearly everything in heaven is <u>white.</u> NO BLACK!

"The King is preparing Himself and His armies for the major event this writer calls *"God's Super Bowl On A Sunday"*. "His angel stood in the sun and cried with a loud voice, saying to all the fowls that fly in the midst of heaven, "Come and gather yourselves together unto the supper of the great God, that you may eat the flesh of kings, and the flesh of captains, and the flesh of mighty men, and the flesh of horses, and of them that sit on them, and the flesh of all men both free and bond, both small and great." (Revelation 19th Chapter) Now is the results of *"God's Super Bowl On A Sunday,"* and this writer prays, that neither you, nor your children, nor any of your friends or loved ones will be the flesh for the *buzzards* at God's Great Supper.

<u>"Corn Shelling Time"</u> is warning you about the judgment of the whore, which is the *church,* because there is no separation between the *Universal Catholic Church* and the *harlot protestant churches*. There is no separation between organized religion and the government. Both factions are unholy. "Without holiness no man shall see the Lord."(Hebrews 12: 14).

It is a shame on you that you have not come out of "Her"; and what is worse, you did not teach your children to come out of "Her," "Her" has been explained in previous chapters is Mystery, Babylon, which is made up of the organized religion and the governments of the world, and the worldly people, the atheist, the agnostic, and the rest of the people that are ignorant sinners. One more time, before God's Grand Finale and His destruction of Mystery, Babylon and everyone that did not "Shell Down the Corn" and confess to the Lord Christ Jesus, and everyone that did not come out of "Her", please obey Christ Jesus' warning and commandment in (Revelation 18:4), and "Come Out of "Her", My people." Also, in (II Corinthians Chapter 6 and verse 14) to not be unequally yoked together with anything that is unholy and unclean, like the hypocrite "Christians", or the lying, stealing, murdering politicians that run the government and load men down with *laws* too heavy and grievous to be borne or carried. Read God's Word for yourself. (I John 2:27) "You have no need for any man to teach you." So, please "Shell Down the Corn" to Christ Jesus, (confess) and "Come Out Of "Her"", My people, that you be not partakers of "Her" sins, and that you receive not of "Her" plagues." (Revelation 18:4)

THIS is an insert in the book, **"CORN SHELLING TIME"** and **MICHAEL DUISHKA** with some of his belief. There is an enormous amount of Israel bashing happening all over the world, and it makes me so sad to read the comments of the fools that hate the Jews and Israel. **"But I say unto you, whosoever is angry with his brother without cause shall be in danger of the Judgment: And whosoever shall say unto his brother, raca, shall be in danger of the council, but whosoever shall say you fool, *(To brother),*shall be in danger of Hell Fire"**. (Matthew 5: 22) From my point of view, I am not calling my brother a fool, because scripture says anyone that curses Israel is cursed himself. I am not a brother to anyone that does not believe CHRIST JESUS, who is God. God gave the land of Israel as an inheritance to Abraham, to his son, Isaac God made an everlasting covenant to him and his seed forever. (Genesis 17:28). Isaac's seed was Jacob, that God changed his name to ISRAEL who has a written deed to the smallest Nation on earth, which the boundary includes Gaza, West Bank, Judea, Samaria, Golan Heights, also the East Bank of the Jordan River, which is a part of the Nation, JORDAN, and more. Fools do not believe God, and do not believe that God Created the earth and has ownership to the earth and the fullness thereof, including all the Gold, Silver, Cattle on a thousand hills, and DUISHKA, and all humans that believe Him. All *the fools* **that do not believe Him are condemned already.** (John 3:18) God divided the earth and gave portions of His land to all people and set boundaries for all nations, giving the smallest portion to the Israelite, and greater amounts of the earth He gave to the Arabs, which are descendants of Ishmael,

Keturah, which are Abraham's children, but are not the children of PROMISE, which God promised the covenant to Abraham's son Isaac. Now the greedy, covetous, misled, robbers of God's people want to steal what God wrote a written deed and gave the nation to His chosen people Israel. (Genesis 17:28) Recorded with God's seal in THE HOLY WORD OF GOD WHO CANNOT LIE: Now listen up all you fools that do not believe CHRIST JESUS, what has been decided will be done,makes no matter what Hamas, Islam, ISIS, Iran, Obama, France, *The Anti-Christ Pope,* Turkey, Syria, Europe, United Nations, and all the other followers of Satan, which are all enemies of God Almighty, (PANTAKRATOR), Israel will never be taken by violence. They will voluntarily sign a treaty with the Anti-Christ, that seduces them with all kind of promises and flattery, which will be all lies in order to gain control of the tiny Nation for the last seven years of all fools lives, which will culminate in what DUISHKA called *"GODS SUPER BOWL ON A SUNDAY"*, But God called it **"ARMAGEDDON"** which is the table God is preparing for the fowls of the air with the flesh of fools that do not believe CHRIST JESUS, WHO IS GOD. The majority of unbelievers will already be eliminated by plagues before the Super Bowl, when the blood of God haters will flow down through Israel up to the bridles of horses. The Israel *Bashers* do not know they are fighting God when they say anything bad about Israel, His chosen people. What ever Israel does is rebellion against their Holy one Christ Jesus, and He is the only one that can discipline His people. Israel is God's servant, and He said who are you to judge another man's servant? The WORD of God says **ALL** Nations will be gathered together against Israel, so God can judge all the Gentiles and the Jews at the same time in the arena in Israel called the valley of decision, also the valley of megiddo, also megeddon, also MICHAEL DUISHKA calls it *"GOD'S SUPER BOWL ON A SUNDAY"*, But God said He gathered them together into a place called in the Hebrew tongue, **ARMAGEDDON.**

Chapter 25

"Corn Shelling Time" is a mystery, just like the Mystery of Godliness. Just like the written Word is man made, out of flesh. Also the Word is Spirit, (not a spirit), not separately in parts, but all, total, spirit. That is why it is so hard to understand God was manifest in the flesh. (I Timothy 3:16) The Word was God in the form of a man that God named Jesus. **"Corn Shelling Time"** is revealing the Mystery of Godliness, and the Mystery of Babylons, which will deliver you from the latter if you desire to be delivered from total destruction.

The word Babylon cannot be defined by the dictionary, that is why it is not found in most dictionaries. That is why the writer put an **S** on the word Babylon. There are two meanings to Babylon. One meaning is literal, and the other meaning is spiritual. The definition is self-explanatory: Babel, which is like a little baby that babels before he can talk. So **"Corn Shelling Time"** is going to explain the difference in literal Babylon, and Mystery, Babylon. The difference in natural Babylon and spiritual Babylon, which if you do not "Come Out of "Her", you will be more confused. That is the meaning of Babylon, (*confusion*).

"But the natural man receives not the things of God, for they are foolishness unto him. Neither can he know them, because they are spiritually discerned (judged)." (I Corinthians 2:14) "Which things also we speak, not in the words which man's wisdom teaches, but which the Holy Ghost teaches, comparing spiritual things with spiritual." (I Corinthians 2:13) That is the reason it is so difficult to get the mysteries revealed to you is because you can only comprehend in the natural.

The writer is not boasting when he says he speaks to you with the wisdom of God, because God is no respecter of persons. "If any of you lack wisdom, let him ask of God, that gives to all men liberally, and upbraids not; and it (*wisdom*) shall be given him." (James 1:5)

This writer can see the urgency in you doing what Jesus, (God), said for you to do, so you will not be destroyed. As this **"Corn Shelling Time"** is being written, many horrendous disasters have happened and are happening at this present time. Many casualties are being reported, and many souls went to judgment without being warned and without the opportunity to read **"Corn Shelling Time"**. This writer is saddened for those lost souls, but he is gladdened in the heart that you had the privilege to read the warnings that Jesus is calling you out of "Her" with a loud voice (Ekklesia).

The literal Babylon is the same thing Satan tempted Jesus with, which is the glory of all the kingdoms of this world. (Matthew 4:8,9) That is what you have done already, you have sold your soul to Satan, in exchange for the glory of the kingdoms of this world, that belong to Satan. For short, it is called idolatry. Every time you see the word *church* in the King James Version of the bible, it is an added made up word, which should read Ekklesia, meaning called out, not *church*. Jesus is calling you out of Babylon (idolatry), with as loud a voice as he can call you. First He called you through the many inspired slaves called prophets and apostles of the Holy Greek New Testament.

This writer is neither a prophet nor an apostle, but Christ Jesus is using this slave of the lowest degree to plead with you in the last few days of the dispensation of the Gentiles. This writer is pleading with you by reasons, like: If you are not sinning, how come you are plagued with infirmities? How come you are a doper and try to smooth it over by calling dope, your *medication?* How come you put your trust in man, instead of Christ Jesus? How come you are just like my poor, wretched, miserable, naked loved ones that say they are rich, but are poor and blind? They have striven all of their lives to get rich; and they have lost their souls. They accumulated so many of the things of this world that they were just like the rich man, in (Luke 12:18), that said he would build bigger barns to hold his goods. God called him a fool, and asked him did he know his soul *(life)* would be required of him that night, then God said, "whose will your goods belong to?" In the same identical way, my acquaintances thought their riches could save them. Jesus said whoever tries to save his life will lose it. They built beautiful houses and built safe rooms in the houses to protect them from the four elements. They forgot about the fifth element, which is called Pempte, Ousa, the fifth being, AKA God. They stored up food and water, bought generators for electrical failures. They have mandatory Obama Care Insurance; and like the rich man, they said, "I will sit back and take my ease." Beautiful cars, trucks, boats, cycles, and their belly was their god. They eat the flesh of swine, and catfish, and oysters, until their arteries filled up with that fifty cent word, cholesterol; and God said, "fool, this night your soul shall be required of you, and who will get all your toys?" Other worldly rich ones ate and drank until sores called cancer destroyed them.

There are millions of others being destroyed simply because they do not keep the Commandments of God. "If you love me, keep My Commandments." (John 14:15) "Come out of "Her" is one of His Commandments. (Revelation 18:4)

All of these words in **"Corn Shelling Time"** are to keep you from being destroyed, and having to stand at the Great White Throne Judgment of God. The judgment of the whole world is happening every day by disasters created by the four elements, wind (tornadoes), fire (vegetation-volcanoes), water (floods, mudslides), earth (earthquakes), plus all of the other weapons of Pempte Ousa (the fifth element, or being), which is God Almighty (PANTAKRATOR).

John, my brother, (not a *saint*), saw the One that sat upon the <u>white</u> horse in heaven with His army of the ones on <u>white</u> horses following the One on the <u>white</u> horse, which was the captain of the <u>white</u> team, prepared and ready to go to *"God's Super Bowl, On A Sunday.* And Brother John also saw the beast and the kings of the earth, and all their armies, which is the black team gathered together to make war against Him that sat on the <u>white</u> horse and against His armies in *"God's Super Bowl On A Sunday"*, in the arena called **Armageddon.**

But prior to the Super Bowl, He has to smite the nations of the entire earth with the sharp sword that goes out of His mouth. (Revelation 19:11-19)

But before the Grand Finale of God, Brother John has a commandment to go take the little book out of the mighty angel's hand, that set his right foot upon the sea, and his left foot upon the earth, and eat the book. So Brother John could prophesy again before many peoples, and nations, and tongues, and kings, before the mighty angel swears that by the one that lives for ever and ever, who created heaven, and the things in it, and the earth and the things that are in it, and the sea, and the things that are in it, that there should be time no longer, when the days come when the seventh angel blows his trumpet or at the sound of the seventh angel's voice, that the Mystery of God should be finished. (Revelation 10:5-11) So that is what Brother John did is prophesy to many people, nations, tongues, and kings; and **"Corn Shelling Time"** is reiterating the prophecies of Brother John before the seventh trumpet sounds. But **"Corn Shelling Time"** is revealing more details of Daniel's sealed up book, and the seals of the book of God, and revealing the mysteries of iniquity, Mystery of Godliness, Mystery of Babylon, and the mystery of **"Corn Shelling Time"**.

Daniel's sealed up book is opened when his vision of the seventieth week is included in the seven seals, the lion of the tribe of Judah, the root of David, which is none other than our sacrificial Lamb that was slain on the altar of the tree; and His blood was the price He paid to buy us back from Satan, and redeem us from the second death, and the curse that was upon us, and the sentence to Hell. The Lamb opens the sealed book that reveals the last plagues that will come upon the entire world, and the only ones to escape these plagues are the Holy, and Pure, and Sanctified Holy Ghost Baptized Believers of Christ Jesus, that have washed their hearts in the shed blood of that Lamb, and washed their robes and made them white by the blood of the Lamb. Let me emphasize: "There will not be any thing black in heaven." The One on the white horse and His armies on white horses are being prepared at this very moment in heaven, and also on the earth. To qualify for heaven and to be a soldier in the army of Christ, you have to "Come out of Mystery Babylon", which includes, "Come out of the Whore, which is organized religion.

The *harlot churches* are returning to the hog wallow, the Universal Catholic Whore. Just like the dog going back to lick up his own vomit: Also Mystery, Babylon, includes all governments world wide. You cannot qualify for a citizenship in heaven and vote or be any part of any government or be any kind of a lying, stealing, murdering politician. You cannot be a candidate for God's kingdom and participate in literal Babylon, which is living deliciously and glorifying yourself with things of this world, such as mammon, which is material wealth and selfish gains of this life. You cannot qualify for the first resurrection, if you have any sins that will weight you down and keep you from rising. You are getting your second chance as you read **"Corn Shelling Time"**.

"Therefore to him that knows to do good and does it not, to him it is sin" (James 4:17) And the soul that sins, to him is death. If you "Shell Down the Corn" (confess) to God, you shall live.

While the King of kings and Lord of lords is preparing Himself and His team and making Himself ready for *"God's Super Bowl On A Sunday"*, "He still has a controversy with the inhabitants of the land, because there is no truth nor mercy, nor knowledge of God in the land." (Hosea 4:1) "By swearing, and lying, and killing, and stealing, and committing adultery, they break out, and blood touches blood." (Hosea 4:2) "For, lo, I begin to bring evil on the city which is called by my name, and should you be utterly unpunished? You shall not be unpunished: for I will call for a sword upon all the inhabitants of the earth, saith the Lord of Hosts." (Jeremiah 25:29) "For the Lord has a controversy with all the nations, and will plead with all flesh; that is what the Lord is doing with you right now, through **"Corn Shelling Time"** is pleading with you to confess the Lord Christ Jesus "before you be destroyed from off the land." (Jeremiah 25:31)

God is also pleading with all flesh in many different ways, such as diseases, sickness, infirmities, disasters, deaths, and great storms of the inner man, or the suffering of the broken heart and soul, which this writer calls the great Euroaquilo. Brother Paul went through a great typhonic wind storm on his trip to Rome out in the middle of the Great Sea, AKA the Mediterranean Sea. Everyone on that ship was suffering what looked like, on the surface, as sure death. But God sent an angel to Paul to reassure him that Pempte Ousa, the fifth being, which is (PANTAKRATOR) God Almighty, was testing His faith in Christ Jesus, and Not a soul (life) would be lost.

This writer, and every person that would live Godly must go through a great storm on the inside of them to test them, just like Brother Paul went through a literal storm on the outside to test his faith in Christ Jesus. This writer is showing you how to overcome the worst tempest that will ever come upon you, the kind of storm on the inside of you that just tears the heart right out of you. You feel as though you have lost every thing that matters and every thing that will ever matter, and you would feel better if you could just die. This writer went through such a storm, and he called it the great Euroaquilo.

Everyone must go through this kind of spiritual storm to test their stickability to see if they really trust Jesus or if they fail the test. This is just one of the ways God is pleading with our flesh to "Come out of Mystery, Babylon", and test you to see if you overcome, so He can see if you are fit for the Kingdom of God. Be of good courage, loved one, and let this ole country boy show you how to tie a knot in the end of your rope and keep holding on. Whenever you are holding on to life, and it seems like you are holding on to a rope, or a line, and you think you have come to your end of the rope, and just about to slide off the end of the rope, just tie a knot in the end of your rope and hold on a little longer, because what you cannot see in the knot is Pempte Ousa (the fifth Being), Christ Jesus, and I will personally testify that He will not let you fall, if you will just "Shell Down the Corn" to Him and trust Him.

This writer had the greatest storm, that ever arose in any human, come upon him suddenly; and he was not prepared to deal with it. He lost his wife, and his children, all his riches, and one of those grievous sores, called cancer was just about to end his life. This writer did not want to wait and suffer until the cancer took his life, he wanted to end it all and get it over with. He knew that would calm the great Euroaquilo storm that was raging inside of him, tearing his heart out every awake minute, which was almost 24-seven, because it seemed like he never slept. The storm inside just kept on raging. Taking my life seemed like the right thing to do. Wrong! With the 38 Smith and Wesson cocked and the barrel pointed against his temple, this writer did not have the guts to pull the trigger, and all the time a still small voice was coming up from his heart, (belly) (spirit), saying, "This is not the right way." How can you take a life that does not belong to you? Do you not know that the blood of Christ bought you and redeemed you out of being a slave for Satan? How could you steal something that does not belong to you?" This writer, from that moment to this moment has "Shelled Down the Corn" to God Almighty and gone about telling the whole world how to overcome all the fiery darts of Satan, and how to overcome all the worst storms of life, and how you can do all things through Christ Jesus, which strengthens you. (Philippians 4:13) Nothing by any means shall hurt you after you have overcome the great storm that is raging inside of you. You will know the power of Christ Jesus, and you will not need to teach your troubles how to swim in alcohol, or to ease the pain with pain killer (dope), because you will not have any pain. All will be joy.

The way to overcome the storm, and weather the storm, is to repent of your sins and confess to God your sins, and admit to Christ Jesus that you are a sinner and that you need someone to save you; and the Lord Christ Jesus will save you and command the plague, or storm to go away, and it should obey Jesus. Then the Lord Jesus will set you free from bondage to Satan, and you can shout the victory. If you go and sin no more, and continue being into Christ Jesus, you will be on His team at *"God's Super Bowl On A Sunday"*.

Not only will a great tempestuous storm come on every individual on earth to test them to see if they can qualify to be a citizen in the Kingdom of God; but also a great Euroaquilo is coming on the literal earth to test the inhabitants, because God has a controversy with every inhabitant on the earth, and is pleading with all flesh in many different ways, because it is not God's will that any should perish, but that all should come to repentance, and "Shell Down the Corn" (confess), and live forever. This great storm is already in action with God's four elements, the wind, water, fire, and earth. Many have gone on out into eternity without believing Christ Jesus; but they that turn many to righteousness shall shine as the stars forever and ever. These are they which came out of great tribulation, which is Mystery, Babylon and "Her", and have washed their robes and made them white in the blood of the Lamb; and they will be with the King of kings and Lord of lords at *"God's Super Bowl On A Sunday"*, wearing their robes of <u>white</u> with a new name.

Dear Loved Ones, this believer believes that although he cannot see you, he is looking as though he can see you. He believes that as many in the world, that reads **"Corn Shelling Time"** is gonna believe Christ Jesus and come out of all *churches,* come out of all governments, come out of the things of this world, and come out of darkness, and come to the light, which is Christ Jesus, and not be led by blind leaders any more, but will read (I John 2:26,27), and will let the Holy Spirit of God teach you all things; and you have no need of any man teaching you anything.

The great tempestuous wind is blowing up a great storm over the entire earth to plead with the inhabitants that God has a great controversy with. **"Corn Shelling Time"** is only reiterating some of God's Word to wake you up and wash the sleepy out of your spiritual eyes, so you can see why God is angry with all the nations on the earth, and must deal with them, before His *"Super Bowl On A Sunday"* can manifest.

The *harlot churches* are going back into the hog wallow of their mother, the Whore, *the Universal Catholic Church. The Presbyterian Harlot Church* has sanctioned same sex marriages, which means they are all sodomites by association. If you are not a *queer,* then what are you doing there? Another denomination of abomination. Here is another example of division, or in God's language, devils against devils. This denomination has gone back into the pig sty, or the hog wallow of ignorance, sucking the whore's breasts again, and agreeing with the abominations of the *Mother Catholic Church* to be a *queer* by association. Or else, Come out of "Her", My people.

Such filth that you have just read about is the very reason God has a controversy with the inhabitants of the earth, and the reason a great sword is being sent among you, or a great Euroaquilo storm, which will devour the entire earth. If you do what **"Corn Shelling Time"** directs, you shall be saved from the snare that shall come on all that dwell on the face of the whole earth. You would benefit if you would read the book, "Please Do Not Call Me A "Christian" by Michael Duishka, which tells about the filth and corruption that is contaminating the *harlot churches*. All are trying to cover their sins with the name *church*, or with the name of Jesus.

The governments of the world are just as abominable, when *lizzies* and *queers* are leading all nations into destruction. The Great Satan, the *NewNited States of America* has a leader that is leading the whole world into ObomaNation of Desolation.

Abraham asked God, if He could find ten righteous people in Sodom and Gomorrah, would He destroy them? God answered Abraham, and told him if there were ten righteous people in the cities, He would not destroy them. But He could not find them. There are not many righteous people in this world, and I believe the end is getting to the point that is equivalent to Sodom and Gomorrah, with a world full of whores, *queers,* and fornicators. Idolatry is close to 100%, and God is pleading with the world,with the wind (hurricanes, tornadoes), water (floods, mudslides), fire (burning vegetation), and the earth (earthquakes). But we have a merciful God, that is long suffering, and wants to give every one of His people time to repent and "Shell Down the Corn" (confess), and come out of "Her", Mystery, Babylon, which is the *church* (the whore, the governments, and the world, which is the glory of Satan's Kingdoms).

Brother Paul said there would be a great apostasy, or falling away from the Truth, which is happening right before your eyes, by the exhibition of the harlot *churches,* and governments of the world sanctioning marriage of *lizzies* and *queers*, knowing that the ones that do these things are worthy of death, according to the judgment of God. (Romans 1:32) Not only the ones who do these things are guilty, but also the ones that think these acts of lewdness are O.K. Even the ones that do not openly voice their disapproval are just as guilty, because silence is assent, or having pleasure in those that commit such acts is consent.

"But God is sending these people a strong delusion that they should believe **The Lie** and be damned, because they believed not the Truth, but had pleasure in unrighteousness." (II Thessalonians 2:12)

"Corn Shelling Time" is reiterating what all the Holy Ones of God are warning the entire world about, so they will not receive "Her" (Mystery, Babylon), plagues. "But we are bound to give thanks always to God for you that read **"Corn Shelling Time"**, brothers and sisters, beloved of the Lord, because God has chosen you from the beginning on account of sanctification of the Spirit and belief of the Truth, where unto He called you by the gospel to the obtaining of our Lord Christ Jesus. Therefore, stand fast!

This writer of **"Corn Shelling Time"** is believing that everyone all over the world that reads this book will be chosen of God to receive salvation by true confession to Christ Jesus, and God will not send you a strong delusion, and you will not believe the lie of Satan, and that you will not be damned, because you are going to read the Truth for yourself. (I John 2:27) And let the anointing of God, the Holy Spirit, teach you what is Truth. You have no need for any man to teach you doctrines of devils, or the things of this world. So, since you have already been there and done that, do not go back into the mire and hog wallow of the *harlot church,* or the hog wallow of politics, or governments or the hog wallow of self, living in luxuries of the glory of Satan's Kingdoms; but rather just quit going to your *apostate church,* and let Christ Jesus teach you how to save your self from this wicked and untoward generation. "Do not be joined to any harlot; and do you not know that the members of your body are the members of Christ. Will you then take the members of Christ and join them to, and make them the members of a *harlot (church)?*" (I Corinthians 6:15)

If you work for any level of government, municipal, county, state, federal, you are guilty by reason of association of stealing, murder and destroying God's people, God's property, and God's earth. Your only hope is to quit your job and come out from among them, and touch not the unclean thing, which all the rulers and governments of the world are the filth and abominable trash of Satan. In the Great Satan Country of America, the ugly, and the divided nation, you are living in the ObomaNation of Desolation. The leader of literal Babylon, and the leader of Mystery, Babylon, the City of Babylon the Great is *New York City, USA.* We, at **"Corn Shelling Time"** are praying for all the citizens of the world to take the blinders off their minds, which Satan has deceived you with; and come out of the hog wallow of ignorance and **"come and learn of Me"**, Jesus doing the talking. (Matthew 11:29) No matter how much or how many of you have run to and fro, and no matter how much your knowledge has been increased in worldly knowledge, you are still wallowing in the hog mire of ignorance, because you are still in Mystery, Babylon, and you are partakers of "Her" sins, and you are double dog dead sure to receive of "Her" plagues (*or stripes*). "And men were scorched with great heat, and blasphemed the name of God, which has power over these plagues, (*stripes*); and they repented not to give Him glory." (Revelation 16:15)

But you, dear reader, have repented, are repenting, and will repent, and "Shell Down the Corn", (confess); and your plagues will go away and disappear. Jesus will quit laying the stripes on you when you quit sinning. Quit going to *church*, quit voting for a lying, stealing, murdering politician. If you quit all these sins and receive salvation, it may not be too late to save your children. "My people are destroyed for lack of knowledge; because you have rejected knowledge, I will also reject you, that you shall be no priest to me. Seeing you have forgotten the Law of Your God, I will also forget your children." (Hosea 4:6)

Even if you are too selfish to quit sinning yourself, have mercy on your children, which have been taught by pagan, heathen, "Christian" teachers the ways of the world, and the ways of Satan. Take your children out of the heathen public schools and teach your children to read (I John 2:27) just like you are doing, read it for yourself. Give your children a chance and bring them home, and home school them, teaching them the Commandments of God, which is the Law of God. To reject the Law of God is to reject heaven and the Kingdom of God. To send your children to public school is sending you and your children to Hell. Public schools, which are the property of Satan *(the governments)* have passed a law that you cannot say the Commandments of God, or even mention His name, or the name of the Son of God, Christ Jesus. Without the confession of your sins in the name of Jesus, no flesh can be saved. No other name (Allah, Buddha, Mohammed, God, or any other name can save you), nothing except the blood and the name of Jesus. The government is trying to condemn home schooling. If it comes to a choice to obey the law of the land or obey the Law of God, which will you obey? Will you choose Hell or Heaven? Father God, just like this writer shelled down the corn to his daddy and his daddy used the **SPA** method of correction, which was **S**eize by the hand **P**ossess the razor strop with the other hand, **A**pply stripes to the butt, and just like this writer "Shelled Down the Corn" (confessed his sins) to you and you applied stripes the same way and gave this writer power to be called a son of God, this writer prays in the name of Christ Jesus that you, Father will save and heal every one that reads **"Corn Shelling Time"** and shells down the corn (confesses his sins) and repents and comes out of the harlot *churches,* and Mystery, Babylon, and sin, and Father sanctify him and fill him or her with the Holy Ghost and Fire. In the name of your son Christ Jesus, Amen and Amen.

Chapter 26

ON HIS WAY TO (*"God's Super Bowl On A Sunday"*) **Armageddon**, "Great Babylon came in remembrance before God, to give unto "Her" the cup of the wine of the fierceness of His wrath." (Revelation 16:19)

Corn Shelling Time has told you in previous chapters that literal Babylon is world wide in physical things, such as riches of delicacies, such as merchandise of gold and silver and precious stones and of pearls, and fine linen and purple, and silk, and scarlet, and all thyine wood, and all manner of vessels of most precious wood, and of brass, and iron, and marble, and cinnamon, and odours, and ointments, and frankincense, and wine, and oil, and fine flour, and wheat, and beasts, and sheep, and horses, and chariots, and slaves, and souls of men. These delicacies are with men world wide; but they are procured and obtained via merchants that buy, sell, and trade at the Commercial Trade Center of the whole world, which is in the *NewNited States of America*, with the head of the snake being *New York City, USA*. The great sea port, New York Harbor, is the place the merchants of the whole world load and unload the above merchandise to deliver and sell it to all the nations of the world. So America the ugly and New York City is the literal Babylon; and New York City is that Great City in Revelation 18:16, where they are saying "Alas, alas, that Great City, that was clothed in fine linen and purple and scarlet and decked with gold, etc."

Now the other Babylon, which is Mystery, Babylon, which is spiritual Babylon, is also world wide, and is sin. The sin of Mystery, Babylon is committed by the excessive use of the delicacies of literal Babylon; and since these are the things of the world, the lust of the flesh, the lust of the eyes, and the pride of life, which is idolatry. That is what Christ Jesus is telling you, rather commanding you, to "Come out of "Her," and not to partake of "Her" sins, which is fornication, which is idolatry."

So remember in the previous chapter you were told that God said He had a controversy with all the inhabitants of the land, which is to say He has a controversy with all the ones that are still living in Mystery, Babylon and excessively indulging in the delicacies of literal Babylon, and living deliciously in whoredom, and fornication, and idolatry. So when God remembered The Great Babylon, He did not just remember the great city of Babylon; He remembered all the cities of all the nations of the world. He remembered London, England, France and her cities, German cities, Sweden, Norway, Finland, Poland and their cities, Japan, Russia, Ukraine, Italy, Spain, India, China, Saudi Arabia, Turkey, Syria, Mongolia, Iran, Iraq, Pakistan, Kazakhstan and all their cities, Africa and all her cities, and South America and her cities etc., including all nations and cities on the earth. God deals more harshly with the leaders of all these nations, which is the *NewNited States of America;* and most especially the head of the snake, which is the Great City of Babylon, AKA *New York City, USA.*

You want to know why God deals more harshly with the *NewNited* States of America and New York City, USA. It is because "Therefore to him that knows to do good and does *it* not, to him it is sin." (James 4:17) The North American Continent knew how to do good more than any country of the world; and they did evil instead of good.

Michael Duishka

So it is accounted to the USA as sin. All the American cities that advocate *queers* and homosexuality will be severely judged, and they will fall. **"For unto whomsoever much is given, of him shall be much required; and to whom men have committed much, of him they will ask the more. I am come to send fire on the earth, and what will I, if it be already kindled?" (Luke 12:48,49)**

The USA was given more than any country in the world and more of everything in the world was committed to her; and she betrayed God Almighty, and bit the hand that fed her. America the ugliest nation on God's earth, that used to be called America the beautiful; but that was then, and this is now. America used to be the lender; but since the dead beat, lazy, sluggards, elected their "Christian"president, him and his jack booted thugs have turned America into the ugliest country in the world, that owes more money than any other nation. America is an oligarchy, ruled by Obama, Reid, Pelosi, Clinton, Biden, and a few more like them; and they have turned the Good Ole USA into an ObomaNation of Desolation; and are just wallowing in ignorance until God remembers. He, (the president) lived in Chicago, the same city where Al Capone the gangster led a crime syndicate; and I am not talking about God. (My Opinion)

But you, dear reader, of **"Corn Shelling Time"** are getting your last chance to repent and wash your hands of the blood that the rulers of the world have spilled of God's people. Christ Jesus and His armies are ready to go to the contest at *"God's Super Bowl On A Sunday,"* but He remembered Great Babylon; and Christ Jesus turned His angels loose to pour out the vials, *(bowls)*, and sound the trumpets to bring the last plagues upon all the ones that did not come out of "Her". All the four elements, the wind, the water, the fire, and the earth, led by the fifth element, Pemptos Ousa, which **is** The Fifth Element, which is God Almighty, (PANTAKRATOR).

Remember the four angels that were bound in the Great Euphrates River holding the four winds until God's slaves could receive the seal of God in their forehead. Well, "the Lord shall roar from on high; and the sixth trumpet shall sound and loose the four angels over the wind; and God gives a mighty shout as they that tread all the inhabitants of the earth. A noise shall come to the ends of the earth, for the Lord has a controversy with the nations. He will plead with all flesh. He will give them that are wicked to the sword, saith the Lord." "Thus saith the Lord of Hosts, behold evil shall go forth from nation to nation, and a great whirlwind shall be raised up from the coasts of the earth, and the slain of the Lord shall be at that day from one end of the earth even unto the other end of the earth. They shall not be lamented, neither gathered, nor buried. They shall be dung upon the ground." (Jeremiah 25:32,33) Also, the winds dried up the River Euphrates so the kings of the east could go over to God's Super Bowl and wait for *Sunday*.

After the whirlwinds came from one end of the earth even to the other end of the earth that caused great floods to come, "and the serpent cast out of his mouth water as a flood after the woman that he might cause her to be carried away of the flood, and the earth helped the woman, and the earth opened her mouth and swallowed up the flood which the dragon cast out of his mouth." (Revelation 12:15,16) Now **"Corn Shelling Time"** has brought to observation another character, which is another woman. This woman is a symbol, which represents the repented Jews that have Christ Jesus as their savior; also, the repented Gentiles that are no longer Gentiles, but rather are adopted Jews, even us whom He has called, not of the Jews only, but also of the Gentiles. (Romans 9:24)

You, dear reader, can be an adopted Jew if you will "Shell Down the Corn" and confess Christ Jesus. "That is, they which are the children of the flesh, these are not the children of God."(Romans 9:8) Some of the ignorant and unlearned "Christians" and Muslims, and Islams say in their heart, "I do not want to be a Jew!" This is the reason they will be destroyed according to Hosea, when he was speaking by the inspiration of God Almighty, (PANTAKRATOR); and it is written: "My people are destroyed for lack of knowledge. Because you have rejected knowledge, I will also reject you that you shall be no priest to me. Seeing you have forgotten the law of your God, I will also forget your children. As they were increased, so they sinned against Me. Therefore, I will change their glory into shame." (Hosea 4:6,7) God is talking directly to you, dear reader, of **"Corn Shelling Time"**. If you are one that says, "I do not want to be a Jew, because my Lord Jesus said, **"You know not what you worship. We know what we worship: For salvation is of the Jews."** (John 4:22) My Lord Jesus continued saying: **"But the time is coming and now is, when the true worshipers shall worship the Father in Spirit and in Truth, for the Father seeks such to worship Him. God is spirit, and they that worship Him, must worship Him in Spirit and in Truth."** (John 4:23,24) The writer of **"Corn Shelling Time"** is not wandering, because he found it necessary to show you what God is showing you in Revelation 12, about the other woman, which is a symbol of the ones that "Jesus promised He would keep you from the hour of temptation, which shall come upon all the world." (Revelation 3:10) Notice that the woman in Revelation 12 has come into the light, and is clothed with the sun. This sun clothed woman is symbolic for all the believers in the world that have gained spiritual knowledge and have come out of the other woman in Revelation 17:5, which is symbolic for the ones that lack knowledge and believe the *church* is going to save them, and are married or joined in union to the Harlot *Church*, or the Whore, Mystery, Babylon.

Dig, dear reader, dig a little deeper into what this writer is revealing to you about the Mystery of God, and about the Mystery of Iniquity, which **is** the Mystery, Babylon. You do not have to be destroyed for lack of knowledge. You can be an adopted Jew that has been grafted into the True Vine. You do not have to be a dead branch that is cast into the fire. You are a blessed vessel if you do not reject knowledge and keep the Commandments of Jesus and prove that you love Him. The last Commandment that Jesus gave to you in the bible is to come out of "Her", so you can follow the Sun Clothed Woman into the place prepared for her, and you will not be destroyed by the dragon, Satan, and <u>you</u> will be in the army of the one sitting on the <u>white</u> horse, clothed in clean fine <u>white</u> linen, that has washed himself in the Word of God. You will be on the winning team and be in the contest of *"God's Super Bowl On A Sunday"*.

This knowledge is not the worldly knowledge that you can learn by the click of a mouse, or read in a Theological Seminary. So do not reject this knowledge, or God will reject your children. This knowledge will provide you with "a way of escape in the time of temptation." (Revelation 3:10) There is a difference between a spiritual Jew and a natural Jew. The spiritual Jew is anyone that has asked the Lord Jesus to save him and believes that He did. A natural Jew is under condemnation because they are not in Christ Jesus and will not "Shell Down the Corn", (confess). So the natural Jew is still in Mystery, Babylon, just like any other country of the world that will not come out of "Her". Israel is the land of the Jew, the ones that rejected knowledge; and God said: "For I begin to bring evil on the city which is called by My Name, *(Jerusalem)*. Should you be utterly unpunished? You shall not be unpunished. For I will call for a sword upon all the inhabitants of the earth, saith the Lord of Hosts." (Jeremiah 25:29). So Israel and the natural Jews are under condemnation and will be destroyed from the land, if they do not repent and call on the Name of Jesus.

Israel is condemned just like every country on earth, because sin is rampant, with Israel sanctioning same sex marriages, which is men lying with men, and *lizzies* marrying *lizzies,* plus all kinds of fornication which is abomination of the earth. So God is bringing His wrath down on Israel, but He said, "<u>You</u> shall not go unpunished." The only way for you to miss the weeping and wailing and gnashing of teeth is to "Shell Down the Corn" to Christ Jesus and confess your sins to Him, and ask Him to forgive you, and believe that He did. Read the bible and also **"Corn Shelling Time"** for "The one doctrine for reproof, for correction and for instruction in righteousness." (II Timothy 3:16) You may go to sleep before the one on the white horse arrives at *"God's Super Bowl On A Sunday"*, and if you have "Shelled Down the Corn", confessed Christ Jesus, you will be clothed in clean, fine, white linen riding on a white horse alongside of Jesus, the WORD, going to *"God's Super Bowl On A Sunday"*. But if you go to sleep without "Shelling Down the Corn" (confessing), you will sleep on until the Great White Throne Judgment and the second resurrection. Oh me! I want to be in the first resurrection.

Right at this moment, wherever you are on this earth, the beginning of sorrows is happening in every country in the world by some kind of disaster. Perhaps you have been warned by a near windstorm or by an earth tremor, or maybe you suffered loss by a flood, or possibly by a great fire. All of these four elements, the wind, water, earth, or fire are ruled by an angel that God has appointed to be the ruler over each one of these four elements; but the ruler over all these angels and elements is Pempte Ousa, which is the fifth being, called Almighty God, AKA (PANTAKRATOR). If per chance you escaped the four elements, maybe a deadly disease has overtaken you, or you are hungry on account of the famine that is going through the land.

"There is a great famine in every nation, country, and people of this beginning of sorrows. There are many dead bodies in every nation on account of the famine. "Not a famine of bread, nor a thirst for water, but of hearing the Words of the Lord". (Amos 8:11)

The end has already come upon the people of God in Israel, but the end is coming upon you, whichever land or people you are in. Because of the famine of hearing the Words of the Lord, there are many dead bodies everywhere. The Lord said, "I will not again pass by them anymore. Pay attention! **"Corn Shelling Time"** is the last time you will ever hear the true Word of the Lord, until God's angels bring the everlasting gospel, saying, "Fear God, give God glory." **"Corn Shelling Time"** is the last time God will pass by you with His bread of life and His living water until you be destroyed off the land, if you do not repent. If you will "Shell Down the Corn", that means confess that you are a sinner to Christ Jesus, and ask Him to save you, that is one of His many promises; and He will save you.

If one of the four elements, the wind, water, earth, or fire does not destroy you, the famine of not hearing the true Word of the Lord will cause some calamity to come upon you. The people of God have been held in captivity by the famine of not hearing the Words of the Lord for 400 years, from 1611 A.D., when the King James Bible was published, until 2011 A. D., when Michael Duishka boldly proclaimed the true Word of God in His book called "Please, Do Not Call Me a "Christian". And now God's last warning in (Revelation 18:4), "And I heard another voice from heaven saying, "Come out of "Her", My people, that you be not partakers of "Her" sins, and that you receive not of "Her" plagues." **"Corn Shelling Time"** is God's scribe and crier to warn the entire world that Christ Jesus is mounted on His white horse and on His ride to "God's Super Bowl On A Sunday". Babylon the Great came to His remembrance in the meantime, while waiting for the grand finale of *"God's Super Bowl On A Sunday."* The beginning of sorrows is escalating with great intensity, and will continue to increase with a greater degree of force until 2018, when the last plagues will start to occur on Mystery, Babylon.

The parable of the fig tree will come to fruition and understanding of the mystery of the parable of (Matthew 24:32) will begin to come into focus in 2018, **"When his branch is yet tender and puts forth leaves, then you will know that summer is nigh."** The angels will start sounding the trumpets and pouring out their vials or bowls of wrath all over the earth. "The first angel sounded and there followed hail and fire mingled with blood, and they were cast upon the earth, and the third part of the trees was burnt up and all the green grass was burnt up." (Revelation 8:7)

Notice the parable of the fig tree in (Matthew 24:32) says, **"Then you will know that summer is nigh,"** and here all the green grass was burnt up; and the grass is only green in summertime. One of Pempte Ousa's four elements, fire, is manifest. "And I saw another sign in heaven, great and marvelous, seven angels having the seven last plagues, *(stripes)*, for in them is filled up the wrath of God." (Revelation 15:1) Notice, the word plague, which is playgay, in Greek meaning a wound from the stripes that God puts upon disobedient ones. Thank God you are obedient to God's command to "Come out of "Her", and go and sin no more.

The writer of **"Corn Shelling Time"** thanks God for the stripes his daddy put on him with the razor strop, and then "the stripes God put on him to let him know he was not a bastard, but rather a child of God." (Hebrews12:8)

But these last plagues are deadly judgments to destroy the ones that have taken the mark, number, or the name of the beast, which rules the Anti-Christ. But you, dear reader, have "Shelled Down the Corn" to Christ Jesus, (confessed your sins), and God will be a covert with His wings spread for you.

"And the first angel poured out his vial upon the earth, and there fell a noisome and grievous sore upon the men which had the mark of the beast, and upon them which worshiped his image." (Revelation 16:2) "Christians" already have the mark; believers already have the seal of God. "Christians" are the wife of Satan, the harlots, the daughters of the Great Whore. "Christians" are married to a harlot *church* that have pleasure in *queers, lizzies,* idolaters, fornicators, and heathen holidays. They vote and elect such filth and abominable pagans to rule over them and have turned the world into an ObomaNation of Desolation. God's people are being punished with stripes for voting for the heathen rulers.

"Only he who now lets will let until he be taken out of the way." (II Thessalonians 2:7). What Brother Paul is talking about is happening as you read **"Corn Shelling Time"**. The door of the ark of safety is almost closed. "Let no man deceive you by any means, for that day shall not come, except there come a falling away first, and that man of sin be revealed, the Son of Perdition." (II Thessalonians 2:3) "For the Mystery of Iniquity does already work." (II Thessalonians 2:7) Open your eyes and observe all the plagues that have already escalated to great heights all over the earth. Better yet, examine yourself and observe the calamities that are happening to you. The doctor you are going to is prescribing dope that will kill your senses and cause worse dysfunctions of your God-given organs. The Mystery of Iniquity is already working in you because you are plagued with all kinds of problems, like the habitual anesthetic you fill your body, soul, and spirit with, called alcohol or dope, that produces loss of the senses of your body, soul, and your spirit, and causes many to commit suicide. Whether it is prescribed by a doctor, or you call it legal or illegal, it is still killing you, which is working iniquity called lawlessness of God. Such habits, which are prevalent over all of the earth are manifesting the great apostasy, or the falling away from God Almighty, (PANTAKRATOR). (II Thessalonians 2:3) You are (anathema) accursed. "Thus saith the Lord, cursed be the man that trusts in man, and makes flesh his arm, and whose heart departs *(apostasy)* from the Lord." (Jeremiah 17:5)

Stop! Do not click that mouse, or go refill your drink, or light another cigarette, or cigar; but pray to Christ Jesus and ask Him to forgive you and promise Him you will renounce Satan, sin, and iniquity. In other words, just "Shell Down the Corn".

"Corn Shelling Time" is the only source in the world where you can find the pure Word of God deciphered, and the parables, puzzles, and mysteries solved and manifested. You cannot find the solution to your problems in *church,* or in the government, or in any organization of the world, or from any man, woman, child, or animal, plant, invention, or anything in the earth, sea, or Hell! The only one that can solve your problem is Christ Jesus; and **"Corn Shelling Time"** is the answer to revealing the Mystery of Iniquity, the Mystery, Babylon, and most importantly the Mystery of God Almighty, (PANTAKRATOR). Study the bible to hear the Word of God, and then study the revealing of the mysteries of the bible in **"Corn Shelling Time"**, so you can overcome the doctrines, *(teachings)* of devils,and the traditions of men. (I Timothy 4:1)

In defense of some of the preachers, and in defense of some of the "Christians", and in defense of some of the *church goers,* and in defense of some of the ones that are trapped in Mystery, Babylon, they search the scriptures and think they have eternal life. (John 5:39) Oh! Look what thoughts will do. In the Greek, dokeism is a false doctrine of (I think) or (it seems), which is what the doctrines of devils are.

The above mentioned people, preachers, "Christians", church goers, and the ones trapped in Mystery, Babylon, are in part deceived by Satan, that has blinded their minds; because they believed not (II Corinthians 4:3,4). They are lost because they did not know and hear the conclusion of the whole matter, "Fear God and keep His Commandments, for this is the whole duty of man." (Ecclesiastes 12:13) They did not live by "every Word that proceeds from the mouth of God." (Matthew 4:4) If these people do not repent and "Shell Down the Corn" to Christ Jesus, they will be destroyed for lack of knowledge. But if they read **"Corn Shelling Time"** in it's entirety, they will not lack knowledge. They will not be ignorant any more. They have been warned already. But ignorance is no excuse for being lost. You repent and confess, "Shell Down the Corn".

To the remainder of the preachers, and the "Christians", and the *church goers,* and the ones that choose to stay in Mystery, Babylon, because you are hard headed, hard of heart disobedient, disbelieving, unthankful, unholy, (II Timothy 2:2): You have a Lake of Fire that is prepared for the Devil and his angels, and his ministers, except you repent and "Shell Down the Corn", (that means confess), and read and do what **"Corn Shelling Time"** tells you to do. You have already read the bible; and you know the Word and the scriptures from the front to the back; and it was just like pouring water on a duck's back, it just ran off. The remainder of the preachers, "Christians", *church goers,* the ones that are in Mystery, Babylon have spoken lies in hypocrisy for so long that their consciences are seared. All the ones mentioned above, if their conscience is not already seared, are ministers of Satan, and are doing deception for Satan, to receive all the glory of Satan's kingdoms of this world as their rewards, knowing fully well that their judgment will be at the Great White Throne Judgment.

Now that you have read this far in **"Corn Shelling Time"**, you, dear reader, know how to do good; and if you do not do good, it will be sin to you. "The soul that sins will surely die. Therefore, to him that knows to do good, and does it not, to him it is sin." (James 4:17) **"Corn Shelling Time"** has been God's crier and scribe to proclaim the Truth of God and His last warning to "Come out of "Her", and receive not of "Her" plagues, and be not partakers of "Her" sins". (Revelation 18:4)

So now Brother John will show you "Her" plagues. Mystery, Babylon's plagues are already coming on all the nations, tongues, kindreds, and people, because Christ Jesus is pouring the wrath of His fierceness out upon the entire earth.

There are so many contingencies, or conditional promises, in the scriptures that it is hard to make an absolute statement. That is why God is so much bigger and wiser than any man. The starting of this chapter told how the rider on the white horse in Revelation Chapter 19 was preparing to go to the contest at *"God's Super Bowl On A Sunday"*, when He remembered the Great Babylon, which is a different Babylon from Mystery, Babylon. Mystery, Babylon is the worldwide spirit of rebellion to the Word of God, which is the spirit of Satan. The Great Babylon is literal, physical, material, which is the Good Ole USA, AKA America. That great city, that mighty city Babylon is *New York City, USA.* Before God pours out His wrath on literal Babylon, He deals with Mystery, Babylon,which is worldwide. That is where His ministers, (angels), trigger the last plagues on the ones who are disobedient to God but are followers of Satan.

Daniel's book was sealed up along with the book in the right hand of Him that sat on the throne, a book written within and on the backside, sealed with seven seals. Daniel's book is a sealed up revelation of what is to befall the Israelite s, which are Daniel's people, the Jews. (Revelation 5:1) Now God is no respecter of persons, but He requires more from the sons of Jacob than He does from the Gentiles, so God deals differently with them than He does the nations. Why does He deal differently with them? "Moreover, it is required in stewards, that a man be found faithful." (I Corinthians 4:2) The Israelite s, (Jews), were entrusted with the key of salvation for the entire human race, and they were found to be unfaithful, and committed spiritual adultery, because they were married to God. God chose them and entrusted them with His valuable secrets; and they betrayed God; and they went into idolatry, AKA, Mystery, Babylon. "And that servant which knew his Lord's will and prepared not himself, neither did according to his will, shall be beaten with many stripes." (Luke 12:47) That is what is revealed in Daniel's sealed up book, how the Jews will be beaten with many stripes, because they knew God's will and were disobedient. Pay attention! Dear reader, what is good for the goose, is also good for the gander. Only a remnant of the Israelite s will be saved. They were God's chosen people and were given more than most. You, dear reader, please have enough discernment to know that you were entrusted with the same key to salvation as was entrusted to the Jews, which is the Jew, Christ Jesus. He is the Ark. He is the Jew. He is God. He is the **"I Am"** (Eyo Ei Mi). He is the Messiah. He is the Son of God. His Spirit is the Holy Spirit. He and the Father are One. One God Almighty (PANTAKRATOR). Do not be hard headed, hard of heart; but you can not pray to God effectively without using the only name whereby men might be saved under heaven, which is the Name Christ Jesus. You, dear reader, have freely received the savior, the blood, the once for all times, and all sacrifices, so freely give to the ones that do not know about them.

Jesus is very long suffering and has been prolonging destroying the ones that are destroying the earth. He has been making intersession for His people to come out of killing, stealing, and destroying for almost two thousand years before He closes the door of entry into the Kingdom of God. When He tells His <u>white</u> horse to giddy-up and go to *"God's Super Bowl On A Sunday,"***Armageddon**, He is ready to pour out His wrath on all the earth, to the Jew first, and then the Gentiles. He has had His witnesses warning His people for almost six thousand years; and now He has His scribe and witness crying out His last warning to come out of Mystery, Babylon to the whole world, in (Revelation 18:4) through this scroll called. **"Corn Shelling Time"**. PASSPORT TO KINGDOM OF GOD. DO YOU QUALIFY?

Have you asked the King to accept you into His kingdom? Have you shelled down the corn, that is confessed you are a sinner? Have you had a bath and washed away your sins by the blood of JESUS, the SON OF GOD? Have you quit sinning, that is disobeying GOD? Do you keep THE KING'S commandments? Have you let go of the love of the things of this kingdom (world), which is ruled by another king called Satan? Do you love your neighbor more than yourself? Do you hate anyone or any thing that GOD has made? Do you kill anything that God has made, or vote or assent to those that do, such as politicians, police, capitol punishment, War, abortion,Government run public schools that teach the lie evolution,secular humanism, homosexuality, idolatry, fornication, abominable filth,which is unholy,and will disqualify your passport to the kingdom of GOD? Are you HOLY? Do you steal your neighbor's wife, or husband, or anything that belongs to anyone else? Do you destroy God's earth by taking minerals, oil, trees,vegetation, water, excessively out of the ground, and replace it with poisonous waste? Do you pollute the fountains, rivers, lakes, streams, and other sources of water? Do you contribute to destroying the air and ozone by driving multiple, unnecessary automobiles,trucks, boats, trains, planes, cycles etc.? Do you wear anything black? Why do you want to enter into this land that does not have any the above mentioned things? What is your purpose for wanting to come to this place that has only Holiness? Do you enjoy watching the celebrities and sex symbols on television? Do you have any baggage you wish to bring on your journey, such as,television,radio, computer, smart phone, money, watch, gun, black hoodie, knife, medication, alcohol, jewelry, musical instruments, tobacco,snuff, or anything of this world? Do you believe you are fit for the kingdom of GOD? What have you ever done for GOD? Anything? Do you believe Jesus is God? Do you believe God came down from heaven to this world in the flesh as a man? DO you believe that Hell is hot? Do you believe in *queers*? Do you believe in fornication, adultery? Has the HOLY SPIRIT taught you anything that Jesus said? Has the HOLY SPIRIT showed you anything that is to happen in the future? Have you been justified? Have you been Sanctified? Do you know what is the difference between Justification and Sanctification? What is Glorification? Do you believe Jesus, or believe in Jesus? Do you believe the devils believe in Jesus? Do you know your children are being taught homosexuality by *queers*, and heathen councilors are poisoning their minds, that God made a mistake and males should be females, and many other lies of the devil, in the public school system? Do you know GOD said take your children out of Babylon, and you come out of Her also? Do you believe you are condemned according to JOHN 3; 18? Whom should you obey, man, or GOD? Do you believe this passport into the Holy Kingdom OF GOD will be issued to you? Do you ever call on the name of CHRIST JESUS? Do you know how to teach your children how to pray, how to enter into THE KINGDOM OF GOD? Shell down the corn, (confess you are a sinner) REPENT, ask Jesus to save you, and BELIEVE Him!!!

Chapter 27

THE BEGINNING OF SORROWS, to the Jew first and then to the Gentiles. Why to the Jew first, because they were the first to reject God and kill their savior. This chapter of **"Corn Shelling Time"** is to remind the Jews all over the world, but mostly in Israel, what the Prophets, Moses, Isaiah, Jeremiah, Ezekiel, Daniel, Hosea, Zechariah, and your hero, David, warned you about and what would befall you in the latter days, which you are in the latter days now. I know you believe these foreseers because not one word has failed to come to pass that God inspired them to speak to you, the tribes of Judah and Benjamin and the ten dispersed tribes.

"Corn Shelling Time" is not endeavoring to convert you to any doctrine or religion, but warning you about the abomination of desolation that Daniel spoke of in (Daniel 12:11). The seventieth week that Daniel spoke of is shut up in Daniel's book; and you cannot open Daniel's book, because you are unbelievers. **"Corn Shelling Time"** is a believer and will reveal to the Jew first what the book of Daniel is, that the Angel Gabriel, told Daniel to shut up. (Daniel 12:4) Since this is getting close to the time of the end of all transgressions, Daniel's book has been opened up to believers only. Inside of Daniel's book are the things, or troubles, that will befall Daniel's people, which you are, in the time of the end. (Daniel 10:14)

Ever since the diaspora, when Babylon took the Jews out of Israel and destroyed their temple, violence has ever been present with the Jews. Jeremiah said: "We have heard a voice of trembling, of fear, and not of peace. Ask you now and see whether a man does travail with child? Wherefore Do I see every man with his hands on his loins, as a woman in travail; and all faces are turned into paleness? Alas! For that day *is* great, so that none *is* like it. It *is* even the time of Jacob's trouble; but he shall be saved out of it." (Jeremiah 30:5,6,7) "And at that time Michael shall stand up, the great Prince which stands for the children of your people; and there shall be a time of trouble, such as never was since there was a nation, even to that same time; and at that time your people shall be delivered, everyone that shall be found written in the book." (Daniel 12:1) This is your God talking to you through Jeremiah and Daniel, which you can read for yourselves.

But what book is Daniel talking about? When will that time be when Daniel's people shall be delivered? You, Jews and Israelite s, cannot answer these questions, because the answer was given to these questions by the one you do not believe; and you received another spirit, which is not the Holy Spirit. Daniel's book was shut and sealed until the time of the end. This period of time is the end time. (Daniel 12:4) No one can open Daniel's sealed up book, except the Lamb of God, that you Jews killed by turning the Lion of the tribe of Judah, the root of David, which was Jesus, which was God, over to the ruler of the Romans, called Pilate, that nailed your God to a tree; and His blood is the only way anyone can be redeemed from their sins is to believe the blood of Jesus, the Lamb of God, covers you and washes your sins away. Since you Jews do not believe that, you cannot know what is contained in Daniel's sealed up book. If you believed Jesus, you would have the key to open the door to the Ark of safety.

Jeremiah said Jacob, talking about you descendants of Jacob, was gonna go through trouble. Daniel said it would be a time of trouble, such as never was since there was a nation, even to that same time. **<u>"Corn Shelling Time"</u>** is a believer of the Word that was made flesh, and that flesh was God manifested and called Jesus, your messiah. **Corn Shelling Time"** is a believer of every Word that proceeds out of the mouth of God Almighty, (PANTAKRATOR), which is God the Father, God the Son, (Jesus), God the Holy Spirit, (the Spirit of Jesus), and has the credentials to have the key of authority to unlock the door to the Ark of safety, which door is Jesus. **"Corn Shelling time"** is gonna reveal to you Jews first the trouble you must suffer, because you are not believers.

Daniel's book that was shut and sealed is contained in the book that was written within, and on the backside, sealed with seven scals that was in the right hand of Him that sat on the throne. (Revelation 5:1). Then Brother John beheld a Lamb go take the book out of the right hand of the One that sat upon the throne, because He was the only one worthy to open the seven sealed book. (Revelation 5:9). Contained in the book sealed with the seven seals is Daniel's book along with other books that contain all the plagues that will befall, not only Daniel's people, (the sons of Jacob), Jacob being the one that wrestled with God, until God blessed him and changed Jacob's name to Israel, which has God's name, El in it, but also every nation on earth. Condemnation has already been pronounced on the nation of Israel as a whole, because they do not believe (John 3:16). Then in (John 3:18) the Word says: "He that believes Him is not condemned; but he that believes not is condemned already,_because he has not believed the Name of the only begotten Son of God."

(Daniel 11:36) " For that that is determined shall be done." "Seventy weeks are determined upon your people, and upon your holy city, to finish the transgression, and to make an end of sins, and to make reconciliation for iniquity, and to bring in everlasting righteousness, and to seal up the vision of prophecy,and to anoint the Most Holy." (Daniel 9:24) All of the seventy weeks have already come to pass except the last week, which are the last 7 years of this age, which is the seventieth week that you can read about; but you cannot understand what will happen in the seventieth week, because the spiritual knowledge is sealed up and can only be opened by the Lamb that was slain by you; and the Lamb reveals this knowledge to His blood covered believers that "overcome him, (the Devil), by the blood of the Lamb and by the Word of their testimony; and they loved not their lives unto the death." (Revelation 12:11)

The writer of **"Corn Shelling Time"**, Michael Duishka, is one of those blood covered believers that has the testimony of the Word of Christ Jesus and will overcome him, the dragon, that old serpent, called the Devil and Satan, because I love not this life unto the death. Israel as a whole is condemned; but it is every man for himself. Any individual can be saved, whether Jew or Gentile, if he will repent and "Shell Down the Corn", which means confess he is a sinner to Christ Jesus. You, Jews, believe there is one God, so do I. But God is Spirit, and can manifest Himself in human flesh, which He did in Jesus The Christ, or Messiah. So God is a triune God, which is the Father, the Son, the Holy Spirit, that is one God called the trinity, three entities, but ONE GOD.

Daniel said the seventieth week, which is the last 7 years of time, that it would end all transgression. So when the seventh trumpet sounds, that will finish the Mystery of God. **"Corn Shelling Time"** will reveal to you Jews what is the Mystery of Iniquity, Mystery, Babylon, and the Mystery of Godliness and the Mystery of God.

You Israelites are the most coveted race of people in the world. Every Country in the world hates you for no apparent reason. Is it because they are jealous of all your delicacies? Some of you are descendants of the children of Israel that God made a covenant with in the twentieth chapter of Exodus, called the 10 Commandments. In (Exodus 19:8) all the people agreed together, and said: "All that the Lord has spoken, we will do." Moses was a witness to that covenant. They also said: "Do **not** let the Lord speak to us lest we die." (Exodus 20:19) So from that time till this the Lord God has only spoken to you Israelis through a prophet like Moses, or Daniel, or that prophet, which was

Jesus. You hardhearted, stiff necked sons of Israel are being destroyed for lack of knowledge, because you do not believe Jesus. Now God is speaking to you through this book, **"Corn Shelling Time".**

You have been praying to God for almost 2,000 years; and God has not heard one prayer you prayed, because you never used the name of Jesus. If you could only understand. "In the beginning was the Word, and the Word was with God, and the Word was God. And the Word was made flesh." (John 1:1-14) "And without controversy great is the Mystery of Godliness: God was manifest in the flesh, justified in the Spirit, seen of angels, preached unto the Gentiles, believed on in the world, received up into glory." (I Timothy 3:16) So since God is Spirit, He talks in spiritual voice, that you cannot understand, because you do not have the Holy Ghost. So God had to manifest Himself in fleshly bodies, such as the one that talked to Abraham, or the "I Am", on the mountain, or in fleshly bodies of prophets, apostles, JESUS, Holy Ghost filled witnesses that talk in an audible fleshly voice that you can hear. Isaiah heard the voice of the Lord, which was a spiritual voice, saying: "Whom shall I send? And who will go for Us?" (Interruption) Who was God talking about when He said Us? (Answer) God the Father, God the Son, God the Holy Spirit, which is One God, which was the Word. Back to the voice Isaiah heard. "Then said I, here am I, send me." "And He said, Go, and tell this people, (talking about you), hear you indeed, but understand not, and see you, indeed, but perceive not." (Isaiah 6:8,9). Your ancestors made an everlasting contract, (covenant), for you, when they agreed to do all God said to do. Here is some of the covenant:

"And God spake all these Words saying: I Am the Lord your God, which have brought you out of the land of Egypt, out of the house of bondage. You shall have no other gods before Me. You shall not make unto you any graven image, or any likeness *of* anything that is in heaven above, or that is in the earth beneath, or that is in the water under the earth. You shall not bow down yourself to them nor serve them: for I the Lord your God am a jealous God, visiting the iniquity (lawlessness) of the fathers upon the children, unto the third and fourth generation of them that hate Me, and showing mercy unto thousands of them that love Me, and keep My Commandments. You shall not take the Name of the Lord your God in vain, (Reverend is His Name), for the Lord will not hold him guiltless that takes His Name in vain. Remember the Sabbath day, to keep it holy. Six days shall you labor, and do all your work, but the seventh day is the Sabbath of the Lord your God, in it you shall not do any work, you, nor your son, nor your daughter, your man servant, nor your maid servant, nor your cattle, nor your stranger that is within your gates: for *in* six days the Lord made heaven and earth, the sea, and all that in them is, and rested the seventh day: wherefore the Lord blessed the Sabbath day and hallowed it. Honor your father and your mother that your days may be long upon the land which the Lord your God gives you. You shall not kill. You shall not commit adultery. You shall not steal. You shall not bear false witness against your neighbor. You shall not covet your neighbor's house, you shall not covet your neighbor's wife, nor his man servant, nor his maid servant, nor his ox, nor his ass, nor anything that is your neighbors." (Exodus 20:1-20) All of these commandments are the ones that your forefathers agreed to do. They broke the covenant, and you are following in your forefathers' footsteps. Only you are more heathenish than they were.

"The Lord thy God shall raise up unto you a prophet from the midst of you, of your brethren like unto me, unto him you shall hearken." (Deuteronomy 18:15) But you did not dunnit. Oh me! God raised Himself up in the form of that prophet manifested in the flesh, and called Him Jesus. God overshadowed a virgin named Mary; and she conceived by the Holy Spirit of God; and God was manifested in the flesh and named Him Jesus, whom you and the Romans killed. He was buried in a tomb where His body lay for three nights and three days, while His Spirit went to the prisoners in Hell and preached to them. Then God raised His Spirit out of Hell, and He stopped on earth just long enough to pick up His body; and His body, soul, and spirit was received up into glory, where He is your High Priest to intercede for you to God Almighty (PANTAKRATOR); but you are trying to enter in to God by another door, so that makes you a thief and a robber. (John 10:1) You have been crying to God for almost 2,000 years; and you have never received an answer from Him in all this time, because you did not come to God in the Name of Jesus. "Jesus saith unto him, I am the way, the truth, and the life. No man comes unto the Father but by Me." (John 14:6) So when you pray, the heavens are solid and your words never get through, because you do not go by Christ Jesus. But that that is determined shall be done.

But you modern Israelis are just like the false prophets of Baal and Ahab the King that had forsaken God's Commandments; and you will be destroyed just like every soul that transgresses the Commandments of God. You are waiting for your Messiah, the anointed one, to come. He has already come; and you killed Him. You lied to God and broke the covenant which is contained in the Mystery of Iniquity, which is called lawlessness, or breaking God's laws.

As we will see later on when Daniel's book and the book of the one sitting on the throne is opened, that the cities of your nation will be destroyed and you with them, if you do not do what **"Corn Shelling Time"** reiterates to you; and that is to repent and "Shell Down the Corn", (confess to Christ Jesus) to God in the Name of Jesus; and Gabriel the angel told Daniel his people would be delivered, (delivered from what or who?) Delivered from Mystery, Babylon, and sin, and Satan. "Shell Down the Corn and confess that you are a lawbreaker and you are a sinner and quit committing fornication, which is idolatry, and do what Jesus said to do. Go and sin no more. Behold your house is left unto you desolate. You have no seers, no prophets, no teachers, no evangelist, no man of God. You have one thing going for you; and that is you will not have to answer for the righteous blood shed upon the earth, because Jesus said that blood would be upon the generation of scribes, pharisees, and Sadducees at His time. But you will have to answer for rejecting your Savior, which was God; also for rejecting the blood that He shed on the tree as a sacrifice for your sins. Michael Duishka confesses that he is not a prophet, nor he is not an apostle, or a teacher; and "Please Do Not Call Me a "Christian". I confess I am a sanctified, Holy Ghost filled, blood covered believer of Christ Jesus; and I believe **"Corn Shelling Time"** is anointed to be a crier to the whole world to warn every soul on earth to come out of Mystery, Babylon, which includes organized religious institutions, such as the Mother of Harlots and all the Harlots, AKA the *Catholic Church at Rome,* and **all** *churches* all over the world, which are the Harlots. All governments, politicians, judges, lawyers, law enforcement are included in Mystery, Babylon; and last of the list is all worldly people that have pleasure in idolatry, such as public, government funded schools and their sinful teachers, sports idols, Hollywood, television, computers, *queers, lizzies,* DHS recipients (AKA bums), unemployed lazy dopers, and slow bellies that lust after what they see and lust after what their flesh desires, and the pride of their worldly accomplishments, *(self for short).* All the people that vote all over the world are sinners, because they vote for a devil filled liar, thief, killer, and a destroyer of God's people and God's earth, and the created teachers that teach evolution, safe sex, planned parenthood, abortion, same sex marriage, NAACP, mandatory hiring of blacks, mandatory insurance of any kind, car, house, healthcare, boats or anything else. All of these things are sinful, because not a one puts their trust into Jesus.

But you Israelis have already forgotten your heritage; and just like Esau, you sold your birthright for a bowl of soup. The Jews used to be God's pure race; but that was then; and this is now. Not only are the women lying with Canaanites; but the men are lying with men, turning God's pure people into whores and *queers,* just like Sodom and Gomorrah. That is why God calls "that great city where also our Lord was crucified, spiritual Sodom." (Revelation 11:8) Jerusalem used to be God's holy city. Now He calls it spiritual Sodom and Egypt.

Leaders of Israel, like Golda Meir, and Moshe Dayan have gone by the wayside; and the country is no longer ruled by God. There are not any more prophets, seers, or men of God, because you rejected and killed your God, the anointed One, the Holy One of Israel, Christ Jesus. You killed your Messiah.

Daniel's book has been opened to Michael Duishka, and he is revealing what was shut up and sealed until the time of the end in his book called **"Corn Shelling Time"**, which means it is time for the whole world to "Shell Down the Corn". Just in case you missed it, to "Shell Down the Corn" means to confess and pour your black heart full of sins out to Christ Jesus, and tell Him that you are sorry for rejecting Him, and will He forgive you; and you promise Him you will go and sin no more. If you believe Him, when He said: "Though your sins be as scarlet, they shall be white as snow." (Isaiah 1:18)

You Israelis will not have any more prophets until the two witnesses in the 11th chapter of Revelation, because your forefathers killed them; and your leader at that time will kill the two witnesses in the street in the spiritual city of Sodom and Egypt, where also our Lord was crucified. Your leader at that time will be the Beast, which is the Anti-Christ, which fools you into thinking he is God.

Mister Nethanyahu, if you are still the leader of Israel when the events that Daniel's book reveals, **"Corn Shelling Time"** is the closest thing to God's Word as you will ever hear. I am not a prophet, I am not an apostle, I am not on the same level as a sheep herder. My credentials are the anointing of God the Father, God the Son, (Christ Jesus), God the Holy Spirit, which is one God Almighty, (PANTAKRATOR). He has anointed me to be a witness for Him to reiterate the warning of Christ Jesus to His people to come out of "Her.", "Her" being Mystery, Babylon, Mystery, Babylon being the Great Whore, the world system. (Revelation 18:4) My witness is being written in this book, **"Corn Shelling Time"**, Mister Nethanyahu. Daniel said you would have a Holy Place to offer the oblation and sacrifice. This prince will deceive you by making a holy covenant, which will be the seventieth week of Daniel's seventy weeks. But this prince will break the peace treaty he has made with you and pollute the holy place that he caused to be built for you by flattery. You know, like Oboma did with the *NewNited States of America* and the whole world by giving the riches of America to welfare bums and terrorists of the world, even Hamas, that is set to destroy Israel. Mister Nethenyahu, if you are still the leader when this flattering Devil deceives you, then you will recall what **"Corn Sheling Time"** has warned you about. Daniel said the prince would do wickedly against the covenant which he shall corrupt by flattery. Daniel said he, the prince, would take away the daily sacrifice; and they shall place the abomination that makes desolate. So, listen to this Mister Nethenyahu: If you ever see Oboma stand in your holy place, you will know that he is the ObomaNation of Desolation. Listen (BiBi), I call you that with all respect, because I am your friend. I am a friend of all of God's people. Oboma has made America an ObomaNation of Desolation and is on a world wide campaign to bring desolation to Israel by flattery. Christ Jesus, my Lord my God said: "When you therefore shall see the abomination of desolation, spoken of by Daniel the prophet, stand in the holy place, (whoso reads let him understand)." (Matthew 24:15). This reader understands, and **"Corn Shelling Time"** is making it plain so the world can understand.

God created an arena in Israel for His main event, the Grand Finale, called God's Super Bowl, to take place on a Sunday. He is already mounted on His <u>white</u> horse, ready to ride; "but the Great Babylon came in remembrance before God." (Revelation 16:19) So He put off going to the Super Bowl in His Arena called **Armageddon.** The reason He put it off is so He could give unto "Her" the cup of the wine of the fierceness of His wrath. (Revelation 16:19) Keep in mind that the great Babylon is the *NewNited* States of America; and the great city is none other than *New York City, USA*. So that is why, if you ever see Oboma stand in your holy place, you that are in Judea flee into the mountains. (Matthew 24:16) When these events take place, this is when Brother John saw another angel fly in the midst of heaven, having the everlasting gospel to preach unto them that dwell on the earth, and to every nation, and kindred, and tongue, and people, saying with a loud voice, "Fear God and give glory to Him, for the hour of His judgment is come, and worship Him that made heaven and earth, and the sea, and the fountains of waters." (Revelation 14:7)

But when the great Babylon came in remembrance of God, Brother John heard another voice with God's last warning, saying: "Come out of "Her", My people, that you be not partakers of "Her" sins, and that you receive not of "Her" plagues." (Revelation 18:4). This is a two fold meaning talking about the great literal Babylon, but also the Mystery, Babylon, which includes all organized religions, AKA churches, the great Whore, the Catholic Church of Rome, the mother of Harlots, which are all churches; and included in the Mystery, Babylon are all governments of the world and every one that has chosen to give his allegiance to the beast, which is the Mystery of Iniquity, which is lawlessness. And Brother John heard and saw another angel following saying. "Babylon is fallen, is fallen, that great city, (New York City, USA), because she made all nations drink of the wine of the wrath of "Her" fornication." (Revelation 14:8) So if all nations participated in "Her" fornication, (which is idolatry), then all nations must suffer the plagues of "Her" sins. That is why **"Corn Shelling Time"** is showing you "the patience of the Holy Ones, the ones that keep the Commandments of God, and the faith of Jesus." (Revelation 14:12) Listen: "Hear, O Israel, Jesus said: "You believe God, believe also Me." (John 14:1)

BiBi, my brother, please do not be like Nicodemus in the 3rd chapter of John. Nicodemus was a ruler of the Jews, as you are. You are a master in Israel, so you know these things. The writer of **"Corn Shelling Time"** is warning you to do not believe anything Oboma says. The only time he lies is when his mouth opens. He lied to the ignorant people in the USA, and not one of his promises (flattery) did he keep. So Brother BiBi just like he turned America into an ObomaNation of Desolation, he will turn Israel into an ObomaNation of Desolation, and not only Israel and the USA, but also the whole world. I know you believe God. He spoke through Jeremiah and said: "For lo I begin to bring evil on the city which is called by My name, which is Jerusalem. Golda Meir and Moshe Dayan took back some of the land inherited from Abraham. Prime ministers before you, gave it back in the name of peace. My Brother Paul wrote to the Thessalonians and said, "For when they shall say peace and safety, then sudden destruction comes upon them, as travail upon a woman with child, and they shall not escape." (I Thessalonians 5:3). So your country, Israel, will sign a treaty for peace and safety with the Anti-Christ and sudden destruction comes upon you.

There is a way that all Israel can receive the key to the Ark of safety, and that key is Christ Jesus. Believe Him: "Believe His Words for they are spirit and they are life." (John 6:63) **"O Jerusalem, Jerusalem you that kills the prophets and stones them which are sent unto you, how often would I have gathered your children together, even as a hen gathers her chickens under her wings, and you would not."** (Matthew 23:37) Brother Paul, a Benjaminite, was very sad on account of Israel's sad fate; and he said: "Brethren my heart's desire and prayer to God for Israel is, that they might be saved. For I bear them record that they have a zeal of God, but not according to knowledge." (Romans 10:1,2) That is why Hosea said: "My people are destroyed for lack of knowledge: because you have rejected knowledge, I will also reject you, that you shall be no priest to Me, seeing you have forgotten the law of your God, I will also forget your children." (Hosea 4:6)

But what did Daniel's book say about the Anti-Christ that will seduce you ignorant Jews with flattery like Oboma did to the ignorant "Christians" in the Good Ole USA? Daniel said in his book: "And the King (Anti-Christ) shall do according to his will; and he shall exalt himself, and magnify himself above every god, and shall speak marvelous things against the God of gods, (like Oboma did), and shall prosper (like Oboma did) til the indignation be accomplished. for that that is determined shall be done." (Daniel 11:36)

"And all the kingdoms of the world shall drink of the wine cup of this fury at My hand, and cause all the nations to whom I send you to drink it. And they shall drink, and be moved, and be mad, because of the sword that I will send among them. Then I took the cup at the Lord's hand, and made all the nations to drink unto whom the Lord had sent me: To wit: Jerusalem, and the cities of Judah, and the kings thereof, and the princes thereof, to make them a desolation, and astonishment, an hissing, and a curse, as *it is* this day." (Jeremiah 25:15,16,17,18) "For, lo, I begin to bring evil on the city which is called by My Name, and should you be utterly unpunished? You shall not be unpunished, for I will call for a sword upon **All** the inhabitants of the earth, saith the Lord of Hosts." (Jeremiah 25:29) To the Jew first, then the Gentile. "Behold the day of the Lord comes, and your spoil shall be divided in the midst of you, (like Oboma did in the USA), for I will gather **All** nations against Jerusalem, to battle, and half of the city shall go forth into captivity, then shall the Lord go forth and fight against those nations, (all the nations of the world, in *"God's Super Bowl On A Sunday"*, at His Arena called **Armageddon**). And His feet shall stand in that day upon the Mount of Olives, which is before Jerusalem on the east; and the Mount of Olives shall cleave in the midst thereof toward the east and toward the west." (Zechariah 14:1-4) When Jesus touches the Mount of Olives, that triggers the chain of earthquakes all over the earth, including the one in literal Babylon called *New York City, USA*. "And there were voices, thunders, and lightnings; and there was a great earthquake, such as was not since men were upon the earth, so mighty an earthquake, *and* so great; and the great city was divided into three parts; and the cities of the nations fell; and Great Babylon came in remembrance before God, to give unto "Her" the cup of the wine of the fierceness of His wrath. And every island fled away, and the mountains were not found. And there fell upon men a great hail out of heaven, every stone about the weight of a talent, and men blasphemed God because of the plague of the hail for the plague thereof was exceeding great, (114 pounds a piece)." (Revelation 16:18-21) This is one of the plagues that are a result of the sins of Babylon, which is a mystery to you. But **"Corn Shelling**

Time" is revealing the Mystery, Babylon, which is the world system, led by New York City, USA, and the United Nations, led by the King of Babylon called Oboma, making the world an Obomanation of Desolation by robbing, killing and destroying by flattery, dividing the spoils, by spreading wealth around, the wealth of the USA that God gave to His people. But now let us open the book to reveal the restitution to be made to end all transgressions.

THIS is an insert in the book, "CORN SHELLING TIME", and MICHAEL DUISHKA,clarifying statements made that had extenuating circumstances that altered the absolute belief, such as recipients of DHS (Department of Human Services). Some of God's people are bona fide, genuine, qualified,deserving, recipients, and the writer is not speaking of that group of people. The book is speaking about the group of people that are milking the system by lying,and fraudulently falsifying their sworn statement that their statement is true, when at that time it is a bald face lie.   Some of God's people are bona fide, genuine, qualified, deserving, patients that are honestly sick, or mangled, or dying that has need to have a physician attend to them. The book is definitely not speaking about this group of people. The book is exposing the hypochondriacs that imagine they have many kinds of ailments, just to *jilflirt* the physician into writing them a prescription for pain pills(dope) the system calls medication that in many cases the scammer sells on the street for megabucks to add to his, or her false obtained Welfare check, food stamps, all kinds of Oboma stimulus subsidies so they will have security to not work, and March, Loot, Steal, Kill, and Destroy at the expense of the honest,hard working, middle class, taxpaying, true American, "That's What I AM Talking About".

Some of God's people are bona fide, genuine, so called "Christians" that sincerely think they are doing God's will, and doing their best to work for God. God said they were being destroyed for lack of knowledge(ignorance), and being deceived by the deceiver aka Satan. That is why Jesus commanded you to come out of her my people.

Churches are tools of Satan that he is using to do his work in the name of God. The MOTHER of Harlots, the Universal Babylonian Catholic *Church,* has brought all the Babylonian idols of worship and incorporated them into a false organized religion called Christianity that is a deception in itself. My GOD said He is wearied by you calling evil good and good evil. There is no way any good thing can come out of a Babylonian house of idolatry called *church.* There is very little difference in protestant *churches* and their MOTHER. THE king James Bible writers adopted the same man made words as the pagan catholic bible, such as *Church, Saint, Cross, Sunday* Worship, *Easter Sunday, Christmas, Halloween,* Trees, all kinds of Idol worship, which is why JESUS is telling His people to come out of Her, Seeing that He is LORD of heaven and earth, dwells **NOT** in temples made with hands. ACTS (17: 24). DUISHKA is not talking about bona fide, sincere, ignorant, so called"Christians", but rather heathen sinners masquerading as "born again "Christians"

Chapter 28

"CORN SHELLING TIME" FLIES the flag at half staff to memorialize fallen America. It is too late for this to symbolize distress of America, but the flag is raised to half staff to show whoever observes it that we are in mourning for fallen America and the people God called His people that did not come out of "Her". America is dying, just like "Christians".

Previous chapters of **"Corn Shelling Time"** proclaim the belief that America is literal Babylon; and New York City is the City of Babylon that the angel is to cry out to in the near future, "Babylon the Great is fallen, is fallen." Not only are we mourning the destruction of this once America the Beautiful; but mostly, we are mourning for God's people that were destroyed and will be destroyed. When the devil possessed people voted for the ones that are descendants of Cain to steal and plunder, that is when America was in distress. Now America is past being in distress. She has fallen past the point of no_return. (PNR) What **"Corn Shelling Time"** is defining as returning is different from what the worldly people think of returning. Worldly people only think of sinful things like deceit; how they can make a personal gain in everything they say or do; how they can look like they are good, honest, and righteous, when all the time the spirit of the wicked one is guiding them to cheat and deceive their neighbor. Worldly people only look at every contact and every transaction how they can profit economically from that contact. So the worldly person is always thinking how they can cheat, steal, rob, kill or destroy their neighbor, and still appear as a righteous person. So the worldly person thinks that returning is to return to a thieving economy. That is the reason God is bringing the plagues and judgments on the entire world. God said He had some righteous people left in the world; and wherever they are, they are out working with their hands, so they can give to the ones in need.

God's believers think of returning as a change of heart and return to their creator, and to repent and keep His Commandments. America as a whole has fallen past the point of no return, because America is the *Great Babylon, and New York City is the Great City.* That is why God anointed **"Corn Shelling Time"** to cry out to the whole world for His people to come out of Mystery, Babylon, which is the worldly system of lying, cheating, and stealing, so they will not receive the plagues of total destruction. **"Corn Shelling Time"** is telling each individual on this earth to repent, and Shell Down the Corn, (which means confess), to Christ Jesus, and return to honesty and holiness to God. "Without holiness no man shall see God." (Hebrews 12:14)

Christ Jesus, the one sitting on the white horse with His army following Him, sitting on white horses, also is ready to go to God's Super Bowl, that great event that will happen on your pagan worship day of your Sun God Day called *Sunday*. This main event will not happen on the seventh day of the week, because that is the Sabbath Day; and God and all of His people remember the Sabbath Day and keep it holy. They do not do any work on the Sabbath Day; but they rest so they can work in *"God's Super Bowl On A Sunday"* in God's arena, AKA **Armageddon.** Dear reader, please know that this event is double dog dead sure to come, just as sure as God made little green apples. God is a merciful, long suffering God, full of grace; but He has been pleading with His people for 6,000 years to keep His Commandments, and He is still pleading with you in this book, **"Corn Shelling Time"**, and will keep on pleading and warning you for just a short time more; until He tells His angels to sound the trumpets, and He tells His angels to pour out the vials; and His long suffering will come to an end; and His mercy will turn into wrath; and your days of grace will come to an end; and there will be wailing and blasphemies, and gnashing of teeth on account of all the plagues that comes upon them, plagues of pain and sores, and great hail; and they repented not, but blasphemed God instead.

Dear reader, you take this correction, and divorce the harlot *church* you are joined to, (*married to*). Quit voting, quit robbing, killing, and destroying God's people by enforcing the laws of the land, which are robbing, killing, and destroying God's creation, and quit teaching God's little ones to commit fornication, which is idolatry. Quit drawing welfare checks, food stamps, unemployment checks, so you will not have time to march and riot, and burn, and steal, and destroy, and protest against the hand that feeds you. Do you not know when you are rioting and loud mouthing for justice, that God will be a just God, and will give you justice at the Great White Throne Judgment? You raise your children up from babies to think the white people owes them a right to take what does not belong to them; and when they get caught and killed for their crime, then you start rioting, marching, protesting without cause, loud mouthing for justice. You will get your justice at the Great White Throne Judgment of God Almighty, (PANTAKRATOR).

All you white protestors that contribute to the sins of the heathen uncivilized Babylonians will be rewarded double with God's wrath, because you are giving your body, soul, and spirit to the works of Satan. You are committing the unpardonable sin of unbelief. Oh Me! You will get what you want, and be turned into a black puff of smoke that ascends up forever, and ever. "If any man worships the beast and his image, and receives his mark in his forehead, or in his hand, the same shall drink of the wine of the wrath of God, which is poured out without measure into the cup of His indignation; and he shall be tormented with fire and brimstone in the presence of the holy angels and in the presence of the Lamb. And the smoke of their torment ascends up forever and ever." (Revelation 14:9,10,11) You white heathen are being marked with the mark of the beast when you are allied with black heathen protestors that are stealing, killing, and destroying for their god, Satan. That is what the thief came to do, rob, kill, and destroy.

All the blacks that are marching and rioting, burning, stealing, killing, and destroying for equal rights will get their reward according to their works, and the white people that are allied with the children of darkness will be rewarded double. "Reward her even as she rewarded you, and double unto her double according to "Her" works in the cup which she has filled, fill to "Her" double." (Revelation 18:6) The black women are having illegitimate babies, drawing illegitimate welfare checks, going to free medical hospitals and clinics paid for by Obama Care, get prescriptions for pain pills, *(dope)*, then sell the pain pills; and some are knocking down thousand of dollars every month that they support a lazy shack job, boy friend, that is drawing unemployment benefits, that Obama just keeps extending, selling dope, stealing, killing, and destroying, having time and money to protest and break all the laws that would land a white man in jail.

White people are too busy working with their hands making an honest living for their families, while the lazy, dope dealing, loud mouth bums are busy protesting the hand that feeds them. The honest hard working class of people are paying an enormous amount of taxes to the government, while Obama is spreading the wealth of America around to welfare bums, terrorists, bail outs, stimulus, tarp, and all kinds of abominable acts to flatter people world wide. All of this corruption is what is causing Mystery, Babylon and literal Babylon the Great to come in remembrance of God, to reward "Her" double for "Her" sins.

The "Christians" are the biggest enemy of God and His people, by putting such filth into the seat of authority, by voting for the

ObomaNation of Desolation and his hoodies. That is the reason our flag is lowered to half staff, to signify our mourning for the Great City of Babylon, which is *New York City, USA,* and the Great Babylon of America, which has passed the falling point of no return. (PNR). God is on His way to reward her double, according to the rewards she gave to God's holy ones. Oh Me!

What the problem with you, dear reader, is you never did "Shell Down the Corn" to Christ Jesus and confess to Him just like Solomon did in (I Kings 3:7) when he said: "I am but a child. I know not how to go out or come in." That is what the writer of **"Corn Shelling Time"** did, and is doing, and will continue to do; and you will be ignorant of God and wisdom as long as you reject confessing that you are as ignorant as a little child to Christ Jesus, and ask Him for wisdom, "which He gives to all, liberally to those that ask." (James 1:5)

Warning: "Do not run to and fro to seek the Word of the Lord, because you will not find it." (Amos 8:12). As before stated in Daniel's book: "Many shall run to and fro, and knowledge shall be increased." (Daniel 12:4) "This is not the knowledge that the Spirit gives." (I Corinthians 12:8) This is your problem. You are very intelligent, and you are increased with so much knowledge your head is about to burst. You have read every commentary, and know every doctrine of devils that all the English Bibles afford. "You are ever learning and never able to come to the knowledge of the truth." (II Timothy 3:7) You never will be able to know the truth until you renounce the knowledge you have acquired from the worldly teachers, and obey the Word of God that John revealed to you in (I John 2:26,27): "These things have I written to you concerning them that seduce you. But the anointing (Holy Spirit), which you have received of Him abides in you, and you need not that any man teach you: But as the same anointing (Holy Spirit) teaches you of all things, and is truth, and is no lie, and even as He has taught you, you shall abide in Him." (I John 2:26,27)

Let me interrupt the Holy Spirit, (Please forgive me Lord Jesus), to insert this testimony. Michael Duishka had to renounce the deceiver and all the commandments of men, and doctrines of devils that were seductive and luring, and tempting me to enter into **"the wide gate and the broad way, that leads to destruction, and many there be which go in thereat."** (Matthew 7:13) "Jesus said: **Believe me that I am in the Father, and the Father in Me, or else believe me for the very work's sake."** (John 14:11)

Here is the key and contingency, and condition to all the promises of God. **"If you love Me, keep My Commandments."** (John 14:15) This is what makes all men liars. If you ask them, "Do you love Jesus?" The answer is always, "Yes," which is a lie, because they do not keep His Commandments. They say, "I am a "Christian", which is synonymous with heathen or pagan. **"And why call you Me Lord, Lord and do not the things which I say?"** (Luke 6:46) *(Commandments)* "If you keep all the contingencies, which I did, He said: **"And I will pray the Father, and He will give you another comforter that He may abide with you forever."** (John 14:16) **"Howbeit, when He, the Spirit of truth is come, He will guide you into all truth: for He shall not speak of himself; but whatsoever He shall hear, that shall He speak; and He will show you things to come."** (John 16:13) Jesus did to me just what He said He would do; and I was taught by no man, because He anointed me and sent the Holy Spirit, which is the anointing, to teach me these things I am writing to you, so you can come out of "Her" and touch not the unclean things, and separate yourself from your unbelieving acquaintances, and the Holy Spirit will show you things to come, just like He showed me, and I am going to show you.

"You will run to and fro, from sea to sea, and from the north even to the east to seek the Word of the Lord and shall not find it, because the Lord has sent a famine in the land, not a famine of bread, nor a thirst of water, but of hearing the words of the Lord." (Amos 8:11,12)

"But they rose up early and corrupted all their doings. Therefore you wait upon Me saith the Lord, until the day that I rise up to the prey." Warning: You are the prey, if you do not repent and "Shell Down the Corn", (confess) to Christ Jesus, who is on His way to *"God's Super Bowl On A Sunday"*. "For My determination is to gather the nations, that I may assemble the kingdoms, to pour upon them mine indignation, all My fierce anger: for all the earth shall be devoured with the fire of My jealousy. Thus saith the Lord." (Zephaniah 3:8) "Hold your peace at the presence of the Lord God, for the day of the Lord *is* at hand, for the Lord has prepared a sacrifice, He has bid His guests." (Zephaniah 1:7) Now a lot of theologians and commentaries think the guests that God bids to come to His sacrifice are people. Wrong! "And I saw another angel standing in the sun; and he cried with a loud voice, saying to all the fowls that fly in the midst of heaven, "Come and gather yourselves together unto the supper of the Great God, that you may eat the flesh of kings, and the flesh of captains, and the flesh of horses, and the flesh of them that sit on them, and the flesh of all men, both free and bond, both small and great." (Revelation 19:18). These are God's guests He bids to eat His sacrifice. I pray, dear reader, that you will not be the sacrifice. "What has been determined will be done, and God has determined to gather all nations and kingdoms together so He can get vengeance for all the sins and make restitution for all transgression. "And He gathered them into a place called in the Hebrew tongue **Armageddon,** *" God's Super Bowl On A Sunday"!*

It is your reasonable service, *(duty)*, to voluntarily present yourself a sacrifice to God while you are still alive. The sacrifice He is preparing for His guests, *(the fowls of the air)*, are dead rebellious bodies. I pray that you, dear reader, will not be *buzzard bait.*

This writer had a so called "Preacher", a "Christian" to tell me I was a liar. I agreed with him and told him I was quitting lying. He erred, not knowing the scriptures or the power of God. The scriptures say, "let all men be liars, but God's Word be truth."

As stated in previous pages, as God was on His way to the Great Super Bowl event, Great Babylon came into His remembrance. Also all of Mystery, Babylon, which includes all of the people on the earth. Even the Holy Ones: "Many shall be purified, and made <u>white,</u> and tested; but the wicked shall do wickedly and none of the wicked shall understand." I interject here with the fact that the wicked cannot in any way receive the Holy Ghost, which is the only way anyone can have wisdom and understanding. "But the wise shall understand." (Daniel 12:10) Remember this is the time of trouble, such as never was since there was a nation, even to that same time; and at that time your people shall be delivered, every one that shall be found written in the book." (Daniel 12:1) What book? "And whosoever was not found written in the Book of Life was cast into the Lake of Fire." (Revelation 20:15)

"The first angel sounded (blew his trumpet), and there followed hail and fire, mingled with blood; and they were cast upon the earth; and the third part of trees and all the green grass was burned up," which means no hay for the cattle of the field. (Revelation 8:7) "How do the beasts groan, the herds of cattle are perplexed, because they have no pasture, yea the flocks of sheep are made desolate. Oh Lord, to you will I cry, for the fire has devoured the pastures of the wilderness, and the flame has burned all the trees of the field. The beasts of the field cry also unto you, for the rivers of waters are dried up, and the fire has devoured the pastures of the wilderness." (Joel 1:18,19,20)

I thank Christ Jesus that "My Fancy Jewel" and "Izmi", our snow <u>white</u> Arabians do not and will not suffer the blowing of the first trumpet, and the seven other angels with the seven vials having the last seven plagues. These angels were clothed in linen that was pure and <u>white.</u> Notice: There is no black in heaven. "And the first angel poured out his vial, and there fell a noisome and grievous sore upon the men which had the mark of the beast and upon them which worshiped his image." (Revelation 15:6-16:2) Radiation from the chip embedded in your hand or your forehead. "Christians" already have the mark. Believers already have the seal of God.

It is so sad to this writer to see loved ones that are rebellious to Christ Jesus. Some of my loved ones do not even have a form of Godliness to deny the Power of God thereof. Some of my loved ones are "Christians" and say they love Jesus; but they do right the opposite of what He said. Some of my loved ones are selfish and strictly of the world, and know nothing about the Word of God or Christ Jesus. All I can do for them is pray and turn them over to God. Nearly All of my loved ones have distanced themselves a long way from me; but there is no distance in prayer. Amen.

The beginning of sorrows has escalated so fervently til it is hard to discern the difference between them and the plagues of God's wrath. In 2011 the beginning of sorrows escalated to great heights and will continue to rise in all the four elements of earth, water, fire, and wind. These four elements will continue to escalate until all sinful people are destroyed from off the face of the earth. Then, after all sin and transgressions have come to an end in this dispensation, God will start a 1,000 year age of trial for people without the devil's presence to tempt and lie to people. There will be 1,000 years of peace with no tempter; and the people will still follow the devil after he is loosed at the end of the 1,000 years. (Revelation 20:3) "Blessed and holy is he that has part in the first resurrection." (Revelation 20:6)

"Corn Shelling Time" could tell you, dear reader, of a lot of disasters that will come to pass on the entire earth, worldwide. But I will not tell them, because it would come to pass sooner than God intended for them to happen. The devil would take the words that I say and pass them on to his evil followers, and the results would be death for thousands of people. The Lord Jesus said "The words you speak are life, or death." He called **"Corn Shelling Time"** to speak words of life to those that repent, and confess, and come out of "Her". Death has already been spoken to the ones that the devil has blinded their minds, because they believe not, and "he that believes not is condemned already." (John 3:18) Even though you are a "Christian" and believe not, you can still have life and life more abundantly, if you repent and "Shell Down the Corn", (confess), to Christ Jesus. If you will confess to the High Priest, (Jesus), that you wasted the life He gave you by being disobedient to His laws and His Commandments by putting other gods in His place, such as all the pleasures of sin in worldly sensual gratification, lust of the flesh, lust of the eye, pride of life, and renounce the god of this world. If you do this with a broken heart and a contrite spirit, with tears flowing out of your eyes and snot running out of your nose into your mouth, (just like this writer of **"Corn Shelling Time"** did), it is possible "the Spirit of God will draw you to Christ Jesus; and He will save you and raise you up in the last day." (John 6:44) Then if you believe Christ forgave you and saved you, you will be a believer instead of a "Christian".

Michael Duishka wrote a book called, "Please Do Not Call Me a "Christian", that is at the book stores, and on the internet with iUniverse Publishing, which it is imperative for you to read. He said a "Christian" professes to know about a man named Jesus Christ. All believers possess Christ Jesus, which is God Almighty, (PANTAKRATOR). That makes a "Christian" a professor; and a believer is a possessor of God the Father, God the Son, God the Holy Ghost. A believer has put off the old man and has been generated from above, *(not born again)*, and is holy; and Jesus will fill him or her with the Holy Spirit. Then God will sanctify him or her and cause him or her to be pure and holy, then set him or her apart from the *church*, politics, world, and set him or her apart for His use. Anyone that tells you he or she is *born again* has not been regenerated from above or received the Holy Spirit. It is not my mission to give Greek lessons; but that is where millions of "Christians" have erred is by reading the KJV version of (John 3:3,4,5) and never let the generator charge them or plug the generator into them. The Greek Scripture does not ever use the word *again* in (John 3:3,4,5), which in Greek language is another meaning (from above). Likewise, the scriptures do not use the word *born*, but rather (gennao), meaning generated, which the scriptures goes on to say "a man must be generated from the water also the Spirit to enter the Kingdom of God." (John 3:5) Then Jesus states that when a man is sired, or generated, by his daddy, which is flesh, is of the substance, flesh, (sarx); and that which is generated of the Spirit is Spirit, called in the Greek language (Pnooma), which is a different substance than flesh. There is only One Entity that is Spirit, (Pnooma), and that Entity is Above (Anothen), which is the Sovereign God; so He is the Generator that is Above that generates His Spirit (Pnooma) into the candidate for the Kingdom of God. He said, a man must be generated by the water, which the water means the vehicle or engine from the noun, Logos, which is God, by Rhema, or the saying of the Logos (Word). (Ephesians 5:26) So it is interpreted all wrong in the Catholic and the English KJV Bibles. Correct doctrine is, "You must be generated by God's Holy Spirit; and you must have a bath by the sayings of the Word, which was God, which was Jesus." **"The words I speak,** *they* **are Spirit and** *they* **are Life."** (John 6:63)

Jesus told John the baptizer, **"Suffer it to be so now, for this is the way that becomes us to fulfill all righteousness."** ((Matthew 3:15) So it is right to be baptized in water; but it is being submerged a dry sinner, and coming up out of the water a wet sinner, if you do not do what the Baptizer said to do in (Matthew 3:11); and that is be baptized into Jesus, and let Him baptize you with the Holy Ghost and fire, which does not mean you are *"born again"*, but rather it means you have had a bath in the water by the Sayings (Rhemah) of the Word (Jesus) and generated from above by God the Holy Spirit. You cannot receive the generation from above, unless you have washed your garments in the soul cleansing blood that Jesus sacrificed on the altar of the tree to make you pure and holy. His blood is the only way you can be pure and holy. "Follow peace with all and holiness, without which no man shall see the Lord." (Hebrews 12:14)

If the leading nation of the world has turned into an ObomaNation of Desolation and festered up with the filth and corruption and the scum of the earth is leading the Satan deceived people of America into destruction, where does that leave the rest of the pagan, heathen nations that worship anything from monkeys to cows? We at **"Corn Shelling Time"** are mourning for America and New York City, because like Phinehas' wife I have written "Ichabod" over the portals of America, meaning the glory is departed; and she is spiritually dead. Our flag is lowered to half staff. "Taps" is the new theme song. Whenever they say or play "God Bless America", they are slinging it in God's face. God has already been there and done that; and the heathen "Christians" let foreigners flatter them and gain control of them, and convert them into laws that rob, kill, and destroy lives. Obama and all his sick perverted constituents have come to the point that they do not know whether to _ _ _ _ or go blind. So they just shut one eye and _ _ _ _. The inhabitants of the land are in great perplexity; and everything they try is the wrong thing; and the lying News Media try to lie and cover up the mistakes and wrong decisions the educated fools make. "He that sits in the heavens shall laugh. The Lord shall have them in derision."(Psalms 2:4) The Lord said the nations would be in distress, with perplexity, (Luke 21:25)(*which means no way out*), and that is happening as I speak.

At this present time Michael Duishka is God's man on this earth to cry out and proclaim the gospel, the Truth, until the two witnesses of God come on the scene that God will give power to prophesy a thousand two hundred threescore days (1,260 days). (Revelation 11:3) God has chosen and ordained Michael Duishka to reiterate the Word of God through the books, **"Please Do Not Call Me A "Christian"** and this manuscript, **"Corn Shelling time."** The counterfeit "Christians" have all kinds of political agenda trying to promote their cause by using the title "Christian"; and so called "Christians" are buying into the cloak, or covering, they put on deceiving the ignorant and unlearned. One of the phony organizations is the (IDC) In Defense of "Christians" that advocate bringing awareness of any eastern religious groups that rob, kill, and destroy God's creation in the guise of religion of "Christians". Believers of Christ Jesus do not need any defense group, because "Believers have an advocate with the Father, the righteous Christ Jesus, and He is the propitiation for our sins; and not only for our sins, but also for the whole world." (I John 2:1,2) The blood of the righteous One covers believers; and if the "Christians" believed Christ Jesus, He would be their defense; and they would not need any group of men to defend them, such as the (IDC).

All of these "Christian" groups from all over the world, whether western, eastern, northern, or southern are harlots, the daughters of the Great Whore that sits upon many waters. Many waters shows the misled peoples that are under the influence of Mystery, Babylon, which includes the Great Whore, the Mother of Harlots, which are the unholy *Roman Catholic Church, (the Mother)*, and the Harlots being <u>all</u> the other *churches* and religions of the world, including, Baptist, Anglican, Catholic, Orthodox, or Pentecostal, or Orthodox Coptic. They are still divided and separated from the pure, sanctified, Holy Ghost filled Believers of Christ Jesus. Mohammed had epileptic seizures; and his followers thought it was a spiritual gift from God; but it was really an attack by an evil spirit, just like the event in (Mark 9:25), when Christ Jesus said to the dumb and deaf spirit. **"I charge you come out of him and enter no more into him."** That is what happened to Mohammed and what started Islam, because Jesus was not present to rebuke the foul spirit that collided with Mohammed. Now natural people, that do not possess the Spirit of God, call the foul unclean spirits epilepsy and other names; but "the natural man receives not the things of the Spirit of God." (I Corinthians 2:14)

A. "For they are foolishness unto him, neither can he know them, because they are spiritually discerned." (I Corinthians 2:14) B. "But he that is spiritual judges all things. Yet he himself is judged of no man." (I Corinthians 2:15)

All these religions world wide help to make Mystery Babylon. All the fornication, idolatry, and great riches make literal *Babylon, which is USA;* and the *City is New York City, USA.*

All religions are filled with hatred toward Abraham's descendants, the "Jews". Even America, that has always been allied with Israel, now has a president and vice president and others that dis Israel for defending itself against the Palestinians, and Hamas, and Islam, Muslims, Jihadists, and other terrorist groups. God made Abraham a promise and said: "And I will make of you a great nation, (which He did, Israel); and I will bless you and make your name great, (which He did through his children named Isaac and his grandson called Jacob, who wrestled with God until God blessed him and changed his name from Jacob to Israel.)" God made Abraham another promise that carried over to Abraham's descendants called Israelites, to wit: "I will bless them that bless you, and curse them that curse you; and in you shall all families of the earth be blessed." (Genesis 12:2,3) God kept His promise, "In Abraham all families would be blessed, *(saved),* by the Christ, the savior of the world, God manifest in the flesh, called Jesus." Jesus in the flesh was a Jew, a descendant of Abraham, who was the blessing promised to all the families of the earth. In the spiritual body He was God the Son. "And Simon Peter answered and said, "You are the Christ, the Son of the living God." (Matthew 16:16) Anyone that does not confess that Jesus is **The Christ,** the Son of the Living God, is lost.

My daddy loved me; and I loved my parents; and he never withheld that double razor strop from leaving stripes on my butt and legs. Neither did he wait until he had access to the razor strop. If there was a hickory limb close by, he would get a keen switch and use the SPA method on me. The SPA meaning Seize, Possess, and Apply. Daddy would Seize me with his left hand, and Possess the instrument (razor strop, limb, belt, switch, cotton stalk) with his right hand, and Apply the correction to my butt, legs, or back. That is called the SPA method of correction. Sometimes daddy called it, "hickory tea".

That is one of the reasons the world is in such a chaotic mess. The unorganized system has Satan for their god. He is the god of this world. My God said, "Withhold not correction from the child, for if you beat him with the rod, he will not die. You shall beat him with the rod, and shall deliver his soul from Hell." (Proverbs 23:13,14) The system would have accused my daddy of child abuse, and the unjust judges would have sent him to the penitentiary for life or have given him the electric chair. But according to my God, the whole system are child abusers by sending parents to jail for whipping their child, calling correction child abuse. They *(the system)* are the child abusers. Moreover, anyone that does not whip his child hard enough to leave stripes on his butt, legs, back, does not love his child; and the child winds up like all the devil filled children that hear voices and go on killing sprees and rob, kill, or destroy, and wind up dead themselves, because their parents were too ignorant to beat the hell out of him, or her. I do not even know the families at the Colorado, (Columbine), Sandy Hook, (Connecticut), Florida, Missouri, (Ferguson), and on and on. But I discern that these children were not whipped and taught not to steal, kill, and destroy. They came from broken homes with parents that were too selfish to take time to teach the children about Christ Jesus and the stripes He puts on His children, which this writer is a child of Christ Jesus, because of the stripes my daddy put on my butt, and because of the stripes Christ Jesus put on my body, and called me His son. "But if you be without chastisement, *(which all the system is)*, whereof all are partakers, then you are bastards, and not sons." (Hebrews 12:8) It does not matter what century, or race, or background you are in, you are a bastard and not a son if you do not receive the stripes that Christ Jesus puts on you, because "He is the same yesterday, today, and forever." (Hebrews 13:8) If your child steals, kills, or destroys because you did not beat his butt, you burn with him. But on the other hand if you whipped your child, and imparted knowledge of Christ Jesus to him or her; and he or she goes bad, you are not guilty and will not burn. All of you are children of darkness if you are children of this world system, to name a few, parents that do not teach knowledge of God to their children,

(I did not say send them to *church*), all you school teachers in public schools, all policemen and their superiors, mayors, councilmen or women, lawyers, senators, representatives, district attorneys, and most especially unjust judges, and all DHS and welfare workers, city code inspectors, governors, presidents, supreme court judges, sheriffs, NAACP, civil rights advocates, rioters, looters, marchers, loud mouth advocates for justice,or any one else that is a parasite and robs, steals, kills, and destroys the children of light. The biggest enemy of God's people are the *harlot churches* and "Christians". "Please do not call me a "Christian." All of the above named titles take hard working people's money illegally, either at gun point or by fraud, by making the laws of the land that steal, kill and destroy God's people and God's earth. These are the ones that take children away from their parents and put them in some pervert's care that rapes them and abuses them; and, yes, I know of instances where the child was murdered. Lay the blame on all the above. These are the ones that give the death penalty to innocent victims. These are the ones that tote guns and shoot innocent people and give tickets to people that do not pay insurance. These are the municipal mafia, county mafia, state mafia, federal mafia, all extracting money in the guise of protection. The honest people that keep these parasites living (walking around dead) are honest hard working people that quit stealing, killing, and destroying, and got a job working with their hands so they could feed the hungry, give water to the thirsty, visit the sick, visit the ones in prison, took in strangers, and clothed the naked. I do not mean do all of this with stolen money (taxes) assessments, confiscation, or condemnation of some one's property, but by carpenters, (like Jesus), plumbers, electricians, air conditioning, heating, roofers, handymen, yard keepers, mowers, flower bed preparers, landscapers, private school teachers of Jesus, nurses, midwives, wild life sanctuaries, cowboys, shepherds, ranchers, and most of all that pleases God most, is farmers. All of these honest, hard working children of light are the ones the parasites are robbing, killing, and destroying. But all these parasites shall go into everlasting punishment. (Matthew 25:46)

All of these parasitic people that get their food (livelihood) from stealing, killing, and destroying never had any discipline and never disciplined their children. That is why their children have all kinds of maladies, which are foul unclean spirits, that believers know to be "demons" from the abyss, which is a part of Hell. Your children hear voices that tell them to steal from anyone that is vulnerable, and voices that tell them to kill, and oft times they either kill their own flesh and blood, or kill strangers, or the saddest thing is the fact that they are killing themselves, *(committing suicide)*. The reason is they never had a SPA treatment; and they never "Shelled Down the Corn", which is confessing their sins to Christ Jesus, which you have not done either.

"Corn Shelling Time" is a wake up call to the whole entire world to come out of sin and darkness and come into the light, which is to come out of "Her", which is Mystery, Babylon. Christ Jesus inspired Michael Duishka to warn the whole world and pull as many out of the flames of hell as will repent and "Shell Down the Corn", which is to confess to Christ Jesus that you have done wrong and are painfully sorry for your sins, and ask Him to forgive you, and go and sin no more. Ask Him to save you and believe Him, because He said, "If you confess, He is faithful and just to forgive you." (I John 1:9) Now all the plagues (stripes) are coming upon you and will destroy you because you are not keeping His commandments. If you do not repent, you will be *buzzard bait* for God's supper.

If you do repent and shell down the corn to Christ Jesus, pray that God will open a door for world wide distribution of this book, **"CORN SHELLING TIME",** not to make any gain for **MICHAEL DUISHKA,** But God's word be preached in all the world, and lead many souls out of destruction of sin and Satan. Amen. One dream of mine is a treasured long shot,and that is to have one of my Japhetic brothers,the honourable descendant of Noah, Vladimir Putin, the highest ranking man in Russia, to find a way to visit Michael Duishka, the most dishonorable man in Babylonian America. I am nothing. But Mavis, my wife and I would love to have you come and eat cornbread and pinto beans with us if you could figure out how to work a miracle vacation, and charge it to the state. Mavis does not know how to bake pirozhki (stuffed buns), but we could russel up some grub, maybe some cabbage with beef and rice if you have not gone back on your raising. The only reason I could think of why a dignitary like you, Mr. Putin, the ruler of the 2nd largest country in the world, would want to visit a couple of old nobodies like Mavis and I (past 4score)would be because the LORD Christ Jesus might want to impart some spiritual gift on you. Pray about it and ask Him. Wait for an answer. Maybe God wants to reveal something about Magog, which is your land that would be a blessing to you. Besides always look ahead, it would be a first, and make the front page. Thank you Mr. Putin for helping brother Snowden, a patriot of his country, he was a stranger and you took him in. Jesus said in (Matthew 25: 38-40) that you done it to Him,when you done it to brother Snowden, also a son of Japheth. The LORD JESUS will give you a special blessing for that, I promise. When you get this book and read this, and have your intelligence to check Michael and Mavis Duishka out, come on over and eat beans and cornbread with us, and share. It is the best we can offer a King like you. You can find us through iUniverse Publishing. LORD JESUS you said you would do any thing I ask in your name and now Father God, in the name of your only begotten Son, Christ Jesus, Mavis and I agree that you will send a special blessing to brother Vladimir Putin and save him and his house and send peace to him and the people of Russia, we ask in the name of Jesus, and everybody said Amen! If you see brother Snowden, tell him all the true Americans are praying for him. I apologize for the degenerated class of people in my country that would elect a party of anti-Americans that are promoting worldwide strife and contentiousness against the true American's will. Because Satan is the god of this world, Christ Jesus has to be invited into someone's heart before He will come into Satan's world. Evidently the Hamitic rulers of America has not invited Christ Jesus,(the prince of peace,) into their heart. So there is only one other spirit that they could have in their heart, and that is the spirit of Anti-Christ, that only comes to steal, kill, and destroy. The God fearing Americans here at home have a terrorist problem with the Hamites that are rioting, stealing, burning, and destroying, but the Hamitic rulers cause the attention to shift from that to trying to police the rest of the globe. The degenerates are trying to jump out of the frying pan into the fire by electing a woman,(some have called Jezebel), because she called the Republican Americans her enemies. Brother Putin I appreciate the kind words you spoke about Donald, which were not words of hate. We need more words of love and kindness to be spoken in every country of the world, do you think it so? Looking forward to hearing from you. I AM your friend and brother, Michael and Mavis Duishka.

Chapter 29

BABYLON IS DEFINED AS confusion. Many many knowledgeable worldly people are in the state of confusion, which is the state of Mystery, Babylon. **"Corn Shelling Time"** has made it's case against Mystery, Babylon and literal Babylon, which is America and that Great City of New York City, USA. So whenever it comes time for God to remember Great Babylon, He has already judged the cities of the nations; and they have already fallen before He remembers the Great Babylon. **"Corn Shelling Time"** has pleaded with you differently from the way God is pleading with you at this very moment. **"Corn Shelling Time"** has been reasoning with you with the Word of God.

But the world has turned a deaf ear to God's Word; and because the world has become a habitation of idol worshipers and "Christians" filled with the spirit of devils, God is pleading with you with stripes. He is chastising more severely now with bodily chastisement with plagues that God calls stripes. "And that servant which knew his Lord's will and prepared not himself, neither did according to His will, shall be beaten with many stripes." (Luke 12:47) Now you do not recognize that Ebola, aids, tuberculosis, arthritis, pneumonia, brain tumors, diabetes, influenza, leukemia, cancer, obesity, epilepsy, prostate, liver, (psoriasis) STD, polio, miscarriages, kidney stones, ulcers, heart attacks, gall bladder, gout and hundreds of more diseases are stripes that God is allowing the devil to beat you with, because you know to quit the sins that are causing these stripes AKA plagues. *"You ain't seen nothing yet."* "But it shall come to pass if you will not hearken to the voice of the Lord your God, to observe to do all His Commandments and statutes, which I command you this day, that all these curses (stripes) shall come upon you and overtake you." (Deuteronomy 28:15) The Lord will smite you with all these curses, and you cannot be healed from the top of your head to the sole of your foot. Is that what is happening to you at this present time? This is only the beginning of sorrows. The end is not yet. You say, "That is only for the Jews", then how come you are cursed? There is a simple way to be healed of your stripes. "Shell Down the Corn" to Christ Jesus, (confess to Him you do not keep His Commandments, that you are a sinner), repent and turn from your wicked ways. If you "Shell Down the Corn (confess), "He is faithful and just to forgive us our sins, and to cleanse us from all unrighteousness." (1 John 1:9)

But on the other hand, if you choose to keep your malady, just keep sinning until you be destroyed from off the land wherever you are on this earth. "The wages of sin *is* death, but the gift of God is eternal life through Christ Jesus our Lord." (Romans 6:23) Greed is a mighty catalyst in the commission of sin. Satan uses you for his agent to covet or lust after more mammon. It makes no difference if it be money, sex, power, or notoriety, self never seems to get enough. God told David, "if you had wanted more women, I would have given you more; but you, David, coveted another man's wife, and even committed murder to satisfy your lust." King Ahab coveted Naboth's vineyard so much that he and his wife, Jezebel, committed murder and killed Naboth, because of greed. The televangelists preach prosperity; and become rich by tickling people's ears. No matter how much money they store up, they still lust for more money, fame, and power. Their reward will be according to their works. **"They compass land and sea to make one proselyte, and when he is made, they make him twofold more the child of Hell than they."** (Matthew 23:15). That is why God is beating you with more stripes, (plagues), because "you know to do good and do not do it, and to you it is sin." (James 4:17)

You succumb to the overpowering force of lust of the eye, when you see the "Christians" dress immodestly, showing their flesh to the point of the burning temptation of the lust of the flesh; and you forget about the vows you made to God; and your pride of "Christianity", that you profess, goes out the window; and you fall into the snare of Satan, which is one of the glories of his kingdom, called sex. You leave the hour long sermon the preacher admonishes you with in *church*, on *Sunday* to go worship one of your idols, the television, and be exposed to many hours of nudity of the flesh until your profession of being a "Christian" is forgotten, and you worship another god, called the goddess of sex, that has burned in your loins.

The "Christian" prosperity preachers incite the lustful greed for money in you and make you believe it is God's will for you to be rich. Jesus said, "It is easier for a camel to go through the eye of a needle, than for a rich man to enter into the Kingdom of God." (Mark 10:25) Do you think it is God's will for you to be rich, so you cannot enter into the Kingdom of God? I trow not. The devil will make you the same proposal he made our Lord Jesus, "If you will bow down and worship me, I will give you all these things, which include all the kingdoms of the world and the glory of them, (the glory of them being power, money, sex, notoriety, fame, and anything your soul lusts for)" Jesus declined Satan's offer; but you fell down and worshiped the god of this world, (Satan), and say like the lying preacher said that God has blessed you, when all the time it was Satan that gave you your riches and made you a twofold more child of Hell than the lying preacher. (Matthew 23:15) You sold your soul to the devil for prosperity, name it and claim it, gab it and grab it, confess it and possess it. You married the Great Whore, Mystery, Babylon. "Please do not call me a "Christian" says Michael Duishka. You have everything this world has to offer. You confess everything except the right thing, which is the sins of "Her" that you are partaking of; but you are receiving "Her" plagues, (stripes). **"Corn Shelling Time"** will warn you again to, "Come out of "Her", My people, that you be not partakers of "Her" sins, and that you receive not of "Her" plagues." (Revelation 18:4)

It is too late to not receive "Her" plagues, because you made a deal with the devil for power, riches, sex, notoriety, fortune, fame; but it is not too late to "Shell Down the Corn", that is to confess to Christ Jesus that you are a sinner and ask Him to save you, and believe Him when He said He would save you. "But faith without works is dead, so He said to sell that you have and give alms." (Luke 12:33). "Christians" confess Jesus Christ, Believers possess Christ Jesus. "Christians" try to use Jesus as a cloak, or a covering, for their sins. Also they use the *church,* which is a Harlot, to try to justify themselves to God; but the only way they can do that is to repent of all their sins and start keeping God's Commandments: "Remember the sabbath day to keep it holy." (Exodus 20:8) "Here is the patience of the holy ones, here are they that keep the commandments of God and the faith of Jesus." (Revelation 14:12)

God is going to give His two witnesses the power to prophesy to the angels with the trumpets, when to sound, and power to prophesy to the angels with the vials, (bowls), when to pour them out. God is pleading with His people kindly through **"Corn Shelling time"** to "Shell Down the Corn" and confess to Christ Jesus all their sins; and "He is faithful and just to forgive us our sins and cleanse us from all unrighteousness." (1 John 1:9)

God is also pleading with His people in many more ways; but that is why He has put a hook in the jaws of all the hate filled rulers in the world to draw them to His *"Super Bowl On A Sunday"* to put an end to all sin and transgression, and to make restitution for all the sins against God. That is another way God is pleading with Satan's people at the Grand Finale called *"God's Super Bowl On A Sunday".* (1st Duishka)

Until the Super Bowl, He is allowing Satan and all unclean spirits to enter into the hate filled rulers of the world to change God's laws and commandments into traditions and doctrines of devils. He is also pleading with His people all over the earth with the four elements, the wind, (tornadoes, hurricanes, and all kinds of whirlwinds), the fire, (volcanoes), forest fires, prairie fires, and all kind of fires, the water, by floods and hail, snow and rain, then the earth, (earthquakes, tsunami, under water volcanoes. Then the fifth element that rules over the other four is Pemptos Ousa, the fifth being, which is the triune God Almighty, (PANTAKRATOR).

Pempte Ousa, (Christ Jesus), said: **"I Am come to send fire on the earth, and what will I, if it be already kindled."** (Luke 12:49) The four arch angels God has appointed over the four elements are very powerful angels, exacting judgments all over the earth on account of man's greed. The angels over the four elements are actually restraining or holding the elements to keep them from destroying the fools that are destroying the earth. (Revelation 11:18)

There are not any believers that are loud mouthed activists going around hollering, "We want equal rights, or we want justice." There are no lazy believers that draw unemployment benefits. God has plenty of work for believers. There are no believers or candidates for the Kingdom of God that gang up in masses stealing, killing, destroying, looting and burning other people's property. These are Satan's people on their way to the Lake of Fire prepared for the devil and his angels. (Revelation 20:15) There are no believers that beg the DHS for handouts to resale for drug money. There are no believers that think they have the right to other people's possessions by marching and protesting. Those that do such things are waiting for the elevator going down. A believer is quiet, calm, never loud, and always abases himself because he knows his rewards are greater in the Kingdom of God than they are here in Satan's kingdoms.

Ever since the year 2011, when the sorrows of mankind escalated and the days of vengeance grew more intense, the days of God's justice have already started. (Luke 21:22) God does not go around loud mouthing, hollering for justice. He lets the four elements exact justice in as much as the seas and waves roaring. (Luke 21:25). Jesus said: **"I am come to send fire on earth, and what will I if it be <u>already</u> kindled?"** (Luke 12:49)

All the protestors all over the planet earth, are the reason God is pouring out His wrath on the people that are participating in the sins of the Great Whore, Mystery, Babylon, by all kinds of plagues that are destroying the ones that do not come out of "Her".

"And the blood shall be to you for a token upon the houses where you are; and when I see the blood, I will pass over you; and the plague shall not be upon you to destroy you." (Exodus 12:13) Now, the promise is if the blood of Christ Jesus is applied to your heart, and you are covered with the blood of the Lamb, the plague shall not be upon you. It is easy for a believer to discern (judge) that the pagan, "Christian", heathens do not so much as know what the blood of the Lamb is. A believer can look on every side and see "Christians", pagans, heathen, that are being destroyed every day, because they received of "Her" plagues. They made light of the holy, sacred Passover, thereby desecrating their way of escape from the destroying plague. The pagans changed the action of Almighty God, (PANTAKRATOR), that passed over the blood covered door posts, to the goddess of sex called Ishtar (Easter), which is falling away from life into death, "Seeing they crucify to themselves the Son of God afresh, and put Him to an open shame." (Hebrews 6:6) "Were they ashamed when they had committed abominations? Nay, they were not at all ashamed, neither could they blush: Therefore shall they fall; in the time of their visitation they shall be cast down, saith the Lord." (Jeremiah 8:12) This present time is the time of their visitation; and therefore they are falling from all the plagues of their affiliation with the Great Whore AKA Mystery, Babylon, and refuse to come out of "Her".

"Corn Shelling Time" is one of God's agents He has sent to remind His people of all the promises He made to them, to warn them, and also to reward them before the time of their visitation. The rich man that was buried lift his eyes up in Hell and prayed for Abraham to send someone from the dead to testify to his brothers. Abraham told the rich man if they would not believe Moses and the prophets, they would not believe if one from the dead testified to them. Abraham was talking about Christ Jesus that was dead and is alive. (Revelation 2:8) But Michael Duishka is one that was walking around dead, just like you, that was dead in trespasses and sins of stealing, killing, and destroying for Satan, the god of this world; but God had mercy on me and let the light of the glorious gospel of Christ, who is the image of God, shine unto me, then I repented of my sins that all passed before my eyes; and this ole country boy "Shelled Down the Corn", and confessed to Christ Jesus that I was the baddest of all of the bad seed, the lowest of all the sinners, and there was no good thing in me, and begged Christ Jesus to please have mercy on me; and I believed Him; and He did have mercy on me. The Lord and master of me brought me back from the dead to testify to my millions of brothers and sisters, and tell them that Christ Jesus is no respecter of persons; and He will do the same thing for you, if you will just "Shell Down the Corn", and confess to Him.

The sad part of the testimony of Christ Jesus is the condemnation of the created ones that do not believe Him. (John 3:18) The unbelievers think that when their body goes back to dust, that is the end of their existence. Since they lack knowledge of inanimate beings, they are destroyed, but do not cease to exist. They still exist in a different entity.

The joyful part of the testimony of Christ Jesus is the eternal life of the created ones that believe Him by faith and do not have to have anything proven, but have changed from death to life by faith. (John

3:16) That is the difference between a "Christian" and a believer. A "Christian" professes to be filled with the Holy Spirit and walks around blind, because the god of this world has blinded his mind and causes him to believe not the Word, which is synonymous with not believing Christ Jesus. They are the ones that believe in Jesus Christ, just like the demons; but they do not believe Him. A believer has the mind of Christ Jesus and can see things by faith, and is not destroyed, because he does not lack knowledge, because he, (the believer), possesses the Holy Spirit in him. The Holy Spirit is the anointing; and the anointing teaches the believer all things; and the believer has no need of a man to teach him. (1 John 2:27) A believer lives by every Word that proceeds out of the mouth of God, and affirms that confession by acting upon the Word that God spoke.

One of the many contingencies to salvation and other benefits of God is found in (II Chronicles 7:14), to wit: "If My people, which are called by My Name, shall humble themselves, and pray, and seek My face, and turn from their wicked ways, then will I hear from heaven, and will forgive their sin, and will heal their land." Now it is beneficial for you to parse every contingency and to analyze each specific word, since this is God talking. First of all He calls us His people. The same wicked ones He calls His people in Revelation 18:4, where He warns us to come out of "Her", My people. Now God must be talking to the "Christians", since these are the only people that are called by His name, (Christ). The next step is to humble themselves, which the professors of self esteem find so difficult to do, when they are obsessed with exaltation. Jesus said, **"And whosoever shall exalt himself shall be abased: And he that humbles himself shall be exalted."** (Matthew 23:12) The next step is to pray, but most "Christians" do not know how to pray. They do not know how to use kneeology, (bend their knees), and bow before the Almighty (PANTAKRATOR), with a broken heart and a contrite spirit, and go through Christ Jesus to reach God. Jesus said unto him, "I am they way, the truth, and the life: No man comes to the Father, but by Me." (John 14:6) That is the reason God never hears your prayer, because you do not call on Him, in the Name of Jesus. The next step is "seek My face", God doing the talking. To seek His face means you have to call unto Him for a longer time than two minutes, and that depends on how long it takes you to generate enough power to worship the Father in Spirit and Truth. **"The hour is coming, and now is, when the true worshipers shall worship the Father in Spirit and in Truth, for the Father seeks such to worship Him."** (John 4:23)

Paul, my brother, said, "praying always with all prayer and supplication in the Spirit." (Ephesians 6:18); but it is impossible to pray in the Spirit if you do not have the Holy Spirit dwelling in you. "Christians" have the Holy Spirit with them: Believers have the Holy Spirit in them. If you ever seek His face long enough to see Him, then you have to turn from your wicked ways. You say you do not have any wicked ways. God said you have to turn from your wicked way. Now who is lying, you or God? Since God cannot lie, it would have to be you that is lying, so here is what you need to do. Get down on your knees and cry out to God in the Name of Jesus, and "Shell Down the Corn, (confess), that you are a wicked sinner, and promise Him you repent, which is to turn from your wicked ways and renounce the god of this world, (which is Satan), and the things of this world, and go and sin no more, and believe Jesus, and He will hear you from heaven and forgive your sins, and He will heal your land. (II Chronicles 7:14)

If you do these contingencies, God will answer your prayer and do more for you than you asked. He cannot lie. This is **"Corn Shelling Time"**, so quit playing with God and lying to Him, before it is time for your visitation. Your visitation time will be when the death angel comes for you, and he will be looking for the blood of Jesus. If you are not covered with the blood of Jesus, the death angel will not pass over you, but you can call on the Easter Bunny and see if he can save you. Or maybe Santa Claus will save you, or perhaps Obama, or Mandela, or Michael Jackson, or possibly Reverend King, or Jesse, or Al, or perchance Oprah, or the degenerated girl, maybe the witch at

Halloween will let you ride her broom to safety, possibly Mohammed will pick you up on his horse, maybe you can rub Buddha's belly and say "Buddha, Buddha, bring me luck", or maybe the Virgin Mary, mother of Jesus will hear your hail Mary, or arguably the ISIS, Islam State, or the Muslim Quran, perhaps you will evolve, or maybe the *harlot church*, or even the Mother of Harlots, or possibly the Mystery, Babylon that you are in will rapture you out of this world. Nonetheless, the only other alternative you have that will work for you; is to "Shell Down the Corn" to Christ Jesus, since, "Neither is there salvation in any other, for there is none other name under heaven whereby we must be saved." (Acts 4:12) That means confess your sins to Him and ask Him to save you. Then, **BELIEVE HIM.**

Warning! It is such a short time until you will go to sleep with your people, which at that time you will not be given any more chances to talk for yourself. You will be silent after the judgment. Plead your case to Christ Jesus while you are conscious and aware of the charges against you. At the judgment you will not be able to speak, because the books will be opened, and they will have every word written that you spoke when you were conscious and aware of the words you had spoken. If you "Shell Down the Corn" now and confess your sins while you are able to think and talk, you have a mouthpiece, lawyer, an advocate, an intercessor, Christ Jesus, to plead your case for you. If you do not "Shell Down the Corn" while you can talk, and confess to Christ Jesus, He will say to you at judgment, **"Depart from Me you that work iniquity, (lawlessness), I never knew you."** (I John 2:1) – (Matthew 7:23)

Remember, you do not want to go around loud mouthing for justice, like the black "Christians" that try to make criminals into victims of injustice. They need to be crying out to Christ Jesus like blind Bartimaeus did when he said, "You son of David have mercy on me." (Mark 10:46) Every time some black is killed after committing a crime, his kind gang up and march, stealing, killing and destroying by looting, burning and destroying, hollering, "We want justice;" and at the Great White Throne Judgment, justice is just what they will get. But you believers know that we are all guilty and deserve death; but **"Corn Shelling Time"** has a way of escape. Just "Shell Down the Corn" and confess you are guilty, and plead for mercy from Jesus.

"Christians" used to be decent examples of morality, exhibiting the highest standards of respectability. That was then, and this is now. At this present time so called "Christians" do not draw any respect in their speech, or their dress, and most especially their conduct. They cannot be distinguished from the heathen. The women dress like whores, showing all the flesh the law allows, tempting men into rape or molestation, or sexual assault. Then after the seed is planted and a life is formed in their belly, they commit a worse crime and murder their own baby, their own flesh and blood. They add to their immorality by voting for a *queer* politician that votes for a bill that allows murder, stealing and destroying God's creation.

This writer personally knew a doctor that aborted a baby in a young woman, and they (the law of the land) tried the doctor for murder. Now they protect the baby killers, and the politicians, and the judges that made murder legal. **"But the children of the kingdom shall be cast out into outer darkness: There shall be weeping and gnashing of teeth."** (Matthew 8:12)

"The woman shall not wear that which pertains unto a man. Neither shall a man put on a woman's garment, for all that do so are abomination unto the Lord thy God." (Deuteronomy 22:5) Now, not only are the men wearing women' apparel; but men are getting sex changes turning men into women. "Men lying with men, which are called *queers,* who knowing the judgment of God, that they which commit such things are worthy of death, not only do the same, but have pleasure in them that do them." (Romans 1:32)

Now, the *Pope,* the highest ranked "Christian" says, "The Catholic *Church* should not dismiss gay marriage." He speaks the sentiment of the majority of so called "Christians", whether Catholic or protestant, no difference.

If there are any believers of Christ Jesus, "Wherefore come out from among them, and be you separate, " saith the Lord, "And touch not the unclean thing; and I will receive you." (II Corinthians 6:17) "Come out of "Her", My people, that you be not partakers of "Her" sins, and that you receive not of "Her" plagues." (Revelation 18:4) This is God's last warning in the bible to His people; and the only way to come out of "Her" is to "Shell Down the Corn" to Christ Jesus, which means confess all your sins to Him, and ask God Almighty (PANTAKRATOR) to save you in the name of Jesus.

"Corn Shelling Time" is reiterating the pleading of God the Father, God the Son, God the Holy Ghost, the One God. You, dear readers are partakers in the sins of the world, the Great Whore that sits on many waters. "And the woman was arrayed in purple and scarlet colour, and decked with gold, and precious stones, and pearls, having a golden cup in "Her" hand full of abominations and filthiness of "Her" fornication: And upon "Her" forehead was a name written, MYSTERY, BABYLON THE GREAT, THE MOTHER OF HARLOTS AND ABOMINATIONS OF THE EARTH." (Revelation 17:1-5)

The first word is Mystery, which is known only by revelation. Since this word could fill up volumes of books, **"Corn Shelling Time"** is going to cut through to the chase and call it Mystery shortcut. Since Mystery shortcut is talking about abominations and filthiness of the Great Whore that sits on many waters means the sins of the entire world. The Mystery of Iniquity, which is lawlessness, or disobedience of God's laws or commandments.

The next word written on Her forehead is Babylon, which means confusion that is deceiving everyone on the earth, except the believers that have come out of "Her". These unbelieving "Christians",

Muslims, Confucianism, Buddhism, Taoism, Communism, and all other philosophical cults of the world causes the two words to join, forming Mystery, Babylon.

The next two words made another setting and place. The Great created another Babylon, which is the leader of Mystery, Babylon in all the iniquities, or lawlessness of the entire earth. This Babylon, The Great, is the *newnited States of America;* and The Great Babylon City is *New York City,* the home of the stock exchange, home of the trade center of the world, home of the great New York Harbor,and home of the United Nations of the Mother Of Harlots And Abominations Of The Earth. This is the Great Babylon that is remembered by God to give unto "Her" the cup of the wine of the fierceness of His wrath. (Revelation 16:19)

But before God can serve "Her" the cup of wine of the fierceness of His wrath, He is going to make reconciliation for the iniquity of all the sins of the nations, and to fulfill all the desolation that has been determined in the book of Daniel. When we open it up with the seven sealed up books of Revelation and open the vision and prophecy, the Most Holy One has been anointed to judge and make war. (Revelation 19:11) The true and faithful judge is sitting on His white horse with His army following Him, waiting for His angels to sound their trumpets and pour out their bowl of wrath on all of Mystery, Babylon and the Great Babylon (*newnited States of America*), and the Great City, *New York City, U.S.A.*

As **"Corn Shelling time"** has faithfully showed you, the reader, how to "Shell Down the Corn" confess to Christ Jesus all your iniquities, (lawlessness), and reiterated God's last warning to you, which is come out of Her, My people, and told you how to escape all your plagues, which are stripes of chastisement, also how, Pempte Ousa, the fifth being, over the four elements, the earth, the wind, the water, the fire, has shown you a way of escape of what you call natural disasters, also how the anointing will teach you all things,

(I John 2:27), we are going into the spirit of prophecy, which is the testimony of Jesus, and follow the one on the white horse and His army on to *"God's Super Bowl On A Sunday"*, but GOD called it **ARMAGEDDON.**

This is an insert in the book, **"CORN SHELLING TIME"**, and **MICHAEL DUISHKA** with some of his additional belief. The Media took a poll which is always a big lie to promote what they want to happen, and usually it happens, The consensus is there are more secular than "Christians". The belief of DUISHKA is there are not any difference in "Christians", Secular Humanism, Atheist, Pagans, Heathen,Agnostic, or the *CHURCH* of Satan, since they all steal kill and destroy, either literally, or by proxy. They put on a mask, cloak, or covering, by promoting their title as to what they say, to cover up their actions. They say is always a lie. RIGHT?!!!!! They all vote for a jack booted thug that passes laws that steal, kill, or destroy God's property or else they are silent, which is consent to do lawlessness, (iniquity), (SIN), (DEATH PENALTY). These silent people are committing sins of omission. They vowed in their confession to salvation to obey and serve the One who is saving them, and He said if you love Him, keep His commandments, which is go be a witness for Him, not to be silent. If you keep His commandments, you know you would be doing good. But if you do not keep His commandments, you are sinning. He that knows to do good and does it not to him it is sin. (JAMES 4:17). There is, in my opinion, no such thing as a true Christian, because "Christians" belong to a *church*. They are married to a *church*, which is either a daughter of the HARLOT MOTHER, or THE MOTHER HARLOT herself. Revelation:17;5. There is no such thing as the *true church of Jesus Christ,* because there is no such scripture as *Jesus Christ* in the Holy Greek Scriptures. Christ is not Jesus' last name. In the Holy Greek Scriptures there is either CHRIST JESUS, or JESUS THE CHRIST. The Greek scriptures are written in part like Hebrew from right to left, and the UNHOLY ROMAN CATHOLIC BIBLE interpreted the scriptures basackered, So when the UNHOLY, UNTOWARD, INTERPRETERS of the King James Bible were acting under duress and threats from the king, they just for the most part copied the UNHOLY CATHOLIC BIBLE. Tyndale wrote the first correct interpretation of Greek Scriptures to English in I believe 1525 AD, and the king of England killed Tyndale. King James came on the scene later, and told his interpreters to not use any of Tyndale' writings. But they used his interpretations anyway, and the most of the only TRUTH in the KJV is Tyndale Copy. There is a true body of CHRIST that is connected together by THE HOLY SPIRIT of GOD. No one knows who they are except they, themselves. No one knows where they are except they themselves, and their Master, CHRIST JESUS. There was no such word *church* in the HOLY SCRIPTURES. *Church* is a man made word. *SAINT* is a dead catholic. Cross is a pagan symbol for the "T" in the heathen god Tammuz. All "Christians" blaspheme CHRIST JESUS by following the heathen worm eaten murderer, Herod, in calling the MOST HOLY PASSOVER, *Easter*. Acts: 4:12. Preacher, "Christian", makes no matter how much you profess to know CHRIST JESUS, I believe you have trampled on the Son of God and you have the blood of the covenant where with He was sanctified:an unholy thing, and have done despite to the spirit of grace? Hebrews: 10:29. Makes no matter how rich and haughty,prideful, famous you are, you cannot justify adopting catholic pagan gods and pagan words, trying to turn them into holy words of GOD. You will Not find a member of the body of CHRIST in a *church*, because the LORD of heaven and earth dwells not in temples made with hands. YOU are the temple of God, not a man made building. Teachers of error think when Brother John said come out of her my people, that He was talking about THE MOTHER HARLOT only: Revelation 18:4, WRONG! He was talking about the daughters also Revelation17: 5. BLOOD COVERED HOLY GHOST, SANCTIFIED, BELIEVERS, are the body of CHRIST, and no one knows who they are.

Chapter 30

"**Corn Shelling Time**" is going to illuminate the awful events that the man in <u>white</u> linen and the Angel Gabriel showed Daniel would befall his people at the time of the end of the dispensation of the Gentiles. Daniel shut up an enormous amount of knowledge in his book that is opened up when the seven sealed books or seven addendum to the book that was in the right hand of Him that sat on the throne, (Revelation 5:1) and was opened by the Lamb of God that was slain and has redeemed us to God by His blood out of every kindred, and tongue, and people, and nation. These books can reveal knowledge to you, the reader; but only God Almighty can give you the wisdom to show you how to apply the knowledge that you will receive from **"Corn Shelling Time"**. "And they that be wise shall shine as the brightness of the firmament, and they that turn many to righteousness as the stars forever and ever." (Daniel 12:3)

As it has been written in the first of **"Corn Shelling Time"**, "Many shall run to and fro, and knowledge shall be increased", this has already manifested to this generation we live in at the present time. This generation is the most intelligent species of the human race since God created man. But, as someone once said, "They are a generation of educated fools," because the knowledge they possess is worldly knowledge and will profit them zilch.

But you, dear reader, are in the position to ask God for the wisdom to apply the knowledge you will receive from **"Corn Shelling Time"** to make, to turn many to righteousness and to shine as the firmament. You do not need any worldly credentials like BA's or MA's, or PHD, because the Lord Christ Jesus will send you His Holy Spirit and anoint you to do His work to tell His people to come out of the things of this world and turn to righteousness.

"Then said He unto the disciples, "It is impossible but that offenses will come; but woe unto him, through whom they come." (Luke 17:1) Offenses started coming on America when Truman, the President, got America into Korea, then Kennedy got America into the Vietnam War and started the biggest welfare give away to followers of Martin Luther King Jr., which some say led to their assassination. It just happened that all of these negative things were caused by these two democratic presidents. But the trigger that really stirred up God's wrath was the next democratic president, Bill Clinton, that as far as the evidence against him shows, he turned the office of president of the *NewNited* States of America into a pig sty, or hog wallow. He nominated Janet Reno, *(some believe she was deranged),* to be Attorney General, and left Stephen E. Higgins, the Director of the BATFE, (Bureau of Alcohol, Tobacco, Firearms, and Explosives). He left William S. Sessions as Director of the Federal Bureau of Investigations, when the Waco, Texas, fiasco was initiated, which resulted in the murder of men, women, and children at the Branch Davidian Compound near Waco, Texas. Bill Clinton stated: "The buck stopped with me." So Bill Clinton, the Democratic President, turned his gangs of jack booted thugs, (according to George H. Bush) loose on all the innocent men, women, and little children at the home of David Koresh, that resulted in the massacre of at least 76 human beings.

These main players are not the only guilty ones; but there are too many to name; but to name a few additional ones was Ann Richards, Governor of Texas, Phillip Choinacki, Chuck Sarabyn, Jeff Jamar,

Richard Rogers, and many, many more. This writer would be lax to leave out the special *FBI agent involved in the Waco siege, Bob Ricks*. All of these above named are what has triggered God's wrath to start manifestation on the whole world. They caused the offenses to come on God's little ones, "And it were better for them that a millstone were hanged about their neck and be cast into the sea, than they should offend one of these little ones." Their only escape is to repent and humble themselves before God and "Shell Down the Corn" to God Almighty, (PANTAKRATOR). That means (confess), plead guilty, ask Christ Jesus to save you. Not only are these main players guilty, but also every soul that had pleasure in their acts of evil, and the ones that voted for those children of darkness. Oh me, there will be weeping and gnashing of teeth. Nero fiddled while Rome burned. Bill committed fornication while the little children of God burned in Waco. It makes no difference what they accused Vernon Wayne Howell, AKA David Koresh, of, nobody has the authority to convict someone and execute them before a trial, like they did at Waco. But even after the Waco fiasco, the ignorant immoral fools voted the democrat back into office and made him an idol even after he was impeached. Now his liberal wife that is against women being homemakers is trying to be a president after the voters voted for a black waffling flatterer before her. She is against everything God told women to be.

The ignorant voters jumped out of the frying pan into the fire and elected a black democrat that, in my opinion, is destroying America. But I am not second guessing God, because God put this Hamite into the high office to punish the gluttons for punishment, and finish setting the stage for *"God's Super Bowl On A Sunday"*, and bringing transgressions and sin to an end. God allowed all the heathen, "Christian", pagan, anti-Christ politicians to acquire power over the peon subjects of the world, so He could manifest His power when His trumpet angels start sounding, and the angels with the *bowls* start pouring out the seven last plagues, "for in them is filled up the wrath of God." (Revelation 15:1)

Even before the trumpets sound and the bowls are poured out, God is allowing Satan to fill all the unbelieving recipients of the world with the spirit of stealing, killing, and destruction to the point where: **"No flesh should be saved except those days should be shortened; but for the elect's sake, those days shall be shortened."** (Matthew 24:22) In the meantime the blood of the prophets, and holy ones is being spilled. (Revelation 18:24)

Nearly all of the "Christian" population thinks they are going to be raptured either by pre-tribulation, or mid-tribulation, or post-tribulation. **"Corn Shelling Time"** takes a pessimistic view of the *rapture*, and bursts the bubble of the "Christian" view. Just like many cognate words in the KJB (King James Bible), *rapture* is not in the bible. Neither is *"God's Super Bowl On A Sunday"* Forgive me LORD Jesu

When we opened Daniel's book, we read: "And many of them that sleep in the dust of the earth shall awake, some to everlasting life, and some to shame and everlasting contempt." (Daniel 12:2)

"Then Jesus said: **"Verily, verily, I say unto you, the time is coming, and now is, when the dead shall hear the voice of the Son of God: and they that hear shall live."** (John 5:25) **"Marvel not at this, for the time is coming in the which all that are in the graves shall hear His voice, and shall come forth, they that have done good, unto the resurrection of life."** (John 5:28,29). This is the first resurrection and the only resurrection for the ones that have done good, that is those that believed Jesus. The rest of Verse 29 continues **"and they that have done evil, unto the resurrection of damnation."** (John 5:29) These are the only two risings that happen, and this includes the first fruits, Jesus being the first, and many holy ones that were prisoners in the compartment of Hell, called Paradise. (Matthew 27:52,53). The 144,000 virgin Jews, (Revelation 7), the multitude of holy ones that go through the tribulation (Revelation7:9), then the two witnesses in

(Revelation 11), which will be the trigger to the general resurrection of all the ones that are asleep in Jesus. (I Thessalonians 4:13-18) God will bring all the spirits of the ones that are asleep in Christ Jesus to be joined together with their bodies; and all the holy ones will rise to attend the banquet of the Marriage Supper of the Lamb; and there everyone will receive their rewards, including Christ Jesus, who will receive His title King of Kings and Lord of Lords. That is everyone in Christ Jesus, who will be in the first resurrection. There will not be a single believer left on earth; but there will be a lot of "Christians" who went to *church* on *Sunday,* who did not keep His commandments. "And why call you me Lord, Lord, and do not the things which I say?" (Luke 6:46) This scripture has been repeated in **"Corn Shelling Time"** to make double dog dead sure that this writer will not have any blood of any reader on his hands.

Because of these erring "Christians", pagans, and heathen, is why God remembered Babylon, and why He is bringing judgment on all the nations, tongues, and people of the world; but because He is a merciful God, "He is holding back the angels with the trumpets, and the angels with the vials *(bowls),* and the angels over the four elements, (the earth, fire, water, and wind), until we have sealed the servants of our God in their foreheads." The servants of our God are the ones that have "Come out of "Her", the Mystery, Babylon. (Revelation 7:13) After all the servants of God have been sealed in their foreheads, the angels will be ready to bring the ultimate end to the cities, mountains, nations, and all sin including the Great Babylon, *(America),* and the Great Babylon City, which is *New York City, USA.*

Now the false prophets and the false apostles have gotten a new lie going, saying they have heard the voice of the Lord wanting to extend the call of the Lord to the "Christians". Jesus said: **"And many false prophets shall arise and shall deceive many; and because iniquity shall abound, the love of many shall wax cold; but he that shall endure to the end, the same shall**

be saved." (Matthew 24:12,13) At this moment in the present time iniquity, which is lawlessness to God's commandments, is abounding to the extremes. The false prophets and false apostles are begging you for money so they can pray and fight in the war against Satan. Where were the false prophets and apostles of Satan when Kennedy was joining America to be sympathetic to the blood bath of the Vietnam War? Also, he sanctioned the loud mouthed Martin Luther King Jr., which was anti-American, to my belief, because that started the black terrorists to burning, looting, and marching against America. Where were the false prophets then? It is worse now than then. Where are the false prophets and false apostles of God now? Where in God's word did He say to steal, kill, and destroy? That is what the blacks have been doing ever since Kennedy let King get away with rioting, looting, burning and terrorism. Where were the false prophets, that want your money, when the Clinton terrorists were killing and burning the family and innocent children, and residents of the Vernon Wayne Howell Compound in Waco, AKA David Koresh and his Davidians at Mount Carmel? Where were the false prophets when the men, women, and little children were screaming, crying out to God, when Bill Clinton's appointed Attorney General, Janet Reno, gave the order for the jack booted thugs to shoot the gas into the compound that resulted in the precious creation of God being cremated? All of the murderers said they were "Christians." I agree with Michael Duishka in his book, "Please Do Not Call Me a "Christian". (Read it)

One more time, this writer is not a prophet or an apostle, but you be the judge of the ATF, and the FBI, the USA Military, all the Clinton administration, including Janet Reno, George Stephanopoulos, Bob Ricks, William Sessions, Ann Richards, and all the Texas state law enforcement participants, and most especially the Judas that was planted in the compound to snitch on Koresh and the Davidians, the Waco Tribune Herald, publisher of "The Sinful Messiah", a series of derogatory gossip fiction articles written by Mark England, and Darlene McCormick, and the UPS driver that said a package

Michael Duishka

broke open and he revealed the contents. (how do you think the package broke open?), also Chief Deputy Daniel Weyenberg, and every person that voted for Bill Clinton, and every person that had pleasure and agreed with the fiasco of the mass murder of the Branch Davidians at or near Waco, Texas. How do you judge? The Lord said, "Judge righteously." Then the stupid fools jumped out of the frying pan into the fire and voted Obama in as president to lead America into the ObomaNation of Desolation. The Great Babylon *New York City, USA* is anticipating the final destruction. The false apostles, prophets, preachers, *catholic pope,* and bishops are coming out of the closet, taking pride in being *queers,* but still calling themselves "Christians". Oh me!

People are leaving America to join rebel forces that say, "Obama, we are coming after you." These rebel factions are Al Qaeda, Hamas, Isis, Isil, Jihaddis, and others. This writer believes Obama is the instigator of the rebel rousing in Egypt, Libya, Syria, and possibly the Palestine fiasco.

"For many shall come in My name, saying I am "Christ, ian", and shall deceive many. And you shall hear of wars and rumors of wars: See that you be not troubled: For all these things must come to pass, but the end is not yet." (Matthew 24:5,6). This was **that** prophet, Jesus, prophesying 2000 years ago about what is happening today at this present time. But keep in mind that all these things are the trigger via *"God's Super Bowl On A Sunday,"* which is the Battle of **Armageddon,** which will be the end. (Revelation 16:16)

God has already set His plan of action into motion. He is making the whole earth into designated labels that He has chosen an angel to be the ambassador over each label or marking. He (God) has already given His ambassador angels specific boundaries and limitations to their authorities. The angel that is the ambassador over the fire will have specific areas of trees to equal a third part of all the trees to be burned on the earth at the specific time the first angel with the golden trumpet sounds. This is not all of the things the ambassador angel over the fire burns up, (Revelation 8:7) when the fourth angel of the seven angels that were given seven golden vials *(bowls)* full of the wrath of God pours out his vial upon the sun, and power was given unto him to scorch men with fire. (Revelation 16:8)

Scientist's understanding about this minimal warming of the earth at this present time is very little, but their understanding of the bible is nil. It is too late for nations as a whole to repent and turn to God, because "that that has been determined shall be done." (Daniel 11:36) "The men that were scorched when the angel poured out his vial on the sun blasphemed the name of God, which has power over these plagues, and they repented not to give Him glory." (Revelation 16:9)

But you, dear reader, do not turn a deaf ear to His calling you to repentance through this book, **"Corn Shelling Time"**. These events have a designated time and a designated area to take place, and **"Corn Shelling Time"** is giving you a preview of events to happen before *"God's Super Bowl On A Sunday"*.

The next of the four elements that God (Pempte Ousa) puts His ambassador angel over is the water. At this present time, God is still pleading with this sinful generation to "Come out of Her", which is the Mystery of Iniquity, which is lawlessness. "Christians" are lost on account of that word lawlessness. They, ("Christians"), are *bamboosled* by the KJV of the bible, and by unlearned, false preaching, to believe lawlessness is the disobedience of the laws of the land. Wrong! Whosoever obeys the laws of the land is disobeying the laws of God. The Master said: **"Whosoever therefore shall break one of these least commandments, (laws), and shall teach men so, he shall be called the least in the Kingdom of heaven, but whosoever shall <u>do</u> and teach the same shall be called great in the Kingdom of Heaven."** (Matthew 5:19) Duishka is putting in his assessment, and that is, if the one breaking the laws of God does not repent, he or she will not be in the Kingdom of Heaven to be called anything,(I believe).

The ambassador angel is holding off the plagues that have already been determined to contaminate the fountains of waters. The beginning of sorrows is linked to mankind that is destroying the earth, which includes destroying the water. The ambassador angel delegated to control the plagues connected to the future water supply will not exercise his authority until Pempte Ousa (the Fifth Being) commands the third trumpet to sound, and the third vial is poured out on the fountains of waters, and the star called Wormwood falls from heaven, causing the waters to turn bitter, and many men died. (Revelation 8:11 - Revelation 16:4) Mankind is polluting the rivers, streams, fountains and even underground water with all kinds of waste; and many settlements of people are finding it necessary to boil their water before they can safely drink the water. Soon there will be no water to boil.

"All things were made by Him, and without Him was not anything made that was made." (John 1:3) Him, being the Word of God, who is God. (John 1:1) All things that were made by Him, including the four elements, (fire, water, wind, and earth), were made by Him for mankind's benefit to live. Without any one of these elements man cannot survive. These are the days where greedy men are destroying the earth for their personal gain. Jesus said: **"And except those days should be shortened, there should no flesh be saved. But for the elect's sake, those days shall be shortened."** (Matthew 24:22) Pay attention to the word elect's sake, in Greek is Eklektos, meaning His chosen ones. Many are called, which is the true Greek word Ekklesia, that is a compound word which means "calling out" and not the counterfeit Catholic English word (*church*), but few are chosen. The misled "Christians" think they are the chosen ones; but they are the called out ones that Christ Jesus is calling to "Come out of "her", My people." (Revelation 18:4) This means you, whosoever is reading this; and if you repent and "Shell

Down the Corn", (confess your sins), then Christ Jesus will choose you; and you will be the very elect, (Eklektos). Do not say I have plenty of time to call on the Lord Jesus, because you do not have much time. If you could only understand that the Lord is merciful to you by making it possible for you to read this book before your life is required. Do not linger to call on the Lord Christ Jesus. Your time is shorter than you think.

Another ambassador angel that God has appointed over the element wind will not let the four angels that are holding back the wind that it hurt not the trees, or sea, or earth, until the servants of God have received His seal in their foreheads. The "Christians" that do not repent and "Shell Down the Corn to Christ Jesus will take the mark of the beast. The believers of Christ Jesus that "Come out of the Mystery of Iniquity" will receive the seal of God. The whirlwinds will be withheld until the seal of God is put upon the foreheads of His servants.

The last of the four elements that (Pempte Ousa), the Fifth Being, which is (PANTAKRATOR), Almighty God is holding back is the ambassador angel that has been delegated to have authority over the earth element. All the ambassador angels are working continuously to keep evil, greedy, lying, perverse, deceitful, rapacious, (living off prey), parasitic (blacks on DHS), warmongering, devil possessed murdering men from destroying the earth before their time will be cut short, or shortened. All of the above mentioned people are mostly politicians, and "Christians" that vote for them. But the ambassador angels that have been delegated to have authority over the elements are restraining these wicked people from destroying all flesh. (Matthew 24:22) until ***"God's Super Bowl On A Sunday"***. God is allowing the wicked, devil possessed, idolatrous people to pollute the wind, (which is the breath of God), rape and use the fire to burn the forestland, and pollute the fountains, streams, rivers, and lakes, and even the seas with human dung and piss, and toxic wastes, until all water will become bitter, AKA poison. The angel ambassador over the earth is working his helpers continually to keep the thing that Jeremiah saw from happening before the purposed time of *"God's Super Bowl On A Sunday"*.

Here is what Jeremiah saw: "I beheld the earth, and, lo, it was without form and void, and the heavens they had no light. I beheld the mountains, and, lo, they trembled, and all the hills moved lightly. I beheld, and, lo, there was no man, all the birds of the heavens were fled. I beheld, and, lo, the fruitful place was a wilderness; and all the cities thereof were broken down at the presence of the Lord and by His fierce anger. For thus has the Lord said, "The whole land shall be desolate, yet I will not make a full end." (Jeremiah 4:23,24,25,26,27) This is what the ambassador angel is holding back where greedy wicked men have made cavities all in the earth by taking the minerals, all the ores, such as gold, silver, iron, brass, platinum, uranium, copper, lead, diamonds, lime, sand, gravel, and many more that this writer is not smart enough to name, plus all the gases and liquids, such as oil, water, and if there are any others the writer is not knowledgeable enough to know. But all of the above are enough substances to cause the earth to quake and tremble with weakness from all this support being removed from it.

"And there were voices, and thunders, and lightnings, and there was a great earthquake, such as was not since men were upon the earth, so mighty an earthquake, and so great. And the great city was divided into three parts, and the cities of the nations fell, and Great Babylon came in remembrance before God, to give unto "Her" the cup of the wine of the fierceness of His wrath. And every island fled away, and the mountains were not found." (Revelation 16:18,19,20)

Readers, please pay attention, because many "prophets?", "Theologians?", commentaries, and others have said the Great City, mentioned above is Jerusalem. But **"Corn Shelling Time"** says, "No!" Others believe it is the ancient city of Rome. But **"Corn Shelling Time"** says, "No!" Others believe it is the Great Whore, the city of Rome that is the Mother of all Harlots, the city of the Catholic Church; but **"Corn /Shelling Time"** says "No!" Not anyone in the world says it is *New York City USA,* except Michael Duishka, the man God chose to herald His last warning in the bible in the Eighteenth Chapter and the Fourth verse of Revelation to the whole entire universe, which is; "And I heard another voice from heaven, saying, "Come out of "Her", My people, that you be not partakers of "Her" sins, and that you receive not of "Her" plagues" (Revelation 18:4) This writer believes God is giving the few that will be chosen a chance to repent before they fall with the cities of the nations, and one of the four elements destroys them. As of 2011 A.D. The sorrows have escalated to great heights, and the stage is being set for the grand finale and *"God's Super Bowl On A Sunday"* that will happen on this wise. When the world fills up with iniquity, as this writer fails to see any cities of the world that are not like Sodom and Gomorrah. But like God said: "He has 7,000 just ones that have not bowed their knee to Satan and idolatry. Whenever there are not ten righteous believers found in the cities of the nations, then the earth will be full of iniquity; and then God will cause His ambassador angels over the fire, water, wind, and earth to cause all the cities of the nations to fall; and all the kings and their armies will be drawn to participate in *"God's Super Bowl On A Sunday."* God called it **Armageddon.**

As before stated in this book, every king, president, prime minister, ruler or soldier has an evil spirit ruling over him. Satan is the ruler of all the evil spirits that rule over all the children of darkness. The Word of the Lord came unto Ezekiel in the 38th chapter of Ezekiel, saying: "Son of man set your face against Gog, the land of Magog." All "theologians, "prophets", commentators say that Gog will be the ruler or earthly president over the land of Magog. But Duishka says this Gog is the evil spirit, or the prince over all the fleshly rulers in the land of Magog, which are the lands that are settled with the descendants of Japheth, which are his sons' descendants. "The sons of Japheth are Magog, Gomer, Madai and Javan, and Tubal, and

Meshech, and Tyras. These are the race of God's creation. By these were the isles of the Gentiles divided in their lands every one after his tongue, after their families, in their nations. (Genesis 10:2) (Genesis 10:5) So when God told Ezekiel to prophesy against Gog, Ezekiel was prophesying to evil spirits that would enter in to kings and rulers of the earth and to their captains and armies in the latter days to sacrifice their flesh *(bodies)* to the fowls of heaven and to the wild beasts of the earth that the angel standing in the sun, (Revelation 19:27) cried with a loud voice to "gather yourselves together unto the Supper of the Great God to eat the sacrifice of the loser at ***"God's Super Bowl On A Sunday"***, AKA *buzzard bait!* Ezekiel prophesied what God said to Gog the evil spirit of Satan that rules many, many people in the land of Magog, the He, (God), would put hooks into your jaws; "and I, (God), will bring you forth with Persia, *(modern day Iran)*, Ethiopia, *(modern day continent of Africa),* and Libya, (northern country of Africa), Gomer, *(Germany and all his bans of Europe)* and Togarmah, *(modern day Turkey and all his bands),* and many people with you." (Ezekiel 38:4,5,6)

All of the above is just a part of the other team opposing the one called Faithful and True, sitting on a white horse. (Revelation 19:11) The remainder of all the kings of the earth and the whole world will be drawn to ***"God's Super Bowl On A Sunday"*** in this manner. Brother John said: "And I saw three unclean spirits like frogs come out of the mouth of the dragon, and out of the mouth of the beast, and out of the mouth of the false prophet, which go forth unto the kings of the earth and of the whole world to gather them to the battle of that great day of God Almighty (PANTAKRATOR)," (Revelation 16:13,14) AKA ***"God's Super Bowl On A Sunday"***. The reason this writer believes God's Super Bowl will be on a *Sunday* is because God would never work or allow His slaves to work on His holy sabbath, the seventh day of the week. Since rebellious man wants to desecrate God's sabbath and obey the man made *Sunday,* for every abomination on earth, God will say "Come on down, come on down, and be baptized in your own blood on a *Sunday.* Call the beast of the field and the fowls of the air so they can drink of the blood of the mighty until they are drunken." (Ezekiel 39:19) This will be the blood of the ones who do not "Come out of "Her". "God has put in their hearts to fulfill His will, and to agree, and give their kingdom unto the beast Apollyon) until the words of God shall be fulfilled." (Revelation 17:17) All of this blood bath in the entire earth is futuristic and ignorant people say: "I have heard that all my life and it has not happened yet." This is why you, dear reader, and the rest of the population of the world will not be innocent. Jesus said: **"And this gospel of the kingdom shall be preaached in all the world for a witness unto all nations, and then shall the end come."** (Matthew 24:14)

"Corn Shelling Time" is one of those witnesses that is being preached to the whole world in God's last warning. This is God's last warning, "Come out of "Her", My people, that you be not partakers of "Her" sins, and that you receive not of "Her" plagues." (Revelation 18:4) Jesus still talking, **"When you therefore shall see the abomination of desolation, spoken of by Daniel the Prophet, stand in the Holy Place, (whoso reads, let him understand)."** (Matthew 24:15) This has already come to pass in America, except there is not any holy place in America for the abomination to stand, so the ObomaNation of Desolation is sitting in the White House, which is now the black house, and America is already the ObomaNation of Desolation. **"Corn Shelling Time"** is preaching the gospel of the kingdom as a witness for Christ Jesus. So like the angel told the women at the tomb, He is risen, and you shall see Him if you will "Shell Down the Corn, (confess). Lo, I have told you. (Matthew 28:7)

After this gospel has been preached in all the world as a warning and a witness for Christ Jesus, then will come the end, which is *"God's Super Bowl On A Sunday"*. All the invitations will be sent to all the kings and leaders of all the nations of the world to gather them and their armies to the battle in the Valley of Decision, which is

God's Super Bowl in Israel by the three unclean spirits that came out of the mouth of the dragon, and out of the mouth of the beast, and out of the mouth of the false prophet. (Revelation 16:13) Ezekiel sent Gog an invitation, which is to all the land of Magog, which is Russia, Germany, all European nations, along with Persia, Ethiopia, Libya, and Togarmah, (*Turkey*), and some Asia Minor nations. "God said to Gog and I will turn you back, and put hooks into your jaws." (Ezekiel 38:4)"Then God will have the sixth angel with the vials, (*bowls*), to pour out his vial on the great river Euphrates, and the water thereof was dried up that the way of the kings of the East might be prepared." (Revelation 16:12) All the kings of the world and all their armies will be there at *"God's Super Bowl On A Sunday"* to fight against the King of kings and the Lord of lords. So everyone that did not "Come out of "Her"" will be against the Lord Christ Jesus and His armies. When God has gathered them together at His arena, (*the Super Bowl*), His angel will call all the fowls of heaven to God's great supper, and another angel will cry with a loud voice, "Come and see", let the game begin. The controversy that has been going on for aeons of time will come to an end at that great day of the Lord God Almighty (PANTAKRATOR). This great and notable day of the Lord will bring an end to all transgression and sin, which is disobedience and rebellion against God's Word. This day will reveal the Mystery of Iniquity, which will be manifest on that day; and there will be no more iniquity or mysteries in the Kingdom of God. Then the Theocratic Government of God will be set up, and man will not be a free moral agent, but it will be mandatory to obey God. +This writer asked Christ Jesus to hire him to work in His government, and His answer was you have not chosen me, but I have chosen you, and ordained you, that you should go and bring forth fruit, and your fruit should remain, that whatsoever you shall ask of the Father in my name He may give it you. John: 15:16. I have chosen you to work in my government, and also my vineyard. One of my duties is to warn the entire world about how to be saved from the wrath of my terrible GOD, which there is no other GOD except Him, CHRIST JESUS. To one of the kings of the East, XI

Jinping, king of Republic of China. You are one of God's people and God loves you, and I do too. God set you over the largest Nation on earth. I like the way you mind your own business, and not meddle in every body else business. I would like very much to have you to come visit me, the lowest person on God's earth, to share with the greatest king on God's earth, about the KING of kings and LORD of lords, CHRIST JESUS, before *"GODS SUPER BOWL ON A SUNDAY"* That GOD calls **ARMAGEDDON.** XI, that would be the greatest miracle of God, to happen on this earth. If you can pull it off, I hope you like beans and taters. I am nothing. DUISHKA. Check with brother Putin, and come eat with Mavis and I when brother Putin comes to visit us. OK?

Chapter 31

THE CURTAIN RISES ON the world stage; but the focus is on the abomination that makes desolate, which shows itself in Israel during the last half of the seventieth week of Daniel's prophecy. This will start the beginning of the end of Jacob's trouble. Also it will be the preliminaries to *"God's Super Bowl On A Sunday"*.

God told Moses to prophesy to Pharaoh the upcoming plague that was to come on the Egyptians; and it happened just the way Aaron, Moses' brother said it would. The same play action is going to happen in the last 42 months of the 70th week of Daniel's book. "And I will give power unto My two witnesses, and they shall prophesy a thousand two hundred and threescore days, clothed in sackcloth." The two witnesses prophesy the plague that is to come upon the earth; and the ambassador angel of God tells the trumpet angel to sound his voice; and when the trumpet sounds, the plague happens. The same pattern is for the vials *(bowls)*. The two witnesses prophesy the plague, the ambassador angel tells the angel with the vial to pour it out, and the plague of the Mystery, Babylon is poured out into the earth. The two witnesses will have power to call down (*prophesy*) any plague on the earth. So the witnesses tell the first angel to pour out his vial on the earth, "and there fell a noisome and grievous sore upon the men which had the mark of the beast, and upon them which worshiped his image." (Revelation 16:2) "The first trumpet angel sounded, and there followed hail and fire mingled with blood; and they were cast upon the earth: And the third part of trees were burnt up; and all green grass was burnt up." (Revelation 8:7).

"And the second angel sounded, *(blew his trumpet)*,; and as it were a great mountain burning with fire was cast into the sea. And the third part of the sea became blood; and the third part of the creatures, which were in the sea and had life died; and the third part of the ships were destroyed." (Revelation 8:8,9) "And the second angel poured out his vial upon the sea, and it became as the blood of a dead man, and every living soul died in the sea." (Revelation 16:3)

The two witnesses have the power to call the plagues upon the earth the way Moses did, and the power to shut heaven that it rain not, just like Elijah. "They can withhold the rain for forty-two months, which is the length of their prophecy." (Revelation 11:6)

At this time, the time of the trumpets and vials, men' hearts are just like Pharaoh's heart, hardened! The voice out of heaven told the angels with the seven vials to go and pour out their vials of God's wrath upon the earth. "And the first angel went and poured out his vial upon the earth, and there fell a noisome and grievous sore, *(cancer)*, upon the men which had the mark of the beast, and upon them which worshiped his image." (Revelation 16:1,2) Yes, I know I repeated this event of the first angel pouring out the vial of God's wrath, so **"Corn Shelling Time"** could draw your attention to the fact that grievous sores, *(cancer)*, are already on mankind; and "Christians" are dying and not repenting of their desecration of the law of God, the Ten Commandments, most especially the fourth command to: "Remember the sabbath day, to keep it holy. Six days shall you labor and do all your work: But the seventh day is the sabbath of the Lord your God. In it you shall not do any work, you, nor your son, nor your daughter, your man servant, nor your maid servant, nor your cattle, nor your stranger that is within your gates: For in six days the Lord made heaven and earth, the sea, and all that in them are, and rested the seventh day: Wherefore the Lord blessed the sabbath day and hallowed it." (Exodus 20:8,9,10,11)

The ones breaking God's commandments are the ones that have the mark of the beast. These are the ones that receive the plagues of the wrath of God. If you are a good "Christian" that obeys the laws of the land, which are man's laws, then you are breaking God's law; and you already have the mark of the beast. The ones that keep the laws of God are already sealed by God in their forehead. You cannot be loyal to two masters. The ones that are married to a *harlot (church)* cannot be in the bride of Christ. The ones that are in a *church* are in Mystery, Babylon. The ones in the ekklesia (called out ones) have an opportunity to be the chosen (ekklektos) ones of Christ, the holy ones, *(not saints)*. Saints are dead, and none of God's chosen ones are dead, but rather they are alive and sealed with everlasting life. Even before the angels blow the trumpets, and before the angels pour out the vials of God's wrath on the earth, the Devil is taking authority over ignorant, sinful people to oppress and possess them.

The reason the people are ignorant, (lack of knowledge), is because they do not know that the Devil does not have any authority, or power, to bring any kind of *cancer (sore)* on them, except they give him the power to do so by sinning. Whenever a person sins, that gives place to the Devil to possess them and cause all kinds of sickness and disease and infirmities to come upon a person; and the person does not know it was their disobedience to God's laws. The person had rather have the grievous sores on him or her than to quit sinning.

The same thing happens with the elements. Man pollutes the land, seas, the air, and rapes the forests; and Satan causes all kinds of disasters, such as tornadoes, earthquakes, mudslides, tsunami to come upon people. My wife, Mavis Duishka, saw a swarm of tornadoes in a night vision; and the tornadoes were headed for some school children. She said she saw an individual devil that looked like a man in each tornado. She rebuked each tornado, in the name of Jesus, and the tornadoes became nothing. So the tsunami that hit New Orleans was powered by Satan, because that is one of the most sinful cities in the world; and the citizens sinned; and that gave place to the evil spirits to inflict a plague on that city. Then the powerful hurricane, the climatologists named "Sandy" hit the sinful state of New Jersey, where the gambling is running rampant in Atlantic City, New Jersey; then proceeded on to the Great City Babylon, AKA *New York City, USA.* The powers of the air came to do their job, which is to kill, steal and destroy. God is warning His people every way possible, and they harden their hearts, and still will not "Shell Down the Corn" and repent of their evil ways.

Everyone that says he or she does not judge is a liar, and the truth is not in them. In my country, which is *Babylon USA,* there are terrorists of all different races. The majority of terrorists are black. The blacks imitate their leader, Martin Luther King, Jr.. He was the engine that started the looting, burning, killing, stealing, and destroying of American's property in the guise of peaceful protests, which they are everything but peaceful. Remember the Selma, Alabama, Peace March? Ha, Ha, Ha, all the murders, injuries, looting, stealing, destroying was by the blacks. The same thing happened in Los Angeles in the 60's, then again in the 90's, now again in 2014. The blacks are looking for any kind of an excuse so they can steal, kill, and destroy America. Then they always get away with the terror by saying they are "Afro American". The thefts and the killings are too numerous for **"Corn Shelling Time"** to mention, but the property damage was in the billions. Let us not forget about the trigger, Katrina, the hurricane, that hit New Orleans, Louisiana, with property damage in the millions; but the looting and destroying by blacks was greater than the damage done by Katrina. Not only did the blacks loot and destroy in New Orleans, but they invaded Baton Rouge and other cities. The New Orleans police were also in on the act of looting in New Orleans. Do not leave out every place a tornado hits. The blacks take advantage of the victims of that disaster. As soon as the devil in the tornado has destroyed property, the devil filled blacks start their looting before the dead are found and before the injured can be rescued. If the police confront the thieves, they just say they are helping in the rescue of the victims; and the gullible believe whatever they are told. Because this writer of **"Corn Shelling Time"** has seen everything he says happen, there are lazy, cursed, whites, that are milking the system for everything they can, that tell me I have a heart filled with hate for the blacks. This writer just considers the source from where the criticizing comes from; and the white critics have the same conduct as the blacks, which is *Jill flirting* the system by saying they have a disability and cannot work, or cash in on some kind of give away program that the Democrats invented to fill their pockets with filthy lucre, *(money)*. This is this writer's opinion and belief. This writer has a black neighbor that cannot be helped, refuses to be helped, that destroyed my stockade fence so their vicious pit bulldogs could come into my yard and attack me. They destroyed a fence that would cost 3 to 5 thousand dollars to replace. When they were confronted, they do like the majority of blacks, and turned the volume of their tonsils up to the highest decibel, saying they were African Americans; and they had rights to have pit bulldogs, evading the destruction of my property, with advice that if they wanted to be Americans, they should act like Americans. With that the scripture that Brother Peter said came to me: "But the face of the Lord is against them that do evil. And who is he that will harm you, if you be followers of that which is good? But, if you suffer for righteousness' sake, blessed are you and be not afraid of their terror, neither be troubled; but sanctify the Lord God in your hearts, and be ready always to give an answer to every man that asks you a reason of the hope that is in you with meekness and fear." (1 Peter 3:12,13,14,15)

While **"Corn Shelling Time"** is writing down just infinitesimal evils that blacks are doing to my country, and your country, if you are not anti-American or anti-Christ does not mean my heart (spirit) is full of hate. The only thing to hate is the devil and the works of the devil, which is to rob, kill and destroy. (John 10:10) But the last part of (John 10:10) says: **"I am come that they might have life, and that they might have it more abundantly."** (John 10:10)

But the Devil does not want you to have life eternal, so he causes his subjects to rob, kill, and destroy, like the blacks are doing in many cities of the *NewNited* States of America, not United, but *NewNited*. Every faction in the 50 states of America is divided: The husband and wife are divided, the children are divided against parents, the government is against parents (no discipline), *churches* are divided, (denominations), schools are divided, teaching safe sex, cities are divided, states are divided, congress is divided, the President is divided against the congress (*dictator*), the Supreme Court Judges are divided against the Constitution, every voter is divided, races are divided, but they broke out of their boundaries. The blacks came to America, and they are destroying the hand that feeds them. Just like in Sanford, Florida. A big black teenager jumped on a man, but the man killed the black in self defense. The blacks wanted to mob rule and started protesting, causing stealing, killing, and destroying. Another 18 year old black was trying to get a policeman's gun and wound up dead. The National Guard was called out to try to stop the stealing, killing, and destroying by burning. Another black man killed by cops in NYC, USA caused riots all over these *NewNited States of America*, resulting in stealing, killing, and destroying. This writer is not blind, and his heart is not full of hate just because white "Christians" say so. They say is always a lie. Two NYC police officers were ambushed and murdered by a black man that committed suicide. There was no rioting or protesting. How come? Because the killer was black. Hate, or fact?

The black president of the *NewNited States of America* and his black attorney general are instigators of the black people rioting and burning; but they say they are "Christians". Then what **"Corn Shelling Time"** is concerned with are these ignorant "Christians" loud mouthing, "We want justice", and then tell this writer, "Judge not." (Matthew 7:1) They can quote "Judge not lest you be not judged.

But the 2nd verse says, "for with what judgment you judge, you shall be judged: And with what measure you mete, it shall be measured to you again." If this writer was still stealing, killing, and destroying, I would expect to be judged with the same measure of judgment that is meted out by me. The only thing is I believe the Lord Christ Jesus, and He said to judge righteously, and to judge with mercy, which **<u>"Corn Shelling Time"</u>** judges with mercy.

All the world can hear ever since the Murrah Building Bombing in Oklahoma City, Oklahoma on April 19, 1995, is the loud mouth blacks hollering: "We want justice." The same ones will get justice at the Great White Throne Judgment. This writer was a victim of that bombing, as is stated in this book in previous pages. But now here are some of the details. On April 19, 1995, at 8:55 A.M. My phone rang. With a "Hello!" the Greek accented voice on the other end of the line was the owner of the Athenian Restaurant, which was located directly north across the street from the Alfred P. Murrah Federal Building at 200 N. W. 5th Street, in Oklahoma City, Oklahoma. This would be Fotis Bargeliotes that owned and operated the Athenian Restaurant with his beautiful wife, Fofo. This writer was working on the 2nd floor of the Athenian Building. Fotis said in his accented voice: "Meekey, Fofo has breakfast ready, come on down and eat." I said: "I cannot come down until later Fotis, because I have to go to City Hall and buy some permits; and I will be down later. We ended the conversation at 9:00 A.M., when I received another call from another customer that had a business close to the Athenian. We had just started talking when the glass windows in my house blew out in my floor with a deafening bang. I told the lady on the other end of the phone, "Pat, I have to go now, because the {*Democrats*} are bombing me." She said, "They are bombing me too." Some of the blacks in my neighborhood had been arrested for suspected bomb making. On the television it told where the bomb blast hit, "The Murrah Building," and said they needed volunteers. By the time a friend and I got within two blocks of the site, the FBI and police would not allow us to proceed any closer. Fotis and Fofo were both injured, but thank you Lord Jesus, they were still <u>ALIVE</u>. The bomb had gone off at 9:02 A.M., as I was talking to Pat, one of my customers, There were two white men this writer knows of that suffered extraordinarily bad heart wrenching loss that stated publicly that they forgave. Also some blacks that suffered loss were hollering, "We want justice." The same chant that is going on as the terrorists are marching in the USA today. This is why the trumpets and the vials will be activated in the near future.

"And the third angel sounded, and there fell a great star from heaven, burning as it were a lamp; and it fell upon the third part of the rivers, and upon the fountains of waters; and the name of the star is called, "Wormwood": And the third part of the waters became wormwood; and many men died of the waters, because they were made bitter." (Revelation 8:10,11)

And the fourth angel sounded; and the third part of the sun was smitten, and the third part of the moon, and the third part of the stars, so as the third part of them was darkened; and the day shone not for a third part of it, and the night likewise. And I beheld and heard an angel flying through the midst of heaven, saying with a loud voice, "Woe, Woe, Woe, to the inhabiters of the earth by reason of the other voices of the trumpet of the three angels which are yet to sound." (Revelation 8:12,13) All these plagues are to come upon the earth before *"God's Super Bowl on a Sunday"* begins.

"And the third angel poured out his vial upon the rivers and fountains of waters; and they became blood. And I heard the angel of the waters say, "You are righteous, O Lord, which are, and was, and shall be, because you have judged thus. For they have shed the blood of the holy ones and prophets, and you have given them blood to drink, for they are worthy." (Revelation 16:4,5,6)

"And the fourth angel poured out his vial upon the sun; and power was given unto him to scorch men with fire. And men were scorched with great heat, and blasphemed the name of God, which has power over these plagues: And they repented not to give Him glory." (Revelation 16:8,9)

All of these plagues are happening at this present time, but not with the magnitude of the last plagues. The plagues that are attacking people now are minor compared to these last, end time plagues. But people will not repent and give God glory; and they are dying in their sins, and will to not come out of Mystery, Babylon. **"Corn Shelling Time"** shows you how to escape. If you are busy fighting wars, and cutting people's heads off, policing all other countries, protesting, rioting, burning, stealing, killing, destroying, campaigning for politicians, watching all kinds of sports, and busy making the celebs of Hollywood your idols, you will be too busy to read, "Please Do Not Call Me A "Christian" or **"Corn Shelling Time"** by **Michael Duihka** and save your soul *(life)*. God has someone on this earth that is a true believer with an excessive amount of money that will promote these books with advertising that will preach the gospel to all the world. These believers whoever they are has a barn full of money, with little chance of going to the Kingdom of God, except they help promote God's Word and be fit to inherit eternal life. These believers will get a call from God the HOLY SPIRIT, so be attentive.

"And this gospel of the Kingdom shall be preached in all the world for a witness unto all nations, and then shall the end come." (Matthew 24:14)

This writer is depending on Christ Jesus to spread His Word in these books abroad. Thank you, God Almighty (PANTAKRATOR), in the Name of Jesus for that person that wants to promote your gospel in all the world by **"Corn Shelling Time"**. "And above all things have fervent charity among yourselves: For charity shall cover the multitude of sins." (1 Peter 4:8) You know, the Holy Spirit is talking to you. You have all those riches laid back looking for some place to put them before your life is required. To promote these books would be preaching this gospel of the Kingdom in all the world. "Then Jesus said unto His disciples: **"Verily I say unto you, that a rich man shall hardly enter into the kingdom of Heaven."** (Matthew 19:23) **"And again I say unto you. It is easier for a camel to go through the eye of a needle than for a rich man to enter into the Kingdom of God."** (Matthew 19:24) Michael Duishka is just showing you another option of how you can enter into the Kingdom of God. Promote this gospel.

There was a man in Moore, Oklahoma, that worked in a food processing place that took one of his tools he worked with, and stabbed a woman several times, then cut her head off. This tool he worked with was a knife. Before I reveal what race the man was, please be truthful with yourself and admit that you judged in your own mind what race he was. Be honest with yourself and admit that whatever race the man was, you had to judge if the man was civilized or not. Was he urbane or naive? Would you judge that any man that would commit such a horrendous act was cultivated or wild? Regardless of what race or nationality, creed, color, religion or belief you are, you are a liar if you say you do not have an opinion as to whether this man was civilized or a barbarian. So, your opinion is judging. The Lord said to judge righteously. This man that committed this heinous evil act was black. How did you judge? **"Corn Shelling Time"** judged this man righteously and racist. Call me a racist and judge me as having hate in my heart. Then the racist that calls me a racist and tells me my heart is full of hate, out of the other side of his mouth says he does not judge, and quotes, (Matthew 7:1) that says, "Judge not," but these lying hypocrites are *church* going "Christians". (Matthew 12:33) "The tree is judged by his fruit." Whenever you tell anyone about the evil ways of the racists that are destroying this land, which is my land, the old man inside of them that is supposed to be dead, raises up and comes alive with anger, and their fruit is rotten and shows that tree is corrupt.

Brother Paul said: "Brethren be followers together of me, and mark (*judge*) them which walk so as you have us, (Timothy, Titus, Epaphroditus)." (Philippians 3:17) How can you mark them without judging which ones to mark? For an example, "For many walk, of whom I have told you often, and now tell you even weeping, that they are the enemies of the stake of Christ, whose end is destruction, whose God is their belly, and whose glory is in their shame, who mind earthly things." (Philippians 3:18,19) If these scriptures fit you, take this opportunity right now to "Shell Down the Corn, (confess), and repent, and make Christ Jesus your God instead of your belly. Brother Paul also said: "Now I beseech you, brethren, mark, {*judge*}, them which cause divisions and offenses contrary to the doctrine which you have learned, and avoid them." (Romans 16:17) Question: How can you mark them without judging them? How can you avoid them without judging them? Answer: You cannot. Anyone that says he does not judge is a liar, and the truth is not in him.

The meaning of these scriptures, which are commandments for believers, (not "Christians") is to put the mark on the ones that do not believe Christ Jesus. Brother Paul is speaking by the Spirit of Christ Jesus, and these are commandments. All "Christians" cause division, Catholic, Baptist, Anglican, etc. All "Christians" do not keep the commandments of Christ. That is why **"Corn Shelling Time"** is begging the good, devout, honest people of God in all *churches* to "Come Out of "Her". You may say that is your opinion, or that is your interpretation, and you are correct, that is my interpretation; but it is a commandment of Christ Jesus." (Revelation 18:4) You read it and interpret it any way you want. Jesus said, "Come Out of "Her," so He commanded His people to come out of something, so you judge what to come out of. You judge who "Her" is. All "Christians" do not keep this commandment. (Revelation 18:4) **"Corn Shelling Time"** is praying for God's ignorant, deceived, sincere "Christians" to come out of something called "Her". You good people are sincere, but sincerely wrong. That is why you are being destroyed by "Her" plagues.

"Woe, woe, woe, to the inhabitants of the earth, and of the sea! For the Devil is come down unto you, having great wrath, because he knows that he has but a short time." (Revelation 12:12) "And the fifth angel sounded, and I saw a star fall from heaven unto the earth: and to him was given the key to the bottomless pit. And he opened the bottomless pit, and there arose a smoke out of the pit, as the smoke of a great furnace; and the sun and the air were darkened by reason of the smoke of the pit. And there came out of the smoke locusts upon the earth. And unto them was given power, as the scorpions of the earth have power. And it was commanded them that they should not hurt the grass of the earth, neither any green thing, neither any tree, but only those men which have not the seal of God in their foreheads. And to them it was given that they should not kill them, but that they should be tormented five months, and their torment was as the torment of a scorpion, when he strikes a man. And in those days shall men seek death, and shall not find it, and shall desire to die, and death shall flee from them. And the shapes of the locusts were like unto horses prepared unto battle, and on their heads were as it were crowns like gold, and their faces were as the faces of men. And they had hair as the hair of women, and their teeth were as the teeth of lions, and they had breastplates as it were breastplates of iron, and the sound of their wings were as the sound of chariots of many horses running to battle. And they had tails like unto scorpions, and there were stings in their tails: And their power was to hurt men five months, and they had a king over them, which is the angel of the bottomless pit, whose name in the Hebrew tongue is Abaddon, A-bad-don, but in the Greek tongue has his name, Apollyon. One woe is past, and behold, there come two woes more hereafter." (Revelation 9:1-12) And the fifth angel poured out his vial upon the seat of the beast, and his kingdom was full of darkness, and they gnawed their tongues for pain and blasphemed the God of heaven, because of their pains and their sores, and repented not of their deeds." (Revelation 16:10,11)

Michael Duishka

This writer can testify that he "Shelled Down the Corn" to Christ Jesus, (confessed his sins), asked the Lord to forgive him of all his iniquity, (lawlessness), and came out of "Her", repented, and turned from his wicked ways; and God healed his land, (that means God healed me of those sores and pains.) No more doctors, no more drugs, no more idolatry, no more world system, no more *church*, no more defeat, only victory. Praise be to God through Christ Jesus, my Lord. He will do the same for you, if you will "Shell Down the Corn"! (CONFESS AND REPENT)

The writer of **"Corn Shelling Time"** wants to beg the readers indulgence and to ask them to please bear with me while a short story is told about an incident that happened in the Athenian Building, the evening of April 18,1995, which was the day prior to the bombing of the Murrah Building on April 19, 1995. Almost all the news coverage was on the Murrah Building, and very little on the surrounding buildings. As was stated before, this writer was working to revamp the 2nd floor of the Athenian. My helper and myself were working at that particular time on the ladies rest room, which was not in any condition to be used. The 2nd floor had at least one or two occupants renting apartments from the owner of the building. The reason **"Corn Shelling Time"** is mentioning this incident is solely to pay tribute and my respect to one of the occupants in the Athenian. At that time I did not even know the lady's name. But all the commodes were disassembled from the drains; and surprisingly a lady said to me, "I need to use the rest room. What am I going to do?" "No problem," I told her. "Just go across the hall and use the men' rest room, because there are no men up here except my helper and myself, and no one will bother you." She said, "Are you sure?" I told her, "I am sure." So the lady went across the hall and into the men' rest room, as we continued with our work in the women' rest room. A few minutes later I looked up from my work and the lady was standing there, and I asked her, "Well did anybody bother you?" She said, "No, dang it!" Then I knew she was my kind of person by her jive. Because that is the way my life is, no sad times, only joy and happiness. Little did either one of us know that the next morning at 9:02 A.M. The bomb at the Murrah Building would also destroy the Athenian Building, and also kill the beautiful lady that joked with me. This lady was civilized, this lady was urbane, this lady was cultivated, this lady was educated, this lady was black. She was not like the rioters, looters, arsonists, killers, destroyers, barbarians, anti-American, anti-Christ, protestors that incite terror that aids and abets these crimes. I read later the victims' names; and I was devastated and set back to hear of her demise. I salute you Anita Christine Hightower.

This is why it is so important to read **"Corn Shelling Time"**, because maybe you did not know that everything bad that happens to you or to anyone is a warning to people to plead with them to wake up and to know that their precious life could be required at any moment; and then it would be too late to repent. God told or inspired His scribes to warn His people in the bible from Genesis to Revelation; but broad and wide is the gate to destruction, and many enter in it. But the last warning God gives His people before *"God's Super Bowl On A Sunday"* AKA **Armageddon**, is in (Revelation 18:4) "And I heard another voice from heaven, saying, Come Out of "Her", My people, that you be not partakers of "Her" sins, and that you receive not of "Her" plagues." Now, you can interpret this scripture any way you want to. But it is a lead pipe cinch that Jesus said to come out of something called "Her". You judge, discern, opine what or who "Her" is. Then whoever or whatever "Her" is, Jesus said for you to not be a partaker of "Her" sins. That is a fact that "Her" is sinning, and you are taking part in "Her" sins. The incentive for you to come out of "Her" and quit sinning is so that you do not receive "Her" plagues, of which are all the trumpet's plagues, plus all the vials which are the last plagues, and the vials are full of God's wrath to "Her". But this writer knows that you are already receiving "Her" plagues, and they are warning you to "Shell Down the Corn" to Christ Jesus, (confess you are a sinner), and ask the Lord Jesus to save you and repent, and above all things, Believe Him, CHRIST JESUS!

If you have any kind of disease, if you have any kind of sickness, if you have any kind of infirmity, if your life was spared in any kind of accident, if your life was spared in any kind of disaster, that means you are sinning and God is merciful to warn you to "Come out of "Her", whatever or whoever you deem "Her" to be. So you cannot say it is my interpretation. Sin and Satan are the only thing that causes sickness, diseases, infirmities, or disasters. So if you come out of "Her" and do not take part in "Her" sins, you will not receive any of "Her" plagues. My interpretation and opinion are in this book many times; but you form your own opinion and interpretation; but it is double dog dead sure you need to come out of something. "Her" is the glories of the kingdom of this world, that the ruler of this world tried to give to Jesus. Jesus would not bow down and worship Satan, so Satan made you the same offer, and you took him up on his offer. Now God's people are in the Kingdom of Satan enjoying all the glory of Satan's Kingdom, which is Mystery, Babylon the Great, the Mother of *Harlots* and abominations of the earth. (Revelation 17:5)

My interpretation is as follows: Mystery, Babylon, is the opposite of the Mystery of Godliness, which is the Mystery of iniquity, which is the disobedience to God's Commandments, which is "Come out of "Her", the Mystery of Iniquity. Next, is Babylon the Great, which is all the idols of the world, "The lust of the flesh, and the lust of the eyes, and the pride of life, is not of the Father, but is of the world." (1 John 2:16) Next is, "the Mother of Harlots and abomination of the earth." (Revelation 17:5) The Mother is the *Roman Catholic Church.* The Harlots are all *churches*, which are the daughters of the Mother; which is the abomination of the earth. The body of Babylon the Great is America, the Serpent; and the Great City of Babylon is the *New York City,* the head of the Serpent. The world leaders have conspired for years trying to usher in the One World Government, which will marry the religion and the state together to make the two of them one. The *churches* all over the world will join or marry the One World Government; and She will ride or be carried by the beast, *(Anti-Christ),* which will be the world ruler until the kings of the earth hate the whore, and make "Her" desolate and naked, and shall eat "Her" flesh, and burn "Her" with fire." (Revelation 17:16) "Also, thus with violence shall that Great City Babylon be thrown down, and shall be found no more at all." (Revelation 18:21)

"That in the mouth of two or three witnesses every word may be established." (Matthew 18:16) This writer is going to make God's case to establish in the mouth of two or three or four witnesses. "Come out of "Her", Babylon, may be established: "Flee out of the midst of Babylon and deliver every man his soul: be not cut off in "Her" iniquity: For this is the time of the Lord's vengeance. He will render to "Her" a recompense." (Jeremiah 51:6) "My people, go you out of the midst of "Her" and deliver every man his soul from the fierce anger of the Lord." (Jeremiah 51:45) "Go you forth of Babylon, flee you from the Chaldeans with a voice of singing declare you, tell this, utter it even unto the end of the earth: Say you, the Lord has redeemed His servant Jacob, (Israel)." (Isaiah 48:20) These are prophecies from Jeremiah and Isaiah about the end time, not of old Babylon, but the Babylon the angel told Brother John about, when he said: "And I heard another voice from heaven, saying, "Come out of "Her", My people, that you be not partakers of "Her" (Babylon's) sins, and that you receive not of "Her" plagues." (Revelation 18:4)

Now, listen to Duishka, "Shell Down the Corn": There was an old Babylon that has been destroyed and will be no more. It will never be rebuilt. Saddam Hussein tried to rebuild it, but failed. God said it would never exist any more. Then there is literal Babylon the Great, which envelopes the entire physical things of the whole world, which is all the glory of Satan's world. Satan owns all the inanimate things of the world, which are dead things, things which do not have life, which includes you. All these things make up the literal Babylon. Satan owns everything in literal Babylon, including you, if you do not "Come out of "Her". These are some of the possessions of Babylon. All governments, and all the people that work for the governments, all the lawmakers that make the laws of the lands that rob, kill, and destroy. Every animate being of God are the things that God gave life to. God gave life to His believers and put His seal in their foreheads. These that are with Him are called, (klay-tos') from Ekklesia, called out ones (*not church*) and chosen, (Eklektos'), elect, favorite ones, and faithful (pis-tos') believers. (Revelation 17:14) These are not saints. Saints are inanimate, dead. If you work for any government in the world, you are in Babylon; and you belong to Satan. All people in governments are ruled by the "principalities, (evil spirits), powers, (evil spirits), rulers of darkness of this world, (evil spirits), wickedness in high places, (evil spirits)," (Ephesians 6:12) then by Satan himself, who owns all the evil spirits and the governments of the world, and all the people that work for him. (Ephesians 2:2) Next are the "Christians" and all the *churches,* which are all inanimate (walking dead). These are the whore, or harlot, and all harlots, which "She" is the mother of. (Revelation 17:5) If you are joined to any church, or if you are a member of any *church,* you are joined or married to a harlot, *(whore),* you are dead. You are in Babylon, you are in "Her". (Revelation 18:4)

God's last warning in the bible is to you, which are deceived, good, honest people of God. But God is commanding you to come out of "Her, My people, so you do not receive "Her" plagues. The last group of people are ignorant Idolators, sinners, historians, atheists, agnostics, and people wanting equal rights and justice. These are all inanimate, *(dead).* But Jesus, who is the Christ, who is God, came to give you life, and life more abundantly. (John 10:10) But you have to "Shell Down the Corn", (confess to God that you are a sinner), come out of "Her" and believe Jesus. He said **"REPENT"**

Then literal Babylon has a leading country, which is the *NewNited States of America.* Then the leading country has that Great City, where the headquarters of Babylon is located. That Great City is *New York City, USA.* There are many reasons why Duishka believes this to be true. This city rules the entire world by proxy through the United Nations. That Great City Babylon, it's merchants were the great men of the earth, "for by your sorceries were all nations deceived." (Revelation 18:23) The evidence that this is New York City is the New York Stock Exchange; and Wall Street is deceiving all nations to buy falling stock. "The mighty angel took up a stone like a great millstone and cast it into the sea, saying, "thus with violence shall that Great City Babylon be thrown down, and shall be found no more at all." (Revelation 18:21)

New York City, USA, is the target city of the world terrorists to bring down with violence. Two attempts have been made to destroy New York City. Why not Tokyo, London, Moscow, Beijing, Washington D.C., Los Angeles, or Vatican City, that theologians believe is Babylon? It is because all the terrorist nations of the world hate America, *(the snake)*, and want to destroy the Snake's head, *(New York City)*, which they call the Great Satan. No other city of the world could be the Great City Babylon.

Then there is Mystery, Babylon the Great, which is where interpreters, and theologians get confused. But this is the way I believe it is going to go down. The *Pope* is trying to walk away from his stance on same sex marriages, which is the same as men lying with men and women that change the natural use into that which is against nature. This is the same as *queer* or homosexual, the same as sin worthy of death, according to God's judgment. (Romans 1:32) The Pope is the head of the Whore, the Mother of harlots, or the Mother Church of "Christians", and mother of <u>all</u> *churches* and all "Christians" world wide. The *Pope* admits that all the *queer* priests and pedophile priests in the past were wrong, but is allied with the *queers* of the world by having pleasure in those that are guilty of sin. The president and vice president of the USA are having pleasure with *queers*, sanctioning same sex joining together. The Pope is warming up to all the members of the United Nations by agreeing with their sinful ways.

When Daniel's seventieth week begins, the Anti-Christ will sneak into the back door of the United Nations, and he will become allied with Israel, deceiving them with flattery. The *Pope* will be allied with the Anti-Christ, which will be causing the United Nations in New York City to be at his every step. The Anti-Christ will flatter Israel by giving them all kinds of concessions, and cause them to enter into a 7 year Peace Treaty that will go awry; and in the middle of the 7 years, the Anti-Christ will cause Jacob's trouble to begin. (Jeremiah 30:7)

"Corn Shelling Time" just heard that Benjamin Netanyahu was re-elected as head of Israel's Likud Party, which gives us all indication that more than likely Brother "BiBi" you will be in the driver's seat when this prophecy comes to pass. Brother "BiBi" I know you believe Jeremiah the prophet for Israel. You read the 30th Chapter. "The Word that came to Jeremiah from the Lord, saying, thus speaketh the Lord God of Israel, saying, write you all the words that I have spoken to you in a book. For, lo, the days come, saith the Lord, that I will bring again the captivity of My people Israel and Judah, saith the Lord, and I will cause them to return to the land that I gave to their fathers; and they shall possess it. And these are the words that the Lord spake concerning Israel and concerning Judah. For thus saith the Lord, We have heard a voice of trembling, of fear, and **not** of peace. Ask you now and see whether a man does travail with child? Wherefore do I see every man with his hands on his loins, as a woman in travail, and all faces are turned into paleness? Alas for that day is great, so that none is like it. It is even the time of Jacob's trouble; but he shall be saved out of it." Brother "BiBi" this writer believes you will be living when this prophecy comes to pass. (Jeremiah 30:1-7) But you need to read on about the yoke God has upon Jacob's neck, and see if you will be saved, in the name of Jesus. Brother "BiBi" do not believe anything the *Pope* or the president of the United States of America promises you. They have been found of God Almighty, (PANTAKRATOR), to be liars. Brother "BiBi" God said you would be deceived by flattery. (Daniel 11:21) Brother Benjamin read all of **"Corn Shelling Time"** and Romans 10:9-13) Then after the Anti-Christ has ruled Israel by proxy from America, alias the United Nations in the Great City Babylon, which is *New York*

City, he will set up shop in Israel and rule the world for 42 months until ***"God's Super Bowl On A Sunday",*** AKA **Armageddon.**

Now the power of authority in the days of God's vengeance has been given to Jesus on this wise. The eleven disciples went away into Galilee, into a mountain where Jesus had appointed to meet them. And when they saw him, they worshiped him, but some doubted. (Matthew 28:16,17) "And Jesus came and spake unto them, saying, **"All power is given unto me in heaven and in earth".** (Matthew 28:18) So, the order of command starts at Jesus, then goes to His archangel on down to the two witnesses, which prophesy to the ambassador angel, which tells the trumpet angels to sound, which lets the angel over the angels with the vials know when to pour out the plagues on the sinful people that are still in the Mystery, Babylon that have the mark of the beast, whose names have not been written in the Book of Life from the foundation of the world, and do not have the seal of God in their forehead.

So the order was given for the sixth angel to sound. At this time of the tribulation the two witnesses are killed; and when the voice out of heaven says, "Come up here," the spirit of life comes into the two witnesses and to everybody that is asleep in Christ Jesus. At this time will be the first resurrection. This will manifest all of the raptures into one. "And when they, the two witnesses, shall have finished their testimony, the beast that ascends out of the bottomless pit shall make war against them, and shall overcome them, and kill them; and their dead bodies shall lie in the street of the great city, which spiritually is called Sodom and Egypt, where also our Lord was crucified." (Revelation 11:7,8) "And after three days and an half the Spirit of God entered into them, and they stood upon their feet, and great fear fell upon them which saw them; and they heard a great voice from heaven saying unto them, "Come up hither;" and they ascended up to heaven in a cloud; and their enemies beheld them." (Revelation 11:11,12) "And the same hour there was a great earthquake, and the tenth part of the city fell, and in the earthquake were slain of men seven thousand: And the remnant were affrighted and gave glory to the God of heaven." "The second woe is past, and behold, the third woe comes quickly." (Revelation 11:13,14)

At this time Jesus comes back in the clouds and does not touch the earth; but just like the voice the two witnesses heard, which was great, "For the Lord himself shall descend from heaven, with a shout, with the voice of the archangel, and with the trump of God, (*not the trumpets of His angels*). And the dead in Christ shall rise first, then we which are alive and remain shall be caught up together with them in the clouds, to meet the Lord in the air; and so shall we ever be with the Lord." (1 Thessalonians 4:16,17) Notice the Lord comes first for His Holy Ones, (*not saints*); and when He comes to earth, He brings His Holy Ones with Him. Only the ones that are sanctified, washed, and clothed in <u>white</u> *git* to go with Him.

THIS is an insert in the book, **"CORN SHELLING TIME"** and **MICHAEL DUISHKA** with some of his additional belief. CHRIST JESUS said the believers were to be witnesses for Him in all the world. Michael Duishka believes Jesus so **"CORN SHELLING TIME"** is a witness for Him plus, here is a personal testimony. Not to give place to the devil or glorify Satan, but as has already been written, I was the lowest of all sinners if sin has any measure. I admit I did it because I was ignorant, which is no excuse, just a fact. I cannot name each of the millions of trespasses I committed against God and man, but I repeatedly broke all of the ten commandments that I never knew existed which was worthy of death, but I was an arrogant, belligerent, domineering, haughty, insulting, egotistical, vengeful, do unto you before you did it to me, showing no signs of mercy, destitute of compassion, selfish, sadistic, ignorant, unforgiving fool. My daddy, and my mama, and all my siblings were just the opposite of all those adjectives describing me, and they are all gone on to their rewards. When my LORD, CHRIST JESUS found me, because I was the One lost sheep, instead of Him getting revenge on me, He took every one of those evil traits one by one, and with patience He transformed each one of those evil traits into right the opposite of their description, and gave me life more abundantly on this earth, plus eternal life with HIM!!!! AMEN. Christ Jesus is no respecter of persons, and He will do the same for you if you will ask Him, and believe Him, HE SAID HE WOULD DO IT FOR YOU.

Chapter 32

UP TO THIS FIRST resurrection **<u>"Corn Shelling Time"</u>** has been reiterating God's last warning, where He told His people to "Come out of "Her". (Revelation 18:4) You still have time to come out of "Her", "Shell Down the Corn", (confess to Christ Jesus), repent, ask God, in the name of Jesus to forgive you for all your lawlessness, iniquity, sins: and believe Him when He said He would remember your sins no more. "For I will be merciful to their unrighteousness, and their sins and iniquities will I remember no more.." (Hebrews 8:12) If you will do this, Michael and Mavis Duishka are personally inviting you to come to the Marriage Supper of the Lamb. "And he said unto me, write, "Blessed are they which are called unto the Marriage Supper of the Lamb, and he said unto me, "These are the true sayings of God." (Revelation 19:9) Just for the record, by the authority vested in us, Michael and Mavis Duishka are calling you, dear reader, to the Marriage Supper of the Lamb. You have the time to be one of God's chosen ones; but remember you have to be clothed in <u>white,</u> you have to be clean, you have to be sanctified, and consecrated. "Husbands love your wives, even as Christ also loved the Called Out Ones, and gave himself for them, that He might sanctify and cleanse them with the washing of water by the **<u>Word,</u>** that He might present them to himself a glorious congregation, not having spot, or wrinkle, or any such thing, but that they should be Holy and without blemish." (Ephesians 5:25,26,27) (not transubstantiation, but Holy and sanctified, clean).

"And the great dragon was cast out, that old serpent, called the Devil, and Satan, which deceives the whole world: he was cast out into the earth, and his angels were cast out with him." (Revelation 12:9) Michael and his angels won the war with the dragon and his angels, and the dragon was really mad, having great wrath, because he knows that he has but a short time. Woe to the inhabiters of the earth and of the sea! For the devil is come down unto you. So the dragon gives authority to the beast that the angel that had the key to the bottomless pit let out. The dragon set the beast up a kingdom and put him on a throne, (seat of the beast) and gave the beast great power. (Revelation 13:2) The beast that came up out of the bottomless pit was a spirit which was evil. He was an angel, a ministering spirit of Satan, the dragon. The dragon, Satan, gave the beast a kingdom and power and great authority. Remember all the kingdoms of this world belong to the dragon, which is Satan, the Devil. Satan can give all this power to whomsoever he wills to give it to. (Luke 4:5,6). But the spirits have to have some kind of fleshly body to enter into. The beast is A-bad-don, and he enters into a man, which will be the Anti Christ. The Anti Christ will deceive the whole world and come in peaceably, and obtain the kingdom by flattery. (Daniel 11:21) This Anti Christ will negotiate a treaty with the Jews and set them up a temple with all their oblations and sacrifices in the great city Jerusalem, the city of the Great King. (Matthew 5:35) This treaty the Anti Christ will negotiate will be for a 7 year period of time, which will be the seventieth week in Daniel's book (Daniel 9:24), which is seven years in prophetical time. The Anti Christ will rule out of *New York City, USA* for the first three and one half years, then "he will cause the oblation to cease and he will cause the daily sacrifice to be taken away, and the Abomination that makes desolate set up. There shall be a thousand two hundred and ninety days." (Daniel 12:11) Then the Anti Christ will let the spirit of the beast enter into him, and "he opposes and exalts himself above all that is called, or that is worshiped, so that he as God sits in the temple of God, shewing himself that he is god." (2 Thessalonians 2:4) "The dragon gives the beast, *(which is the Anti Christ)*, his power, and his throne (seat), and great authority." (Revelation 13:2)

Remember the dragon was cast out of heaven by Michael, and the dragon's angels were cast out with him. These angels are all spirits, and have to have a fleshly body to enter into. The dragon's angels are one third of the angels in heaven, which are millions. These evil spirits enter into all the rulers of the nations of the world; and it is called perdition, which means destruction. These disembodied spirits go into any human that is naive, and green, and permits the evil unclean spirit to possess their body, which destroys the body with some kind of malady, which is some kind of disease that destroys the body, or mind, or both of the ignorant victim. That is why God said; "My people are destroyed for lack of knowledge." (Hosea 4:6) Any people, race, nation, or language with the lack of knowledge of Christ Jesus, which is God, will go into perdition, destruction. The hireling preachers in <u>all</u> *churches* make fun of devil *caster outers* and teach doctrines of devils and giving heed to seducing spirits, because they are ignorant, and green, and are destitute of knowledge of God. (1 Timothy 4:1) Pay attention, dear reader, to the above knowledge you have just read. The hirelings tell you about the miracles, and the fishes, and loaves that Jesus did; but they do not know how to tell you about the controversy God has with you, because you lack knowledge of God when He told you about the lies the hireling preachers tell you about how God loves you; and there is no such thing as everlasting fire. (Matthew 25:41) "For the Lord has a controversy with the inhabitants of the land, because there is no truth, nor mercy, nor knowledge of God in the land. By swearing, lying, and killing, and stealing, and committing adultery, they break out, and blood touches blood." (Hosea 4:1,2)

It is just about time for the trumpets to start sounding, and the vials of God's wrath to start pouring out on the land. Listen! Dear reader, the evil spirits are invisible. You cannot see them. That is why you do not believe they are causing your malady, which is some kind of infirmity of your body or mind. What caused your infirmity? You do not know, do you? When you first recognized your disease, you just did not think about it until it became worse and unbearable. Then you went to get help from someone that needed help themselves. You sought help from some deranged doctor, or some deranged preacher, or in most cases, you went to the drugstore first, then to the doctor, back to the drug store, then to the preacher in the *devil's church;* and because the drugs deadened your senses to where you could not see, hear, smell, or feel the sensation, you thought you were healed. Wrong! This is how the evil spirit deceived you. By causing you to think the ignorant doctor, or the ignorant preacher had the answer to your ignorant problem. Listen carefully, **"Corn Shelling Time"** does not have enough paper, time, or patience to argue with a world full of ignorant sick ones that God has a controversy with. Secular Humanism will get you a front seat in Hell. Jesus gives you life. You make your own bed.

The book of Daniel comes back into play: "But you, O Daniel, shut up the words, and seal the book, to the time of the end. Many shall run to and fro, and knowledge shall be increased." (Daniel 12:4) Do you not know that God is opening up Daniel's book in **"Corn Shelling Time"** just for you. You are not ignorant in worldly knowledge, the doctor is not ignorant in worldly knowledge, the school teacher is not ignorant in worldly knowledge, the rulers of the world are not ignorant in worldly knowledge: this is the knowledge Daniel said would be increased, which all of the above mentioned possess. This worldly knowledge is the power the dragon gives to the beast, and the power the dragon's angels gives to you. The evil spirits *(ministering spirits of the devil)* have educated the ignorant people; and someone said a long time ago, "they are educated fools." They possess all the knowledge about the world, they possess all knowledge about God; but they do not possess God. You profess God, which makes you a professor. If you possessed God, you would be a possessor. But the evil spirit in you causes your mind to be deranged and argue that you know Jesus, which is a lie, or you would be free from those evil spirits that causes your maladies. Jesus does not know you and will say, "get away from Me, you that work iniquity, (sin), I never knew you." Jesus never did say go to a doctor, but only those that are sick need a physician. Jesus never did say go to school. He said, "The Holy Spirit would teach you." (1 John 2:27) *He never did say come to church, or come to a hireling preacher;* but He did say, **"Come unto Me, all you that labour and are heavy laden, and I will give you rest."** (Matthew 11:28) "Jesus said whoever says to his brother, you fool, shall be in danger of hell fire." (Matthew 5:22) This writer is not in any danger, because he does not have any brothers that are sick. All my brothers are healed, because they "Shelled Down the Corn", (confessed), to Jesus, and repented, and commanded the evil, unclean spirits to loose them in the name of Christ Jesus. All of these educated fools are the ones God has a controversy with. They have knowledge of the world, but they are destitute for knowledge of Christ Jesus, God the Son. Listen! Do not be an educated fool. The fool says there is no God. It is the same thing with the one that does not believe God. You lie when you say you believe God. If you believed God, you would not have the plague you have.

"God is Spirit." (John 4:24) The only way God talks to most people is by a man that is flesh and blood like Moses, David, Jeremiah, Isaiah, Daniel, Ezekiel, Hosea, or one of the other prophets, or by **That** prophet, which was Jesus. Jesus said no man had seen the Father except Him, the one that came down from the Father. **"All things are delivered to Me of My Father, and no man knows who the Son is, but the Father, and who the Father is, but the Son, and to whom the Son will reveal Him."** (Luke 10:22) Since God is Spirit, He chooses to speak through a human. So God manifested Himself in a fleshly body called Jesus. "Jesus is the Word. The Word is God." (John 1:1) Jesus is God in the flesh; "And the Word was made flesh, and dwelt among us." (John 1:14) "And without controversy great is the Mystery of Godliness.

God was manifest in the flesh, justified in the Spirit, seen of angels, preached unto the Gentiles, believed on in the world, received up into glory." (1 Timothy 3:16) So Jesus is God talking in the Word. Jesus revealed the Father to Michael Duishka according to His will, and **"Corn Shelling Time"** is reiterating what the Word, Jesus, said. **"It is the Spirit (God), that quickens, (makes alive), the flesh profits nothing: The words that I speak unto you are Spirit, and are life." (John 6:63)**

So here is the Word of God to you. "Shell Down the Corn", (confess your sins), "If we confess our sins, He is faithful and just to forgive us our sins, and to cleanse us from all unrighteousness." (1 John 1:9) Then you repent, which means quit sinning. Sinning is breaking the Commandments of God. "Remember the Sabbath day to keep it Holy. Without holiness no man shall see God." (Hebrews 12:14) The seventh day is the Sabbath day, *(not the first day – not Sunday)*. The Word says to "Have faith of God." (Mark 11:22) **"For verily I say unto you, that whosoever shall say unto this mountain, be thou removed, and be thou cast into the sea, and shall not doubt in his heart** (your spirit), **but shall believe that those things which he** (you) **says shall come to pass, he** (you) **shall have whatsoever he** (you) **says."** (Mark 11:23) Believe what you say. But here is the most important part. **"And when you stand praying, forgive, if you have ought against any that your Father also which is in heaven may forgive you your trespasses. But if you do not forgive, neither will your Father which is in heaven forgive your trespasses."** (Mark 11:25,26) "Now you have the power to start commanding those evil unclean spirits to obey you. **"Behold I give unto you power to tread on serpents and scorpions, and over all the power of the enemy, and nothing shall by any means hurt you." "Notwithstanding in this rejoice not, that the spirits are subject unto you, but rather rejoice because your names are written in heaven."** (Luke 10:19,20) If you have done everything the Word, Jesus, God, said to do, your names are written in heaven, so do not do anything to get your names blotted out of the Book of Life. You promised God in the name of Christ Jesus that you would go and sin no more and keep His Commandments. He commanded you to be not unequally yoked together with unbelievers:"For what fellowship has righteousness with unrighteousness? And what communion has light with darkness? And what concord has Christ with Belial? Or what part has he that believes with an infidel? And what agreement has the temple of God with idols? "For you are the temple of the Living God, as God has said, I will dwell in them, and walk in them, and I will be their God, and they shall be My people. Wherefore come out from among them and be you separate, saith the Lord, and touch not the unclean thing; and I will receive you, and will be a Father unto you; and you shall be My sons and daughters, saith the Lord Almighty, (PANTAKRATOR)." (2 Corinthians 6:14,15,16,17,18) God just called you His people if you come out from the infidels, so here comes another commandment to "Come out of "Her", My people." (Revelation 18:4)

Do not go back into the hog wallow of the *"christian" church*. You have been there already and done that, and that is where you received your maladies, disease of body and mind. "For you have escaped the pollutions of the world through the knowledge of the Lord and Saviour, Christ Jesus." (2 Peter 2:20) This is the one that will save you, so do not get entangled again with hireling preachers, churches, and the world. "For it had been better for them not to have known the way of righteousness, than, after they have known it, to turn from the Holy Commandment delivered unto them." (2 Peter 2:21) "But it is happened to them according to the true proverb, the dog is turned to his own vomit again; and the sow that was washed to her wallowing in the mire." (2 Peter 2:22) Mavis said that she saw in a dream a woman that said she was a genuine hog washed "Christian".

<u>"Corn Shelling Time"</u> is your last chance of escape. There are many kinds of religions and beliefs in the world, but all religions are double dog dead sure to cut you off from God. Any religion is just like a pair of limb lobbers that cut a limb off a tree and it is cast into the everlasting fire. There cannot be found salvation in any organized or unorganized religion. "For there is none other name under heaven given among men, whereby we must be saved except in the name of Christ Jesus." (Acts 4:12) All "Christians" that think they can use His name to proclaim self "Christianity", and use His name for a cloak to cover their sins, and obtain salvation are deceiving themselves. It does not matter if you are a Jew, Gentile, heathen, Islam, Muslim, "Christian", black, white, "Afro American" President, prime minister, king, queen, grand duke, governor, ayatollah, shah, emperor, sheikh, imir, prince, priest, *pope,* bishop, cardinal, any kind of monarch, you have to be covered by the blood of Jesus. Symbolically you have to have his blood to wash you and cover your sins. To do this you have to humble yourself and surrender everything you have, give it all up to the savior of the ones that believe this.

Back to the woes of the world when Michael cast out the dragon to the earth. The dragon was full of wrath and set the beast upon a throne and gave him a seat of authority and power; and the beast possessed the Anti Christ: and "it was given to the beast which ruled the Anti Christ to make war with the Holy Ones of God, (*not the churches)*, and overcome them." (Revelation 13:7) He did not overcome the *saints,* because there is no such thing as a *saint,* but rather "the beast and Anti Christ overcame the Holy Ones, the ones that did not take the mark in their right hand, or in their forehead, or the number of the beast." (Revelation 13:17)

At this time when the fifth angel pours out his vial that is full of the wrath of God on the seat of the beast, and his kingdom is full of darkness; and when the beast makes war with the Holy Ones of God and overcomes them, he also makes war with the two witnesses and kills them; and that is all of the Holy Ones left upon the earth at that time. (Revelation 11:7) After that the beast kills the two witnesses and their dead bodies shall lie in the street of the great city, which is spiritually called Sodom and Egypt, where also our Lord was crucified." (Revelation 11:8) Interruption - **"Corn Shelling Time"** wants to draw to your attention that the great city, {Jerusalem}, at that time is spiritually called Sodom, which means it has become filled up with *queers,* commonly called homosexuals, and also Egypt, which signifies that it is full of all kinds of idols and is no longer a holy city. - "And after the two witnesses' dead bodies lay dead in the street for three and one half days, the Spirit of Life from God entered into them, and they stood upon their feet, and fear fell upon them which saw them. And they heard a great voice from heaven saying unto them, "Come up here," and they ascended up to heaven in a cloud; and their enemies beheld them." (Revelation 11:8,9,10,11,12) Simultaneously all the Holy Ones, them which also sleep in Jesus, will God bring with Him. These are the spirits of all the ones that died in Christ, including "the souls under the altar that were slain for the Word of God and for the testimony they held." (Revelation 6:9) Also in this first resurrection are the multitude John saw "which no man could number, of all nations, and kindred, and people, and tongues, clothed in white robes." (Revelation 7:9) Also will be resurrected "the 144,000 Jews which were sealed with the seal of God in their foreheads." (Revelation 7:3,4) "Included in this first resurrection are all the ones on earth that are in graves that are asleep in Christ Jesus. "Then we which are alive and remain, that is the mystery, Holy Ones, that shall not sleep but shall be changed in a moment in the twinkling of an eye at the last trump. For the trumpet shall sound, and the dead shall be raised incorruptible; and we shall be changed." (1 Thessalonians 4:15) and 1 Corinthians 15:51,52) This last trumpet sound is just like the silver trumpets God told Moses to make to gather the children altogether in (Numbers 10:2) This first resurrection happens simultaneously at the last trump when the Spirit of Life comes back into the two witnesses; and they hear a great voice saying "step up here". "Blessed and holy is he that has part in the first resurrection: on such the second death has no power; but they shall be priests of God and of Christ, and shall reign with Him a thousand years." (Revelation 20:6)

All those that the "Christians" called *raptured* actually have been murdered by "Christians" in the Catholic churches, and the Anglican churches, which are the churches of England, and by the laws of the lands that steal, kill, and destroy those believers, which are blessed and Holy. The "Christians" are still murdering by proxy, by voting for the war mongers that pass laws to go to foreign lands to kill the inhabitants, and steal their oil, gold, silver and all their possessions in the guise of helping them. Yes, you murdering "Christians" are the guilty ones that voted for the politicians that made it lawful to murder babies; and say the baby was not alive. Oh Me! Then you say we will be *raptured* out and miss the tribulation. I do not believe so. Then you say we will be kings and priests in God's Kingdom. I do not believe Christ Jesus, my Lord, would want anyone in His kingdom that voted for thieves, murderers, destroyers and the ObomaNation of Desolation that makes desolate God's creation. No buddy! You "Christians already have the mark spiritually; and when the false prophet tells you to take the mark literally, your hireling preacher will be the first one to stick his right hand out and say, "Oh this is not the mark of the beast;" and all you "Christians" will run over each other going to *church,* where the mark will be given TO YOU.

"The ten horns which you saw upon the beast, (ten kings), these shall hate the whore, and shall make "Her" desolate and naked, and shall eat "Her" flesh, and burn "Her" with fire." (Revelation 17:16) You "Christians" are the harlot daughters of the whore. But **"Corn Shelling Time"** is still reiterating Christ Jesus' Commandment while you still have the chance that you are going to beg Him for, "to come out of "Her". God told Jeremiah, "Because you speak this word, behold I will make my words in your mouth fire, and this people wood, and it shall devour them." (Jeremiah 5:14)

Try to think spiritually, and do not be like the "Christians", that say they have the Holy Ghost, and think in natural thoughts, and receive all the plagues that are being poured out on them, because the plagues only affect the ones that do not have the seal of God in their forehead. The only ones that have the seal of God in their forehead are the ones that obey God and keep His Commandments, and are sanctified, holy and pure. They are clothed in white.

After the fifth trumpet sounds and the star falls from heaven and unlocks the bottomless pit to let out the beast, Apollyon, A-Bad-Don, the ruler of the locusts, the dragon (Satan) gave him a seat of authority and power over all the Gentile nations, which are so called "Christians" and the "Christians" will have to either "Come out of "Her", (Mystery, Babylon) or be subject to the rule of the dragon, Satan, Devil, that old serpent. When the fifth angel pours out his vial on the seat of the beast (Revelation 16:10), the nations (Gentiles) were angry, (Revelation 11:18) because God's wrath is come: At this time the seat of the beast is moved from New York City to the new temple of worship of the Jews in Jerusalem, Israel. The retaliation of the beast is he makes war with the Holy Ones, the ones that have the seal of God in their forehead, and overcomes them. That means he kills all the ones that do not join his army.

The sixth angel with the vials that are full of God's wrath pours out his vial on the great Euphrates river and looses the four angels that have been prepared for a certain year, and a certain month of the year, and a certain day of the month, and a certain hour of that certain day. These four angels were prepared to slay a third part of men, but they do more damage than that, because since the Holy Ones have been killed two woes are past; (Revelation 11:14) Behold the third woe comes quickly. There was a great earthquake, and the tenth part of the city fell, and in the earthquake seven thousand men were slain.

The four angels that were loosed on the great Euphrates river are the four angels over the four elements of the earth, which are the earth, the fire, the water, and the wind. They cause the river to dry up so the way of the kings of the east might be prepared. (Revelation 14:12) Why is the way prepared for the kings of the east? Answer: So they and their armies can be one of the players in *"God's Super Bowl On A Sunday"* in the arena which is the valley around the mountain of Megiddo, which Duishka calls *God's Super Bowl;* but God called it in the Hebrew tongue **Armageddon.** (Revelation 16:16)

"After the sixth vial is poured out, John saw three unclean spirits, like frogs come out of the mouth of the dragon, and out of the mouth of the beast, and out of the mouth of the false prophet, for they are spirits of devils, working miracles, which go forth unto the kings of the earth, and of the whole world, to gather them to the battle of that great day of God Almighty (PANTAKRATOR)." (Revelation 16:13,14)

God said in (Jeremiah 25:29,30) "For lo I begin to bring evil on the city which is called by My name, *(Jerusalem)*. Should you be utterly unpunished? You shall not be unpunished: for I will call for a sword upon all the inhabitants of the earth, saith the Lord of Hosts." "But the court which is without the temple leave out, and measure it not, for it is given unto the Gentiles." (Revelation 11:2) This will be the evil that God brings against the city, which is called by His name, *(Jerusalem)*. "And the holy city shall they *(Gentiles)* tread under foot forty and two months." The holy city is not holy any more at that point in time. It is full of queers (homosexuals), and God called it spiritual Sodom. And they worshiped pagan idols, such as Ishtar, Goddess of Sex, and *Easter,* (desecration of the holy passover), so God also called His city Egypt. (Revelation 11:8) God is allowing the nations, (Gentiles), to punish the Israelites until all the filth and abominable people in His city are destroyed; and after His Super Bowl He intervenes and saves a remnant.

In the meantime on His way to the *Super Bowl* on His <u>white</u> horse with His armies following on <u>white</u> horses, Great Babylon came in remembrance before God to give unto "Her" the cup of the wine of the fierceness of His wrath. (Revelation 16:19) "And a mighty angel took up a stone like a great millstone and cast it into the sea, saying thus with violence shall that great city Babylon be thrown down, and shall be found no more at all." (Revelation 18:21) Good bye to *New York City, USA*. "Reward her even as she rewarded you, and double unto her double according to her works. In the cup which she has filled, fill to her double." (Revelation 18:6) "After these things I saw another angel come down from heaven having great power; and the earth was lightened with his glory, and he cried mightily with a strong voice, saying, Babylon the great is fallen, is fallen." (Revelation 18:1,2) "Therefore shall her plagues come in one day, death, and mourning; and she shall be utterly burned with fire; and the kings of the earth who have committed fornication and lived deliciously with her shall bewail her, and lament for her, when they shall see the smoke of her burning, standing afar off for the fear of her torment, saying, Alas, alas, that great city Babylon, that mighty city; for in one hour is thy judgments come." (Revelation 18:8,9,10) These judgments are because the United Nations with the United States of America have robbed, killed, and destroyed in almost every country in the world, and supported the heathen terrorists to stir up uprisings in almost all countries of the world, even the blacks in American cities in the name of Civil Liberties, even killing police in Babylon City, *(New York City)*. The Lord said to pay her back double and with violence; and the four elements destroy her.

After all the Holy Ones have been killed and resurrected, "and they overcame him, *(the accuser of the brethren, Satan),* by the blood of the Lamb, and by the word of their testimony, and they loved not their lives unto death." (Revelation 12:11), God is really angry. He turns up the intensity of His power and strength to command His forces to bring vengeance upon all the earth. The four angels over the four elements, which are the fire, earth, water, and wind are deployed to bring death to all the impenitent of the ones that did not come out of the churches, the governments, and the idolatry of this world. These four elements, fire, earth, wind and water were created by Christ Jesus to give life, and life more abundantly; but at the time between the first sound of the first trumpet and the seventh sound of the seventh trumpet, and between the pouring out of the first vial *(bowl)* full of the plagues of God's wrath, the life giving elements escalate into death and destruction.

God is pleading with you through **"Corn Shelling Time"** to repent before it is too late; and do not be like the evil ones that were "scorched with great heat, and blasphemed God, the one that had power over all these plagues; and they repented not." (Revelation 16:9)

"The second angel sounded, and as a great mountain of fire was cast into the sea, and the third part of the sea became blood, and the third part of the creatures in the sea died, and the third part of the ships were destroyed. The third angel sounded, and there fell a great star from heaven, burning as it were a lamp, and it fell upon the third part of the rivers and upon the fountains of waters, and the name of the star is called Wormwood. And the third part of the waters became Wormwood, and many men died of the waters, because they were made bitter." (Revelation 8:8,9,10,11,12) It is amazing how God could foresee a disaster like Chernobyl, which say some, that the Ukrainian meaning for Chernobyl is Wormwood. The Chernobyl Nuclear Disaster fits the description of the star named Wormwood that made the waters bitter and killed many men and is still killing many by nuclear radiation, causing grievous sores *(cancer)* on an entire generation in many countries. The name of the burning star is called Wormwood.

The fire and the water are destroying agents of God; and the wind, which all of these elements are to be taken with a two fold meaning. One meaning is spiritual and the other meaning is literal. The spiritual meaning of wind is God's Holy Spirit. (John 3:8) "That we henceforth *(hereafter)* be no more children, tossed to an fro, and carried about with every wind of doctrine, by the sleight of men, and cunning craftiness, whereby they lie in wait to deceive." (Ephesians 4:14) This is talking about the evil winds that come from the four corners of the earth to deceive "Christians" and teach them "false doctrines from the Prince of the Powers of the Air." (Ephesians 2:2)

When the four angels loose the four winds of the earth, God's people will have the seal of God in their forehead, and the deceiver cannot seduce them, because they are the chosen ones, the very elect.

"God told Jeremiah to take the wine cup of this fury at My hand, and cause all the nations, to whom I send you to drink, and they shall drink, and be moved, and be mad, because of the sword that I will send among them." (Jeremiah 25:15,16) "And all the kings of the north, far and near, one with another, and all the kingdoms of the world, which are upon the face of the earth." (Jeremiah 25:26) "Therefore, you shall say unto them, thus saith the Lord of Hosts, the God of Israel, drink you, and be drunken, and spue, and fall, and rise no more because of the sword I will send among you." (Jeremiah 25:27) "And it shall be if they refuse to take the cup at your hand to drink, then you shall say unto them, thus saith the Lord of Hosts, you shall certainly drink." (Jeremiah 25:28)

Pay attention, America (*Babylon*), **"Corn Shelling Time"** has told you before, Duishka is not a prophet, apostle, "Christian", or a blind guide. Duishka is not deceiving himself. Duishka is nothing. But God cannot lie, and He told Jeremiah all nations (Gentiles) would drink of His cup of wrath. It is happening right before your eyes. The King of Babylon, *America,* has started to turn the nation into an ObomaNation of Desolation to be a perpetual desolation. Thus saith the Lord: I will bring the King of Babylon (*America*), My servant against this land, and against the inhabitants thereof, and against all these nations (Gentiles) round about, and will utterly destroy them and make them a perpetual A-bum-a-Nation of Desolation. The King of Babylon (*America*) is employed by God to bring God's wrath on His people. The king, a servant of Satan, is being used by the true God, Christ Jesus, as an instrument to correct God's people and to call them out of "Her". The King of Babylon (*America*) has string pullers telling him what to do to bring total perpetual desolation to the enemies of God. The "Christians" voted for the destroyer, robber, and killer of God's people.

<u>"Corn Shelling Time"</u> has risen up early and stayed up late at night to warn the world about the cup of the wrath of God that you shall certainly drink. The four elements, earth, water, fire, and wind, with their ruler (PEMPTE OUSA), (the fifth being), are part of God's armies, that are demonstrating their powers in different places of the earth to plead with the wise people of God to separate themselves from the "Christians", heathen, pagan unbelievers, and "come out from among them, and you be separate, saith the Lord, and touch not the unclean; and I will receive you." (2 Corinthians 6:17)

If you would listen to what **<u>"Corn Shelling Time"</u>** is reiterating of the Word of God, you would not be affected by the hurricanes, or the tornadoes, or tsunami, or mudslides, or earthquakes, or fires, or terrorists, or by Muslims cutting off the heads and killing your loved ones, or by the terrorist organization Hamas, or by Jihad or Islam or any other terror by night. If you would do, not say, what Jesus done, you would not be catching any communicable disease, because you would come out from among them and separate yourselves from the unclean. Stay out of long lines, rubbing up against filthy people, breathing their germs when they cough, or sneeze. Do not be hugging unbelievers, such as "Christians" in church. If you shake hands with anyone, wipe your hands with a hand-i-wipe. Do not be committing adultery, or fornication, or sodomy to catch a STD. Do not hate anyone, but stay away from "Christians", Muslims, Buddhist, Islamic, heathen, pagans, Judaism, Taoism, Polytheism, Hinduism, Yoga, Gnostic, Satan, Occults, or Scientology, all of these are infidels. Do not lie, *(or your nose may grow longer.)* Above all do not be lazy. Lazy people always come to an end with some kind of obese disease, such as diabetes, kidney malfunction, gall bladder, liver, heart malfunction, or hip or knee joint wear out from carrying too much weight. Do not get on welfare, DHS, or Obama Care, as all who do so wind up going to doctors and become legalized dopers, and eventually lose all their senses, smell, taste, hearing, sight, and feeling. Come out from among schools, police, politics, sporting events, most especially *"God's Super Bowl On A Sunday"*, where you will become buzzard bait. Forsake the assembling of yourselves together with unsanctified enemies of God, unholy, unthankful, diseased up slo-bellies full of demons. Stay out of restaurants, and every place where diseases are spread. While we are waiting for that great and terrible day of the Lord, the sorrows that began to escalate with extreme intensity in 2011, have expanded to be occurring more densely. The four elements are giving a preview of the terrible velocity of their power before that great and terrible day of the Lord. Wars are occurring all over the world. Earthquakes are shifting the layers of the earth, getting the earth ready for "the great earthquake, such as was not since men were upon the earth." (Revelation 16:18)

In 2011 Duishka unlocked the ones bound by the King James Version of the Bible that has deceived God's people for 400 years, from 1611 to 2011, when Michael Duishka told of the misinterpretation and mistranslation of the pure words of our God, Christ Jesus. Duishka expounded on this subject in a book called "Please Do Not Call Me A "Christian", that would set the ones deceived by the KJV of the bible free. Also Amos said: "Behold the days come, saith the Lord God, that I will send a famine in the land, not a famine of bread, not a thirst for water, but of hearing the words of the Lord." (Amos 8:11) "They shall wander from sea to sea, and from the north even unto the east. They shall run to and fro to seek the word of the Lord, and shall not find it." (Amos 8:12) Current Event!

Those days are here <u>already.</u> "Christians" think they have the word of the Lord in the perverted KJV of the bible, when all the time the misleading words such as *cross, saints, church, "Christians"*, happy, and on and on never were spoken by the Christ Jesus or any of His apostles, prophets, disciples, followers, or holy ones. All of the above words are invented by man, including *Sunday* for the man made sabbath. **"Corn Shelling Time"** is tormenting everyone that reads it, if they are not wise. This book is bread for the ones that hunger for righteousness. This book is living water for the ones that are thirsty for righteousness. The famine of the true Word of God is here *(rat)* now;. Go into any church in the world, and you will find a lying preacher, deceiving the ignorant ones into thinking he or she is really proclaiming God's Word, when all the time they are in competition with some other misguided false prophet like the one in Texas that has more proselytes than anyone else, and has made them a two fold child of hell more than himself; but their prosperity will burn with them. **"He that believes Me, the works that I do shall he do also; and greater works than these shall he do, because I go unto My Father."** (John 14:12) There must not be any left on earth that believes Him, because there are not any works being done that are like He did, much less greater works. There are a lot of professors, but possessors cannot be found. There are not any true prophets, or true apostles, or true preachers that preach what Jesus said to do. "Come out of "Her", or any separation from the unclean. Churches are not forsaking the assembling of themselves together with fornicators, adulterers, *queers, lizzies,* politicians, police, black protestors that march to steal, kill, and destroy the people's businesses that feed the welfare bums. They do not work, or they would not have the time to break into businesses, and steal the good man's possessions, and then set his business on fire. All that march and protest are guilty by association and instigating the works of the devil. If they did not get subsidies from their leader, such as free DHS money, food stamps, Obama Care, extended unemployment checks, feigned disability checks, all kinds of grants and loans, they never pay back, they would not have time to destroy the hand that feeds them, *(Babylon)*

"Corn Shelling Time" is reiterating God's promises to believers. Let the heathen rage. **"Because you have kept the word of My patience, I also will keep you from the hour of temptation, which shall come upon all the world, to test them that dwell**

upon the earth." (Revelation 3:10) When it comes time to flee the ObomaNation of Desolation, do not run into a church, because: "And the ten horns that you saw upon the beast, these shall hate the Whore, {*and "Her" daughters, the Harlots*}, and shall make "Her" desolate and naked, and shall eat "Her" flesh, and burn "Her" with fire." (Revelation 17:16) If you run into a church or a public building, God's promise is not for you. He only keeps the ones that keep His Commandments from the hour of temptation; and "Christians", churches, and the world do not keep His Commandments.

America (*Babylon*) is a land flowing with zombies, who have all of their senses deadened. The democrats have passed laws to give America's wealth away to lazy shiftless bums that get money, food, and drugs from the DHS (Department of Human Services) (*welfare*), that are supported by the working class of honest people. Doctors go to school to learn how to write a prescription for drugs, not to learn how to cure diseases. The Pharmaceutical Companies are paying doctors to prescribe their drugs to the feigned sick, that either get their drugs paid for by Obama Care or other insurance companies that the democrats make mandatory for the honest hard working class to pay for in taxes. The republican wimps get paid off by special interest groups to be quiet and not tell the secret scams. The drugged up zombies call it taking their medication to keep it legal. The illegals call it getting a fix. Any way you slice it, all the addicts are zombies that cannot feel, hear, smell, see, or taste fully, because their senses are deadened on account of dope, either legal or illegal.

"Know you not that you are the temple of God, and that the spirit of God dwell in you? If any man defile the temple of God, him shall God destroy; for the temple of God is holy, which temple you are." (1 Corinthians 3:16,17) You zombies go around filling God's temple with all kinds of drugs, which is defiling God's temple with filth and abominations of the earth. That is the reason God will destroy you with "Her" plagues, if you do not "Shell Down the Corn", (confess to God), and REPENT.

After the fifth trumpet sounds, all the locusts will sting men, and they cannot die for five months; and they will seek death and cannot die.

When the sixth trumpet sounds, the four angels are loosed, which brings the Anti Christ against God and His holy ones. "These shall make war with the Lamb; and the Lamb shall overcome them, for He is Lord of lords, and King of kings. And they that are with Him are <u>called</u> and <u>chosen,</u> and <u>faithful.</u>" (Revelation 17:14) The man made World War III has started "when the sixth angel pours out his vial on the earth, and the River Euphrates is dried up to let the kings of the east join the battle. The four elements are loosed with the four angels that were prepared for a year, and a month, and a day, and an hour." (Revelation 9:15) These angels were prepared for a certain date, which only God knows what date it is that these angels will slay the third part of all the men on the earth.

In a previous chapter of **"Corn Shelling Time"** some of the fault lines were listed, which the smaller quakes that are happening today are preparing the shift of the earth for the great earthquake.

"Behold I am against you, O you most proud, saith the Lord God of Hosts, for your day has come; the time that I will visit you; and the most proud shall stumble and fall; and none shall raise him up: And I will kindle a fire in his cities, and it shall devour all around about him." (Jeremiah 50:31,32) This is God speaking to individuals as well as to Babylon the Great.

The *Pope*, which is the head of the Whore, has altered his views of sodomy, to be parallel with the views of the king of Babylon, who calls himself a "Christian"; and the two # hash tag "Christians" are sanctioning same sex marriages, just like the heathen they are. The *Pope* is scheduled to come to Babylon at a later time to corroborate the "Christian" marriage to pagans. I believe the religious leader of the great Whore is the *Pope*, which is influential in causing the presidents, (kings) of many countries to make sinful decisions by laws that are allied with the decisions of Satan to rob, kill, and destroy God's people. I believe the President of the *NewNited States of America* to be the political leader of the world, which is influential in causing the leaders of many countries to make sinful decisions by laws that are allied with the designs of Satan to rob, kill, and destroy God's people, most especially the holy, sanctified, Holy Ghost filled, Chosen Ones of Christ Jesus. I believe the *NewNited States of America* to be the leader of literal Babylon. I believe *New York City* is the Great City, Babylon, which causes all the merchants of the earth to be prosperous by the Tower of Babel, (*The World Trade Center*), the tallest tower of the west. I believe, at this time, the president of the *NewNited States of America* to be the king of literal Babylon, which he himself does not have enough sense to rule anything, even his own family, but his string pullers, (*secret advisers*) tell him frog, and he says, "How far?" I believe the religious leader of the Whore will form a coalition with the political leader of literal Babylon for the common purpose to rule the entire world.

The *Pope* is **a** false prophet, but he is not **the** false prophet. The President of the *NewNited States of America* is **a** Anti Christ ("Christian"), but he is not **the** Anti Christ. But the Catholic Church, the great Whore, the Mother of harlots, will be stripped naked, (*exposed of "Her" lies and deceptions*), burned with fire, and brought to total desolation by the ten horns (kings) of the beast. (Revelation 17:16), which is spiritual Babylon that God is commanding His people to come out of "Her". (Revelation 18:4). Also the Whore is the Mother of the Harlots, which are the *churches* of the world, that includes <u>all</u> denominations, creeds, isms, beliefs, doctrines, theories, dualisms, and, yes, even the church of Satan. She is the head of the old serpent. This and more is Mystery, Babylon. Literal Babylon will be destroyed doubly with the cup of God's wrath that she will have to drink, indubitably. He that has any wisdom, please let him or her understand that *New York City, (Babylon City)*, or America, leader of all Babylon,is not the entirety of Babylon. The cup that the Babylon City drinks is going down like this: Not only will she be brought down by violence, but she will also be brought down by the four elements of God, the earth, water, wind, and fire. The king of Babylon is the president of *the NewNited States of America,* who is trying to police all the countries of the world, except the terrorist countries like Iran, Syria, Yemen, Hamas, Palistine, Boko Haram, Lebanon, and other countries that burn the American Flag. The king gives support with the money from the working class of American citizens. The king gives support to the black Americans that burn, loot, kill and destroy the people and property of true Americans. Could that be because he is a racist for the blacks? Could it be that he is a Muslim? Could it be that he showed a bible at election time and just said he was a "Christian"? Michael Duishka authored a book called "Please Do Not Call Me A "Christian"; and the reason he did this was so he would not be stereotyped with "Christians" like the king of Babylon. The terrorist countries will drop an atomic bomb or some greater vehicle of explosives on Babylon, the Great City; and that will cause an earthquake such as was not since men were upon the earth, so mighty an earthquake, and so great that it started a chain reaction to all the fault lines all around the earth; "and the cities of the nations fell along with Babylon the Great City, which was divided into three parts; and she was drinking the cup of the wine of the fierceness of His, (God's) wrath." (Revelation 16:18,19) "Because she said I sit as a queen and shall see no sorrow, and lived deliciously, as she is doing at this present time." As **"Corn Shelling Time"** is telling you what God said would happen to Babylon the Great City, which I believe is *New York City, USA.* Just like the great Whore, she shall be utterly burned with fire, another one of God's elements. The earthquake will cause a tsunami that will throw down Babylon, the Great City, and she shall be found no more at all. (Revelation 18:21)

Can you imagine the Murrah Building and the Athenian Building bomb of Oklahoma City, will be as insignificant as a firecracker compared to the Great City, Babylon that will become desolate in one hour. (Revelation 18:19? Can you imagine the Tower of Babel, (*The World Trade Center),* falling with all the people that did not come out of "Her"; and all the gold, silver, jewels, food, computers, (the evil inventions of the Devil), money, and many other riches, falling to be seen no more? Can you imagine how big the fire will be that will burn the great city, compared to Pat and Katy O'Leary's cow and the Chicago fire of 1871, which would look like a boy scout campfire in comparison? Can you imagine the greatness of the fire of Babylon City, compared to the fire that burned San Francisco, caused by an earthquake in 1906? "All the ship masters and sailors, and as many as trade by sea, stood afar off, and cried when they saw the smoke of her burning." (Revelation 18:17,18) The Statue of Liberty will fall just like the Philistines god Dagon. Only the Statue of Liberty will fall to be seen no more. The United Nations Headquarters will be destroyed in less than one hour. The New York Stock Exchange will go belly up. Central Park will be the home of devil spirits and every unclean and hateful bird called *buzzards*, which will eat the flesh of *queers, lizzies,* fornicators, dope heads, (legal and illegal), because the *buzzards* are scavengers that only eat dead things. All of the people that did not come out of "Her" were dead while they were alive. In "Her" was found the blood of prophets, and of holy ones, and all that were slain upon the earth." (Revelation 18:24)

<u>"Corn Shelling Time"</u> is going to cut right through to the chase, and leave out the most of the gory details of the vials of God's wrath and plagues being poured out; and the most of the bloody details that happens when the trumpets sound the preliminaries that eliminate some of the contestants of *"God's Super Bowl On A Sunday"*. Until the Super Bowl happens, God allows the destruction of the unbelievers that succumb to the deception of the beast and Anti Christ. All of the earth will be gathered by the angel with the sharp cycle. (Revelation 14:19) They will be thrown into the wine press of God with the exception of the ones that kept the word of Christ's patience, and He promised to keep them from the time of temptation. (Revelation 3:10)

Also the sun clothed woman that fled into the wilderness, where she has a place prepared of God, that they should feed her there a thousand two hundred and three score days. (Revelation 12:6) These are the Jews and the Gentiles that have been grafted into the vine by becoming holy, and becoming a Jew by adoption. All the holy ones all over the earth, (not saints, not "Christians", not the idol worshipers), the ones that keep the Commandments of God, and are covered by the blood of Christ, and are not ashamed to testify that they are joined to Christ Jesus, the Son of the Living God. These will flee into the wilderness and into Edom, Petra, Bozrah, Moab, and Ammon, and other refugees to escape the Anti Christ and the beast and his mark. God will feed them until the harvest, these holy ones that have come out of Babylon, either Mystery, or literal Babylon, which consists of the Great Whore, the Mother Catholic Church, and the Harlots, all churches, and all governments and all the glories of the kingdoms of the world will receive the promises of Christ Jesus. The holy ones are the ones that overcome the accuser of the brethren, Satan, by the blood of the Lamb, and by the word of their testimony; and they loved not their lives unto the death. (Revelation 12:11)

"Christians" and *church goers* cannot be in these holy ones, because they do not keep the Commandments of God; but they keep the commandments of men by not remembering the Sabbath Day to keep it holy. Instead they are allied with the Mother Whore, by worshiping the *Sunday* god, the same god that Herod called *Easter* in Acts 4:12. And most *church goers* and "Christians" deny the blood of Christ Jesus, which causes the death angel to pass over you. That was the sacrifice Christ Jesus gave the ultimate, called the Passover, not *Easter.* Churches are a mixture of Babylonianism and "Christians", both heathen. Just like their Mother Whore, "Christians" worship the *Christmas Tree* with a star or a statue of an angel on top of it, with images of other pagan symbols all around it, teaching the children lies about baby Jesus. Christ was a grown man that hung on a torture stake, a tree, and suffered all that pain for "Christians"; and they blaspheme Christ's name, and desecrate His gift of life by worshiping Babylonian idols, changing the *"T"* sign of the Pagan God Tammuz into a sign of the *cross,* which is <u>not</u> a holy word that God ever spoke.

A young man from a Baptist *Church* was sincerely trying to be a witness for the Baptist *Church*, he and his young wife, he was married to, when he was asked if he was a *saint*? His reply was, yes, I am a *saint*. This is another fallacy of the mother Whore that the hireling preachers will have to answer for. Every word that proceeds out of the mouth of God did not include, *church, saint, cross, "Christian", Easter, Christmas, Saint Valentine, Halloween, football, Hollywood, medication, (dope), or a bunch of other heathen practices that the Mother Whore and "Her" harlot churches promote:* All people that are living deliciously with all the riches of literal Babylon committing fornication, (idolatry), *sorceries, (medication dope)*, homosexuality, (men lying with men, women changing their natural use into that which is against nature), all kinds of unrighteousness. "Come Out of her: Jesus is calling out loud for you to come out from among all the above unrighteousness and be separate from the unclean thing and He will receive you." (II Corinthians 6:14 – 17) EKKLESIA, Called Out Ones. (n*ot church*)

Christ Jesus anointed Michael Duishka to plead with you by reiterating His last warning to "Come Out of "Her"! (Revelation 18:4) Just like my daddy's razor strop caused me to "Shell Down the Corn", (confess), God's Holy Spirit caused me to "Shell Down the Corn" to Him, (confess my sins). "He is faithful and just to forgive us our sins and to cleanse us from all unrighteousness (I John 1:9) "Today is the accepted time of salvation." Any way you slice it, right now is **"Corn Shelling Time"**.

THIS is an insert in the book, **"CORN SHELLING TIME"** and **MICHAEL DUISHKA** with some of his belief. The LORD CHRIST JESUS has blessed this slave of His, more abundantly than any of HIS **CHOSEN ONES,** because He called me to iterate His Love for you that He wrote in His Love Letters that perhaps you may have never read. Maybe you have speedily glanced over the love letters, and not have understood the depth of intimacy of His warmth, or maybe you did recognize His personal presence when He covered you with His Love. He will not leave you to fend for yourself in a world full of unclean spirits, aka devils, but He does not talk to you audibly, because He is Spirit, and talks in Spiritual language which you can only understand whenever you are by yourself, quite,and intently listening for a voice that comes out of your belly and you hear it with your conscience, and act on the belief of what you heard. If the thought comes into your mind and makes you think it is God talking, do not be deceived, it is not God, but it is the devil talking to you, telling you to do some evil thing that is not in the bible, where His love letters are found, YOU go hide your self in some secluded place and wait until you know it is the holy spirit of Christ filling you with HIS LOVE and His Spirit. Michael Duishka thought he knew how God works and just how it would happen. WRONG!!! God let Michael Duishka know He,(GOD), was running things, and that the way He does things are past finding out. Here is an Oklahoma guarantee, but better than that here is Christ's WORD **" I will not leave you comfortless: I will come to you"**. JOHN 14:18 DUISHKA is nothing, CHRIST is EVERYTHING!

Chapter 33

"God's Super Bowl on a Sunday" is the culmination of the mystery of iniquity that has been working and escalating ever since that wicked one, (Satan), has rebelled against God Almighty, (PANTAKRATOR), "whose coming is after the working of Satan with all power, and signs, and lying wonders, and with; all deceivableness of unrighteousness in them that perish, because they received not the love of the Truth, (Christ Jesus), that they might be saved." (2 Thessalonians 2:9,10) The Super Bowl is for all the marbles, which is a match up of the Mystery of Iniquity against the Mystery of Godliness. The winner has already been revealed, although the deceived ones do not believe the Word. The KING of kings and LORD of lords is the winner and champion of all righteousness. Duishka calls the up and coming event, ***"God's Super Bowl On A Sunday",*** which is something made up and manufactured by Duishka. God's Word plainly calls the place in the Hebrew tongue **Armageddon.**

God has been merciful and long suffering for over two thousand years, pleading with His ignorant people to come out of "Her", which is Mystery, Babylon. God is Spirit, but He manifested Himself in the flesh through Christ Jesus, which was the Word; "and the Word was made flesh and dwelt among us." (John 1:14) God sent all His prophets of old to warn and plead with His people; and they killed all the prophets. God sent His only begotten Son to plead with His people, and they killed Him. They killed God in the flesh. Then God sent His Holy Apostles and prophets to plead with His people; and they killed them. Now He has sent Michael Duishka to warn and plead with His people to come out of "Her", Babylon; and **?** What will happen to him**?** Brother Paul said: "Having made known unto us the mystery of His will according to His good pleasure, He has proposed in Himself." (Ephesians 1:9)

Before the Super Bowl there are many preliminaries that God lets His armies, which are all the hosts of heaven and earth, work for Him. "Christ Jesus is God manifested in the flesh." (1Timothy 3:16) When the religious people killed Christ Jesus, (God), they started killing all the apostles. When they had killed the prophets and apostles, they proceeded to kill the written Word of God. There was an Emperor named Constantine, who was the sovereign ruler of the Roman Empire, who was the ruler of the whole inhabited world at that time. He was compromising Babylonian worship and so called Christianity, and adopted the Babylonian gods and beliefs, that are still active in the world at this present time. God, (Christ Jesus), could foresee, and He told His Apostle John to warn the people of God to come out of "Her", Babylon; but they would not. God has warned His people of the plagues they will receive if they continue to sin and continue in iniquity, which is a mystery. The Word of God plainly tells what iniquity is: Iniquity is lawlessness, breaking the Ten Commandments, which is the Law of God. The bottom line is, iniquity is sin. **+**For sin is the transgression of the law.(1John 3:4)

Jesus foretold the beginning of sorrows in (Matthew 24:8), which are earthquakes, wars, famines and pestilences, which bring diseases, and are diseases. Duishka told about the escalation of all of these sorrows in a book called, "Please Do Not Call Me A "Christian". The book tells about the abounding rate of iniquity that causes the abounding escalation of woe occurring all over the universe.

Now, this book, **"Corn Shelling Time"**, is reiterating the warning to come out of the Mystery of Iniquity, (lawlessness), before the *Super Bowl,* because the door of God's mercy and grace will be closed at the time of that event. All that wait until that gathering will be people that have committed the unpardonable sin, which is unbelief, sinning against the Holy Spirit. The sorrows are increasing so fast, that it will be hard to discern when the plagues of the trumpets and vials begin, because the wars are happening all over; and the earthquakes are preparing the earth for the big quake that will be the last one. The little tremors happening in Oklahoma have caused Oklahoma USA to be christened the Earthquake Capitol of the World, because there are so many tremors. Other warnings are happening in Oklahoma, such as the EF5 Tornado, May 20, 2013, that hit Moore, Oklahoma, killing and destroying.

There is not enough room in this book to name all of the fires, earthquakes, floods, and wind storms that God has allowed Satan to attack His people with. This writer is pleading with a people that does not want to be pleaded with. Many are committing the unpardonable sin. They are sinning against the Holy Spirit, and will be destroyed by the plagues that are happening as you read this. I pray that you are not one that says, "I do not want to be pleaded with, I do not want to know what God, or the Bible, or **"Corn Shelling Time"** is telling me." If you have your mind made up that you are bound for Hell, and you will have a lot of company, then you need to listen to what the Holy Spirit is saying to you, before you sin against the Holy Spirit. "Now the Spirit speaks expressly that in the latter times, *(last days)*, some shall depart from the faith, giving heed to seducing spirits, and doctrines *(teachings)* of devils, speaking lies in hypocrisy, having their conscience seared with a hot iron." (I Timothy 4:1,2)

Maybe you are one of a billion people that Michael Duishka wrote about in the book, "Please Do Not Call Me A "Christian", that go to the *harlot church,* and has called on the name of Jesus, and was baptized in water a dry sinner and came up out of the water a wet sinner; and say, "Well that is it, I am saved, and my preacher said once saved always saved." Maybe you even witness for your *harlot church* you are married to. Maybe you give some of your excessive filthy lucre to the Whore; and say, "Well the preacher and the board gives to the widow, the orphan, the hungry, the thirsty, the naked, the stranger, the sick, the prisoners, the poor;" but your conscience does not pull and draw you anymore. You feel like the *harlot church* covers your idolatry, you <u>think</u>, (dokeism), you are justified. Your conscience is seared. You are close to sinning the unpardonable sin. You are close to sinning against the Holy Spirit. Come out of "Her", confess, "Shell Down the Corn", repent, and see if God will save you before you become like America, come to the PNR, **Point of No Return**. What has been determined will be done. **"Corn Shelling Time"** is gleaning the scattered wheat from among the tares, that the harvesters missed, and storing it in God's garner, before He gathers the tares to bind them up and throw them into the fire.

When the angel looses the four angels bound in the Euphrates River, God's wrath has reached it's apex, and He starts His judgment on the entire world. The four elements, the angels over the fire, water, earth, and wind start their plagues with "the seas and waves roaring." (Luke 21:25) Distress of nations with perplexity, such as the tsunami, earthquakes, fires, tornadoes, floods, mud slides, and the sword. The tyrant rulers of America are God's sword against the ignorant people of God to punish them for voting for tyrants. The tornadoes, earthquakes, floods, and fires are to chastise the sinners that are living deliciously in iniquity, (lawlessness). "Jeshurun waxed fat and kicked." (Deuteronomy 32:15). The ObomaNation that is making America desolate is to plead with the deceived people to repent and turn back to God. But the nation as a whole has come to their PNR, (Point of No Return). **"Corn Shelling Time"** is a gleaner to rescue the souls the reapers missed: The ones that believe Jesus, and love Him, and keep His commandments, (*all of them, not just some of them*).

So God is going to bring evil on the people that are rebellious to His commandments, to the hypocritical nation of Israel (Jew) first, and He used the heathen to plead with them and to bring judgment upon them by the sword.

"The sixth trumpet sounded, and he was told to loose the four angels that are bound right now in the Great Euphrates River. In turn the four angels loose the four angels standing on the four corners of the earth, holding the four winds of the earth." (Revelation 7:1) The four angels in the Euphrates have been trained to kill a third part of men on the earth, because they were prepared to start their campaign for a year, and a month, and a day, and an hour. Brother John had not ever seen any atomic inventions, so he described these spirits as horses that had smoke, fire, and brimstone, *(sulphur)*, which were no doubt some kind of mechanical vehicle that shot projectiles that were like the fire and brimstone that destroyed Sodom and Gomorrah. Their power came out of their mouth and their tails. Not only did these two hundred thousand thousand kill one third of the men on earth, (Revelation 9:15), but Joel said, "The day of the Lord comes and is nigh at hand, a day of gloominess, a day of clouds, and of thick darkness. As the morning spread upon the mountains, a great people and a strong: there has not been ever the like, neither shall be any more after it, to the years of many generations. A fire devours before them, and behind them a flame burns the land as the garden of Eden before them, and behind them a desolate wilderness, and nothing shall escape them." (Joel 2:2,3) These are the angels of God, and they cannot be killed, because if they fall upon a sword, it will not hurt them. This is part of the destruction by fire. " And the rest of the men which were not killed by these plagues repented not of the works of their hands, that they should not worship devils, and idols of gold, and silver, and brass, and wood, and of stone, which neither can see, nor hear, nor walk. Neither repented they of their murders, nor of their *sorceries, (drugs)*, nor of their fornication, nor of their thefts." (Revelation 9:20,21) Not only are the supernatural forces of heaven going to fight against the Jews, but also "God said I will gather all nations, *(Gentiles)*, against Jerusalem to battle; and the city shall be taken, and the houses rifled, and the women ravished, and half of the city shall go forth into captivity; and the residue of the people shall not be cut off from the city." (Zechariah 14:2,3) "In that day I will make Jerusalem a burdensome stone for all people: All that burden themselves with it shall be cut in pieces. Though all the people of the earth be gathered together against it, behold I will make Jerusalem a cup of trembling unto all the people round about, when they shall be in the siege both against Judah and against Jerusalem." (Zechariah 12:2,3)

"Behold evil shall go forth from nation to nation, and a great whirlwind (hurricane, tornado, cyclone), shall be raised up from the coasts of the earth. And the slain of the Lord shall be at that day from one end of the earth even unto the other end of the earth: They shall not be lamented, neither gathered, nor buried, they shall be dung upon the ground.. Thus saith the Lord of Hosts." (Jeremiah 25:32,33)

God said whoever blesses Israel, He will bless them, but whoever curses Israel, He will curse them. Listen! Brother "BiBi", what has been determined will be done, so your prophet Daniel said. There are a lot of believers that are praying to Christ Jesus for you and your people, Israel, even though the king of Babylon, the President of these *NewNited States*, seems to be allied with Hamas and Iran; and the heathen democrats are turning against Israel; but God said He would gather all the nations of the earth against Jerusalem; and that is the way it will be. But Brother, BiBi, **"Corn Shelling Time"** is praying for you and your wife, Sara, and family to call on the name of Christ Jesus, so you and your house will be saved, in the Name of Christ Jesus, (Acts 16:31), the Messiah of Israel. King David believed Him.

(Ezekiel 38) Ezekiel turned his face toward heaven and prophesied to Gog. This is why people are miserable, wretched, and poor, and blind, and naked is because they are soulish, (natural), even the educated commentators do not know that Gog is a spirit that rules the children of Japheth; and he, (Gog), has been ruling the kings of Magog, which have a lot of princes, *(rulers)* over Meshech and Tubal; but Gog is the Chief Spirit over all of the descendants of Japheth. He is the spiritual ruler over the natural sons of Japheth, which are Gomer, and Magog, and Javan, and Tubal, and Madai, and Meshech, and Tiras, and also Togarmah, the grandson of Noah. And when all of the natural kings of the earth gather together at *"God's Super Bowl On A Sunday"*, these spiritual rulers that work for the dragon (Satan) and the beast, the angel out of the bottomless pit are the ones that are the three unclean spirits like frogs that come out of the mouth of the dragon, and the mouth of the beast, and out of the mouth of the false prophet. "For they are the spirits of devils, working miracles, which go forth unto the kings of the earth and of the whole world to gather them to the battle of that great day of God Almighty, (PANTAKRATOR)." (Revelation 16:13,14) Not only do these spirits go to tell Gog to bring the fleshly kings of Meshech and Tubal to the main event; but these are the hooks God puts in Gog's jaws to turn him back, and bring him to the battle. (Ezekiel 38:4) Also, brother BiBi, your nemesis, Iran, which God called Persia, will come over to your land with the kings of Gog, which will be the ten nations of the European Union, and all the land of Magog, which I believe to be Russia, Germany, France, Greece, Poland, Romania, Italy, Ukraine, Belgium, and possibly England, possibly Turkey. (Ezekiel 38:4,5,6) tells Gog to bring all his allies with him, Persia, which is modern day Iran, also one of your enemies, Ethiopia *(with Uganda)*, and Libya with them, Gomer and all his bands, the house of Togarmah, which could be Turkey, and Syria. The unclean spirits go forth to every nation of the world, including Babylon, which I believe to be *America the ugly*, and the Great City, *New York City*. America was once like the Garden of Eden, but the destroyer has turned it into desolation. That was then and this is now.

The dragon, the beast, and the other beast, called the false prophet, know they are losing the warfare with the Jews and the believers of Christ Jesus, so they send three unclean spirits like frogs to summon all the rulers of principalities, powers, the rulers of darkness of this world, spiritual wickedness in high places, which all of these wicked spirits that control the kings, presidents, prime ministers and all rulers of the world will cause these rulers of the world to gather against God and His Holy Spirit filled believers, that are possessors of the generated Spirit of God from above. "Christians" are professors of the Spirit of God. Believers are possessors of the Holy Spirit of God generated (An'othen) from above. (John 3:3) Not born again. An'othen does not mean again. You must be gennao an'othen, generated from above, *(not born again)*

The spirit of Gog brings all of his armies, the spirits of Persia, *(which is modern day Iran)*, along with all of his armies and allies, like Libya and America the ugly with all of it's armies and all of the United Nations with their armies; and World War III erupts world wide; but mostly in Israel, which is Jacob's trouble. (Jeremiah 30:7) All of these kings with their armies march into Israel, which is so small that they cannot hold all of the armies of the earth, so the World War III begins with the beast and his false prophet setting the statue, *(the abomination that makes desolate)*, that we find Daniel spoke of in his book. The beast and the Anti Christ are synonymous, and the dragon gave him his power, and his seat, and great authority. (Revelation 13:2) The beast has his seat in the Holy Place in Jerusalem. But other kingdoms are vying for the dominance of the One World Government, plus the Jews are still fighting to take back their country; and God is not going to intervene until the Jews drink the cup of the fierceness of God's wrath for rejecting God. So God allows the Gentiles, which are ruled by the dragon, Satan, Devil, that old serpent, to chastise Israel until only a remnant is left of the Jews. "Behold the day of the Lord comes; and when it does your spoils shall be divided in the midst of you." (Zechariah 14:1) "For I will gather all nations against Jerusalem, *(World War III)*; and the city shall be taken, and the houses riffled, and the women ravished, and half of the city shall go forth into captivity, and the residue of the people shall not be cut off from the city." (Zechariah 14:2)

"Blow ye the trumpet in Zion, and sound an alarm in My holy mountain; let all the inhabitants of the land tremble." (Joel 2:1) "I will also gather all nations and bring them down into the Valley of Jehoshaphat, and will plead with them there for my people and for My heritage, Israel, whom they have scattered among the nations and parted My land." (Joel 5:2) This parting of God's land, Israel, is happening at this present time, as the Palestinians have gained consent from Babylon; to make it a two state land, thus Palestine and Israel. Multitudes, multitudes in the valley of decision, for the day of the Lord is near in the valley of decision, (*AKA "God's Super Bowl On A Sunday"*. The valley of Jehoshaphat is the valley of decision, the mountain of Megiddo with the valley of Megiddo is **Armageddon**, which is God's Arena for the great battle. The Great Euphrates River is dried up when the sixth angel pours out his vial, and the way is prepared for the Kings of the east to fight against the Anti Christ. The Anti Christ has his body possessed with the spirit of the beast who gets his power and authority from the dragon, and the Anti Christ is the ruler of the ten nations of the European Union; also it is allied with the armies of Magog, which are ruled by the Spirit Gog. These are the devil spirits fighting against each other trying to take the spoils of the world, and the smallest country of the world, Israel.

Christ Jesus and all His host and different armies will not intervene to save any seed of Jacob, (Israel), until all of the sodomites, (*queers*), have been annihilated from Jerusalem. He will not intervene until all of the evil ones are eradicated from Jerusalem, that He has given an alias of Sodom and Egypt. (Revelation 11:8). Lord Jesus will not come to the rescue of Israel until all the city shall be taken and the houses riffled, and the women ravished. After the Lord God has brought evil upon His city that carries His name, Jerusalem, then He will bring a sword upon all of the inhabitants of the earth. (Jeremiah 25:29)

He starts at the *Great Babylon City of New York City, USA*. "And Great Babylon came in remembrance before God, to give unto "Her" the cup of wine of the fierceness of His wrath." (Revelation 16:19) This is the same cup that Jerusalem has already drunk, and now all nations must drink. By this time the land of beauty has turned into a land of desolate waste. The ObomaNation of Desolation has manifested into a land of filth and corruption. The people of God have already come out of "Her"; and "the Holy Ones have already overcome him (the devil, Satan, dragon, that old serpent, the accuser of our brethren), by the blood of the Lamb, and by the word of their testimony; and they loved not their lives unto the death." (Revelation 12:11) The beautiful has turned ugly. The amber waves of grain have turned into tares, and concrete jungles. The grace of God that Katharine Lee Bates said God shed on her back in 1913 has turned into a curse. The only ones left in Babylon at this time are the ones that have the mark of the beast, and so called "Christians", and politicians. The world is at World War III, and America has become the habitation of devils. (Revelation 18:2). God is avenging the blood of the heroes that the war mongering presidents sacrificed for their gain. God is telling you to reward "Her" double as she rewarded you. (Revelation 18:6) God not only brings a sword against "Her"; but He puts His elements in action; and "She" shall be utterly burned with fire: for the Lord is strong who judges "Her". (Revelation 18:8)

"The ten horns on the beast are ten kings which shall hate the Whore, *(Catholic Church)*, and shall make "Her" desolate, and naked, and shall eat "Her" flesh, and burn "Her" with fire. (Revelation 17:16) "And the cities of the nations fell." (Revelation 16:19) By this time in the World Clock, it has come to two minutes before 12:00 O ' Clock.

The whole world is full of Sodomites, *(Queers)*, and the last vials having the last plagues by this time have been poured out; and the *queers* and their partners are in much pain with aids, begging to die, seeking death and death flees from them. They should sue God for discrimination;. The last plagues the angels pour out are diseases that there are no cure for. The foremost city for homosexuals *(queers)* is San Francisco or Saint Petersburg, Florida. San Francisco will be buried by the earthquake. Saint Petersburg will be leveled by the whirlwind. All manner of sin and idolatry are being committed at this time; and nuclear warfare is being used to destroy and burn all of God's creation with atomic bombs exploding and weapons that cause the elements in the air to cause fire to fall from heaven. "And he, (the 2nd beast) does great wonders, so that he makes fire come down from heaven on the earth in the sight of men; and deceives them that dwell on the earth by those miracles which he had power to do in the sight of the beast, saying to them that dwell on the earth, *(that is you)*, that they should make an image to the beast, which had the wound by a sword and did live. And he had power to give life unto the image of the beast, that the image of the beast should both speak, and cause that as many as would not worship the image of the beast should be killed. And he causes all both small and great, rich and poor, free and bond, to receive a mark in their right hand or in their foreheads; and that no man might buy or sell, save he that had the mark, or the name of the beast, or the number of his name. Here is wisdom, let him that has understanding count the number of the beast, for it is the number of a man; and his number is six hundred threescore and six, (666)." (Revelation 13:12-18)

At this time the last plagues are so great and so many that the atomic warfare would destroy all flesh. **"Except those days should be shortened, there should no flesh be saved; but for the elects' sake those days shall be shortened".** (Matthew 24:22)

The Lord said if you have a dream, tell it like a dream: Duishka has told you that he is not an apostle, or a prophet; but that he is not deceiving himself, he is nothing. God sent Duishka to reiterate the warnings and prophesies of what the brothers have already prophesied. But God did give Duishka a dream that went like this: I was standing inside of a fenced in area of the great Air Force Base in Oklahoma City, Oklahoma, which is also called Tinker field. In the dream I looked up and behold I saw three bombs descending in the form of a triangle. Each bomb had a parachute attached to it that caused it to descend slowly. I started to run; but I said to myself, "It is too late to run now." I never saw the bombs explode or even land, but this was a night vision that was too plain to be from eating a big pickle; and I know that the devil would not warn you. So I kept the vision in my heart until now. Then the scene in the vision changed to a huge building that looked as though a bomb had gutted it, by that I mean all of the windows, doors, wall and all of the contents were gone. Then coming into the building where I was standing, there were a number of uniformed soldiers with automatic weapons; and I started to run; but another group of soldiers were coming in the opening of the building I was going to run out. These soldiers captured me and took me prisoner. They did not shoot me, because I surrendered. These soldiers were all Caucasians of the white race; but they spoke with a language that was foreign to me. This was a night vision I believe to be from Christ Jesus; but I will not attempt to interpret it, for there is too much room for error. Duishka told it as a dream. You can interpret it the way you see it. (1st Duishka). This is just a theory, but I thought this was three atomic bombs coming down in the form of a triangle, meaning three different cities, with Oklahoma City, Oklahoma, being one of the three. These were the sons of Japheth taking Americans prisoners.

God sent me to be His scribe and remind His people to come out of the Mystery, Babylon, which is the iniquity of this world, and to rebuke Satan, the author of confusion, which is Babylon, in the name of Christ Jesus. **"Corn Shelling Time"** is what God told me to write. He also told me to write the book that is already published, called "Please Do Not Call Me A "Christian". I was obedient and wrote them; but I do not have enough money to display the books on the market. I believe God has a brother or sister into Christ Jesus, with enough money to help market these books. I believe God has a person reading this book **"Corn /Shelling Time"** that needs to get rid of some of their filthy lucre and will help promote this book to spread God's Word world wide. Anyway that is only if the Holy Spirit of God lays it on your heart to do it. Remember how hard it is for a rich man or woman to enter into the kingdom of heaven. "Go to now, you rich men weep and howl for your miseries that shall come upon you, your riches are corrupted, and your garments are moth eaten. Your gold and silver is cankered; and the rust of them shall be a witness against you, and shall eat your flesh as it were fire. You have heaped treasure together for the last days." (James 5:1,2,3) This is the last days, and you need to repent of your greedy ways, and "Shell Down the Corn" to Christ Jesus, (confess your sins), and miss the plagues of the cup of God's fierceness of His wrath, and "bring forth therefore fruits meet for repentance." (Matthew 3:8) But God does not want you to help Him promote this book if you came by your riches by illegal gains, or by stealing or robbing your neighbor. Maybe you want to do like Zacchaeus the chief among publicans; and you are rich; and you are seeking the kingdom of God and His righteousness, which is Christ Jesus. (Matthew 6:33) Zack climbed a Sycamore tree to see Jesus. **"Zacchaeus, make haste, and come down, for today I must abide at your house."** So you be like Zacchaeus and receive Christ into your house and your heart and confess to Jesus, and "Shell Down the Corn"; and Christ Jesus will say to you. **"This day is salvation come to this house, forsomuch as he also is a son of Abraham, for the Son of Man is come to seek and save that which was lost."** (Luke 19:2-10) So if the Lord lays it on your heart to promote **"Corn Shelling Time" and "Please Do Not Call Me A "Christian"**, leave your phone number or your email address with the Publishing Company, and Duishka will contact you, or any other method of contact you might have. Do not try to contact me unless God quickens you. God would have to speak to your Spirit, (heart), for me to accept.

And now I have told you most of the preliminaries that will qualify you for *buzzard bait* at God's Arena; or if you have repented, and "Shelled Down the Corn", (confessed your sins), you will qualify to ride on a <u>white</u> horse with Jesus at *"God's Super Bowl On A Sunday"*.

Father God in the name of Christ Jesus I pray fervently for the one that reads **"Corn Shelling Time"** or "Please Do Not Call Me A

"Christian" by Michael Duishka, and Mavis agrees with me that you will save them from the top of their head to the soles of their feet and make them whole. Father baptize them with Your Holy Spirit and with fire according to Your promise. Anoint them Father and give them the power and wisdom to bind and loose according to (Matthew 18:18,19), and cause them to be a witness for You. In The Name Of CHRIST JESUS Mavis and I agree and SAY AMEN!

THIS is an insert in the book, **"CORN SHELLING TIME"** and **MICHAEL DUISHKA** with some of his belief. **"And again I say unto you, that if two of you shall agree on earth as touching anything that they shall ask, it shall be done for them of my Father which is in heaven"**. (Matthew 18:19) It is this writer's belief that there are not any two people in the entire world that can agree on what Jesus was talking about or who HE was talking to. First HE was talking to generated from above, blood bought disciples, that believed Him, not like the "Christians" in this present time, just believe in Jesus, but do not believe Him. Jesus was not talking about agreeing on the things of this world, because the things of this world belong to the ruler of this world, which is Satan. Since Jesus' Father which is in heaven does not own anything of this world, The Father cannot give away something that does not belong to Him. The only thing in this world that belongs to The Father is life, which Jesus and His disciples were ONE that were joined together in conjunction by the HOLY SPIRIT. But the ones that are joined to a harlot are one flesh, who are walking around dead, and they are the property of Satan, So what agreement has the temple of GOD with idols? (2 Corinthians 6:16). That is the reason not any two can agree as touching anything is because all the "Christians" are in some way or another in agreement with some kind of idol. To mention some forms of idolatry there is Television, Computers, Hollywood, Sex idols, Politics, Sports, Wars, Automobiles, Cycles, Boats, Fornication, Sodomy, (*Queers, & Lizzies*), Adultery, Family member's accomplishments, Voting, *Church*, Pride, Jealousy, Covetousness, SIN, just to name a few things of this world that God does not own. Here are some of the things God does own and can give to the Holy Ones that belong to Him. If you are into Him, you are joined to Him by His HOLY SPIRIT and you and Jesus and GOD are ONE SPIRIT, so you can agree for anything Spiritual, such as Salvation, which means you are being saved in your body, Soul, and SPIRIT. You can agree for any of the promises Christ Jesus made, such as being baptized with The HOLY GHOST and FIRE. (Matthew 3:11). Then after you have received power from on high, you are qualified to agree on the promise where Jesus said: **Behold I give unto you power to tread on serpents and scorpions, and over all the power on the enemy: And nothing by any means shall hurt you.** (Luke 10:19). And you can agree on the promise of the spirit of TRUTH: **"Howbeit when HE, the SPIRIT of TRUTH, is come, HE will guide you into all TRUTH. For He shall not speak of himself: but whatsoever He shall hear, *that* shall He speak; and He will show you things to come".** (John 16:13) But you must remember that these gifts He gave to you are not for you to be selfish and puffed up with pride, but on the contrary, they are for your neighbor's benefit so you can cast out devils that is making your neighbor sick, or depressed, or oppressed, or possessed with serpents, or scorpions, or any uncleanness that is a result of unclean spirits. How the gift of the HOLY SPIRIT will help you is HE will lead you, and teach you, and guide you into ALL TRUTH, which is cause for you to remember the WORD JESUS spoke. **"It is the SPIRIT that quickens; the flesh profits nothing: the words that I speak unto you *they* are SPIRIT and *they* are LIFE".** (John 6:63). But the anointing, (HOLY SPIRIT) which you have received of HIM abides in you, and you need not that any man teach you. But as the same anointing, (HOLY SPIRIT) teaches you of all things, and is truth, and is no lie, and even as HE has taught you, you shall abide in HIM. (1 John 2: 27). NO man taught me anything, The anointing I received from HIM taught DUISHKA: Can anyone agree with me?

Chapter 34

"GOD'S SUPER BOWL ON A Sunday" is the last event of this age. It is the finale of the Mystery of God, when the seventh trumpet sounds. "But in the days of the voice of the seventh angel, when he shall begin to sound, the Mystery of God should be finished, as He has declared to His servants the prophets." (Revelation 10:7)

The scene that starts the movie is so spectacular and colorful that the splendor cannot be duplicated by carnal man's imagination. The colors in heaven are so magnificent because there is nothing black whatsoever in the third heaven. The most beautiful colors that the natural people on earth have never seen. Beautiful pastels and chartreuse like had just adorned the festivities of the "Marriage Supper of the Lamb, where the wife of the Lamb has made herself ready and was granted that she should be arrayed in fine linen, clean and white. For the fine linen is the righteousness of the Holy Ones." (Revelation 19:8)

Brother John is the one telling this story. In fact Brother John, the Revelator, is the narrator of all the events that lead up to *"God's Super Bowl On A Sunday"* down on earth in the arena called the Valley of Decision. Brother John is the color man of this great event. But right now the scene on the movie screen changes; and Brother John said: "And I saw heaven opened, and behold a white horse; and He that sat upon him was called faithful and true; and in righteousness He does judge and make war." (Revelation 19:11) "His eyes were as a flame of fire, and on His head were many crowns; and He had a name written, that no man knew, but He Himself. And He was clothed in a vesture dipped in blood: (figuratively blood of grapes), And His Name is called the **WORD** of God. And the armies which were in heaven followed Him upon white horses, clothed in fine linen, white and clean. And out of His mouth goes a sharp sword, that with it He should smite the nations (Gentiles), and He shall rule them with a rod of iron, and He treads the wine press (blood of grapes) of the fierceness and wrath of Almighty God (PANTAKRATOR). And He has on His vesture and on His thigh a Name written, KING OF kings, AND LORD OF lords." (Revelation 19:12 – 16)

Where He received all of these crowns and names was at His wedding, where the Father God bestowed upon Him His awards and rewards. Also at this banquet is where all the resurrected Holy Ones receive their crowns and awards and rewards and thrones. "And he said unto me, write "Blessed are they which are called unto the Marriage Supper of the Lamb"; and he said unto me, "These are the true sayings of God." (Revelation 19:9)

God gave Michael and Mavis Duishka the authority to call you to this supper. We are officially inviting you to come to the Marriage Supper of the Lamb; and God will recognize this as a bonafide invitation. Amen!

The one mounted upon the white horse is going to make war with the dragon and the beast that were persecuting the sun clothed woman and her man child. She was given two wings of a great eagle that she might fly into the wilderness, where she is nourished for a time, and times, and half a time from the face of the serpent, which is equivalent to forty two months, or three and one half years.(Rev. 12:6).

"Come near you nations, (Gentiles), to hear, and hearken, you people: Let the earth hear, and all that is therein, the world, and all things that come forth of it. For the indignation of the Lord is upon all nations, (Gentiles); and His fury upon all their armies. He has utterly destroyed them. He has delivered them to the slaughter. Their slain also shall be cast out, and their stink shall come up out of their carcases, and the mountains shall be melted with their blood. For My sword shall be bathed in heaven. Behold it shall come down upon Idumea, and upon all the people of My curse, to judgment." (Isaiah 34:1 – 5) Idumea is one of the places where the sun clothed woman flees to, and Satan and his armies, called the dragon, and serpent, who persecutes the woman which has run to many places on earth; but the first place Jesus told His believers to flee to was the wilderness, which was Idumea in Israel south of the Dead Sea. The repented Jews, and the repented Gentiles, that have been grafted into the Olive Tree, which is the remnant of the Jews that repented. (Romans 11:19) This woman flees into Idumea first, and then into Edom, which is where Bozrah is located. So this is where the Lord starts His campaign with His sword coming down with a great slaughter of the dragon's armies in Idumea. "Then He, the Lord, has a sacrifice in Bozrah, which is a place in Edom, where God's people are being persecuted by the serpent. But the One that sits on the <u>white</u> horse with His armies brings down His sword, which was bathed in heaven on the armies of the dragon and protects His people in the wilderness of Idumea and Bozrah." (Isaiah 34:5)

All of the previous plagues that are being poured out world wide on all people, that God has cursed, should cause them to repent; but instead of repenting, they only blaspheme God more. When they find out that Christ Jesus has a "Super Bowl On A Sunday" the heathen join the armies of the kings of the world, so they can go fight against God and His armies. You judge who is gonna win. The plagues are being manifested as you are reading this book, and will continue to intensify until you be destroyed by the sword, or by the diseases, or by one of the four elements of God. Except you Repent!

The fools that do not know Christ Jesus and do not believe Him just keep on loud mouthing for their right to sin, and march, and protest against righteousness, so they can kill, steal, and destroy: Voicing to the highest decibel of sound, "We want justice;" and they will get just what they are asking for at the Great White Throne Judgment. Jesus said there would be weeping and gnashing of teeth, and I believe Him, do you?

World War III has already begun, and will grow more intense to the point where "all the people that have fought against Jerusalem, their flesh shall consume away while they stand upon their feet, and their eyes shall consume away in their holes, and their tongue shall consume away in their mouth." (Zechariah 14:12) This is what happened on August 6, 1945, to Hiroshima and Nagasaki Japan, when the United States of America dropped the first atomic bomb on these cities and made these cities desolate. So get ready America, whoever lives by the sword shall die by the sword, "whatsoever a man sows, that shall he reap." (Galatians 6:7)

Every individual that is reading this writing has a choice to either believe what **"Corn Shelling Time"** reiterates from God's Truth, (Jesus), or a choice of Satan, not to believe God's Truth, (Jesus). If you believe the Truth, (Jesus), and do what He says, you will live forever, His promise: If you do not believe, you have chosen to commit the unpardonable sin, which is believing the lie Satan told Eve, "You will not surely die." You **will** surely die. Listen! You have the right to choose right now, either what everybody is doing and be damned, or choose to come out from among everybody and separate yourself from the masses and be a loner, and reject what your peers and friends tell you and what they do, before you reach the PNR, (Point of no Return), and sin against the Holy Spirit. Whichever way you choose right now is a choice to die or live. If you say I will think about it, and make a decision later, you just made your choice to die. If you choose to live you must forget what your misguided people tell you, and do what the Truth, (Jesus), tells you. "Repent", which means quit sinning. Quit having illicit sex. Quit being friends with everybody. Jesus said He is the only friend you need. Do not vote. If you vote, you are voting for Satan. Do what (I John 2:26,27) says. Do not get advice from a "Christian" or any of mankind. That is what the scripture, Truth, (Jesus), says. That is the commandment Michael Duishka obeyed and no man taught him anything, only the anointing that he received of Him. The Truth, (Jesus), lives in Duishka, and Duishka needed not that any man teach him anything. But as the same anointing, (Holy Ghost), teaches me of all things and is Truth, (Jesus), and is no lie, and even as He has taught me, I shall abide, (Live), in Him. If you made a choice right now to live, it is necessary, imperative for you to obey the Commandments of God, who is Christ Jesus, who is the **WORD**, who is the Holy Spirit. (I John 2:27). If you do not choose to live under the yoke of Christ Jesus right now, that means you chose to die under the yoke of Satan, yoked to unbelievers, idolators, fornicators, sorcery *(drugs)*, doctrines *(teachings)*, of devils, and obeying the rulers of darkness of this world, which is filth and abomination of this world. Warning! You are headed to PNR, (Point of no Return), the unpardonable sin, which is unbelief, which is sinning against the Holy Spirit.

Listen! Pay close attention! If you are white or black and march for equal rights, you are lost, and separated from God, because that is why the Arch Angel Lucifer got kicked out of heaven for wanting equal rights to be equal with the Most High God. (Isaiah 14:14) Do you think that you can march with the blacks and cause a diversion for the devils that loot, kill, steal, burn and destroy other people's property? I trow not. "Your rewards will be according to your works." (II Corinthians 11:15) You will no doubt be *buzzard bait.* Oh me!

Blood is thicker than water, meaning the black president is biased against any Jew, or any Caucasoid, which is of the white race. He *(the president)* is not only a racist, he is allied with every anti "Christian" commandment of the Quran; or so it has been said. This is only the belief of Duishka. I believe "he is wearing out the Holy Ones of the

Most High and thinks to change the times and the laws." (Daniel 7:25) I believe he has appointed foreigners to the bible, to infiltrate the Supreme Court; and the justices have violated the Constitution, The Bill of Rights, and the Amendments. He has allowed terrorists to serve in our armed forces, until terrorists massacre real Americans. I believe he is appointing Muslims, blacks, and every white turncoat he can to his cabinet of Apostate Americans, so he can have their support to try to be a dictator. I believe God Almighty, (PANTAKRATOR) has allowed, the enemy of God and God's people to be the Extortioner which will come to an end. (Isaiah 16:4)

Duishka can only warn God's people with this pen. He cannot get into politics and expose the corrupt rulers of the world physically; but he can expose them with the finger of God, which is this pen. Rudy Guiliani said he did not think the president loved America. I agree with Guiliani. How could he love America and destroy all of the freedoms which the dead heroes gave their lives for, and turn this used to be land which was given to God's people into a land of ObomaNation of Desolation. This writer has seen all of the things that have eroded America into a nation of devils that rob, kill, and destroy. This writer cannot see any good thing that the president has done for the real American people or the country. This writer can see all of the freedoms that have been destroyed since he, Oboma, lied about what he would do that never happened. He gave all of his kind, *(black welfare recipients)* a license to commit crime; and after cities are looted, burned, and destroyed he has his appointed anti-Americans to make law abiding white people to resign or suffer the consequences. My God knows this is going on, and He is our *(American's)* King. The Satan run news media and the Satan led democrats, and the greedy lawyers, and the wimpy republicans have suppressed our freedom of speech, annulled the Amendments. No longer can a hunter have a gun if he has been convicted of any felony that he was falsely convicted of. The blacks can say anything as loud as they can holler; but if a white whispers anything that is not politically correct, he is put in prison or exiled from his own land. Example: Snowden, who exposed the traitors in our government of spying on American people and other countries of the world. Snowden is a patriot.

"Corn Shelling Time" is telling you what will happen to all of the enemies of God that have been mentioned above. They will be buzzard bait. Instead of people apologizing for telling the truth, they should use their speech which is not free any more to proclaim the truth. For example: There was some communist acting traitor Jew, that said "Guiliani" was trying to kindle a fire that had gone out. He had freedom of speech, but Guiliani was criticized for telling the truth. Rudy Guiliani should have kept on talking and exposed more of the president's anti American activities, and started a campaign, "Guiliani for president", on the independent ticket. By the time Duishka gets enough money to publish **"Corn Shelling Time"** all of these politicians will have changed in their stature and standings, and ?Duishka may have gone underground to dodge the King of Babylon, to show God's people more of the things that Christ Jesus said that are coming to pass. There are so many people that only read a little of the bible; and they only read what is free about "Please Do Not Call Me A "Christian" by Michael Duishka; and they do not read enough of **"Corn Shelling Time"** by Michael Duishka to be classified as a believer, because they do not know whom to believe.

I have received comments from people that said they would pray for me to get an answer to my question. In the first place, Duishka does not have any questions. In the second place, Duishka does not want you praying for him, because you do not know how to pray; and you do not know that Christ Jesus is the answer to every question. There are millions of professors that falsely profess that they know Christ Jesus; but there are only a few that are possessors, that are truly possessors of Christ Jesus. Possessors of Christ Jesus believe Him, *(not believe in Him)*. Possessors do not go to any kind of a doctor. Possessors do not take medicine of any kind. Possessors have Christ Jesus for an advocate, *(attorney)*. Possessors do not have guns for protection, because their big brother,(Christ Jesus) protects them. Possessors have no fear of men that can kill the body, but they fear God that can kill the spirit and soul. Possessors of Christ Jesus do not vote. Possessors do not join any kind of mobs of killers, such as police, army, navy, marines, air force, or any military service. Possessors of Christ Jesus do not break any of His commandments, such as desecrate the Sabbath day and worship the *Sun god* on *Sunday*. Possessors do not march with the heathen blacks that kill, steal, and destroy, loot and burn, and protest if one of the criminals gets killed, and holler "We want justice." Possessors of Christ Jesus do not partake in sodomy, fornication, idolatry, or whoredoms. Professors of Christ Jesus do all of the above sins and claim to be justified. They are unholy, and have little chance for the kingdom of God.

Duishka and his wife, Mavis, have no need of anything except more of Christ Jesus. But God has a need for someone that has an excessive amount of filthy lucre laid up to redeem their soul and promote **"Corn Shelling Time"** and {**Please Do Not Call Me A "Christian"** by advertising these books world wide, not to make money, but to promote God's **WORD** like He said unto them: **"Go ye into all the world, and preach the gospel to every creature. He that believes and is baptized shall be saved, but he that believes not shall be damned."** (Mark 16:15,16) This book and **"Please Do Not Call Me A "Christian"** are the only way Duishka can go into the whole world and preach the gospel, not for money or fortune or fame, but as an obedience to the Lord's commandment. You can be a partaker in preaching the gospel to the world and be a disciple of Christ, if you want to help promote God's **WORD** by buying ads on all the networks of the world or getting these books translated into foreign languages. God does not need you, but you need to show some fruits of repentance. (Matthew 3:8) If you do help, you will be able to flee from the wrath to come. Help spread the gospel of Christ Jesus. You can be a partaker in preaching the gospel of Christ Jesus by buying ads to promote **"Corn Shelling Time"** and **"Please Do Not Call Me A "Christian"** on the internet or any media; and you will build your treasure up in the Kingdom of

God. This is Friday the 13th, which is a bad luck day to superstitious "Christians"; but to this writer and to the rest of the sanctified, Holy Ghost filled believers, this is a day that is blessed, because we are alive, hallelujah! You may think this writer is wandering, but that is the way the bible does, it goes from one faith to another faith in one sentence: **The "wind blows where it will, and you hear the sound thereof, but you cannot tell from where it comes and where it goes. So is everyone that is generated with the Spirit from above."** (John 3:8) You, dear reader, be a possessor instead of a false professor. Cause this is the day that the **LORD** has made! (Psalms 118: 24)

Dear BiBi, I just saw on the headlines where you won the victory to keep your job as Prime Minister of Israel. Congratulations. You won in spite of all the evil spirits of Satan, that leads the news medias of the world, and the anti Christ, anti America, anti Israel, which includes the biggest part of the Democratic Party of America led by Obama. God, (Christ Jesus), is the One to give glory to, because it is a miracle that you won. Amen. Brother BiBi, you are a son of Abraham, and you have bought a little time for Israel, before *"God's Super Bowl On A Sunday"*, AKA, **Armageddon.** God said to Abram: "Get you into a land I will show you, and I will make you a Great Nation, *(Israel)*, and I will bless you and make your name great; and you shall be a blessing; and I will bless them that bless you; and I will curse him that curses you." (Genesis 12:1,2,3)

Michael Duishka and Mavis Duishka are two witnesses that bless you, because you are a seed of Abraham. God also told Abraham that in you shall all families of the earth be blessed. God was talking here about Abraham's seed, the Messiah, the Christ. (Genesis 12:3). So Brother Ben Netanyahu, you have a short time to be a blessing to your people; but first you have to believe Christ Jesus and love Him; Do not do like your forefathers did in the 30's A.D. And reject Him. You are my brother because you came from Shem. I came from Japheth; and your enemy, Obama, is a Canaanite that is from Ham that God cursed, because he went the way of Cain, that killed his brother Abel. Obama is your enemy and America's enemy; and he is going to try to get the UN to pull the support for Israel and give more support to your enemies, the Gentiles (Muslims). You must repent to Christ Jesus and "Shell Down the Corn and ask God (Yehovah) to forgive you of your sins in the name of Jesus, (Yashua). Shell Down the Corn, simply means, confess your sins to God, (Christ Jesus), who is faithful and just to forgive us our sins. (I John 1:9) Pay attention, Brother BiBi, and I will tell you what is going to happen to you and your beloved land of Israel. You or your next prime minister will enter into a peace treaty with the Gentiles, and Israel will build a holy place of worship and renew the old practice of offering up sacrifices of animals in the Holy Place, (Temple). The holy place is built for you by the coordinator of the peace treaty between Israel and the Gentiles. The coordinator will be someone that wins you over with flattery, by giving you many concessions and promises, which will all be false. Just like Obama did to the gullible Americans. Whoever this coordinator will be will come from the region of Syria or Turkey; and he will be the Anti-Christ. God calls him the Assyrian. God also calls him King of Babylon. He will seduce Israel with cajolery, (sweet talk), for three and one half years after the peace treaty is signed. He will cause **Craft** to prosper, and prosperity will flourish. At the end of three and one half years he will cause all the daily sacrifices to cease. He will set himself up in the Temple of God, showing himself that he is God. He opposes anyone that claims to be Godly and; and he exalts himself above all that is called God. This is the Word with the bark on it. This is revealing the Mystery, of iniquity, and MYSTERY, BABYLON. DUISHKA is just iterating the WORD of JESUS.

"Corn Shelling Time" is warning all people to repent and call on the name of Christ Jesus, so they can escape all these things that are coming on the whole world. It does not matter who is prime minister of Israel, or who is president of the *New Nited States of America*, whether you are a Jew or a Gentile, these things are double dog dead sure to happen, because God said they would. "For that, that is determined shall be done." (Daniel 11:36) "And the King (*of Babylon*) shall do according to his will, and he shall exalt himself, and magnify himself above every god, and shall speak marvelous things against the God of gods, and shall prosper until the indignation be accomplished. For that, that is determined shall be done." (Daniel 11:36)

So, Brother BiBi, God said through Noah that I, a Japhethite, was to serve you, a Shemite; and the only way I know how to serve you is to reiterate God's Word to you and Sara, and be telling you to read, and not only read, but believe and do what **"Corn Shelling Time"** instructs, and be transformed from death to life everlasting. If everyone that reads **"Corn Shelling Time"** will do what it instructs them to do, they will live forever in the Kingdom of God, instead of dying two times, and being cast into outer darkness forever, or being buzzard bait at *"God's Super Bowl On A Sunday"*, AKA, **Armageddon.**

Count from the day the peace treaty is signed, the wicked one will after 1260 days, forty two months, three and one half years cause all of the sacrifices to cease and tell the Israelites and all the world that he is god; and they are to worship him, the anti-Christ, who is calling himself god. At that time the peace treaty is broken, and Jacob 's trouble begins. Then you will know the Word that Christ Jesus spoke is <u>TRUTH</u> and is being manifested. **"For then shall be great tribulation, such as was not since the beginning of the world to this time, no, nor ever shall be; and except those days should be shortened, there should no flesh be saved; but for the elect's sake those days shall be shortened."** (Matthew 24:21,22).

After the three and one half years from the signing of the peace treaty, and the Jews are kicked out of their temple, the Anti-Christ that puts himself in the place of God, causes all people on earth, that do not have their names written in the Lamb's Book of Life to take a mark signifying they belong to the beast that receives his power from the dragon, which is Satan. (Revelation 13:2)

This writer puts some parenthetical passages in this non-fiction prophecy of Christ Jesus to warn the unbelievers and the ignorant people of God that are being destroyed by the thousands every day, and do not know how to say the Word that is nigh them even in their mouth, which is Jesus. (Romans 10:8)

This is so difficult to portray the significance of spiritual understanding and natural understanding. Also I have to be concerned about the consequences of God putting stripes on me, if I say one erroneous word. When the movie producer and the movie director portray the indescribable splendor and brilliance of the spiritual realm, it will make the movie, The Ten Commandments, appear vapid. Can you picture seven heavenly angels hearing a great voice out of the Temple in Heaven, saying to the seven angels, go your ways and pour out the vials of the wrath of God upon the earth? (Revelation 16:1)

Then Christ Jesus showed Brother John, *His Color man,* all of the affects and dis pleasures these vials of God's wrath had upon God's creation. These last plagues not only affected mankind with all kinds of grievous sores and pain, so they begged to die and gnawed their tongues, but they also destroyed the cattle of the fields and also the vegetation in the fields. These last plagues turned the waters of the sea, and the rivers, and the fountains of water into blood. These vials of God's wrath that these angels poured out, affected the four elements, the earth, fire, water, and the wind. The movie producer and the director of the movie would have to be very intellectual to create sights and sounds of all that Brother John saw and heard.

"And the Temple of God was opened in heaven, and there was seen in His Temple, *(the one in heaven)* the ark of His testament; and there were lightnings, and voices, and thundering, and an earthquake, and great hail." (Revelation 11:19) This verse of scripture is enough to keep a movie crew busy for a while.

These seven angels of God with the seven vials of God's wrath are just a small portion of all of the marvelous wonders that have already occurred and are occurring as this is being written and will occur with greater intensity.

The scene changes to the altar in the temple, which is the Master Altar of the replica that God showed Moses how to build in the tabernacle tent that Moses built, when the children of Israel came out of Egypt. (Exodus 17:15) "And Moses built an altar, and called it "Yehovah Nissi, (the Lord our Banner)". (Exodus 17:15)

"The angel that was over the offering of the Holy Ones' prayers, took much incense that was given him to put upon the altar out of a golden censer, which he did." (Revelation 8:3). "When the angel offered the incense out of the golden censer upon the golden altar, which was before the throne, the smoke of the incense, which came with the prayers of the Holy Ones, ascended up before God out of the angel's hand." (Revelation 8:4). "And the angel took the censer and filled it with fire of the altar, and cast it into the earth; and there were voices, and thundering, and lightnings, and an earthquake." Probably the same events that occurred in (Revelation 11:19).

The scene changed and Brother John saw the seven angels, which stood before God; and to them were given seven trumpets." (Revelation 8:2) After the first four trumpets sounded, which killed a third part of the trees and green grass by burning with fire, then a mountain of fire was cast into the sea; and the third part of the sea became blood. "And the third part of the creatures which were in the sea and had life died; and the third part of the ships were destroyed."

And a previous chapter describes the third angel sounding, and "a star burning as a lamp fell upon a third part of the rivers, and upon the fountains of waters, and the name of the star was called Wormwood; and many men died of the waters, because they were made bitter, (*poison*)."

"The fourth angel sounded; and the third part of the sun, and a third part of the moon, and a third part of the stars, so as a third of them were smitten; and a third part of them were darkened. And the day shone not for a third part of it; and the night likewise."

Then the scene changes; and Brother John said: "And I saw and heard an angel flying through the midst of heaven saying with a loud voice, "Woe, Woe, Woe, to the inhabiters of the earth by reason of the other voices of the trumpet of the three angels, which are yet to sound." (Revelation 8:3 – 13)

This writer believes that all of these plagues of ulcers that will come upon men, and they will beg to die is a result of nuclear warfare. Whenever Great Babylon came in remembrance before God, (Revelation 16:19), the Great City was divided into three parts, because an atomic bomb has been ignited right in Midtown Manhattan; and all the five boroughs, Manhattan, Staten Island, the Queens, Brooklyn, and the Bronx; not that it makes any difference what the three parts are, because the Great Babylon City, *New York City*, will receive "Her" judgment in one hour. (Revelation 18:10)

"All "Her" plagues will come in one day". (Revelation 18:8) The atomic bomb will cause the great earthquake to set off a tsunami that will cause the Great City to fall. (Revelation 18:21) The great earthquake will have a domino effect on all the fault lines of the earth, and cause the cities of the nations to fall; "And every island fled away, and the mountains were not found." (Revelation 16:19,20)

What **"Corn Shelling Time"** believes will happen is the Muslims will not rest until "the Great Babylon, *(New York City)*, is fallen, is fallen, and is become the habitation of devils, and the hold of every foul spirit, and a cage of every unclean and hateful bird. Therefore shall "Her" plagues come in one day, death, and mourning, and famine; and she shall be utterly burned with fire, for strong is the Lord God who judges "Her". (Revelation 18:2,8) The Islamic Muslims have bombed the World Trade Center two times and brought it to total destruction. But it has been rebuilt in a more magnificent splendor. But it is this writer's belief that a refuge for Muslim terrorists has been built within six hundred feet of ground zero, where the Twin Towers Trade Center was destroyed. This refuge for murderers is built in the name of religion, called a mosque. This mosque has been named Park 51, or P51. It is the opinion of this writer that all Muslims are terrorists, either active, or aid and abet. They are not subject to any rules of Christ Jesus, but only to the hallucinations of a demon possessed radical, that liberals say had a disorder of the nervous system, which history calls epilepsy. So it is this writer's observation that all Gentiles that do not believe Christ Jesus are filled with hate and possessed with evil spirits called demons. It is this writer's discernment that the mosque at 51 Park is designed to be a haven for Muslims that hate the *New Nited States of America* and are under oath to destroy New York City, the Great Babylon on this wise: They will set aside a portion of the mosque to assemble the bomb that will utterly destroy the Babylonian City in one hour. The Muslims will bring in components in suitcases in the name of religion, and in the name of Allah, until they have a bomb big enough to utterly destroy all of *New York City, the Great City of Babylon.* "And there followed another angel saying, "Babylon is fallen, is fallen." (Revelation 14:8)

"And the great city was divided into three parts. The bomb will be placed in the Mosque at Park 51, which is close to the World Trade Center. When the bomb is detonated with violence, it will divide the three islands, Manhattan Island, Staten Island, and Long Island, causing the great earthquake, such as was not since men were upon the earth, so mighty an earthquake, and so great. (Revelation 16:18) The idol Statue of Liberty on Liberty Island, AKA Ellis Island, will fall like the Philistine God Dagon, when they set God's Ark of the

Covenant by Dagon. Dagon fell and both of his hands were cut off. (I Samuel 5:4) The American Idol, the Statue of Liberty, will fall to be seen no more. Not only that, but the commerce faction of the world, the World Trade Complex, which boasts the tallest building in the western half of the earth will be brought down; and all of the smaller buildings in the center will fall to never be seen no more. The United Nation's Headquarters with it's 193 member countries will not function in world politics any more. The World Banks with the New York Stock Exchange will be a bigger crash than it was in 1929. Only this time, it will crash to be revived no more. This will end the monetary power of the whole world. "For in one hour so great riches is come to naught. Every ship master and all the company in ships, and sailors, and as many as trade by sea, stood afar off, and cried when they saw the smoke of "Her" burning, saying, "What city is like unto this great city?" *The reason they were crying was because they were greedy, and their goose that laid their golden egg was being cooked.* "How much She has glorified Herself and lived deliciously, but no more." (Revelation 18:7) Rejoice over "Her", you heaven, and you holy apostles, and prophets, for God has avenged you on "Her". *This is the Great Babylon that God remembered on His way to "God's Super Bowl On A Sunday".* "And a mighty angel took up a stone like a great millstone, and cast it into the sea, saying, "Thus with violence shall that Great City Babylon be thrown down, and shall be found no more at all." (Revelation 18:21,22)

This is "**<u>Corn Shelling Time's</u>**" belief. This is the only way Duishka knows how to expose the corruption of the festered up boil that is double dog dead sure to come to a head. The president of the *New Nited States of America* is knowingly or unknowingly allied with the Muslim Community making a bad deal with Iran, allowing them to make the bomb that will cause the Great Babylon City to fall. The wimpy republicans are too greedy to voice any opposition to the deal, because they are afraid they will lose their cover of milking the system. The news media and everybody that works for them are ruled by Satan and all his unseen evil spirits. "Satan is the

Prince, *(King)* of the Powers of the Air, the spirit that now works in the children of disobedience." (Ephesians 2:2) These unseen forces are not only working in the news media and the airways, but these demons possess every politician, all law enforcement, all Muslims, Islams, "Christians", voters, all professors, all politically correct liars, and everyone else that has a part with one that steals, kills or destroys.

These are all Anti-Christ, Anti-American, Anti-Life, and Anti-Constitutional, "because that when they knew God, they glorified Him not as God, neither were thankful, but became vain in their imaginations, and their foolish heart was darkened. Professing themselves to be wise, they became fools, and changed the glory of the incorruptible God into an image made like to corruptible man, and to birds, and four footed beasts, and creeping things. Wherefore God gave them up to uncleanness through the lusts of their own hearts to dishonor their own bodies between themselves: who changed the Truth of God into a lie, and worshiped and served the creature more than the Creator, who is blessed forever, Amen." (Romans 1:21,22,23,24,25) "For this cause God gave them up to vile affections, for even their women did change the natural use into that which is against nature; and likewise also the men, leaving the natural use of the woman, burned their lust one toward another, men with men working that which is unseemly, and receiving in themselves that recompense of their error which was meet; and even as they did not like to retain God in their knowledge, God gave them over to a reprobate mind, to do those things which are not convenient, being filled with all unrighteousness, fornication, covetousness, maliciousness, full of envy, murder, debate, deceit, malignity, whisperers, backbiters, haters of God, despiteful, proud, boasters, inventors of evil things, disobedient to parents, without understanding, covenant breakers, without natural affection, implacable, unmerciful; Who knowing the judgment of God, that they which commit such things are worthy of death, not only do the same, but have pleasure in them that do them." (Romans 1:26 – 32) They killed Brother Paul for saying these things; and **"Jesus said the slave is not greater than his Lord. If**

they kill me, they will deliver you up to be afflicted, and shall kill you. If they believe me, they will believe you."

But out of all of the above mentioned, there will be just a few believers. But praise God for the few that enter into eternal life. All of these sinners are the reason Babylon will be judged in one hour. The great earthquake will have a domino effect, and set off all the fault lines on the whole earth. There are not any real men left on this earth anymore, except men like Benjamin (BiBi) Netanyahu, Julian Assange, Edward Snowden, Ronald Reagan, who said "Government's first duty is to protect the people, not run their lives. Too late for Obama to learn. Richard Nixon was right on. Reagan said "When you can make them see the light, make them feel the heat." Reagan caused Iran to turn American hostages loose. Obama is giving them time to build a bomb, to bomb America.

The author of **"Corn Shelling Time"**, Michael Duishka, and his wife, Mavis Duishka, are slaves of Christ Jesus, and they do not expect to receive anything different from the heathen than their Lord Christ Jesus suffered, or anything different than all the prophets and apostles, except all of them were something, while the Duishka house is nothing. Duishka is not a prophet nor an apostle, nor a rabbi, but is only a witness for Christ Jesus. Mavis is the only woman I know that is an example of the woman in (Proverbs 31:10 – 31) She is worth more than rubies to me. God inspired Duishka to reiterate His Word through **"Corn Shelling Time"** so the rider on the *white* horse and His armies are on their way to *"God's Super Bowl On A Sunday"*, AKA, known as **ARMAGEDDON.**

This is an insert in the book, **"CORN SHELLING TIME"** and **MICHAEL DUISHKA** with some of his belief. There is a great apostasy, (falling away from the faith in GOD) all over the earth. But this is not to them, but rather to the ones that never did have any faith to fall away from. The ones that do not know what faith is. Duishka is not boasting or complaining, but only confessing that faith was an unknown word to him. Someone said have faith in God, next question, who is God? They would say put your trust in Jesus. Who was Jesus to put my trust in? JESUS is the SON of the living God. (Matthew 16:16) JESUS is GOD. Listen! I can tell you who God is till I am blue in the face, and you still will not know who God is. The reason is you cannot see GOD. You cannot hear God talk. The only way you will ever know God, is to test Him out in your own level of understanding. Think of anything that there is life in, that you have a need for, and it cannot be something inanimate, meaning something of this world made of gold, silver, wood, stone,or any thing that does not pertain to life. It cannot be something you want to add to your riches, but rather something that pertains to your life and your life more abundantly, and simply look up and say Father God, I do not know you, or your son, Jesus, but I would like to know you, and your son, Jesus, and your HOLY SPIRIT. Father I am asking you for that, that you know is only possible to come from above, that no man could give you) in the name of Christ JESUS, And Father I believe that I receive, and I give you my thanks, Amen. You did not hear Him answer yea, nor nay, but you just keep on believing until you get what you asked Him for. This believing Him is called Faith. You will receive what you ask Him for if it pertains to life, and nothing dead, and nothing black, which is death. But remember when you get what you asked Him for, just use a little *kneeology,* which is get down on your knees and Shell Down The CORN, which means for you to say Father GOD, I confess I am a sinner, and I ask you to save me in the name of your son JESUS, THE CHRIST. I renounce Satan, Sin, And the things of this world, and I will go and sin no more, in the name of Jesus. Father I believe you are saving me and I give you thanks in the name of JESUS. AMEN. You have already tasted God and you now know Him even though you cannot see Him, YOU know my God is real. So please do not join the great apostasy and fall away from the faith you just found, or it will be impossible to please GOD without any faith. Father, DUISHKA thanks you in the name of Jesus for the anointing to reiterate ***"GOD'S SUPER BOWL ON A SUNDAY"*** which you call **ARMAGEDDON,** for all unbelievers and God's lawbreakers. Brother Nethanyahu, Mavis and I invites you and Sara to come and eat with us, if you eat, Kosher, as we do, beans and cornbread, (lentils). If you can, come when brother Putin, and Brother XI Jinping come. Contact them to see when.

Chapter 35

"God's Super Bowl On A Sunday" that God called **"Armageddon"**, this is that great and notable Day of the Lord. **"For these be the days of vengeance that all things which are written may be fulfilled."** (Luke 21:22). these days of God's vengeance are the only way the unbelieving wicked educated fools will know for a certainty that God is judging them; and they still will not repent. Instead they just curse God more. When these days come upon the wicked ones unaware, all of the believers will be **(watching and praying always that they do not fall into the snare that is coming upon the whole earth. Pray that you may have the strength to escape all these things that shall come to pass, and to stand before the Son of Man,) which is Christ Jesus.** (Luke 21:35,36)

"Does this vengeance that God is executing make Him unrighteous? God forbid. How then shall God judge the world?" (Romans 3:5,6)

"And to you who are troubled, rest with us when the Lord Jesus shall be revealed from heaven with His Mighty Angels in flaming fire, taking vengeance on them that know not God, and that obey not the gospel of our Lord Christ Jesus." (2 Thessalonians 1:7,8) "Even as Sodom and Gomorrah, and the cities about them in like manner giving themselves over to fornication, and going after strange flesh,

(Queers), are set forth for an example, suffering the vengeance of eternal fire." (Jude 1:7)

Just like the examples that are being set at this present time by world figures, like the *Pope,* the President and the Vice President of these *NewNited States of America,* which is *(Babylon).* Also other people of prominence, like the Clinton', Bill and Hillary, and everybody that voted for all of them. "Likewise, these *filthy* dreamers defile the flesh, despise dominions, and speak evil of dignities." (Jude 1:8)

Brother Paul told Titus to "speak evil of no man". (Titus 3:2) But Brother Paul also said, "to mark these evildoers." How do you mark them without calling out their evil deeds? God set a bunch of filthy dreamers up as dignitaries to rule His people. God said to speak evil of no man; (Titus 3:2) but He did not say to call evil good, and good evil. So, if the dignitaries of God are calling sodomites, *"Gays",* they are calling evil good, and good evil. All of this filth and abomination is turning God's long suffering into the fierceness of His wrath, which is gonna soon manifest into the last plagues, which will culminate into the Grand Finale' that Duishka calls *"God's Super Bowl On A Sunday,"* that God called **Armageddon.**

Even as **"Corn Shelling Time"** is being written, there are so many sorrows and plagues that are currently happening that they cannot all be named in this book. "Yet, you have not hearkened unto Me, saith the Lord, that you might provoke me to anger with the works of your hands to your own hurt. Take the wine cup of My fury and cause all the kingdoms of the world, which are upon the face of the earth to drink. Thus said the Lord God of Israel: You drink and be drunken, and spue, and fall, and rise no more, because of the sword which I will send among you. Thus said the Lord of Hosts. You shall certainly drink, for, lo, I begin to bring evil on the city, *(Jerusalem),* which is called by My Name; and should you be utterly unpunished? You shall not be unpunished: For I will call for a sword *(all kinds of violence)* upon all the inhabitants of the earth, saith the Lord of Hosts.

A noise shall come *even* to the ends of the earth, for the Lord has a controversy with the nations, *(Gentiles)*. He will plead with all flesh *(which He is doing in* "**_Corn Shelling Time_**"*).* He will give them *that are* wicked to the sword, *(all kinds of violence)*, saith the Lord. "Thus saith the Lord of Hosts, Behold, evil shall go forth from nation to nation, and a great whirlwind shall be raised up from the coasts of the earth. And the slain of the Lord shall be at that day from *one* end of the earth even unto the *other* end of the earth. They shall not be lamented neither gathered, nor buried, they shall be dung upon the ground." (This whirlwind has a multiple meaning. It means literal hurricanes, tornadoes, tsunami, earthquakes, etc. But it also means foreign invaders will come with their armies with all kinds of violence like a whirlwind upon every nation of the earth. It will happen so fast you will not have any time to prepare for the great disaster, whether it be by sword or by the four elements (wind, fire, water, or earth). All of the slain ones will be victims of the Lord *(Pempte Ousa)*, the fifth being. Listen! Pay attention, and do not fall into the hands of the fearful God.) "A voice of the cry of the shepherds and an howling of the principal of the flock *shall be heard* for the Lord has spoiled their pasture. And the peaceable habitations are cut down, because of the anger of the Lord. He has forsaken His covert as the lion: for their land is desolate because of the fierceness of the oppressor, and because of His fierce anger; and the shepherds shall have no way to flee, nor the principal of the flock to escape." All of this is in (Jeremiah the 25th Chapter).

What does all of this mean? This will not mean anything to the unbelieving and the abominable ones. But **Michael Duishka** is going to show you that all of this prophecy that has a two fold meaning is talking about the *annihilation* of all of the nations and people, tongues, kindred upon the face of the earth today, except a remnant that God will save for seed to replenish the desolate earth.

"I beheld the earth, and lo it was without form *(Tohu)* and void, *(Bohu)* and the heavens, and they had no light. I beheld the mountains, and, lo, they trembled, and all the hills moved lightly. I beheld, and, lo, *there was* no man, and all the birds of the heavens were fled. I beheld, and, lo, the fruitful place *was* a wilderness, and all the cities were broken down at the presence of the Lord, *and* by His fierce anger. For thus has the Lord said, the whole land shall be desolate, yet will I not make a full end, because I have spoken *it*, I have purposed *it*, and will not repent, neither will I turn back from it." (Jeremiah 4:23 – 28)

The day of God's vengeance is in God's heart (Spirit). This is a prophecy about the form of the earth after the fall of all nations, and the mountains are melted away with blood of animals and men. This is the form of the earth after all the cities of the earth are broken down, including Babylon City, the great city, now known as *New York City, USA*. This is the form of the earth after *"God's Super Bowl On A Sunday"*. This is the form of the earth after God's **Armageddon**. So let us get on with the destruction of this earth, the way Jeremiah beheld it in his vision in (Jeremiah 4:23 – 28)

The evil that shall go forth from nation to nation has already started in the nations of Syria, Iraq, Egypt, Israel, America, Ukraine; and many more nations have encountered evil from different factions. Just like a cancer, it, *(evil)*, will just keep on spreading. All of the other nations have the evil out in the open so that everyone in the world can see. But the evil that has invaded America is more subtle and concealed. This is one of the signs of the times that Christ Jesus told His believers to watch for, the wolf disguised in sheep's clothing. When the divided anti-Americans voted a black sheep to dictate evil, mandatory laws of Satan to this once God fearing nation, that is when God fearing believers knew the black cloud was covering this land, to never leave it any more, until the presence of our Lord. Fellow believers know what Ichabod means. That is what has happened to America. Black signifies evil, wickedness, damnable iniquity the Lord Christ Jesus has determined for this nation of America. The Lord has commissioned this black president, with his black puppets to cause Babylon *(America)* to fall. The only consolation for believers is trust the Lord for a peaceable habitation.

Do you so called "Christian" fools think you can hide in your plush *church house* and call it a place of refuge from the guilt of silence, while the murders of millions of American babies were sacrificed to Satan? Answer: Because you voted for the murderers and did your civil patriotic duty, but sent your souls to the lake of fire, if you do not "Shell Down the Corn", (confess), repent, ask Lord Jesus to forgive you, and believe Him. You Shepherds *(Pastors)* and Principal of the Flock, God said there will be no place you can hide when the full force of evil goes forth to your nation. There shall be a voice of the cry of the Shepherds, and a howling of the Principal of the Flock. The Shepherds shall have no way to flee, nor the Principal of the Flock to escape. The Lord has spoiled their pasture, their pasture being the *church houses* that will be destroyed.

True Christians, when they were first called Christians in Antioch, had the ordination of the Holy Spirit of God. But the "Christians" let evil men rise up out of them, causing divisions and teaching doctrines of devils. Instead of bringing the brothers into unity, they caused the one doctrine of Christ Jesus to be divided into sects and cults, as they are at this present time. This is provoking God to anger by the so called "Christians" learning all the sins of the Babylonians and rubbing it into God's face; and He is bringing His judgment upon the world right now. He has already kindled the fire.

God never had a *church,* because "God that made the world and all things therein; seeing that He is Lord of heaven and earth, dwells not in temples made with hands. Neither is worshiped with men' hands, as though He needed any thing, seeing He gives to all life, and breath, and all things. And hath made of one blood all nations of men for to dwell on all the face of the earth, and hath determined the times before appointed, and the bounds of their habitation." (Acts 17:24,25,26)

Duishka is preparing to do the dance my daddy taught me with his double razor strop, because God is chastising me for exposing the evil His dignitaries are performing against His people. He said: "I have said you are gods, and all of you are children of the most high, but you shall die like men and fall like one of the princes." (Psalms 82:6,7)

"He (God) has called for a sword upon all the inhabitants of the earth, thus saith the Lord of Hosts." (Jeremiah 25:29) "The Lord shall roar from on high, and utter His voice from His holy habitation; He shall mightily roar upon His habitation. He shall give a shout as they that tread the grapes against all the inhabitants of the earth. A noise shall come *even* unto the ends of the earth. For the Lord has a controversy with the nations, (Gentiles). He will plead with all flesh, (which He is doing in this book, **"Corn Shelling Time"**). He will give them *that are* wicked to the sword, thus saith the Lord. Behold evil shall go forth from nation to nation, and a great whirlwind shall be raised up from the coasts of the earth. And the slain of the Lord shall be at that day from *one* end of the earth even to the *other* end of the earth. They shall not be lamented, neither gathered, nor buried. They shall be dung upon the ground." (Jeremiah 25:30,31,32,33) The whirlwind has already started and is escalating, causing all manner of sorrows and heartaches from one end of the earth to the other end. Whoever the producer of the movie, **"Corn Shellling Time"**, will be? Will be the number one in all categories, showing the whirlwind that takes us right into "God's Super Bowl On A Sunday", which God calls **"ARMAGEDDON"**. Blood is already running in the middle east from terrorist groups such as Al Qaeda, Isis, Jihadist, Hamas, Hezbollah, Shiite, Sunni, Kurds, which are all branches of Islam, which is part of the whirlwind going through the world killing, and starting the blood to flow that will finally run as high as the horses' bridles. Another Islamist group of devils is Boko Haram, that are slaughtering men, women, and children in Nigerian towns, villages, and country, also in Dakar and other countries of Africa. All this is the sword, but the whirlwind is also blowing in God's armies of the four elements, wind, earth, water, and fire. Tsunamis and earthquakes are happening in divers places, killing thousands and bringing down hills, and mountains, and destroying buildings, Crops and causing stench that comes from the dead ones that cannot be buried. Tornadoes, and hurricanes, and tropical storms are killing thousands, and bring in torrents of rain that causes flood waters to rise to their peak, wiping out homes and all kinds of food products, that are bringing on famines and pestilences, and all kinds of diseases, such as Ebola, viruses causing infectious diseases in humans, plants, and animals. Also the flooding water drives out wild beasts and reptiles that cause many deaths of unsuspecting victims. Then there is the fourth element, the fire. In just a short time it can and does wipe out millions of acres of forest land, and grass, and other vegetation that gives survival to many humans and animals. "The wheat, and the barley, and corn are being destroyed. The vine is dried up, and the fig tree, pomegranate tree, the palm tree, apple tree, even all the trees of the field are withered: The barns are broken down for the corn is withered. How do the beasts groan! The herds of cattle are perplexed, because they have no pasture. Yea, the flocks of sheep are made desolate. O LORD, to you will I cry, for the fire has devoured the pastures of the wilderness, and the flame has burned all the trees of the field. The beasts of the field cry also unto you: For the rivers of waters are dried up, and the fire has devoured the pastures of the wilderness. For the day of the Lord is coming, for *it is* nigh at hand. A day of clouds and of thick darkness, as the morning spread upon the mountains: A great people, and a strong, there has not been ever the like, neither shall be any more after it, to the years of many generations. A fire devours before them: And behind them a flame burns. The land as the Garden of Eden before them, and behind them a desolate wilderness. Yea, and nothing shall escape them. The appearance is as the appearance of horses; and as horsemen so shall they run. Like the noise of chariots on the tops of mountains shall they leap, like the noise of a flame of fire that devours the stubble, and as a strong people set in battle array. Before their face the people shall be much pained: All faces shall gather blackness. They shall run like mighty men; They shall climb the wall like men of war; and they shall march every one on his ways, and they shall not break their ranks. Neither shall one thrust another; They shall walk every one in his path; and *when* they fall upon the sword, they shall not be wounded. They shall run to and fro in the city, they shall run upon the wall, they shall climb up upon the houses; They shall enter in at the windows like a thief. The earth shall quake before them; The heavens shall tremble: The sun and the moon shall be dark, and the stars shall withdraw their shining: And the Lord shall utter His voice before His army: For His camp is very great for He is strong that executes His Word: For the day of the Lord is great and very terrible, and who can abide it?" (Joel Chapters 1 and 2)

The answer is nobody except the ones with the seal of God. *America, the literal Babylon, the cesspool of all filth and Obomanation, the great Babylon City, (New York City, USA).* America is the height of all immorality of the whole entire world. This immorality is the cause of the vials of God's wrath being poured out upon this wicked, untoward generation of barbarians that professing to be wise, they became fools, and changed the glory of the incorruptible God into an image made like to corruptible man. Wherefore God gave them up to uncleanness through the lusts of their own hearts, to dishonor their own bodies between themselves, men lying with men, (*which Duishka calls queers,* but God calls it sodomy, which cannot be exonerated by all the laws of the land passed by the Satan filled president and nine heathen judges, so called Justices of the Supreme Court.)

God just turned His fierceness of His anger up to plead more severely with His people, to "Come Out of "Her", (Babylon)" and save yourselves from the plagues that are increasing with all ferocity and violence. For this immorality of sodomy, adultery, fornication, thievery, murder, covetousness, unholy, unthankful, disobedient to parents, proud, blasphemers of God, God is bringing more speedily destruction upon the whole entire earth. When the king of Babylon, (*president of America*) and his constituents, including the nine Supreme Court Justices have fulfilled God's will for them, they will go into perdition, which is destruction. These people are blatantly defying God Almighty, (PANTAKRATOR). If they live long enough to fight against the King of kings and the Lord of lords in *"God's Super Bowl On A Sunday"*, they will be *buzzard bait* at **ARMAGEDDON.**

The immoral dogs, sorcerers, murderers, *queers, lizzies,* whore mongers, idolaters, and whosoever loves and makes a lie that rule America, (Babylon), won a battle, and changed the laws of God into a law of Satan, when they made it a law for *queers* to marry. They do not know that they lost the war. "Be not deceived; God is not mocked, for whatsoever a man sows, that shall he also reap. For he that sows to his flesh, shall of the flesh reap corruption." (Galatians 6:7,8) "The Lord is not slack concerning His promise, as some men count slackness, but is long suffering to us ward, not willing that any should perish, but that all should come to repentance." (2 Peter 3:9)

The queers lit the White House up with rainbow colors, mocking God with pink, greenish yellow, and blue, which are the same colors of an atomic bomb that Duishka believes will destroy the White House, just like God destroyed Sodom and Gomorrah with His own atomic bomb made with the elements of the air, called fire and brimstone, which are fire and sulphur that makes a greenish yellow light. When people think that God is not on the side of His people, they need to think again. God said the ones doing such things, (men lying with men, idolatry, fornication, women that changed their natural use into that which is against nature are worthy of death. Also the ones that agreed with them are worthy of death. And before this book is finished, God will bring plagues, and disasters of all sorts on America, (Babylon). All kinds of grievous sores, diseases, and death will come upon the *queers,* and *lizzies;* and they will not be so gay! But you ain't seen nothing yet. Keep reading.

The heathen take scripture out of context and try to justify their sins. (1 John 4:16) has: ("God is love" in it), but to finish, "whom God loves are only those that keep His Commandments." "By this we know that we love the children of God. When we love God, and keep His commandments." (1 John 5:2)

I suppose God loved the *queers* and whore mongers in Sodom and Gomorah; but He still destroyed them with fire, just like He will do to all of the children of darkness. My daddy took his double razor strop off the nail and said to me, "Mick, it is time to "Shell Down the Corn", and confess. God is saying the same thing to you that are looking for equality of sin with righteousness. God is pleading with you children of Satan to "Shell Down the Corn", confess, repent, and believe Him.

"For this is the love of God, that we keep His commandments, and His commandments are not grievous." (1 John 5:2) God commanded us to love our brother, not seduce him, or lay on him. God has put it into the heart of Obama, and all the kings of the earth to fulfill His will. (Revelation 17:17) This is how God brings judgment on all peoples, multitudes, nations, and tongues. God saves the ones that "Come Out of "Her", Mystery, Babylon, the harlot churches, and literal Babylon. But God brings the sword on the wicked ones that stay in the world of sin. I reported the sin of sodomy, adultery, fornication, thievery, and murder to the appropriate authorities and the appropriate authorities were the ones committing sodomy, adultery, fornication, thievery, and murder. The appropriate authorities arrested me.

"God's Super Bowl On A Sunday" is the culmination of all of God's wrath and fierce anger to fulfill His desire for the day of vengeance before the end of all transgression and sin. These things must come to pass all over the earth. Immorality is caused by false preachers, false pastors, false prophets, false apostles, telling lies causing the great apostasy that is happening at this present time. The ignorant fools that dis against the Jews, Israel, Jerusalem, and the true believers of Christ Jesus, which are spiritual Jews: "The Lord will smite all these people that have fought against Jerusalem with this plague, their flesh shall consume away while they stand upon

their feet, and their eyes shall consume away in their holes, and their tongues shall consume away in their mouth. And it shall come to pass in that day, *that* a great tumult shall be among them; and they shall lay hold every one on the hand of his neighbor, and his hand shall rise up against the hand of his neighbor." (Zechariah 14:13)

"Now I beseech you, brethren, mark those which cause divisions and offenses contrary to the doctrine which you have learned, and avoid them." (Romans 16:17)

God's dignitary President of the *NewNited States of America* is marked, because he has caused divisions and offenses, not only in America, but also world wide. He and his jack booted thugs in the Congress and Supreme Court Justices have divided the moral majority and caused them to be the immoral majority. The *queers* against the righteous ones, the blacks against everyone else, divided the poor working man's money and have given it to the rich, wrongly divided the Word of Truth, and turned God's Word into his lie. This President has offended every righteous person in the world with his divisions and offenses.

The free sex hippie generation, and the baby boomers, and the millennial generation will never know how beautiful America was before these ungodly, untoward generations refused to obey God's commandments and God's laws, so they opted for their rulers to be Satan filled heathen that know only how to kill, steal, and destroy. Evil rulers like Kennedy, Carter, Johnson, Clinton, and worse than all of the others put together is Obama, which have turned God's beautiful paradise into Satan's desolation. America the beautiful is only a beautiful memory in the lives of the "In God We Trust" generation.

Even as **"Corn Shelling Time"** is being written, the plagues of God are being poured out in so many ways. The ungodly fools are being destroyed, and they will not repent and turn from their wicked ways. Duishka has lived through all of the above mentioned generations, and has searched fervently for something good to say about these democrat leaders and their followers; but sad to say, not one good word could be found. So God said "their end would be according to their works." (2 Corinthians 11:15)

Since God has been blasphemed in America, the honey bee that pollinates the female part of vegetation has left with God. The crops are failing and honey is scarce; and famine is coming. The ignorant can only comprehend immorality, like sodomy, fornication, idolatry, covetousness, and greed. Even as **"Corn Shelling Time"** is being written the armies of God are busy burning, flooding, tornadoes, hurricanes, and earthquakes are pleading with you and warning you that it is time to "Shell Down the Corn" to God and confess that you are a sinful person; and perhaps God will extend His mercy upon you and save you. The sword is coming from nation to nation to destroy the wicked, which are almost all of the inhabitants of the earth.

"And I will plead against him with pestilence, and with blood, and I will rain upon him, and upon his bands, and upon the many people that *are* with him an overflowing rain, and great hailstones, fire, and brimstone. Thus I will magnify Myself, and sanctify Myself; and I will be known in the eyes of many nations; and they shall know that I *am* the Lord." (Ezekiel 38:22,23)

In 378 A.D. Bishop Demasus made Christianity and Babylonism one religion, which it is the religion of the great whore at this present time. Heathen temples with Babylonian rituals in so called "Christian" *churches*. Private confessions, worship of images, the *cross*, calling themselves *saints, Christmas trees, Easter*, which is blasphemy of the Holy Passover, All *Saints* Day, they call *Halloween, marriage of queers (sodomites)*, marriage of *lesbians*, which is a woman homosexual, that are also called *lizzies*. All of these are directed by false apostles, false prophets, false pastors, which are bringing in the warm up of God's mighty armies before the first quarter of **"God's Super Bowl On**

A Sunday". The sword of the Lord is being bathed in heaven at this present time. "And the dragon gave the beast his power, and his seat, and great authority." (Revelation 13:2)

But let me cut through to the chase and go to the arena of *"God's Super Bowl On A Sunday."* After many natural disasters have occurred in all the Gentile nations, after the great apostasy, or the population of the world have fallen away from the faith of God, after all the ones that obey the laws of the land have taken the mark of the beast, after all of God's holy ones have been killed by the anti-Christ, except God's very elect, after all the inhabitants of the earth worship the dragon (Satan) that gives the first beast his power, after the son of perdition has been revealed, after the Mystery of Iniquity (Babylon) has manifested; then comes God's Grand Finale.

This is an insert in the book, **"Corn Shelling Time"** and **Michael Duishka** with some of his belief. As this writer is approaching the last lap of the race, he is looking ahead to all of the options he has to rectify his short comings of the glory of God. It is too late to look back at the former evil words and deeds that I have done to God's people. When this writer brings these transgressions up in front of the Lord, He only reminds me that He does not remember them because He has forgiven me and has forgotten all my past sins. Like He told everyone that He healed, He said; **"GO and sin no more"**. Even though He has forgiven me for my past transgressions whatsoever a man sows, that shall he reap. That is a wake up call to everyone that reads **"Corn Shelling Time"** Sow good seed! OK?

Chapter 36

"AND HE GATHERED THEM together into a place called in the Hebrew tongue **Armageddon.**" (Revelation 16:16) He is God the Father, God the Son, God the Holy Spirit, AKA God Almighty, in the Greek tongue PANTAKRATOR; them are the armies of the Beast, which is the destroyer, "called in the Hebrew tongue Abaddon; but in the Greek tongue has *his* name Apollyon." (Revelation 9:11) This is a spiritual being incarnated into a fleshly body; and the fleshly body is called Anti-Christ, which means instead of Christ, which is ruled by the Dragon, AKA Satan, that old Serpent called the Devil, and Satan." (Revelation 12:9)

The Arena is the land of Israel in it's entirety, including every place Abraham walked. The Arena is the total area that God gave a deed to Abraham, which includes all the territory that the terrorists, calling themselves the Palestinian owners of Israel, have. All of the original land of Israel, including the Golan Heights, West Bank, Jerusalem, and the Gaza Strip, will be the Arena for God's judgment on the whole world.

The three unclean spirits that Brother John saw come out of the mouth of the dragon, and of the mouth of the beast, and of the mouth of the false prophet: "For they are the spirits of devils, working miracles, which go forth unto the kings of the earth and of the whole world, to gather them to the battle of that great Day of God Almighty (PANTAKRATOR)." (Revelation 16:13,14). "For God has put in their hearts to fulfill His will, (their hearts being the hearts of all the kings of the whole world), and to agree, and give their kingdom unto the beast, until the words of God be fulfilled." (Revelation 17:17)

"And the woman that you saw is that great city, which reigns over the kings of the earth." (Revelation 17:18) The great city as many commentators believe, is not the city of Rome, which is the Great Whore, the Mother of Harlots, because: "And the ten horns which you saw upon the beast, (*the ten kings*), these shall hate the Whore, and shall make "Her" desolate and naked, and shall eat "Her" flesh, and burn "Her" with fire. (Revelation 17:16). This rules out that the city of Rome is that Great City, because the kings destroy "Her", (*Rome, the Whore, the Catholic Church, and "Her" daughters*). Some commentators think the great city is Jerusalem; but Jerusalem never reigns over the kings of the earth, so Jerusalem is not the great city.

""And the angel said unto me, (*me being Brother John*): Wherefore did you marvel? I will tell you the mystery of the Woman and of the Beast that carries "Her"; which has the seven heads and ten horns. The Beast that you saw, and is not. (*Mystery Babylon*); and shall ascend out of the bottomless pit, and go into perdition, (*destruction*): And they that dwell upon the earth, whose names were not written in the Book of Life from the foundation of the world, shall wonder when they behold the Beast that was, and is not, and yet is. (*Mystery Babylon*)" (Revelation 17:7,8) The Whore is part of Mystery Babylon until "She" Shall be no more. The Great City, which I believe to be *New York City, USA,* that is making the merchants of the entire earth rich at the present time are committing fornication with them, which also are known as the kings of the earth; and the inhabitants of the earth have been made drunk with the wine (spirit) of "Her" fornication.

Obama, the present king of Babylon, is spending billions of borrowed money on foreign countries, while the USA is broke and existing on borrowed money. That is known as committing fornication with the kings of the world.

"And I saw heaven opened, and behold a *white* horse, and He that sat upon him was called Faithful and True, and in righteousness he does judge and make war." (Revelation 19:11) Where does He make war? He makes war with the Beast and the kings of the earth and their armies in the Arena called **Armageddon.** (Revelation 17:14). "These shall make war with the Lamb and the Lamb shall overcome them, for He is Lord of lords, and King of kings; and they that are with Him *are* called and chosen, and faithful." (Revelation 17:14)

Duishka hypercritically calls the Arena of **Armageddon**, *God's Super Bowl,* just to add color to the controversy God has with the Gentile heathen pagan nations and all of the nations in the world, except the Jews. Duishka admits that he is acting hypercritically by using words that God did not say like, *"God's Super Bowl On A Sunday",* when God plainly calls the contest, the Battle of **Armageddon.** Duishka coined the title, *"God's Super Bowl On A Sunday"* to add color to the upcoming movie, **"Corn Shelling Time"**, which will be the number one rated movie of all time.

"And the armies *which were* in heaven followed Him, (*The Word of God*), upon white horses, clothed in fine linen, white and clean." (Revelation 19:14) Notice there is **nothing** black in heaven. Where did the armies in heaven follow the One on the white horse to? Answer: "To smite the nations (Gentiles, heathen, pagans), gathered together in the Arena, called **Armageddon.** "And He has on *His* vesture and on His thigh a name written, KING OF KINGS AND LORD OF LORDS." (Revelation 19:16) The reason you know He is headed to the Arena is because Brother John said: "And I saw an angel standing in the sun, and he cried with a loud voice saying to all the fowls that fly in the midst of heaven, come and gather yourselves together unto the Supper of the Great God. That you may eat the flesh of kings, and the flesh of captains, and the flesh of mighty men, and the flesh of horses, and of them that sit on them, and flesh of all *men both* free and bond, both small and great." (Revelation 19:17,18) Duishka's hypercritical cognate word for flesh is *(buzzard bait)*. "And I saw the beast and the kings of the earth, and their armies, gathered together to make war against Him that sat on the horse and against His army." (Revelation 19:19)

"And the Great City, *(New York City, USA)*, was divided into three parts, and the cities of the nations *(Gentiles, heathen, pagans)* fell." (Revelation 16:19) How did the cities of the nations fall? Answer: "And Great Babylon came in remembrance before God, to give unto "Her" the cup of the wine of the fierceness of His wrath." (Revelation 19:19)

"And the seventh angel poured out his vial into the air: And there came a great voice out of the temple of heaven, from the throne, saying it is done." (Revelation 16:17) "And there were voices, and thunders, and lightnings; and there was a great earthquake, such as was not since men were upon the earth, so mighty an earthquake and so great." (Revelation 16:18) This is the earthquake that is the daddy of them all, that starts in *New York City, USA,* the seat of the Beast, *the Great Babylon City,* that causes a chain reaction, that follows the fault lines all over the earth, that causes the cities of the nations to fall. "And every island fled away, and the mountains were not found.." (revelation 16:19,20)

The Grand Finale of God has begun, and the arena of God's main event, the battle of **Armageddon** is well in array. "And there fell upon men a great hail out of heaven, *every stone* about the weight of a talent: *(the weight of a talent is about 114 pounds each)* And men blasphemed God because of the plague of the hail, for the plague thereof was exceeding great." (Revelation 16:21)

This is the time of the last two Holy Ones left on the earth, the two witnesses of God that were slain; "and they were caught up after they lay dead in the street of the great city, which spiritually is Sodom and

Egypt, where also our Lord was crucified." (Revelation 11:10); "And the same hour there was a great earthquake, and the tenth part of the city fell, and in the earthquake were slain of men seven thousand." (Revelation 11:13) Notice the great city of Jerusalem was not divided into three parts. "The second woe is past *and* behold the third woe comes quickly." (Revelation 11:14) "And the seventh angel sounded, and there were great voices in heaven saying: The kingdoms of the world are become the *kingdoms* of our Lord, and of His Christ; and He shall reign forever and ever." (Revelation 11:15)

"And there were lightnings, and voices, and thundering, and an earthquake, and great hail." (Revelation 11:19) This is probably the same earthquake that was worldwide that had all of the elements of God working in a great storm, causing the wind, water, fire, and earth to be active in the Grand Finale' of God.

"God said to Job: Have you entered into the treasures of the snow? Or have you seen the treasures of the hail, which I have reserved against the time of trouble, against the day of battle and war?" (Job 38:22,23) When ("*God's Super Bowl On A Sunday*") **Armageddon** has manifested, this will be the time of trouble, the day of battle and war, that God will call in His treasures of hail He has reserved especially for that time of Jacob's Trouble. This plague of hail is not confined just to the Arena of the battle of Armageddon; but these hail balls will be falling in different places world wide. "And there fell upon men a great hail out of heaven, and men blasphemed God because of the plague of the hail, for the plague thereof was exceeding great." (Revelation 16:21) When the great day of God's judgment is manifesting in His Arena called Armageddon, the side effects are spilling out in all nations of the world. "For the spirits of devils are working miracles that go forth unto the kings of the earth and of the whole world." (Revelation 16:14) Because as **"Corn Shelling Time"** has explained in previous chapters, this world wide battle is a spiritual battle with the rulers of spiritual Babylon, *(which are the evil spirits of the dragon, Satan, the Beast, the False Prophet)* fighting against the spiritual armies of God. Also the evil spirit that rules the world has marked his subjects, and caused the deceived subjects to follow the glamor of the glory of the kingdoms of the world, which is called literal Babylon. The leader of literal Babylon is the *NewNited States of America,* and the Great City Babylon is *New York City, USA.* The United Nations is located in New York City, which rules all the nations of the world.

Michael Duishka is already in trouble with the Lord. Why? Because the dignitaries of this world are being exposed by Michael Duishka in this book, **"Corn Shelling Time"** The dignitaries of this world are wearying the Lord "when you say every one doing evil is good in the sight of the Lord." (Malachi 2:17) Duishka is already receiving chastisement from God Almighty (PANTAKRATOR) for speaking evil about those rulers. And naming the individual perpetrators and reiterating what God said would be their judgment. **"Corn Shelling Time"** did not, is not, or will not ever call acts of evil good. "Woe unto the ones that do such things, for they have gone in the way of Cain, and ran greedily after the error of Balaam for reward, and perished in the gainsaying of Core." (Jude 1:11) It appears to Duishka that nearly every one in the worldly system is guilty, either by acts of evil, or by association with the ones that do the acts of evil. This evil is preparing the Arena for the harvest of the earth. The word anti means oppose, except in the biblical sense, it means one that is instead of the real one, such as the pope, who has placed himself in the place of Christ, and calls himself the Vicar of Christ, who takes the position of Christ, "who opposes and exalts himself above all that is called God, or that is worshiped, so that he as God sits in the Temple of God, showing himself that he is God." (2 Thessalonians 2:4)

Another Anti Christ is the daughters of the Whore, who are the so called "Christian" churches. They call themselves "Christians" but oppose all godliness, in association with the secular laws of the land, calling themselves "Christians", but voting for murderers, extortionists, terrorists, *queers, (same sex marriages)*, killing their babies that they call abortion, but God calls it murder. "And this is that *spirit* of Anti Christ, whereof you have heard that it should come, and even now <u>already</u> is it in the world." (1 John 4:3) Brother John warned us about the anti "Christians" that are <u>already</u> here. Are you guilty of having pleasure in watching the unholy degenerated lost and dying icons, and idols of television and radios, and computers? If you are guilty of being a participant in doing these things that are worthy of death, or if you have pleasure by watching or voting for those that do such things, please repent and "Shell Down the Corn", (confess) to Christ Jesus, and ask Him to forgive you, and believe Him. If you do that, He will lead you out of the arena of destruction and keep you from the hour of temptation which shall come upon the whole world. The arena of destruction is the whole world with **Armageddon** being the manifestation of the destruction of those that destroy the earth. The so called "Christians" and the politicians think silence is golden; but **<u>"Corn Shelling Time"</u>** is exclaiming that silence is the same as consent or approval to condone acts of sin, which God said was worthy of death. The very ones that say they are against abortion *(murder)*, same sex marriage, *(queers)*, are silent in their meeting places, not saying they are for or against abortion, homosexuality, fornication, adultery, or keeping the Sabbath Day holy, or stealing, lying, or having pleasure in those that do such things.

Michael Duishka is "Shelling Down the Corn", confessing to his part in sin and the breaking of God's laws, and the commandments of my Lord, Christ Jesus, which contributed to the evil that has filled this evil world. Duishka is confessing to Christ Jesus that he is guilty of breaking the commandments of God, which is punishable by death, because the soul that sins is sure to die. Duishka is also confessing to whoever reads, **<u>"Corn Shelling Time"</u>**, that he has committed sins that are worthy of death. **<u>"But</u> <u>God</u> so loved the world, that He gave His only begotten Son that whosoever believes Him should not perish but have everlasting life."** (John 3:16)

Since God cannot lie, or fail, if you repent and "Shell Down the Corn" to God, which means confess your sins and wrong doings to Christ Jesus, and believe Him when He said, you shall be saved, you will be covered by His shed blood, that will wash <u>all</u> your guilty sins away. If you do this, confession and not be lying to God, you will miss the **Snare that shall come on all them that dwell on the face of the whole earth.** (Luke 21:35) This is the snare: The devil has deceived you into believing if you sin, you shall not die. This is the lie that he, (Satan), told from the beginning. But Christ Jesus said: **"Behold I come as a thief. Blessed is he that watches, and keeps his garments, lest he walk naked, and they see his shame."** (Revelation 16:15)

"And He gathered them together, (*the kings of the whole world and their armies*), into a place called in the Hebrew tongue **Armageddon.** And the seventh angel poured out his vial into the air, and there came a great voice out of the Temple of Heaven, from the throne, saying; It is done." (Revelation 16:16,17) Please note, whosoever reads these words of Christ Jesus, that these plagues are poured out into the air of the whole earth. Armageddon is just the center stage to the great eventful Day of the Lord, when His judgment comes on the whole entire earth. Dukishka calls it *"God's Super Bowl On A Sunday";* but the true word of God calls it the day of battle, and many more descriptive adjectives; but the main event is called **Armageddon.** So let the Grand Finale' begin.

"But there were voices, and thunders, and lightnings, and there was a great earthquake, such as was not since men were upon the earth, so mighty an earthquake, *and* so great." (Revelation 16:18) This is the earthquake that was portrayed in previous chapters of **"Corn Shelling Time"** as the one that hits all of the fault lines all around the earth. The quake starts in Babylon City, (*New York City, USA*) and divides the Great City into three parts, "and the cities of the nations fell, because Great Babylon came in remembrance before God to

give unto "Her" the cup of the wine of the fierceness of His wrath."
(Revelation 16:19).

Remember the seven angels have the seven golden vials filled with
God's wrath, and they are ordered to pour them out. (Revelation
16:1) Also remember this storm is the greatest storm that ever was,
because there were voices, thunders, and lightnings, and the great
earthquake. "And there fell upon men a great hail out of heaven, *every
stone* about the weight of a talent." (Revelation 16:21) The earthquake
was so great that it caused a tsunami in the ocean, "and every island
fled away, and the mountains were not found." (Revelation 16:20)

"Behold evil shall go forth from nation to nation, (this is the time of
the evil), and a great whirlwind (tornado, hurricane) shall be raised
up from the coasts of the earth." (Jeremiah 25:32) Out of this storm
comes that whirlwind, *(tornadoes).* "And the slain of the Lord shall be
at that day from *one* end of the earth even to the *other* end of the earth:
They shall not be lamented nor buried; they shall be dung upon the
ground." (Jeremiah 25:33) The reason is because there will not be
enough people left upon the earth to lament them, or bury them.
"Destruction upon destruction is cried, for the whole land is spoiled."
(Jeremiah 4:20) "I beheld the earth, and lo, *it was* without form, and
void, (tohu-bohu) and the heavens, and they *had* no light, I beheld the
mountains, and, lo, they trembled, and <u>all</u> the hills moved lightly."
(Jeremiah 4:23,24) "I beheld, and, lo, *there was* no man, *(all were slain),*
and all the birds of the heavens were fled." (Jeremiah 4:25)

The birds of the heavens heard the angel call them to God's Great
Supper. "And I saw an angel standing in the sun, and he cried with
a loud voice saying to all the fowls that fly in the midst of heaven:
"Come and gather yourselves together unto the supper of the great
God., (Revelation 19:17) that you may eat the flesh of kings, and the
flesh of captains, and the flesh of mighty men, and the flesh of horses,
and of them that sit on them, and the flesh of all *men both* free, and
bond, both small and great." (Revelation 19:18) This supper of the

great God is in the Arena of *"God's Super Bowl On A Sunday"* after the event is over.

Meantime as the scene of the fallen cities changes back to **Armageddon,** the city of Jerusalem is compassed with all of the armies of the world; and the armies of God are preparing to fight against the armies of all the kings of the earth, which are being led by the Beast and the Dragon, (Satan). **"And when you shall see Jerusalem compassed with armies, then know that the desolation thereof is nigh."** (Luke 21:20) God is talking to Gog, the Chief Prince of Meshech and Tubal, *(spirit prince)*. "You shall fall upon the mountains of Israel, you and all your bands, and the people that are with you. I will give you to the ravenous birds of every sort, and *to* the beast of the field to be devoured." (Ezekiel 39:4) These are what Duishka calls *buzzard bait.* The people that Gog is leading are the land of Magog, which this writer believes to be Russia, *(Gomer)* Germany, and the Scandinavian people of Sweden, Norway, and Denmark, which are God's most beautiful people that He created. The light, fair, blonde, white Caucasoid race. These people are part of the ones destroying God's earth. The people with them are Persia *(Iran)*, Ethiopia, and Libya, Togarmah *(believed to be Turkey)*. All of these armies will be *buzzard bait* in the Armageddon Arena.

"And then shall that WICKED be revealed, whom the Lord shall consume with the spirit of His mouth, and shall destroy with the brightness of His coming, *even him*, whose coming if after the working of Satan, with all power and signs and lying wonders, and with all deceivableness of unrighteousness in them that perish, because they received not the love of the Truth that they might be saved." (2 Thessalonians 2:8,9,10)

God will consume the wicked beast with the two edged sword, which is the spirit, which is the Word of God that comes out of His mouth. God will destroy the Anti-Christ and the fleshly armies with the brightness of His coming. The brightness of His coming will be the

Holy Ones clothed in fine, clean,bright, white linen. They will be so bright that it blinds the armies of the Beast; and they will kill each other, because they are blinded by the brightness of His coming. "And for this cause God shall send them strong delusion, that they should believe the lie that they all might be damned who believed not the Truth but had pleasure in unrighteousness." (2 Thessalonians 2:11,12)

The first time Jesus comes back He does not ever touch the earth. Since He is God, the Holy Spirit, He brings only the spirits of those Holy Ones that are asleep in Him and causes their bodies to join their spirits in the air, not on the earth. This resurrection is all of the Holy Ones on the earth, including the Two Witnesses, which are asleep (*dead*) in Christ Jesus. All of these Holy Ones have put off corruption, which is flesh and blood, so they can inherit incorruption. (1 Thessalonians 4:13) and (1 Corinthians 15:50). "Then we which are alive *and* remain shall be caught up together with them, (the Holy Ones that have risen), in the clouds, to meet the Lord in the air, (*not on the earth*), and so shall we ever be with the Lord." (1 Thessalonians (4:17)

The question is what happened to the flesh and blood of the ones that were caught up in the air alive? Answer: "Behold, I shew you a mystery, we shall not all sleep, but we shall all be changed, in a moment, in the twinkling of an eye, at the last trump: For the trumpet shall sound, and the dead shall be raised <u>incorruptable</u>, and we shall be changed." (1 Corinthians 15:51,52)

The next question is what about the two prophets, witnesses that the Beast killed and left their bodies lay in the street of the great city, which spiritually is called Sodom and Egypt, where also our Lord was crucified? Answer: "For you will not leave my soul in hell, neither will you suffer (*let*) Mine (*Your*) Holy One to see corruption." (Psalms 16:10) This was a prophecy about the body of our Lord Christ Jesus who never was dead long enough for His body to turn into corruption, and was raised incorruptable in three nights and three days. The Two Witnesses are raised after the same manner as Christ Jesus, <u>incorruptable</u>. This is the Mystery of Godliness. All of the blood and dirty flesh will be gone and our earthly bodies will be changed into spiritual bodies just like our Lord Christ Jesus. So the first resurrection happens before the battle of Armageddon, and all of the Holy Ones that were in Christ Jesus are gone off the earth, but will return with Christ Jesus to earth in spiritual bodies, clothed in clean fine, <u>white</u> linen at the second coming, or at the presence, or appearing of our Lord Christ Jesus. Every eye shall see Him.

Back to the day of battle in the Arena of *"God's Super Bowl On A Sunday"*. The One on the white horse and His armies are in a world wide battle with the Dragon, and the Beast, and the False Prophet, with all their spiritual wonders, plus all the kings of the earth and their armies that are being led by the Anti-Christ. The world wide storm is still occurring with the four elements, the wind, the water, the earth, and the fire, being directed by the fifth Being, PEMTE OUSA. Also the angels with the vials on different elements like the fourth angel poured out his vial on the sun, and power was given him to scorch men with fire. "And men were scorched with great heat and blasphemed the name of God, which has power over these plagues; and they repented not to give Him glory." (Revelation 16:8,9)

In the meantime "the men who had the mark of the Beast and them which worshiped his image had grievous sores upon them because the first angel poured out his vial." (Revelation 16:2)

"And there fell upon men a great hail out of heaven, and men blasphemed God because of the plague of the hail, for the plague thereof was exceeding great." (Revelation 16:21)

As the wine press of God's wrath is being trodden without the city, blood came out of the wine press, even unto the horses bridles, by the space of a thousand *and* six hundred furlongs." (Revelation 14:20)

Commentators calculate this to be a distance of 200 to 250 miles. Duishka believes it runs world wide into the rivers and fountains and over the earth, because the harvest of wicked men is all over the earth. "And the third angel poured out his vial upon the rivers and fountains of waters, and they became blood." (Revelation 16:4) Duishka believes the thousand six hundred furlongs is a metaphor speaking allegorically about a distance that cannot be measured. The bodies of men slain all over the earth would run enough blood to kill every thing in the sea and pollute all the rivers and fountains world wide. "And I heard the angel of the waters say, you are righteous, O Lord, which are, and was, and shall be, because you have judged *this way*. For they have shed the blood of Holy Ones, and prophets, and you have given them blood to drink." (Revelation 16:5,6)

"The seventh trumpet sounded, the seventh angel poured out his vial upon the earth and into the air. And there came a voice out of the Temple of Heaven from the Throne, saying, it is done." (Revelation 16:17) When the voice out of the temple says this, it is to late for repentance, too late to glorify God, too late to "Come out of "Her", (Mystery Babylon and literal Babylon), too late to pray, too late to "Shell Down the Corn" to Christ Jesus, too late to confess to Christ Jesus you are a sinner, too late to ask forgiveness, too late to believe Jesus. Because all of the wicked people have been slain, either by the sword, or the four elements, earth, wind, water, or fire, or by the plagues, pestilence or diseases. All of the righteous people came out of "Her" and were caught up to be with their Lord and Savior Christ Jesus. All the cities of all the nations will fall. Literal Babylon City will fall, which Duishka believes is *New York City, USA*, is literal Babylon City, and America is the leading factor of the rest of the world system, which is Mystery Babylon and literal Babylon also. In previous chapters is detailed belief of how the Great City Babylon will fall.

Back to the battle of Armageddon, which Duishka calls *"God's Super Bowl On A Sunday"*, because the idolatry of America has made that their worship priority instead of God. Nearly all, or most, of the pagan Americans have adopted *Sunday* as their day to worship something instead of keeping the Sabbath Day holy and worshiping God Almighty, (PANTAKRATOR), on the seventh day like God commanded in the Ten Commandments. "Remember the Sabbath Day to keep it holy." (Exodus 20:8) But the heathen desecrate the Sabbath Day by working on the Sabbath Day, which God called the seventh day, and commanded all to rest on that day. But the pagans adopted the man made sabbath as the first day of the week they call *Sunday.* That is why Duishka believes God will culminate His wrath on a *Sunday* to end the controversy between the Dragon, Satan, the archaic serpent, that old lying Devil and his followers.

"But in the days of the voice of the seventh angel, when he shall begin to sound, *(blow his trumpet),* the Mystery of God should be finished, as He has declared to His servants the prophets." (Revelation 10:7)

God rested on the seventh day, which is the sabbath; but the next day, that man calls *Sunday,* God had His angels and armies to manifest His wrath at the battle of **Armageddon** that Duishka calls ***"God's Super Bowl On A Sunday".***

"The one on the <u>white</u> horse is leading His armies *which were* in heaven that are following Him upon white horses, clothed in fine linen, <u>white</u> and clean." (Revelation 19:14) They will destroy their enemies by the brightness of their bright, fine, clean, <u>white</u>, clothing and <u>white</u> horses. Everything will be so bright that it will blind the armies of the Beast and the Anti Christ so that they will be killing each other on account of being blinded by the King of kings and the Lord of lords and His holy, glorified, resurrected, chosen, elect. "And out of His mouth goes a sharp sword, (which is the Word of God)." (Revelation 19:17)

All the time that the battle is going on the elements of God, which are His armies, (the wind, the water, the earth, and the fire, being led by the fifth being, PEMPTE OUSA), are causing the greatest storm that ever was and never will be again to rage, not only in the Arena of the *"Super Bowl On A Sunday"*, but over the entire earth. "The whirlwind *(tornadoes)* is being raised up on the coasts of the whole earth from one end even to the other end of the earth, causing the slain of the Lord to be as dung upon the ground." (Jeremiah 25:32) "And there fell upon men a great hail out of heaven, *every stone* about the weight of a talent: And men blasphemed God, because of the plague of the hail. For the plague thereof was exceeding great." (Revelation 16:21) This hail was made by the cold wind and the water. "And another angel came out from the altar which had power over fire." (Revelation 14:18) "And the wine press *(of God's wrath)* was trodden without the city, and blood came out of the wine press, even unto the horse's bridles, by the space of a thousand *and* six hundred furlongs." (Revelation 14:20) This city is the capitol city of the Arena AKA Jerusalem.

"Corn Shelling Time" is pleading with you by the Word of God to: Whosoever reads this warning of God to "Come Out of "Her", *(Babylon)*, before the angel cries out: "Babylon is fallen, is fallen", then it will be too late to fear God and give glory to Him, and worship Him that made the heavens, and the earth, and the sea, and the fountains of waters. (Revelation 14:6,7)

You, dear reader, do not have to live in New York City, USA, to be living in Babylon. It makes no difference where you live, you are in Babylon. New York City, I believe, is the eye of the world wide storm. The Great City, Babylon, is the trigger that sets off the culmination of destruction of the Mystery of Iniquity, in simple English, the end of sin. I believe the epicenter of the great earthquake, such as was not since men were upon the earth, so mighty an earthquake, *and* so great, (Revelation 16:18), is the Great Babylon City of *New York City, USA*. New York City is the *eye* of the whirlwind that will be raised up from the coasts of the earth, (Jeremiah 25:32) with the rest of the earth being the eye wall of the great storm. The nucleus of the cell, or the center of the world wide storm, being the great city described in the 18th chapter of Revelation, which I believe to be *New York City, USA*, AKA, *Babylon City*. The lust of the flesh, the lust of the eyes, and the pride of life that are manifested in *New York City, USA*, are causing evil to go forth from nation to nation, causing temptation to come upon the whole world, causing the whole world to desire the glory and the power of Satan's kingdom, with the nucleus of his kingdom being *New York City, USA*. *New York City, USA* is gonna be the seat of the Beast, whenever the fifth angel pours out his vial, "And the kingdom of the Beast was full of darkness." (Revelation 16:10) *New York City, USA* is the door to let every foreigner that wants to come into America, enter, whether they are good or evil.

Donald Trump is plain spoken when he said the immigrants that come in are some evil and maybe some good. Donald knows that the radical Muslims and the terrorists that are allowed to enter into the door of America, New York City, USA, are going to be the cause of the Trump Tower, the World Trade Tower, the Wall Street Stock Exchange, the Statue of Liberty, the New York Harbor, and all of the delicacies of Revelation 18 to fall. In a previous chapter of **"Corn Shelling Time"** detailed information was given as to how the Muslims would do this in the name of Allah. Donald Trump is exposing the President of the US for being sympathetic with the immigrants, whether they be good or evil. Duishka wrote Donald Trump a letter and told him to not piss backards. So far, Donald is sticking to his truth. So when the nucleus of the earthquake projects it's tremors world wide, it will start in Babylon City. When the nucleus of the earthquake projects it's tremors out of Babylon City, the tremors set off all the fault lines worldwide, which **"Corn Shelling Time"** has named in a previous chapter of this book. "And the same hour was there a great earthquake, and the tenth part of the city fell, (*Jerusalem*) And in the earthquake were slain of men seven thousand, and the remnant were affrighted, and gave glory to the God of heaven." (Revelation 11:13)

"The second woe is past and the third woe comes quickly; and the seventh angel sounded, and there were great voices in heaven, saying, the kingdoms of this world are become *the* kingdoms of our Lord and of His Christ; and He shall reign forever and ever." (Revelation 11:15)

"And His feet shall stand in that day upon the Mount of Olives, which is before Jerusalem on the east, and the Mount of Olives shall cleave in the midst thereof toward the east and toward the west, *and there shall be* a very great valley, half of the mountain; shall remove toward the north, and half of it toward the south." (Zechariah 14:4) The reason this earthquake is not connected to the worldwide earthquake is because Israel is not in the series of fault lines that are connected to the rest of the earth. Also the Jews did not make cavities in the earth by drilling for oil, and gas, and other minerals. So it takes something more powerful, like the Spirit of God, which is the Lord's feet touching the high Mount of Olives. This ends the second woe that the angel, John beheld and heard flying through the midst of heaven, "saying with a loud voice, Woe, woe, woe." (Revelation 8:13)

And the third woe comes quickly, and the seventh angel sounded, (*blew his trumpet*), and at that time the prophecies of the destruction of iniquity, sin, is being fulfilled; and the Lion has roared, as He came up from His thicket; and the destroyer of the Gentiles is on his way, he has gone forth from his place to make the land desolate, *and* your cities shall be laid waste, without an inhabitant. "My people is foolish, they have not known Me, they *are* sottish children, and they have none understanding: They *are* wise to do evil, but to do good, they have no knowledge. And the cities of the nations, (Gentiles) fell." No more Macy's Parade, no more Mardi Gra's, no more Hollywood, no more Cinco Di Mayo, no more Corridas De Toros, (bull fighting,no more running of the bulls, no more Mecca (Makkah), no more Yuandans, no more Buddhas, no more sports, (*Super Bowls*), no more evil inventions, no more abortions (killings), no more politics, (*stealing*), no more black lives matter (*destruction*), no more idolatry, no more apostate *churches*, no more terrorism, no more Islam, Muslims, no more heathen, pagan, secular holidays, *(such as Christmas, Easter, New Year, Martin Luther King day)*, *no more queers, (same sex marriages), no more women usurping authority over men, no more women rulers or politicians that are feminine, no more popes, no more protests for equal rights,* because all of these above mentioned people will be dead, according to my Lord Christ Jesus. "These people will be dung upon the ground, not lamented, neither gathered, nor buried." (Jeremiah 25:33) " I beheld the earth, and, lo, *it was* without form, (tohu) and void, (bohu) and the heavens, and they *had* no light. I beheld the mountains, and, lo, they trembled, and all the hills moved lightly. I beheld, and, lo, *there was* no man, and all the birds of the heavens were fled. I beheld, and, lo, the fruitful place *was* a wilderness, and **all** the cities were broken down at the presence of the Lord, *and* by His fierce anger. For thus has the Lord said: The whole land shall be desolate. Yet will I not make a full end." (Jeremiah 4:23-27) "Destruction upon destruction is cried; for the whole land is spoiled: (Jeremiah 4:20) And your cities shall be laid waste without an inhabitant." (Jeremiah 4:7)

"Immediately after the tribulation of those days shall the sun be darkened, and the moon shall not give her light, and stars shall fall from heaven, and the powers of the heavens shall be shaken." (Matthew 24:29) The last minutes of time as we know it has run out. *"God's Super Bowl On A Sunday"* is over. Armageddon has been fulfilled. It is all over but the crying, *(weeping and gnashing of teeth)*. That means cursing and blaspheming the One that sat upon the white horse. The winner is the white team. "The Beast was taken and with him the False Prophet that wrought miracles before him, with which he deceived them that had received the mark of the Beast, and them that had worshiped his image. These both were cast alive into a lake of fire burning with brimstone. And the remnant were slain with the sword of Him that sat upon the horse, which *sword* proceeds out of His mouth: And all the fowls were filled with their flesh." (Revelation 19:29,21) **"For wheresoever the carcase is there will the eagles be gathered together."** (Matthew 24:28)

Michael Duishka

"Corn Shelling Time" has made every effort to reiterate God's Word with the Spirit of God putting more emphasis on the plagues that are double dog sure to come, and are <u>already</u> here, but the intensity will increase with more severity of pain and sorrows. When my daddy taught me how to "Shell Down the Corn", (confess), by the action of the double razor strop across my butt, he was showing his love for me. And in that administration of the double razor strop, I thank God Almighty (PANTAKRATOR) for His mercy on me. In the name of Christ Jesus I give thanks to God for His chastening (stripes) (Plagues) to let me know that He is dealing with me as a son. (Hebrews 12:7) When I remembered to "Shell Down the Corn" to God, (Christ Jesus) (confessing) my sins to Him, admitting I was a lost sinner, He (Christ Jesus) washed my heart with His blood, and gave me the gift of His Holy Spirit to lead me and to guide me into all Truth. He is not a respecter of persons, and all the things Christ Jesus has done, and is doing for me, He will do for you, if you will "Shell Down the Corn", (confess) to Christ Jesus; and He will raise you up in the last day. Just like God divided the light from the darkness in (Genesis 1:4) And just like God divided the light from the darkness in me, He will divide the light from the darkness in you. Just "Shell Down the Corn" to Him, (confess). Just like Hank Williams saw the light, just like Michael Duishka saw the light, you are in darkness until you see the light. Christ Jesus is the light. Satan and sin are the darkness in you. Brother John said in his book of (1 John 3:4) that transgression of the law of God is sin. Hell is darkness. There is not any light in Hell. Heaven is light. There is not any darkness in heaven. God will divide the light from darkness in you if you will let the Word of God divide, Christ Jesus, which is the light, from Satan, which is darkness, if you will "Shell Down the Corn". (confess to Christ Jesus). The fool says there is no God. The agnostic says he does not know if there is a God. Both of these people are full of darkness, (Satan). The believer believes there is God, and God diligently rewards the believer with light. The light came to the Apostle Paul. Michael Duishka saw and came to the light. **"Corn Shelling Time"** is impossible to understand if you are a speed reader. The first sentence of a paragraph does not reflect what the paragraph is talking about. **"Corn Shelling Time"** is a reiteration of the Word of God. The inspired WORD of God, the Prophets, spoke in parables, which the ordinary lay person cannot understand. So this book is an iteration of the parables of the Holy Spirit of God, which Christ Jesus said: His Word, or "The Words that I speak, they are spirit and life unto you." (John 6:63). That is why so many people say the bible is too hard to understand. **"Corn Shelling Time"** is a classmate of the bible, and it is better understood if the reader is filled with God's Holy Spirit. "He that believes Him is not condemned, but he that believes not is condemned **already**." (John 3:18) **"Corn Shelling Time"** is also a potpourri of Michael Duishka's experiences with victories over Satan and how Christ Jesus found him. The way God is using Duishka is bringing to your remembrance the warning to "Come Out of Mystery Babylon", and to reveal to you what Mystery Babylon is: Mystery Babylon is the culmination of the Mystery of Iniquity: The Mystery of Iniquity is sin: Sin is the transgression of the law of God: Transgression of the Law of God is to go beyond the limit of the Ten Commandments, which is the divine law of God. (1 John 3:4) "He that commits sin is of the Devil." (1 John 3:8) To come out of "Her" is to come out of sin. To come out of sin is to keep the Ten Commandments of God. Babylon is a metaphor for the world of sin. The Great City Babylon, is a metaphor for the literal capitol of the world of sin, which Duishka believes is the Great City, AKA *New York City, USA.*

Interjection: When the angel in (Revelation 18:2) is saying Babylon the Great is fallen, is fallen, signifies the total destruction of literal Babylon, and the seat of the Beast. Babylon the Great City, which Duishka believes is *New York City, USA.* These metaphors are symbols and representatives of the world system, and the seat of the Beast, *New York City, USA,* which is the political center, the financial center, and the religious center of the whole world. The angel calls "Her" the Whore, the Mother of Harlots, which is *Harlot Churches* and all religious idols of worship, which is fallen, is fallen. Rome, (the Vatican), will be the official city of the Whore, but "She" will be influenced by the other Woman, *(Babylon City the Great)*, AKA The United Nations headquartered in Babylon City AKA *New York City, USA*. The United Nations Headquarters, located in Turtle Bay of Lower Manhattan, New York City Duishka believes rules the world at this present time by intimidation or fear. The former name of this site was Goat Hill. Also the Trump Tower and all the towers of New York City will be gone when the angel declares: Babylon is fallen, is fallen.

After the fall of Babylon City, (that Great City) all of the kings of the earth are gathered together in a place God called **Armageddon** to be annihilated, wiped out completely. Michael Duishka is being facetious and calls this event *"God's Super Bowl On A Sunday"*. "And there came a great voice out of the Temple of Heaven, from the Throne, saying: It is done." (Revelation 16:17) At this time all of the humans left upon the earth are the remnant that God saves for Himself. All the ones that worshiped the Beast and had his mark in their hand or in their forehead were killed. The Called and Chosen Ones and the Holy Ones were resurrected, before the battle of the Lord.

<u>"Corn Shelling Time"</u> is a confession to God Almighty for a lifetime of sin that Duishka committed unwittingly by the acts of disobeying God's Commandments. The only excuse, or cop out, for that disobedience is ignorance. My parents did not teach me about God, and when the Holy Spirit, God, drew me to Christ Jesus, I immediately started searching for a *church* that had a spiritual leader that could teach me the Truth. After many years of searching, there were not found any apostles, prophets, teachers or anointed ones that were qualified according to the standards of the scriptures, that were anointed of God to preach or teach the whole Truth, (Christ Jesus). The preachers and teachers that Duishka spent many hours listening to were deemed to be hirelings. Some of them were sincere in their belief; but judging by the Word of Truth, they were sincerely wrong. Maybe they were anointed by the Holy Spirit at the beginning of their ministry, but the glamor of the gain of mammon caused them to err. After many hours of praying, weeping, and study of the Word, the Holy Spirit led me to the inspired Word that Brother John had written, which was (1 John 2:26,27)

"These things have I written unto you concerning them that seduce you. But the anointing which you have received of Him abides in you, and you need not that any man teach you; but as the same anointing teaches you of all things, and is Truth, and is no lie, and even as He has taught you, you shall abide in Him." (1 John 2:26,27)

Commentators have said that no one can be saved, except they go or belong to a *church*. Churches have good intentions, but there is an idle phrase that says: The road to Hell is paved with good intentions. Like some say to themselves: "I intend to get saved one of these times, but I have plenty of time." Time will pass by you so fast that you will be so preoccupied in the pleasures of sin that all of a sudden you will be at the end of your allotted time here on this earth.

"Corn Shelling Time" is not adding to, or taking away from the one doctrine of God, but only putting color to instruct or correct you in righteousness, so you can be wise unto salvation. Also just cause you to remember what you <u>already</u> know. "He that knows to do good and does it not, to him it is sin. If we confess our sins, He is faithful and just to forgive us our sins, and to cleanse us from all unrighteousness." (1 John 1:9) This is exactly what this writer did to my daddy when he used the double razor strop and exactly what I did to Christ Jesus, the Son of God, and exactly what I am doing at this present time, and exactly what I will be doing if I ever sin again. My daddy called confessing, "Shelling Down the Corn".

"Corn Shelling time" is a warning that all of the plagues of Mystery Babylon are being poured out gradually at this present time. The plagues are in the air, the fire, the water, and the earth. We cannot hide from them. We can shield ourselves from them by applying the shed blood of Christ Jesus to our hearts. How do I apply the shed blood of Jesus to my heart? It is an act of "Shelling Down the Corn" and confessing that you are a sinner. If you say that you have not sinned, you make Him a liar, and His Word is not in us. The Word says all, everybody, has sinned. It will take you a long time to recall all of the sins you have committed; but not to worry, God has put them in a sea of forgetfulness; and He remembers them no more. Of course you must repent, which means you have to quit sinning. If you do sin, be quick to ask God in the name of His Son, Christ Jesus to forgive you. After you have confessed your sins to Christ Jesus, and repented with a broken and contrite spirit, which means to realize you are the reason Christ Jesus suffered and died on the torture stake, and shed His blood as a sacrifice for our sins. If you are remorseful enough to shed a million tears, then you have applied His shed blood to your heart. That is not all that is required of you. This is where faith comes in. You must believe the Words Christ Jesus said. You must believe Him when He said you should live by every Word that proceeds out of the mouth of God. You must not only believe in Him, (as the Devils do), but **<u>Believe Him</u>**. But the most important part of believing is to believe that you shall be saved. But remember that every time Jesus heals and saves He says to go and sin no more. Also mark this down in your day book. You are being saved by GRACE, which is a free gift of God. Not by any good that you have done, or not by any works that you have done. You cannot boast about anything that you or your friends or family have done, because Christ Jesus laid down His life and shed His precious blood, which is the ultimate (*be-all*) sacrifice to pay the debt you owed, so you could be saved. So please remember He died once for all and He cannot die any more for your sins. If you take Him for granted and receive this once for all time gift lightly and slough (sluff) it off by going back into the hog wallow, or pig sty, there is not any more blood that can wash you and cleanse you for your willful sin. Dear reader, also remember "if you do commit a sin and your heart condemns you, God, is greater than your heart." (1 John 3:20)

So, you are alive if you are reading this. **"And whosoever lives and believes me shall never die. Do you believe this?"** (John 11:26) "But do not let it happen unto you according to the true proverb, the dog *is* turned to his own vomit again, and the sow that was washed to her wallowing in the mire." (2 Peter 2:22)

"For we are the circumcision, which worship God in Spirit, and rejoice in Christ Jesus, and have no confidence in the flesh." (Philippians 3:3) "Brethren and sisters be followers together of me." (Philippians 3:17) And do what the other voice from heaven that Brother John heard, saying, "Come Out of "Her", My People, that you be not partakers of "Her" sins, and that you receive not of "Her" plagues." (Revelation 18:4) "Shell Down the Corn" to God Almighty (PANTAKRATOR), that means, confess to Christ Jesus, Repent of your sins, and ask Christ Jesus to save you. And last of all <u>BELIEVE Him.</u>

I do not know the date that any of the things written in the bible and reiterated in this book will manifest, but I do know that your time is awfully short. Your last breath could be at any time The plagues are falling upon you as I speak. As I have said in previous chapters of this book, I am not an apostle, there are not any on this earth. I am not a prophet, there are not any on this earth. They were all martyred. But I do not need to be very smart to discern the signs of the times, and they are indicating that we are in the time of the end. "The Spirit and the Bride say, Come, and let him that hears say, Come, and let him that is athirst Come. And whosoever will, let him take the water of life freely."

Michael and Mavis Duishka say, "Come, to the Marriage Supper of the Lamb. Put on your robe of clean, bright, <u>white</u> linen." And whatever the time of the world clock is, this is a true, for sure saying: It <u>**is "Corn Shelling Time"**</u>.

Michael Duishka

Addendum

THIS WRITER TRULY BELIEVES Brother Peter, when he said, "Judgment begins at the house of God." This writer is Shelling Down the Corn" to all the readers of this book, to Christ Jesus, to God the Father, to God The Holy Spirit, confessing that he is nothing, a sinner being saved by grace and washed by the blood of Christ Jesus. "For if a man think himself to be something, when he is nothing, he deceives himself." (Galatians 6:3) Let these questions be judged by you, the reader.

Who killed Christ Jesus? Was it the Romans, or the Jews, or maybe Pontius Pilate?

Who murdered the men, women, and little children at the Waco, Texas massacre of the Branch Davidians at Mount Carmel? Were the guilty parties, President Bill Clinton, Attorney General Janet Reno, the FBI, the ATF, the United States National Guard, or the so called *"Christian" Americans* that cast their vote for the president that said: "The buck stops with me"? Were you the ones who had pleasure in being allied with Jack Booted Thugs, that were privy to murder?

Who was responsible for the mass murders in the massacre of men, women, and little children in the bombing of the Federal Murrah Building in Oklahoma City, Oklahoma, on April 19, 1995? Was it

Timothy McVeigh, that was getting revenge for the Waco, Texas Massacre, or the President of the United States of America, Bill Clinton, that was the Commander in Chief of the United States army, that taught Timothy McVeigh how to kill; or was it the *anti-"Christian", anti-Americans* that voted for war mongers that taught young McVeigh how to kill? Who was the guilty party that murdered Timothy McVeigh by lethal injection? Was it the one that injected young Tim with the poison, or the judge and jury that sentenced him to die; or was it the so called "Christian" "Americans" that voted for the ones that carried out the murder?

Who is guilty for the 60 million murdered babies that have been aborted, (murdered), since Roe vs Wade? Is it the mothers, or the so called *"doctors"*, the laws of the land, the United States Supreme Court Judges, or the so called *"Christian"* "American" voters that voted the murderers into office?

Who is responsible for the Muslim terrorists in the world, since the misfits of America voted the Muslim, "Christian" President Obama into office?

Who are the black terrorists in America that rob, steal, kill, burn, and destroy the cities of the United States of America? Are they any different from ISIS, Boko Haram, Hamas, or Jihadists?

The murders of thousands of "Americans" in the bombing of the Twin Towers in *Babylon,* New York City, USA, were they committed by Muslims? Am I a racist for telling the Truth?

Were the terrorists that murdered 14 people and injured twenty-two in San Bernadino, California, Muslims?

Was the black man that cut a woman's head off in Moore, Oklahoma a Muslim?

Who is responsible for this world wide terrorism by Muslims, Obama, Congress, democrats, or the misfit people that voted for a black Muslim misfit? Are the misfits that are allied with the President, Queers, black, violent, anti-Christ, bums, that want free money, free food, free medical, free dope, free college, that steal, kill and destroy America? Is it possible that the misfits, blacks, queers, lesbians, murderers, welfare bums, rioters, anti-Christ, would continue the legacy of this Muslim president, and vote in another of their kind that is an alleged killer of millions of people and a participant in Benghazi, abortion, queers and lizzies marrying each other, welcoming the Muslim and Mexican and every criminal immigrant that is illegal into America to finish destroying "Her"? The answer is could it be all of the above?

Michael Duishka is nothing. He wrote a book prior to **"Corn Shelling Time"** titled, **"Please Do Not Call Me A "Christian",** that has paid him a royalty sum of .99 cents so far; but he does not want to make money, but just open the minds of the lost souls, and keep them from being destroyed for lack of knowledge, or at **"GOD'S SUPER BOWL ON A SUNDAY".** (**ARMAGEDDON**) The way of escape is to "Shell Down The Corn" to Christ Jesus. CONFESS!

MICHAEL DUISHKA

Printed in the United States
By Bookmasters